The Economics of Regional Security

Studies in Defence Economics

Edited by Keith Hartley, Centre for Defence Economics, University of York, UK

This series of monographs and edited collections adopts a wide definition of defence economics to cover all aspects of the political economy of defence, disarmament and peace.

The Economics of Regional Security

NATO, the Mediterranean, and Southern Africa

Edited by

Jurgen Brauer
College of Business Administration
Augusta State University, USA

and

Keith Hartley
Centre for Defence Economics
University of York, UK

harwood academic publishers
Australia • Canada • France • Germany • India • Japan
Luxembourg • Malaysia • The Netherlands • Russia
Singapore • Switzerland

Amsteldijk 166
1st Floor
1079 LH Amsterdam
The Netherlands

British Library Cataloguing in Publication Data

A catalogue record for this book is available from the British Library.

ISBN: 90-5823-070-8
ISSN: 1062-046X

To

*Norbert E., Childhood friend and friend still,
and Jesse L., trusted counselor and friend*

—jb

Adam and Rachel

—kh

Contents

vii

PART III: SOUTHERN AFRICA

Figures and tables

Introduction

Keith Hartley and Jurgen Brauer

Defense economics is a relatively new field in the discipline of economics. This volume is a further demonstration of the importance of the field. It shows how concepts from economics and other social science disciplines can be applied to important issues of defense, conflict, and peace at the regional level. Regional studies provide a rich vein of empirical data for testing theories from defense economics and for evaluating different national defense policies. This volume makes an original contribution through its focus on NATO and the economics of regional security in the Mediterranean region and southern Africa.

NATO celebrated its fiftieth anniversary in 1999, but it faces major threats and new challenges. Many of the new threats are in the Mediterranean region. They include the conflict, peacekeeping, and humanitarian aid in Kosovo, the continued tension between Greece and Turkey with its focus on Cyprus, tensions in the Middle East (e.g., over Iraq), and a potential threat from North Africa (e.g., in the form of rogue states, state terrorism, weapons of mass destruction, and a clash of cultures and religions). NATO is also faced with new challenges. It "won" the cold war but, unlike the rival Warsaw Pact, it survived the end of the cold war and has developed new missions and roles embracing peacekeeping, crisis management, humanitarian aid, and disaster relief. NATO has also been enlarged with the entry of new members from the former Warsaw Pact. The relationship between NATO and the European Union (EU) is a further challenge as the EU develops a defense and security identity and a European procurement policy. Additional challenges arise from developments in new technology (the so-called "revolution in military affairs") and questions about the extent of NATO's "out-of-area" operations (e.g., what, if any, are the geographic limits to its military operations?).

Challenges aside, NATO possesses a unique capability: it is the world's only international military alliance with an established command structure and highly trained and well-equipped military forces able to support the United Nations. The Kosovo conflict proved an example of NATO's new roles and missions. The conflict had three distinctive features. First, it was the first time NATO had been involved in military action. Second, it was a new mission in that it was not an Article 5 action (where an attack on one member is regarded as an attack on all members). Third, it was an air campaign only — involving high technology equipment primarily aimed at minimizing casualties to NATO states — demonstrating the opportunities for substitution between air and ground forces.

Defense and peace economists can contribute to an evaluation of the Kosovo conflict by estimating its costs and benefits. On the cost side, for instance, it involved resource costs through the use of scarce resources in the air campaign, injury, trauma and loss of life, as well as damage to property and infrastructure. There were also non-military costs such as humanitarian aid and support for the refugees, as well as indirect costs through the loss of tourism and trade in the conflict areas and the neighboring states. The end of the conflict was followed by a substantial commitment of NATO forces for peacekeeping and massive reconstruction costs for Kosovo and Yugoslavia. The magnitude and distribution of these costs will vary among NATO members, Kosovo, and Yugoslavia. Within NATO there will inevitably be debates about burden-sharing and whether various members paid more than their "fair share" of both the military conflict and the subsequent peace and reconstruction costs.

Part I of this volume focuses on NATO and deals with its European dimension, defense budgets, and future challenges. The opening chapter (Keith Hartley) shows the contribution of defense economics to policy formulation and examines the economic implications of creating a single European market for defense equipment. Pierre Willa analyses the role of the EU in determining the stability of the Mediterranean region in the post-cold war era. Defense economics is about making difficult choices in conditions of uncertainty and such choices are reflected in defense budgets. John Treddenick analyses the economic impact of falling defense budgets on the central economic questions of allocation and efficiency. Part I ends with a chapter by Todd Sandler which shows how defense economists are addressing important questions about the future of NATO. These include NATO's new roles and missions, weapons of mass destruction, terrorism, rogue states, and NATO expansion.

Apart from NATO *per se*, Part II of the volume focuses on the economics of security in the Mediterranean region. Typically, defense spending is criticized for its "crowding-out" of valuable civil investment. Emmanuel Athanassiou and Christos Kollias extend the "crowding-out" debate by assessing the impact of Greek-Turkish rivalry on foreign direct investment. There follow two chapters which assess the evidence on the defense-growth relationship for Greece (Selami Sezgin) and Turkey (Onur Öszoy). Following these chapters on the eastern Mediterranean are two on the western Mediterranean. Carlos Pestana Barros examines the determinants of military spending in the European Catholic countries and the Muslim African states of the western Mediterranean, and Jacques Fontanel and Fanny Coulomb end Part II with a case study of Algeria, a nation about which little has been published in the defense economics literature.

Part III is devoted to southern Africa, including South Africa. This region has been characterized not only by the search for a peace dividend in post-apartheid South Africa but also by continued conflict and civil wars. The southern African region provides case study material on these new threats, some of which could "spill over" to developed nations. It is also a region which has been relatively neglected in the defense and peace economics literature. Part III remedies this deficiency. It starts with an original and novel contribution which presents an economic analysis of civil war in Mozambique, including its effects on output, growth, and distortions in the economic structure (Tilman Brück). South Africa is obviously of major interest in the region. André Roux examines some of the myths and the reality of the search for a peace dividend in South Africa, especially assessing its macroeconomic impacts. Illegal migration is one of the new threats in the post-cold war period, and Michael Hough assesses its impact on official perceptions of threats to national security, especially for South Africa. New thinking is also developing on the concept of security itself. Denis Venter explores attempts to institutionalize regional security by taking a South African perspective of the southern African region. The book concludes by analyzing regional peace as a collective action good (c.f., the literature on the economics of NATO as a military alliance). Jurgen Brauer explores the implications of the public good approach for peacemaking and peacekeeping in southern Africa, for free-riding, and for the design of institutions.

The chapters in this volume are the product of an international conference organized by the *Centro de Estudos sobre África e do Desenvolvimento* (CEsA) of the Technical University of Lisbon in conjunction with the *Instituto da Defesa Nacional* (IDN). The primary conference organizers were CEsA's Professors Carlos Pestana Barros and Manuel Ennes Ferreira. We thank them and their associates for wonderful hospitality, as well as IDN's director, Prof. Severiano Teixeira, at whose splendid facilities the conference was held in Lisbon, 5-6 June 1998. Our thanks also go to Margaret Cafferky for help in preparing this volume for publication. Finally, a thank you to our families for the inevitable sacrifices they made and the support they offered (for Keith Hartley, wife Winifred and children Adam, Lucy and Cecilia and, for Jurgen Brauer, wife Roswitha and children Jonathan, Leon, and Anne).

PART I:

NATO

1 The economics of European defense procurement

Keith Hartley

Introduction

This chapter deals with two issues involving both Europe and NATO. First is the contribution of defense economics to policy formulation, focusing on choices, procurement policy, defense industries, and alternative industrial policies. The second concerns the economic implications of extending the Single European Market (SEM) to defense procurement. This involves a statement of the policy problem, consideration of alternative scenarios, an evaluation of collaboration, and the prospects for creating a European Union defense industrial base.

European and NATO defense equipment markets: the need for difficult choices

Defense policy has to respond to two pressures, namely, constant or falling defense budgets and equipment which is both costly and becoming costlier. For example, the four-nation Eurofighter combat aircraft is estimated to cost over £13 billion for total development and £40.2 million for unit production costs (1997-98 prices; see HCP 695, 1998). Moreover, equipment costs are rising so that on a unit for unit basis, new equipment costs far more than the equipment which it replaces. Typically, the unit production costs of equipment (combat aircraft, warships, missiles) have risen at some 10 percent per annum in real terms, resulting in a doubling in costs every 7.25 years (Kirkpatrick, 1995; Pugh, 1993). These cost increases reflect the technical arms race as a nation seeks superior equipment to its potential rivals, or tries to prevent its forces from falling into a position of inferiority. The result is "technical leapfrogging" reflected in improved performance and effectiveness of equipment, but such improvements are costly.

Rising unit costs and a limited defense budget mean that fewer units can be bought, with adverse impacts on the numerical strength of the armed forces and on the output of national defense industries. For example, in the UK the air force has declined from 5,213 aircraft in 1954 to 1,100 in 1994; and in the 1950s, 27 new types of aircraft were brought into service compared with only two new types in the 1990s (hence suggestions of a future consisting of a one tank army, a one ship navy and one Starship Enterprise air force; Kirkpatrick, 1997, p. 12). Various policy initiatives such as increased defense budgets, increased industrial productivity, and improvements in the efficiency of procurement policy can *delay* but not prevent the impact of rising unit costs (Pugh, 1993, pp.181-182). Thus, for defense policymakers, rising unit equipment costs and constant or falling defense budgets mean that difficult choices cannot be avoided; and these choices have to be made where the future is unknown. Choices require sacrifices. The question is what to choose and what to sacrifice, and can economics help?

In making defense choices, two market developments cannot be ignored. First, the existence of excess capacity in the world's defense industries. Second, the competitive threat from large US defense companies able to exploit economies of scale, learning, and scope, thereby offering modern equipment cheaply and quickly. These developments raise some difficult policy questions for European nations. Is it worth creating or retaining a national defense industrial base; is a European defense industrial base the solution and what might it look like; or should Europeans buy their equipment off-the-shelf from the US?

Changes since 1990: the stylized facts

The trends in defense expenditure and defense industry employment within Europe and NATO over the period 1990-96 are shown in Table 1.1. Following the end of the cold war, there has been a general decline in both expenditure and industry employment with substantial reductions in Germany, the UK, and the US. Over the same period, real equipment expenditure fell by 15 percent in NATO Europe, by 23 percent in the US, and by 20 percent in NATO (SIPRI, 1998). Table 1.1 also shows major reductions in defense industry employment in Germany, Italy, and Spain. For defense industries, the cuts in defense spending have been reflected in cancellations, fewer new projects, smaller production runs, delays in ordering, the stretching out of programs, and a reduced demand for spares and support. Industry has responded with down-sizing, mergers, the search for new military and civil markets, and exits from the industry. But industrial re-structuring has created two problems for policymakers. First, mergers make it increasingly difficult to maintain competition. Second, major gaps in ordering

Table 1.1: Defense expenditure and employment

Country	Defense Expenditure		Defense Industry Employment	
	Index (1996=100)	US $ (million)	Index (1996=100)	Numbers (000s)
	1990	*1996*	*1990*	*1996*
France	111	40,260	130	230
Germany	140	35,100	218	110
Greece	93	4,480	100	15
Italy	114	17,840	200	40
Portugal	94	1,320	167	6
Spain	114	7,370	333	30
Turkey	88	7,000	83	30
UK	134	29,840	142	310
US	134	259,050	143	2,100
EU	121	161,600	153	860
NATO	129	429,500	146	3,090

Note: Expenditure data in millions of US $ at 1993 prices and exchange rates.

Source: BICC (1998).

new equipment could mean the exit of key industrial capabilities from the national defense industrial base. This issue has arisen in the US in relation to the continued existence of the national defense industrial base for bomber aircraft, tanks, and nuclear-powered submarines. In this context, the relevant defense industrial base comprises prime contractors, sub-contractors, and suppliers (Hartley *et al.*, 1997). Policymakers can respond by allowing market forces to work, or they can intervene by offering state support in the form of continued small-scale orders, mid-life up-dates, through technology demonstrators, or by funding the moth-balling of specialized plant and equipment. Each policy option needs to be evaluated in terms of its estimated costs, benefits, and risks (CBO, 1993).

The economics of defense procurement

Defense equipment markets bring together both procurement and defense industries representing the demand and supply sides of the market. The distinctive feature of defense procurement is the importance of government both as a major buyer and as a regulator. For some equipment, the government is a monopsony (e.g., nuclear systems), and as a regulator it can determine profits on defense contracts and whether to permit defense exports. The government can use its buying power to determine the size of the national defense industry, its structure, entry and exit conditions, industry conduct (e.g., R&D, advertising), and industry performance (e.g., pricing, profitability, technical progress, exports).

Equipment procurement involves a set of policy choices about what to buy, who to buy from, how to buy, and the choice criteria. Decisions are needed on the type of equipment to be purchased which will have an impact on technical progress, and choices are also required between air, land, and sea systems and between the quality and quantity of equipment. A contractor has to be chosen involving further choices about the method of selection (competition versus direct negotiation) and between domestic and foreign firms (i.e., entry conditions). A contract type has to be selected ranging between cost-plus, target-incentive, and fixed price contracts (determined by competition or direct negotiation). Finally, in selecting equipment, policymakers have to decide whether to choose on the basis of narrow defense criteria (e.g., equipment performance, price, delivery, and risk) or on the basis of wider economic, political, and social criteria (e.g., jobs, technology, exports, and support for national defense industrial base).

Choices and efficiency are central to economics and their application to defense and procurement policy suggests four guiding principles for defense policymakers faced with the need to make difficult choices:

▸ *Final outputs.* This suggests that policymakers should not focus on the numbers of aircraft, tanks, and warships which are inputs. Instead, the focus needs to be on the contribution of inputs to final output in the form of protection, security, crisis management and, ultimately, peace. Furthermore, the contribution of inputs to output needs to be evaluated on the basis of marginal costs and benefits.

▸ *Substitution.* This suggests that there are alternative methods of achieving protection. Within the equipment sphere there are possibilities of substitution between attack helicopters and tanks, between strike aircraft and ground forces, between cruise missiles and bomber aircraft, and between maritime patrol aircraft and frigates. Some of these substitutions have implications for the traditional monopoly property rights of each of the armed forces. For example, for air defense, army-operated surface-to-air missiles might replace manned fighter aircraft operated by the air force. Of course, in the private sector such substitutions are made in response to competition and the search for profits.

▸ *Competition.* This is a means of promoting efficiency. Here, there are opportunities for nations to open up their defense procurement markets to domestic and foreign competition. A further possibility would be to introduce competition for the life-cycle support of equipment. For example, private contractors could compete with the armed forces for the repair, support, and maintenance of equipment. A more radical possibility would be for firms to compete for the leasing of equipment, so that the armed forces would lease rather than own equipment, thereby transferring responsibility for maintenance from the armed forces to industry (compare car hire: but it is recognized that the leasing of defense equipment involves complex transaction costs for long-term contracts).

▸ *Incentives.* Military personnel and civil servants need employment contracts which provide incentives to economize and save when *purchasing and using* equipment. Problems arise because incentives are either lacking or are perverse. For example, on a one-for-one replacement basis, the armed forces often buy technically improved equipment for the benefits it offers to users without consideration of system-wide costs.

The economics of defense industries

Four economic features are important for understanding defense industries:

▸ *The importance of R&D.* The industry is characterized by high and increasing R&D costs. For example, development costs for the American F-22 Raptor combat aircraft have been estimated at almost $23 billion (1997 prices; CBO, 1997). As a result, it is important to spread such total fixed costs over a large output so as to reduce the unit costs of acquisition.

▸ *The importance of quantity.* Quantity is a major determinant of average costs through the spreading of fixed R&D costs and through lower unit production costs resulting from economies of scale and learning. For example, learning economies in the aerospace industry result in a reduction in unit production costs of about 10 percent for every doubling of cumulative output (Sandler and Hartley, 1995, p. 124).

Table 1.2: Leading aerospace companies, 1998

Company	Country	1998 Aerospace sales (US $, billions)
Boeing	US	55.0
Lockheed-Martin	US	25.5
Raytheon	US	17.5
Aerospatiale	France	15.0
British Aerospace	UK	15.0
Daimler-Benz Aerospace	Germany	10.4
Northrop-Grumman	US	8.3
GEC	UK	8.1
Thomson CSF	France	8.0

Note: Since mid-1998 there has been further restructuring.

Source: Flight (1998).

▸ *The competitiveness of the US defense industry.* Large US defense companies able to achieve economies of learning, scale, and scope are a major competitive threat to European and other nations' defense industries (see Table 1.2). The scale of re-structuring in the US has led to a reduction in the number of major American defense and aerospace companies from 15 in 1990 to 4 in 1998. At the same time, 6 European nations have three times as many firms as the US, supporting a total defense budget less than half that of the US (HCP 675, 1998, p. xiv).

▸ *Defense industries as economically strategic industries.* In addition to their traditional military-strategic significance, defense industries have the features of an economically strategic industry. Such industries are characterized by decreasing costs reflecting scale and learning economies, high technology reflecting major and costly R&D together with technical spill-overs to the rest of the economy, and by monopoly profits resulting from imperfect competition based on national monopolies and oligopolies (e.g., aerospace, electronics, nuclear). As a result, governments might support these industries as part of strategic trade policy (e.g., using subsidies and anti-competitive behavior) as a means of promoting spill-overs and obtaining a share of monopoly profits in world markets (e.g., Airbus).

Alternative industrial policies

The need for difficult choices resulting from rising equipment costs and falling defense budgets remains. Broadly, the policy options range from a review of defense commitments (e.g., abandoning a major commitment) to a review of the major spending areas, namely, equipment and personnel (e.g., use of reserves and contractors). A review of equipment raises the possibility of a radical review of procurement policy involving more competition and contractorization. A key policy question arises over continued support for a national defense industrial base. Is it worth paying the price of independence by buying from a national defense industrial base; why not shop around and buy equipment off-the-shelf from the cheapest suppliers in the world market? These questions are part of more general issues about alternative industrial policies.

There are a variety of methods of purchasing defense equipment. These include support for a national defense industrial base, international collaboration (two or more nations sharing R&D and production), licensed or co-production, imports with or without offsets, and, for the European nations, the possible creation of a European defense industrial base. An economic evaluation of the costs and benefits of alternative industrial policies is needed. Such an evaluation would identify the objectives of policy and consider alternative methods of achieving these objectives, together with an assessment of their costs and benefits. Identifying policy objectives specifies the range of items to be included in the cost-benefit analysis. For example, will the analysis be restricted to military costs and benefits of equipment or will it include wider economic and industrial benefits? Similarly, if the objective is to retain a national defense industrial base, various alternative policies can be used such as ordering technology demonstrators, or dual-use purchasing, or allowing firms to bid for work usually undertaken in-house by the armed forces (contractorization). Table 1.3 presents a framework for evaluating the costs and benefits of procurement choices and the associated alternative industrial policies. Benefits distinguish between the military and strategic features of equipment and wider national and industrial benefits.

Procurement policy and its industrial aspects are often dominated by myths, emotion, and special pleading. There is scope for critical assessment: policies which appear attractive often have their limitations. Some examples are:

▸ *Employment benefits.* It is often claimed that buying equipment from the national defense industry will create and support x number of jobs. However, rarely is it recognized that alternative public expenditures (e.g., construction

Table 1.3: Policy options: a framework for procurement choices

POLICY OPTIONS	COSTS				BENEFITS								
	Acquisition price		Life cycle costs		Military/strategic features				DIB	National economic benefits			
	Unit	Total fleet	Unit	Total fleet	Perfor-mance	Number	Delivery schedule	Standard-ization		Jobs	Techno-logy	Balance of payments	Other
1. National project (independence)													
2. Collaborative project (two or more nations)													
3. Licensed or co-production													
4. Imported equipment:													
i. Off-the-shelf													
ii. With offset													
5. EU Defense Industrial Base (DIB)													

work for schools, hospitals, and roads) are likely to create more jobs than defense procurement. The key question is whether alternative uses of resources currently employed in defense industries would make a greater contribution to employment, technology, balance of payments, and other policy objectives, and ultimately to society's welfare.

▸ *Defense and wider economic objectives.* Are wider economic objectives the proper concern of defense ministries or are they the responsibility of other ministries (e.g., Employment, Trade and Industry)?

▸ *The need for evidence.* Reliable quantitative evidence is needed on the costs and benefits of alternative policies. All too often, procurement choices are based on vague criteria, qualitative assertions, and emotive references to how vital and important a national equipment project is for local industry and the national economy. Such claims usually lack quantitative evidence and an indication of the reliability of any estimates.

▸ *Offsets appear attractive* but appearances can be deceptive. Claims about offsets need to be critically assessed. How much of the offset is genuinely new business; how much technology is involved; does the work benefit defense industries or civil industries; and are offsets "free gifts"?

▸ *Valuing the defense industrial base.* Even where estimates are available on the magnitude of the wider economic benefits (e.g., jobs, exports), policymakers need to place a valuation on these benefits. How much extra is a nation willing to pay for the benefits of a national defense industrial base? For example, is a government willing to pay an extra 20 to 25 percent for such national economic benefits?

Discussion of the defense industrial base usually fails to address the basic question of its definition. Indeed, such a definition is not without its problems. At one level, the definition seems simple, namely, those firms which supply specialized defense equipment to the national armed forces (e.g., combat aircraft, guns, tanks, and warships). But this neglects the supply chain through its various tiers, other suppliers (e.g., food, construction), and the export of equipment and related services. Analysis is further complicated by the lack of data (e.g., most privately-owned defense firms have a civil business; some companies might not be aware that they are involved in defense production). Some of the problems of defining the defense industrial base are shown in Figure 1.1. The extremes in Figure 1.1 are clear: box A shows firms in the defense industrial base and box B shows firms in the civil sector. Problems arise for firms between boxes A and B as shown by paths P1 to P3. In future, the possible greater use of dual-use equipment from the civil sector rather than the traditional defense industrial base will create more complications in defining defense industries (Dunne, 1995).

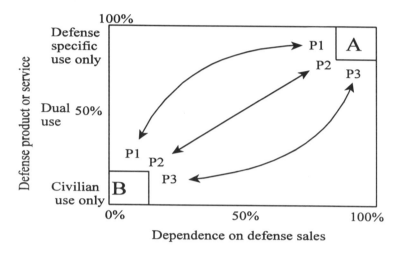

Figure 1.1: Defining the defense industrial base

There are some lessons for countries newly entering defense industrial production (i.e., countries that are developing a new defense industry). Creating a national defense industry with a high technology capability is costly. Nations considering such entry need to answer these questions:

▸ What is meant by a national defense industrial base and why is it needed?
▸ How much is the nation willing to pay for its defense industrial base?
▸ Has there been a careful and critical evaluation of the alternative ways of creating some form of national defense industrial base and the costs of the alternatives?

Nations as potential new entrants might also remember that competition (contestability) is a proven method of achieving value for money in defense procurement (Hartley, 1998). Alternatively, small nations concerned about their lack of buying power in world markets might create international purchasing consortia to provide greater bargaining power when purchasing defense equipment from large foreign contractors.

A Single European Market for the procurement of defense equipment

Defense equipment markets in the European Union (EU) are characterized by inefficiency. Compared with the US, EU nations have too many rival projects and short production runs. The result is duplication of costly R&D and a failure to obtain economies of scale and learning. For example, 6 European nations (France, Germany, Italy, Spain, Sweden, UK) have 14 warship yards compared with 4 in the US; 10 firms manufacturing tanks and armored personnel carriers compared with 2 in the US; 10 missile manufacturers compared with 3 in the US; and 9 aircraft/helicopter firms compared with 5 in the US. Furthermore, these 6 European nations had combined defense budgets of $120 billion compared with a US defense budget of $270 billion in 1997 (HCP 675, 1998, p. xv). Europe has too many relatively small defense firms operating at less than optimal scale.

The European problem is illustrated by combat aircraft. Currently, 6 European nations are developing and producing three different types of combat aircraft (the 4-nation Eurofighter Typhoon; Gripen in Sweden; Rafale in France) involving three costly R&D bills with total production orders of some 1,200 units spread across the three types (i.e., 620 units for Eurofighter and some 300 units each of Gripen and Rafale). The simple economics of standardization shows that the development of one type would have saved two R&D bills and achieved learning economies leading to savings in unit production costs of some 10 to 20 percent from a production run of 1,200 units. In reality, some of the savings in the simple standardization case would be reduced by the need to fund competing prototypes to maintain competition during development and by the possible demands for work sharing and final assembly lines in partner nations. Typically, the larger European nations might each buy 200 to 300 units of an advanced combat aircraft. In contrast, the US plans to buy almost 3,000 units of its new Joint Strike Fighter.

Defense R&D provides a further illustration of the scale differences between Europe and the US. Table 1.4 shows defense R&D in various European nations. The combined total for 14 European states was almost one-third of the US total, but this is misleading since the European total is spread over 14 states. The magnitude of the scale differences is shown by comparing France, the UK, or Germany with the US.

Various scenarios have been proposed for the creation of a Single European Market for the procurement of defense equipment. These are designed to eliminate the major inefficiencies in the current fragmented national arrangements whereby independence through supporting a domestic defense industrial base is costly. Within the EU, each member state's support for its national defense industry has resulted in the duplication of costly R&D programs

Table 1.4: Government defense R&D, 1995-96

	US $ millions (1995 prices)
France	4,900.0
UK	3,200.0
Germany	2,200.0
Sweden	570.0
Spain	310.0
Italy	300.0
Netherlands	100.0
Norway	71.0
Portugal	6.9
Belgium	6.9
Turkey	5.7
Denmark	5.3
Greece	4.3
Luxembourg	1.6
NATO/EU (14 states) total	11,681.7
US total	37,000.0

Source: SIPRI (1998).

and relatively short production runs reflecting small national orders. Three broad scenarios have been proposed for creating a Single European Market for defense equipment, each of which could be the basis for an eventual European Armaments Agency. Each involves different sets of benefits and costs. For each scenario, it is possible to envisage a liberalized competitive market either restricted to firms in member states of the EU or open to firms from the rest of the world. The scenarios are:

▸ *A competitive market* which would simply extend the EU's rules for public procurement in the civil sector to defense procurement (EC, 1996, p. 17). National defense ministries would remain responsible for national procurement, and in principle contracts would be subject to competitive tendering with open and transparent procedures based on objective selection and award criteria. For public procurement in the civil sector, there are also legal remedies for aggrieved contractors and an independent enforcement agency which has investigative powers and can seek corrective measures. Here, there might be a possible role for a European Armaments Agency as a competition and policing authority. Estimates suggest that this scenario might result in lower-bound cost savings of 8.5 to 11 percent of EU defense procurement budgets, depending on whether the market is restricted to EU firms or opened-up to firms from the rest of the world (Hartley, 1998a).

▸ *A centralized purchasing agency* which would replace national defense ministries and would achieve substantial cost savings through purchasing common standardized equipment for all EU nations (i.e., effectively for a single EU army, navy, and air force thereby replicating the US model). A European Armaments Agency could act as such an agency. Lower-bound cost savings for this scenario have been estimated at 14.5 to 17 percent of EU defense equipment budgets with the higher figure applying where the market is opened to firms from the rest of the world (Hartley, 1998a). Of course, whilst this scenario is economically attractive it is politically the most difficult to achieve.

▸ *A twin track approach* which is a mixture of competition and collaboration. Competition would apply to small and medium-size equipment (e.g., small arms, light combat aircraft-trainers, small warships, and small missiles) whilst large-scale air, land, and sea systems would be undertaken on an international collaborative basis. In this scenario, a European Armaments Agency might act as both a competition authority and an agency for promoting and managing collaborative programs (cf. OCCAR, or Organization Conjointe de Coopération pour l'Armament, which is the quadrilateral armaments agency comprising France, Germany, Italy, and the UK). For EU defense equipment budgets, minimum cost savings for this scenario have been estimated at 11 to 14 percent depending on whether competition is restricted to EU firms or open to the rest of the world. In addition to offering substantial cost savings, this scenario is attractive politically in that it offers EU nations possible involvement in collaborative projects in return for opening-up their defense markets to competition (Hartley, 1998a).

Whilst the three Single European Market scenarios offer efficiency improvements and cost savings, the resulting benefits are not costless. It will take time to create a Single European Market and there will be adjustment costs, with some firms and regions being losers in a competitive market (and these costs will be additional to those resulting from disarmament since the end of the cold war). Article 223 of the EC Treaty is also a barrier to creating a Single European

Market for defense procurement since it allows exemptions from the Treaty for "the production of or trade in arms, munitions and war matériel" (EC, 1996, p. 14). Similar barriers to change arise where nations differ in their mix of public and private ownership of defense industries, where cross-border restructuring of defense industries requires government approval, and where nations differ in their arms export policies. Creating a competitive Single European Defense Market also requires a level playing field and non-discriminatory procurement. In addition to anti-competitive behavior on the demand-side of the market (i.e., government), there is potential for similar behavior on the supply-side. If the market is restricted to EU firms, it is likely to be characterized by monopolies, cartels, and collusive tendering with adverse impacts on prices and innovation but higher profits for contractors. A solution to the monopoly problem would be to abolish entry barriers and open up the EU market to firms from the rest of the world. But there would be a trade-off as foreign competition, especially from the US, would have implications for maintaining an EU defense industrial base.

A European defense industrial base: some re-structuring principles

Whilst references are often made to an EU defense industrial base, there has been little economic analysis of the concept. In exploring the concept, the starting point has to be the existing defense industries in each of the member states and especially the domination of the industries in France, Germany, and the UK (both in size and in terms of their range of high technology capabilities in air, land, and sea systems; see Table 1.1). Starting from current positions, questions then arise as to what are the EU's policy objectives in relation to a defense industrial base? One policy objective appears to be the creation of a European defense industrial base which is competitive with the US. But what does this mean? What would it look like? And who would do what? For example, would nations be willing to specialize by comparative advantage and competitiveness? Would nations be willing to sacrifice some national technology and guarantee supply to other EU states? What are the likely constraints on such policy initiatives? Would the losing nations' industries and regions require compensation and would such compensation take the form of other defense work or assistance with resource reallocation (e.g., the KONVER program which was an EU initiative aimed at assisting regions weakened by the decline of defense industries and military facilities; Hooper and Cox, 1996)? In answering these questions, problems arise since the EU lacks an agreed common defense and security policy and an associated set of institutional arrangements for their resolution (cf. WEU,

OCCAR). Ultimately, one solution for the creation of a competitive EU defense industry might require a federal United States of Europe.

European efforts to create a competitive defense industry have focused on applying the US model of a small number of giant companies (Boeing, Lockheed-Martin, Raytheon): hence the need to re-structure Europe's defense industry into a smaller number of larger companies. However, there are problems in applying such re-structuring principles:

- ▸ Uncertainty means that it is not possible to predict accurately the future so that today's winners could be tomorrow's losers. It is possible that completely new forms of industrial organization might emerge, especially with technical progress, which might change a firm's make-or-buy mix. For example, prime contractors need not be vertically-integrated firms owning a complete range of design, development, and production capabilities; instead, they could specialize in systems integration and project management using specialist sub-contractors for various aspects of design, development, and production.
- ▸ Pressures for protectionism and Fortress Europe which, if successful, will have adverse effects on the competitiveness of Europe's defense industry. Such pressures are likely where declining defense equipment budgets are leading to job losses and where nations seek to support their national champions, especially where these are state-owned firms. Protectionism might be further justified in terms of infant industry and strategic trade policy arguments.
- ▸ Large firms require a large market. The US model is based on a large domestic market. On this basis, instructions by European governments that their defense industries should merge or die are fundamentally flawed. Larger European defense companies need a large European market. Economically viable industrial restructuring requires the European governments to combine their demands to create a genuine European market.
- ▸ Re-structuring to create large European companies means the loss of competition in the European market (with potential monopoly problems). The US is faced with a similar problem of a duopoly-oligopoly in its aerospace industry. As a result, both Europe and the US are faced with the challenge of maintaining competition and one solution might be the creation of a NATO free trade area for defense procurement (Hartley, 1998b, p. 69). Nevertheless, even in a NATO free trade area, competition creates conflicts with the European and US aims of maintaining an independent defense industrial base.

European nations are involved in a variety of collaborative defense projects and these could form the basis for creating a European defense industrial base. Aerospace projects dominate European collaboration (e.g., Eurofighter and Eurocopter; Airbus' military division). In contrast, by 1998, Europe had only limited experience of successful collaboration in land and sea systems although economic and budgetary pressures and the formation of OCCAR are leading to new initiatives in these areas.

In its ideal form, collaboration involving two or more nations in the sharing of development costs and the pooling of production orders leads to substantial cost savings (i.e., in development and production via economies of scale and learning). However, actual collaboration departs from the ideal model with cost penalties arising from work sharing rules which allocate work on the basis of equity and fair shares (*juste retour*) rather than on the basis of competition and relative efficiency. For example, the need to provide a balanced spread of technology between the partners results in each nation demanding a share of all aspects of the high technology work which on an aircraft means that each partner requires an involvement in some of the technology on the airframe, engines, and avionics. The management, organizational, policing, and monitoring arrangements embracing industry and governments are a further source of inefficiencies and delays in project completion (Sandler and Hartley, 1995, p. 234). For example, on the four-nation Eurofighter combat aircraft development costs to the UK rose by 47 percent in real terms over the period 1988 to 1997 and by 1998 the project was over three years late (HCP 695, 1998). However, by themselves, such performance indicators can be misleading since similar national projects are also characterized by cost escalation and delays.

There are opportunities for improving the efficiency of collaborative programs. Consider the following policy rules which might be applied by OCCAR:

- ▸ *Rule I: competition.* Introduce more competition into collaborative projects so that work is allocated by competition rather than by *juste retour*.
- ▸ *Rule II: prime contractors.* Appoint a prime contractor with final responsibility for the program and subject the contractor to contractual incentives which place it at risk (e.g., competitively determined fixed price contracts).
- ▸ *Rule III: compensation.* Adequate arrangements are needed to compensate the losers from efficiency-improving policies. However, compensation need not be organized within the program: it could be offered through other defense projects or it could take the form of regional aid and manpower policies (e.g., retraining, mobility).

Conclusion

Defense economics is a relatively new part of the discipline of economics. It can contribute to the evaluation of defense policies in Europe, NATO, the Mediterranean region, and elsewhere by focusing on choices and efficiency. Choices are made in a world of uncertainty and the sacrifices involved in selecting a course of action will reflect an individual's or group's subjective assessment of alternative plans. "There is no reason to suppose that individuals in similar circumstances will make the same assessments and hence reach the same decisions" (Wiseman, 1989, p. 40; Hartley, 1999). Indeed, the world which confronts defense policymakers with planning horizons of forty years or more is dominated by the lack of knowledge of the future and the inevitability of human error. In such a world, characterized by massive uncertainty and continuous change, economists' standard models of market and social equilibrium have little useful meaning and relevance. As a result, the contribution of economists to the formulation of defense policy is at the best modest; but a modest contribution focusing on the advantages of competition and prime contracting continues to offer net benefits.

References

BICC (1998). *Conversion Survey 1998*. Bonn International Center for Conversion. Oxford: Oxford University Press.

CBO (1993). *Alternatives for the US Tank Industrial Base*. Washington, DC: Congressional Budget Office.

CBO (1997). *A Look At Tomorrow's Tactical Air Forces*. Washington, DC: Congressional Budget Office.

Dunne, P. (1995). "The Defense Industrial Base," in *Handbook of Defense Economics*. Amsterdam: Elsevier.

Flight (1998). *Flight International*. Reed Publishing, London, 2-8 September.

EC (1996). *The Challenges Facing the European Defence-Related Industry: A Contribution for Action at the European Level*. Brussels: European Commission, DG XV, CCO/96/08, February.

Hartley, K., *et al.* (1997). *Armoured Fighting Vehicle Supply Chain Analysis: Study of the Value of the Defence Industry to the UK Economy*. University of York: Centre for Defence Economics, September.

Hartley, K. (1998). "Defence Procurement in the UK." *Defence and Peace Economics*. Vol. 9, Nos. 1-2, pp. 39-61.

Hartley, K. (1998a). "UK defence industries," in E. Inbar and B. Zilberfarb (eds.), *The Politics and Economics of Defence Industries*. London: Frank Cass.

Hartley, K. (1998b). "Defence Procurement, the Single Market and the European Armaments Agency," in S. Arrowsmith and A. Davies (eds.), *Public Procurement: Global Revolution*. London: Kluwer Law International.

Hooper, N. and N. Cox (1996). "The European Union KONVER Programme." *Defence and Peace Economics*. Vol. 7, No. 1, pp. 75-94.

Hartley, K. (1999). "Obituary: Jack Wiseman 1919-1991." *Economic Journal*. (forthcoming).

HCP 695 (1998). *Ministry of Defence: Major Projects Report 1997*. National Audit Office. London: The Stationery Office.

HCP 675 (1998). *Aspects of Defence Procurement and Industrial Policy*. House of Commons, Defence Committee, Trade and Industry Committee. London: The Stationery Office.

Kirkpatrick, D.L.I. (1995). "The Rising Unit Cost of Defence Equipment — The Reasons and the Results." *Defence and Peace Economics*. Vol. 6, No. 4, pp. 263-288.

Kirkpatrick, D.L.I. (1997). "Rising Costs, Falling Budgets and their Implications for Defence Policy." *Economic Affairs*. Journal of the Institute of Economic Affairs, Vol. 7, No. 4 (December), pp. 10-14.

Pugh, P. (1993). "The Procurement Nexus." *Defence Economics*. Vol. 4, No. 2, pp. 179-194.

Sandler, T. and K. Hartley (1995). *The Economics of Defense*. Cambridge: Cambridge University Press.

SIPRI (1998). *SIPRI Yearbook 1998: World Armaments and Disarmament*. Stockholm International Peace Research Institute. London: Oxford University Press.

Wiseman, J. (1989). *Cost, Choice and Political Economy*. Aldershot: Elgar.

2 The European Union and Mediterranean stability

Pierre Willa

Introduction

This chapter presents and analyzes the role that the European Union (EU) can play in the stability of the Mediterranean basin in the post-cold war era. Since the end of the 1980s stability has become a recurrent theme in relations between the EU and its periphery. This is particularly true with regards to the Euro-Mediterranean partnership, launched in Barcelona in 1995. The partnership, the latest step in the EU's Mediterranean policy, is based on the Barcelona Partnership Declaration signed by the 15 members of the EU as well as by 12 Mediterranean states (Algeria, Cyprus, Egypt, Israel, Jordan, Lebanon, Malta, Morocco, the Palestinian Authority, Syria, Tunisia, and Turkey). Nevertheless, the partnership is more ambitious than previous initiatives and is wide-ranging in scope, including all manner of political, economic, and cultural interactions. The different actors, namely the governments and the civil society, agreed to meet regularly to push this integrative process forward and to find solutions to common problems. The eventual aim is to transform the Mediterranean into a zone of peace and stability.

The multi-faceted conception of stability embodied in the Barcelona Declaration has rarely been taken into account by mainstream theories of international relations. The latter are usually focused more on security questions than stability as such. In this chapter I adopt a constructivist approach to stability in which stability is understood as a social construct based primarily on the creation of confidence, common understandings, and references. The complex process that leads to stability should eventually drive dependable expectations of peaceful development. Based on this perspective, the chapter proposes a global approach with respect to questions of stability. The approach is applied to the case of the Mediterranean and serves as a reference to assess the EU's actions in this area.

A constructivist approach to stability allows us to take a fresh and challenging look at the EU's possible role in the Mediterranean. The new EU policy as expressed in the Barcelona Partnership encourages lasting stability in the Mediterranean not only by coercion and force but also by establishing common understandings and references, even if mainly on the basis of the EU's perception of reality. But the EU encounters problems in implementing this partnership, in part because of limited EU means. It thus appears that it will be able to play more of an economic than political role. The Euro-Mediterranean Partnership and the EU's actions in the basin must therefore be seen as an indirect and long-term exercise which aspires to transform relations between the EU and the southern countries.

This chapter is divided into three sections. The first deals with some problems of definitions, as well as with history, and it provides the basis and background for the analysis to follow. The second section builds a partial model of stability and establishes benchmarks for comparison and evaluation. On that basis, the third section analyses the present and future role of the EU in the Mediterranean.

The invention of the Mediterranean

The first question when studying the Mediterranean is how to define its extent and limits. The states which border the Mediterranean Sea possess only irregular and loose relations, they belong to at least two geopolitical spheres, and their inhabitants do not usually conceive of the basin as a united entity. Most states along the sea do not consider themselves Mediterranean in the first place, except perhaps for Malta, Cyprus, and to some extent Lebanon and Tunisia. The meaning of "Mediterranean" is consequently vague and undetermined. Economically and politically, the area is characterized more by fragmentation than by unity. It is therefore usually divided among sub-regions such as Europe, the Maghreb, and the Machrek. The trends in the Mediterranean can only be understood in connection to the regions which border it, in our case Europe.

Even if the existence of an identifiable region called the "Mediterranean" is questionable, it seems that the concept of the Mediterranean squares with the ambitions of various key groups, the EU in particular. Following Hobsbawm (1996) one may say that the EU by its policy – the Euro-Mediterranean partnership – is creating, if not inventing, a new political space called the "Mediterranean" with the goal of producing stability in this quite artificial area[1] and to extend its zone of influence into this new space.

From 1992 to 1995 European states launched a number of initiatives in the region, and the Euro-Mediterranean partnership is the result of these previous initiatives. But the Barcelona Partnership is the first example of an official discourse and coherent policy attempt that conceives of the Mediterranean as a whole and means to address present challenges in the basin as a whole. This shift in the discourse and conception of the EU came as a result of assorted events that prompted the EU to change its policy in the region: first, the end of the cold war and the perception of new threats as well as the acceleration of the globalization process; second, the Gulf war and its impact on relations with Arab countries, the peace process in the Middle East, the civil war in Algeria, and in the former Yugoslavia; and third, some European concerns regarding internal equilibrium.

Nevertheless, the concept of the "Mediterranean" and of corollary EU policy is not recent in European institutions. Since its origins, what was then still the EEC inaugurated a Mediterranean policy which developed alongside European institutions. The former colonies of EEC members, the desire to take account of non-member European Mediterranean countries, as well as the containment of any Soviet expansion were the main reasons for this policy. Yet the EEC never imagined the Mediterranean as a region *per se*, but treated it as a basis for bilateral, rather than block (EU-Mediterranean), relations. The energy crisis of the 1970s and the addition of Greece, Spain, and Portugal during the 1980s led to increased EU interest in the area, but with unequal results. The Mediterranean was still not conceived as a region and relations remained mainly bilateral, determined by the superpower rivalry. At the beginning of the 1990s, the end of the cold war brought numerous, albeit slow changes in the Mediterranean, but the EU made only cosmetic modifications to its policy even as the basin gained in relative autonomy. At the time, the EU was preoccupied first and foremost with its east European neighbors.

The Barcelona Partnership and its definition of a "new" Mediterranean region is therefore a contextual choice that helps the EU to build a pillow of stability at its southern border and to more easily manage its relations with its southern neighbors. It is also the result of internal EU politics as well as of a desire to extend its sphere of influence. The EU tries to create a new region and thus a new framework of action for the various Mediterranean actors. The new discourse and policy are meant to legitimate this new conception. (Of course, Mediterranean countries have their own interests in developing relations with the EU, and the "Mediterranean" concept is one way to engage European countries in the region's problems as well as to balance the influence of the United States.) In sum, the EU's Mediterranean rhetoric must be first understood as a way to manage its southern frontier and stabilize its periphery, and only second as a means to foster co-operation in the basin.

Toward a global approach to stability

The meaning of security has evolved since the end of the 1980s. The end of bi-polarity and the phenomenon of globalization have also changed the meaning of sovereignty, and all parties consequently have come to discover new realities, new threats, and have begun to reorient their security discourse. The scope of security has become wider with the end of the internal-external divide and it has come to embody economic, social, and cultural dimensions, especially in the Mediterranean. Rather than disappear, issues of security now comprise a larger portion of reality.

Security and stability thus are increasingly correlated and interdependent. Nevertheless they are still different, involving different theoretic references, attitudes, and potential solutions while keeping an ambiguous relation. Stability uses somewhat different references than security but the theoretical concepts for analyzing stability usually come from security studies. Different concepts in theories of international relations, such as hegemonic stability or governance, can each represent the basis for an approach to stability and its possible meaning.

It is beyond the scope of this chapter to explain conceptual differences in international relations theory, but it is possible to outline them with an approach inspired by a constructivist reading of security communities[2] which, in turn, provides us with a sense of what regional stability in the Mediterranean could look like. Global and regional stability involves inter- and intrastate relations as much as transnational and international transactions, and internal and external questions. It concerns states as much as international organizations, civil societies, and individuals. It affects global, regional, and domestic levels. Stability, as a global phenomenon, is based on material realities, such as specific economic and political situations, a phenomenon hard to grasp even with the help of different theories.

The peculiar nature of stability, understood here as a social construct, is complex as well as methodologically problematic. It is dependent on the inter-subjectivity of the diverse actors since stability is constructed and conceived by them. The stability of a region is therefore contextual and corresponds to the norms and values which are collectively admitted at a given time as the basis for stabilization processes and the expectation of peaceful change.

According to the constructivist approach, the question of stability cannot simply be reduced to anarchy and the use of force. Stability is a dynamic, on-going, and complex process, historically situated, involving coercion as much as the building of common references, understandings, and identities and leading to a normative integration process. The goal of this kind of process is to promote confidence, inducing behavior changes, leading to the creation of collective understandings and norms with the help of growing communication and transactions among the various actors. A core power can foster this process of integration since it is a magnet and has the capacities, as hegemon, to enforce this process by coercion or by its capacity to impose its definition of reality. The different actors may also adhere to this process voluntarily. Stability is therefore based on communication processes that generate the transformation of disparate understandings and knowledge, leading to a harmonization of the norms and different interests that drive dependable expectations of peaceful change.

To implement this approach to stability, and to give a concrete idea of the actual conception of stability in the Mediterranean, I put forward a partial model composed of a number of interdependent elements. This model is drawn from the actual conception of stability within the EU, and partly from the Countries of the South and East Mediterranean (CSEM), as well as from the material reality they interpret. The elements represent norms and values that define the nature of the reality and which are more or less collectively understood as influencing and possibly generating a zone of stability in the Mediterranean. The EU is of course playing the role of a core power, trying to spread its conceptions of stability and reality. Its policies are co-operative but carry a coercive dimension.

The model's elements are divided into five areas, inspired by Buzan (1991).[3] Each of these areas or spheres is contributing to the stability process by the transactions it involves, the change of the material basis, the interdependence the different elements induce, and the mutual confidence and common understandings that develop.

- ▸ *Socio-economic sphere*: balanced development, new economic relations, mutual development strategies, increased aid for transition, technology transfers, regional integration, development of social balance by improved wealth distribution, economic and judicial reforms in the CSEM, adaptation of technical and economic norms, demographic control, common migration management, common fight against international criminality.
- ▸ *Political sphere*: opening of the political system to civil societies, respect for fundamental liberties, non-use of force in inter- and intrastate affairs, rule of law, fight against terrorism, and rejection of the use of violence as a political instrument.
- ▸ *Security and international sphere*: non-use of violence in interstate and state-minority relations, peaceful resolution of conflict, preventive diplomacy, confidence and security building measures (CSBMs), guarantee of treaties, non-intervention in internal affairs, control of armament and disarmament, control of nuclear and biological warfare, stability pact.

- ▸ *Societal sphere*: cultural dialogue and aid for cultural exchange, creation of common references, creation of a common project of society, integrated education, freedom of belief, tolerance, and respect for other cultures.
- ▸ *Ecological sphere*: co-operation for the management of the bio-sphere, the management and equal distribution of water.

The European Union and the stability of the Mediterranean basin

We now turn to the analysis of the European Union and its role in the stability of the Mediterranean region. The main hypothesis of this chapter is that the actions of the EU toward the stability of the region are indirect, carried out especially through the socio-economic sphere. For a variety of reasons, explored later on, it seems that the EU is more effective in stabilizing the Mediterranean region through the use of the socio-economic sphere than the use of politics and the military.

The EU has a specific way of dealing with global politics. Its original internal structures convert it to a new kind of international actor. The EU involves separate European actors which are not the same ones in the different spheres mentioned above. The *Commission*, the *European Council*, and the member states all possess different legitimacy as well as different roles and means. The presentation of the EU in the Euro-Mediterranean process is consequently divided according to this peculiar organization.

The only domain where the EU is unified is the economic domain. It is the only domain where the EU *per se* is the relevant actor and where its internally diverse actors have a common policy. In fact, the EU's socio-economic domain of action is the only one that is integrated and relatively independent of member states' authority. The EU acts therefore on the stability of the Mediterranean region through the impact of its socio-economic policies on the internal situation of the CSEM and on the economic development of the region. In contrast, the Common Foreign and Security Policy (CFSP), in the front line in the politico-military sphere, is not and will not in the near future be a common EU policy. It remains an inter-state affair, under the authority of the *European Council*, and common actions in the Mediterranean remain few even with the principle of abstention. We shall see later the reasons for this state of affairs. Similarly, the societal or cultural spheres remain the domain of shared responsibility whereby the individual actions of member states are fundamental even as some common policies are gradually elaborated and put into place.

In light of the changes brought about by the end of the cold war and its consequences in the Mediterranean region, the European Union is reorientating its Mediterranean policy — the Euro-Mediterranean process. This no doubt marks a shift in relations between the two sea shores. We should not underestimate the weight of continuities however: the Euro-Mediterranean process is tailored primarily to the capacities and expectations of the EU[4] and follows its customs. As we will see, the EU answers assorted challenges with the solution of free trade as its main instrument. The Euro-Mediterranean process is lightly funded with only 4.6 billion Euros and the same amount of possible loans from the European Investment Bank (EIB) for the period 1995-99. Consequently one cannot see this as a fully-fledged development policy.

Political and security "chapter"

The documents of the Barcelona Partnership Declaration contain three "chapters". The first one is the "political and security chapter". It deals with a broad range of issues, such as democracy, the rule of law, and human rights, but also with confidence and peace building measures, non-proliferation, peaceful settlement of disputes, and military and political co-operation. But as already mentioned this domain remains under the authority of the *European Council*, and the Common Foreign and Security Policy (CFSP) is its principal instrument. The politico-military domain is therefore almost exclusively tied to national and intergovernmental policies, as confirmed by the Amsterdam treaty,[5] and not an independent EU policy arena. The CFSP remains therefore the weak point of the EU in the Mediterranean. Many examples of European failures demonstrate its deficiencies, in the Mediterranean as elsewhere.

To determine the limits of European political actions in the Mediterranean one has to understand the main determinants of the CFSP. The European positions in the basin have above all to do with internal considerations, whether European or Atlantic. National idiosyncracies remain very influential even though they may not answer strategic necessities. Competition appears to exist among European states with regard to security, which has provoked a wish to see the United States remain present in Europe.

The CFSP is hence dependent on the level of European integration as well as on the involvement (or not) of the United States, as Awad (1997) has pointed out. The EU will probably not have a policy, in the foreseeable future, that upsets American interests. So long as the US remain involved, a European policy diverging from American interests will be particularly difficult to define and apply. The different relations that various European states have established with what is their main ally are in this regard fundamental to understanding the difficulties in establishing a common external policy, its content, and its extent in the Mediterranean.

The national policies of the major EU member states with regard to the Mediterranean have to be analyzed to understand divergences and convergences so that one can understand, in turn, the common EU elements present in the Mediterranean and evaluate the existence of a shared conception of the basin and of its stability. In other words, the "chapter" of the Euro-Mediterranean process dealing with politico-security issues and the CFSP in the Mediterranean is the result of a balance of forces within the EU and the latter's links across the Atlantic which conditions possible delegations of authority from member states to the EU *per se.*

Some Arab countries have tried to have Europe play an active role in the peace process of the Middle East, hoping that Europeans might balance the exclusive patronage of the United States. These Arab countries are searching for European attitudes that diverge from American ones. Yet any hint of divergent attitudes is dependent on a third party, the United States, which for a number of governments remains indispensable to European equilibrium. Whether or not the Barcelona process will eventually allow a greater role for the EU in the region remains in large part dependent on strictly European issues.

Thus far, the Euro-Mediterranean process provides a coherent and systematic framework for political relations between the member states and the CSEM. Various political meetings within the Euro-Mediterranean process have shown the positive influence the EU can have in the region through the building of a collective understanding of reality. The Barcelona process also reveals a European drive for independence — at least at its frontiers — based on economic power, and it has the aim to establish a European political role in the Mediterranean. The first "chapter" of the partnership document made this quite clear. Although it is not very developed, it represents the first step for the European Union toward a greater commonality of foreign and security policies. Part of this domain is already the responsibility of the European Commission, as for example in the case of the formulation of the Confidence and Security Building Measures (CSBM) for the basin. Indeed, in this regard the Mediterranean seems to be a test case for the EU's CFSP (and its derivatives).

The dimensions of security, in the strict definition given to it in the Barcelona documents, may seem limited. Security is largely constrained to the creation of a continuous political dialogue and the creation of CSBM, something that would lead, in the long run, to a partial disarmament and stability pact to prevent new conflicts from arising. If one conceives of the Euro-Mediterranean process as the sum total of the measures to prevent conflict in the long term (through the development of democracy, the rule of law, common institutions, etc.), the measures put forward in this "chapter" of the Euro-Mediterranean process should help prevent conflicts addressed by force in the medium or short term. In fact, it is interesting to refer — as does Aliboni (1997/1998) — to the perceptions which underlie the security policies as well as to the diverging perspectives between the two shores of the Mediterranean. Such an approach helps explain the multiple difficulties which exist in all forms of security between the North and the South, as well as among the southern countries, and the need to build up common references. A good example is the Israeli-Arab conflict that is undermined by prejudice and misunderstandings.

At present, the European partners do not see any military threats coming from the CSEM. Their worries concern the possibility of future conflicts between any two states or internal problems which could spread to the region with negative consequences for the EU. Indeed, although such a situation would not threaten the security of Europe as such, it could still handicap it, especially by causing destabilization at its borders, in its economic development or with large flows of migrants. And it could limit the positive effects regionalization is expected to bring in the Mediterranean. The advantage for the EU of a co-operative security regime has to do then with a desire not to lose any opportunities because of some weaknesses at its frontiers. In this context, the Barcelona Partnership cannot fulfil the functions of co-operative security without all institutions and political powers taking part in it. Other initiatives are therefore under way such as the American-led peace process in the Middle East which the Euro-Mediterranean process should complement, not substitute. At the moment the EU is trying to build a status that will allow it at a later stage to address by itself problems that affect perceptions of its own security. The EU is also trying to enforce some of its principles to build up a shared understanding of what could be the stability in the basin.

The reactions of Mediterranean countries to the creation of multinational military forces in the Mediterranean, such as EUROFOR and EUROMARFOR, illustrate the apprehensions that exist on the other side of the sea. These countries do not fear an unstable Europe, but their security concerns are linked to North-South relations and to the potential inter- and intrastate conflicts. Western interventions in their region, such as the Gulf war, have produced the image of an all-powerful and invading West, of which Europe is a constituent part together with the United States. Such power is feared and the reactions to the multinational forces illustrate this. Similarly, each move of an army within the region fosters long-held fears by neighboring countries.

Under such conditions, CSBM are an important component to build transparency and confidence between the two shores of the Mediterranean as well as among the CSEM to promote, in the long term, an integrative and normative process. It is important therefore to build up transparency as a principle for the Partnership and its development. The CSBM are not yet sufficiently developed to move toward disarmament, but are indispensable in creating an atmosphere of confidence and openness. Similarly, the prevention of conflict is just beginning in the Mediterranean; it remains, as yet, limited to the interstate level. Nevertheless, since South-North conflicts are highly improbable, CSBM should be of interest to the CSEM as they relate to possible South-South conflicts. The Euro-Mediterranean process seems little advanced on the issue of conflict prevention and confidence, but it remains necessary for its development and success, especially for assuring a stability which would be able to attract investments in the region — something which is the objective of the second part of the process.

Economic and financial "chapter"

The second "chapter" of the Euro-Mediterranean process concerns the economic and financial domain, whose evolution inevitably depends on the stability of the basin. This "chapter" also deals with a broad range of issues such as economic development, and its underlying conceptions, the reduction of the development gap among the partners, the question of international debts and financial assistance, as well as the implementation of a free trade area by 2010. In contrast to the Union's weakness in politico-strategic affairs, the European Union *per se* is in this regard a fully vested actor and represents a new form of political organization, one that diverges significantly from other international organizations.

Although the European Union has enlarged its co-operation to political and security domains in the face of the stakes in the Mediterranean, the main pillar of the partnership remains the numerous bilateral financial and commercial agreements. As mentioned, the main objective is the creation of a free trade zone by 2010. Following tradition, as it were, the EU proposes to rearrange Euro-Mediterranean trade. Free trade — already widespread worldwide and something that could undermine the preferential advantages given to the CSEM by Europe — is one section of the EU's proposal. The CSEM are already heavily dependent on their trade relations with the EU. Therefore, a free trade zone promises the EU an even greater economic role in the Mediterranean.[6] Free trade may lead to positive and negative effects on the stability process, as it leaves the CSEM exposed and dependent on the EU. The latter will in this way obtain possible means to unilaterally influence these countries and this, in turn, could encourage opposition among the CSEM to perceived EU hegemony.

The economic and financial partnership will have decisive consequences on the CSEM, both negative and positive. Bilateral free trade will probably lead to economic integration of the CSEM within the EU zone. The question then arises what kind of integration will take place. Will it increase the dependency of southern states on Europe or will it result in co-operative and egalitarian relations with the EU? Regionalization, the pendent of globalization, does not aim at a common market in the first place and the increase of commercial exchanges since the founding of the World Trade Organization (WTO) has not yet liberalized most economies. Rather, the aim is to integrate national economies to a European whole in the hope that external investments will be attracted into the Mediterranean region. The success of this aspect of regional integration depends in great part on the intensification of investment flows and accompanying policies that the CSEM and the EU will put in place (Chevallier and Bensidoun, 1996; Chevallier and Kébadjian, 1998). These effects depend in great part on the stability of the region.

Note that the Partnership itself does not give the CSEM any better access to the European market. The latter is already largely opened to Mediterranean exporters even as it continues to exclude agriculture products, one of the main products of the CSEM. On the contrary, CSEM will have to open its markets more to European products and they will be asked to dismantle protections put in place to create national import-substitution industries. Last but not least, the CSEM will have to adopt European norms and standards. The constitution of common references is, in this way, also part of this "chapter" as European norms and values have to be adopted by the CSEM. The Partnership is not very egalitarian on this point and, for the time being, it seems to bring rather more advantages to Europeans than anything else. In other words, if it is limited to trade, the impact of a free trade zone will only result in the creation and diversion of commercial trade. There will be few advantages for the CSEM. But the hoped-for indirect effects and the various expected induced developments are more important than direct effects and developments. As Chevallier and Kébadjian (1998) put it, the costs of the creation of a free trade zone are certain and direct whereas the benefits are uncertain and indirect. The internal impact — social, political, and economic — of bilateral trade agreements will be huge and difficult to manage and smooth.

The results one can expect from this partnership will probably differ from one country to another since all possess contrasting trajectories. The free trade zone is likely to create unbalanced development among the CSEM themselves, some countries becoming better integrated into the EU than others. This might not be the best way of increasing the stability of the area and of creating the global normative and integrative process described earlier.

In sum, one may say that the approach offered by the EU is more demanding for the CSEM than for the EU. But it also implies new responsibilities for the EU. This process of regional integration is first of all a political act which marks the will of the participating states to link each other and to respect a certain economic rules and ways of organizing and running a state. The other dimensions of the Partnership, those related to political, security, and cultural domains, are meant to build upon the progress and development of the economic relations and to help create common references. In this respect the development of contacts among civil societies will also be important.

Cultural, social, and human "chapter"

According to many of the participants themselves, the cultural, social, and human "chapter" is not a prime, strategic domain for security and stability. Nevertheless, it is important since it is related to perceptions. It is a way to overcome fears and misunderstandings that, in the Mediterranean, could carry negative consequences. It is also a way to help create common understandings and shared identities. Communication is important in generating transnational civil society.

The goals of the cultural, social, and human chapter remain purposely vague so that they can encompass all that is not dealt with in the two prior "chapters", mainly cultural and religious dialogue, media, education, technological co-operation, health, social rights, terrorism, and the development of civil societies. Since it is thought that commercial and political exchanges have not been and are not sufficient on their own to create regional integration and common understanding, this "chapter" is meant to contribute to what made this region's wealth and stability (such as it is) in the first place, namely a sense of belonging and common references. It is also meant to foster political convergence among member states.

This part of the Euro-Mediterranean process is also important for many non-governmental organizations (NGOs) because of the cultural exchanges and dialogue it speaks of, including questions of democracy and human rights (even if they are already considered in the first "chapter"). Unfortunately, this remains secondary for the Barcelona signatories themselves. Even as respect for democracy and human rights has been written as a basic value into the Partnership documents, there is little doubt that the first two "chapters" will never be conditional to the application of such values. At best a slow process of democratization is expected as a consequence of the contacts between civil societies and the opening of markets, favoring a gradual change in the identities of the CSEM.

The dialogue between and among cultures is sensitive to differences of perception. The points dealt with here are controversial in the Mediterranean countries. Cultural relations in the basin are unbalanced and often one-way in that one party accepts the other's culture without any real exchange taking place. It is more an export of European values than a dialogue between cultures. Still, a concerted effort to come to terms with misunderstandings and prejudices is necessary to diminish the differences in levels of development, neutralize conflicts in the region, and thus eventually to reach the aims set out in the Barcelona partnership. Common socio-economic issues could become the point of departure for contact between civil societies (Calleya, 1998). Economic relations have already led to the creation of numerous chambers of commerce, joint-ventures, and similar commercial associations that, jointly, are the beginning of a process of integration.

Conclusion

In European history, the Mediterranean region once was conceived as part of the center of the world. This changed after Vasco de Gama's travels and subsequent European colonization of the world. Nevertheless, the Mediterranean has remained central to the peaceful development and stability of Europe.

In this chapter, I have applied a constructivist approach to the concept of stability, an approach that helps us not only to take a new look at the notion of stability but helps to underline key points of the EU role in Mediterranean stability that the Barcelona process wants to foster. It shows that lasting stability in the Mediterranean cannot only be a question of coercion and force. It involves a process of building up common understandings and references that are the basis of expectations of peaceful changes. This process is founded as much on the evolution of the knowledge of the actors through mutual learning as on the EU's potential power to impose its vision of reality as the basis for relations in the basin.

The various elements of the model of stability described earlier represent, in part, actual representations of what could be Mediterranean stability. It argues that each one can contribute to the stability process by communication as well as by the changes in the material reality it might bring, one of course linked to the other. Against the different elements of the model one can gauge the possible impact of EU actions on stability in the Mediterranean.

Using this approach, I have shown that the Barcelona Declaration — which is at the origin of the Euro-Mediterranean process — seems to address many of the model's elements. For example, European policy aims at regional integration of the basin, tries to promote growth in the CSEM, and encourages beneficial changes in the administrative and economic structure in these countries; it wants to spread democratic and judicial values, as well as mechanisms to settle conflict peacefully; the third "chapter" favors exchanges among civil societies and cultures so as to limit mutual prejudice.

This said, I have also shown problems with and limitations to the EU policy. One problem is the way the Euro-Mediterranean policy is being implemented. The Euro-Mediterranean process initiated by the EU drives, above all, on the preoccupation to answer European concerns and to expand its values and norms. The EU initiative appears to impose new rules for relations between itself and its southern neighbors and to define new understandings of stability in the region. The stakes that the CSEM face and their perceptions of security are partly taken into account but the solutions offered demand a particular effort of adaptation and reform on the part of these societies. Yet, at the same time, this may present an opportunity for the CSEM to apply reforms that are unavoidable to remain competitive in the global economy. In my view, the success of this attempt at stabilization depends on internal reforms and an improved distribution of wealth that the elites of the CSEM will need to achieve themselves.

A second problem is that the EU at times addresses symptoms of instability rather than causes. The challenges which exist in each area are often dealt with lightly by the EU, in ways that aim to give an impression of change. An egalitarian co-operation has to be at the basis of this process and long term development has to be its principal goal. To reach these goals, the EU should develop and encourage the necessary closer co-operation and communication, among the European member states, among the EU and its southern partners, and even within the CSEM. An important issue in this regard is the adoption of common norms and criteria, beginning with the commercial and economic fields, and developing in other areas afterwards.

A third problem is that the process is a long term exercise and therefore the present results of the Barcelona process are limited. Only a few association agreements are signed and some are not yet ratified. Many problems with these agreements are still not resolved, for example the exclusion of the agricultural sector in the agreement with Egypt and the energy sector in the accords with Algeria. It has to be noted here that International Monetary Fund and World Bank policies can work against EU policy since these institutions affect the CSEM more than the EU does. Indeed, since the EU's policy concentrates primarily on the economic sphere, its influence on the stability of the region is indirect. Its actions are more effective in the socio-economic than in the politico-military sphere. Unfortunately, as noted, the successful results of its socio-economic policies are dependent on evolution in the political sphere.

Politically, a similar problem occurs. Many EU policies are interfered with by US action and intervention, as in the case of the Middle East peace process. This inhibits the Euro-Mediterranean process. But lack of political capacity is the result of lack of political unity within the EU and the absence of any real CFSP and is therefore related to the internal organization and equilibrium of the EU as well as to the hegemonic role of the US.

The EU is not only the instrument of its member states, but itself also shapes new regional realities through its actions. One may note that unity is gradually growing and hence there is hope for the future. Put differently, a political role for the EU is beginning to appear but it will take time to be recognized. In this context, the Mediterranean could represent an opportunity for the EU to develop its common foreign policy: apart from Israel, the CSEM countries are looking for an actor to balance US power in the region. From an Arab perspective, the Euro-Mediterranean process may offer an opportunity to tie Europe to the problems of the region. Similarly, European experiences with co-operative security can be useful in the Mediterranean even if these experiences cannot simply be transferred in wholesale fashion across the sea. The fluid nature of contemporary international relations in the region may give the EU a chance, even as it has to compete with other actors.

Even if the political and socio-economic stability that the Barcelona process hopes for were to be achieved in the medium term, one cannot imagine the establishment of common perceptions and references other than in the long term. Therefore the cultural and human exchanges envisaged in the Partnership might be able to add nicely to the two first "chapters". They will indeed help in the building of co-operation and thus in the development of the common references.

Even if we do not believe that the EU has the power to impose its visions and conceptions, the Partnership remains a unique opportunity to tackle problems that undermine this region and to create common understandings, eventually allowing peaceful changes. The EU remains the principal actor able to foster the basic conditions for stability as the key problems to stability in the basin are essentially socio-economic. In short, as any ambitious and large scale project, this partnership has an uncertain future, but it should permit both Europe and the CSEM to seize the initiative again.

Moreover, analysis of the relations between EU and Mediterranean countries allows us to deal with various fundamental questions regarding the European Union, the Mediterranean, and the complexity of building stability across a region still divided by prejudices and incompatible conceptions of reality. It gives us a fresh look at questions concerning the future of the EU and its neighbors, including the development of the CFSP. The Euro-Mediterranean process is a new trend in North-South relations and a new way to encourage stability for this kind of asymmetric relations. This process of integration between industrialized and developing countries requires more research and analysis to be understood fully.

Notes

1. One may wonder about the framework's potential to answer challenges which are not common to all participant states and which continue to evolve mainly in their regional context. In other words, it would seem that the Euro-Mediterranean process is failing to take into account the sub-regions' evolution. However, this process is merely the first attempt to introduce a policy of co-operation in the Mediterranean that goes beyond the theoretical stage and encourages regular participation irrespective of political events in the basin. It offers, for the first time, the possibility to extend the structures of co-operation and for the countries of the southern and eastern Mediterranean (CSEM) to involve the EU on a regular basis in the challenges they face.

2. A security community is group of individuals organized in political communities, sufficiently integrated so that each member of the community has real insurance that another member will not settle disputes violently. For more details, see K. Deutsch *et al.*, 1957. A security community is far from being achieved in the Mediterranean, but the current Euro-Mediterranean process could be the beginning of such an evolution. Besides this, as we try to think of what could be stability in the basin, the notion of a security community helps us to propose an approach for the concept of stability (see Adler and Barnett, 1998).

3. Due to limitations of space, I cannot develop the motivation for this list. It is presented as a model, but unfortunately lacks an explicit theoretical basis and specific explanation.

4. For example, the EU does not take into account the possibility of an Arab union in this process — it does not consider the Arab League as a whole. Such division of the Arab countries, which the Euro-Mediterranean process implies, raises many questions if not opposition from the CSEM. Some countries even tend to understand the EU initiative as a European attempt to prevent Arab unity, and this is quite problematic since some Arab states would like to associate Persian Gulf countries as well as Libya to the process.

5. The Amsterdam Treaty refers to the latest treaty signed by EU member states. It concerns all of the EU's domains, including the Common Foreign and Security Policy, and delegated new powers to the European Union from its member states, for example the creation of a single currency, the Euro.

6. The EU is the main commercial partner of all the CSEM; some of them, Tunisia for example, handle 70 percent of their trade with the EU. Even Israel conducts around 50 percent of its trade with EU member states.

References

Adler, E. and M. Barnett (1998). *Security Communities*. Cambridge: Cambridge University Press.

Aliboni, R. (1997/1998). "Confidence Building, Conflict Prevention and Arms Control." *Perceptions* (Dec. 1997/Feb. 1998), pp. 73-86.

Awad, I. (1997). "L'intégration européenne, la PESC et la Méditerranée". *Colloque du CEDEJ*. Cairo, 6-8 January.

Buzan, B. (1991). "New Patterns of Global Security in the Twenty-First Century." *International Affairs*. Vol. 67, No. 3, pp. 431-451.

Calleya, S. (1998). "Is the Barcelona Process Working?" Background paper prepared for the roundtable on EU policy in the Eastern Mediterranean, Athens, Philip Morris Institute, Lambrakis Research Foundation, Hellenic Foundation for European & Foreign Policy. 2-3 April.

Chevallier, A. and I. Bensidoun (1996). *Europe-Méditerranée, le pari de l'ouverture*. Paris: Economica.

Chevallier, A. and G. Kébadjian (1998). "L'Euro-Méditerranée entre mondialisation et régionalisation". *Maghreb-Machrek*, Hors-série (December), pp.9-18.

Deutsch, K., S. Burrell, R.A. Kann, M. Lee Jr, M. Lichterman, R.E. Lindgren, F.L. Loewenheim, and R.W. van Wagenen (1957). *Political Community and North Atlantic Area*. Princeton: Princeton University Press.

Hobsbawm, E. and T. Ranger (1996). *The Invention of Tradition*. Cambridge: Cambridge University Press. [1st ed., 1983]

The Euro-Mediterranean Partnership: basic official documents:

Communication from the Commission to the Council and the European Parliament: Strengthening the Mediterranean Policy of the European Union: Establishing a Euro-Mediterranean Partnership. — COM(94)427 final, 19.10.94.

Communication from the Commission to the Council and the European Parliament: Strengthening the Mediterranean Policy of the European Union: Proposals for implementing a Euro-Mediterranean Partnership. — COM(95)972 final, 8.3.95.

The Barcelona declaration.

Joint Report by the Presidency of the Council and the Commission on Mediterranean Policy: follow-up to the Barcelona Conference. — A4-0027/97.

Final Communiqué of the Second Euro-Mediterranean Ministerial Conference, Valetta, 15 and 16 April 1997.

Communication from the Commission on the Euro-Mediterranean Partnership and the Single Market. — COM(98)538 final, 32.9.98.

Final Communiqué of the Second Euro-Mediterranean Ministerial Conference, Stuttgart, 15-16 April 1999.

Euro-Mediterranean Agreements concluded with Tunisia, Jordan, Israel, Morocco, Palestinian Authority.

Regulations of the MEDA programmes and decentralised MED programmes.

3 Modeling defense budget allocations: an application to Canada

John Treddenick

Introduction

The defense planning challenge today is one of managing great change and great uncertainty in the context of greatly diminished resources. Reductions in defense expenditures, particularly when they occur in a period of a dramatically changing security concerns, give rise to issues about the internal allocation of defense budgets, and especially to issues about the efficiency of those allocations. When expenditures and force structures are large, issues of efficiency in internal resource allocation can be deferred much more easily than under more restrictive budgetary conditions. With sharply falling defense budgets the situation becomes reversed. Internal competition for resources becomes more intense, the necessity for tradeoffs becomes more sharply defined, and, as a result, questions of allocation and efficiency become paramount.

Deciding on budget allocations is the heart of defense policy making. It is in the allocation of defense budgets where force structures and force capabilities are ultimately selected and made feasible. In many ways, then, allocation decisions are as important as deciding on the total level of defense spending itself. But evaluating contending allocations of defense resources is excruciatingly complex. In the first instance, there are no objective measures of defense output. It is difficult to agree on just what is being produced by allocating resources to defense. It is harder still to give that output some notion of value. In a perfectly rational and perfectly informed world, resource allocations across the individual services, across different weapons systems, and across the various inputs in the production of defense capabilities would be based on comparisons of marginal contributions to overall defense value. In a less than perfect world such choices are more subjective. They emerge less from rational calculation than they do from political and bureaucratic bargaining and from simple habit and inertia.

The difficulty of output measures aside, the complexity of allocating defense budgets is rooted in other features of the defense environment. The first of these concerns the stock-flow relationship of many defense inputs. It is the stock of equipment and infrastructure, for example, that contributes to the production of current defense capabilities and not the annual budgetary expenditure for them. Annual expenditures contribute to replenishing or augmenting these stocks, but stocks actually available are inherited from the past. They are the result of previous expenditure decisions and are the cumulative result of those decisions. As a result, capital expenditure decisions can impart particular dynamic properties to defense resource allocations. In addition, the allocation of defense budgets must contend with the existence of complicated interdependencies and feedback relationships among defense inputs. Increasing either manpower or equipment levels, for example, will raise demands for increased operations and maintenance support and for infrastructure support. In turn, the resulting increases in operations and maintenance support and infrastructure support will have implications for manpower usage.

This chapter addresses the complexity of defense budgeting through the use of simple economic models. Its intent is to use rather orthodox economic modeling techniques to explore the multiple direct and indirect causal paths, the inter-temporal linkages, the lagged influences and the feedback loops inherent in defense budgeting. It is intended also to provide a structure for performing "what if" experiments on alternative approaches to defense budget distributions.

To set the stage for the modeling exercise, the next section sketches the main contours of the defense resource allocation problem. It attempts to identify the sorts of issues that models of defense resource allocation should attempt to encompass. Previous work which has inspired and informed this exercise is outlined in the third section. The structure of the general models is described in the fourth section while the fifth section discusses their solution. The sixth section presents some illustrative results obtained from applying one version of this model to near-term simulations of Canadian defense budgets. Finally, a concluding section offers some comments about the modeling approach and makes some suggestions for future research.

The defense resource allocation problem

As indicated in Figure 3.1, defense can be viewed as a physical production process where inputs are transformed and given value by producing an output.

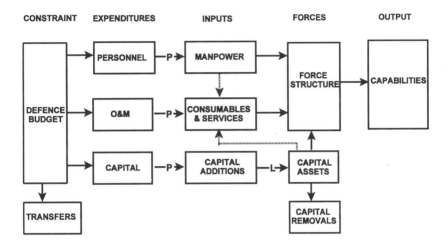

Figure 3.1: Defense budget allocations with input prices (P) and lagged capital stock adjustment (L).

The output of this process can be considered to be a general military capability whose value is determined in political fora rather than in economic markets. The inputs into the production process can be broadly classified as manpower, consumables — comprising such things as petrol, ammunition, and contracted services — and capital, which includes both equipment assets and infrastructure assets such as buildings and other facilities. Actual expenditures on inputs are determined as the product of the physical quantities of inputs acquired and their prices. The corresponding budgetary categories for these inputs are generally denominated as personnel expenditures, operations and maintenance expenditures, and capital expenditures. Capital expenditures are usually further subdivided into equipment expenditures and infrastructure expenditures.

The production of defense capabilities may be regarded as a problem of constrained optimization. From this view, the challenge for defense management is to maximize the military capability achievable from a given budget with a given defense technology and a given set of input prices. It would attempt to achieve this by judiciously choosing the way in which it allocates its expenditure among the inputs. As with goods and services produced in the civilian economy, a given level of defense output can be produced using many different combinations of manpower, consumables, and capital. Depending upon the technology of producing defense, defense managers have the opportunity to substitute among these inputs in attempting to produce a given level of output at minimum cost. Alternatively, with a given budget, it can make these substitutions to maximize the output of defense obtainable from a given budget. Assuming that they are either cost-minimizers or output-maximizers, defense managers will respond to changes in budget levels, changes in defense technology, and changes in defense input prices by reallocating expenditures as required to make appropriate tradeoffs among these inputs. It is important to note, however, that defense managers may be subject to other constraints which may restrict their ability to react to changes in budgets, technology, and input prices. In addition to the budget constraint, for example, there may exist an upper constraint on manpower levels, political constraints on the acquisition of certain weapons, or political constraints on where and how military equipment is to be acquired and where and how military bases are to be maintained.

The manpower input in defense consists of both military and civilian personnel. These are differentiated by contractual differences in working conditions, especially the obligations imposed on military personnel with respect to terms of service, obedience, discipline, and personal liability. The military component will in turn consist of some mix of operational personnel and support personnel. The former includes personnel directly engaged in the production of military capability. The latter include military personnel indirectly contributing to the production of military capability through central administration, financial services, material support, including acquisition services, and personnel support. Civilian personnel will be entirely support personnel. The military support personnel and civilian personnel together comprise the total support manpower. Military personnel can be further classified as regular force, conscript or reserve personnel. With regard to manpower, then, defense planners confront several tradeoff situations: between military and civilian personnel, between operational and support personnel, between military and civilian support, and finally among regular force military personnel, conscripts, and reserve force personnel. The total demand for defense manpower and the desired mix of these various types of manpower will be determined by budget levels, defense technology, the prices of manpower relative to other defense inputs, and the relative prices of the different types of manpower.

Operations and maintenance expenditures represent expenditures for consumables and contracted services made to provide support for personnel, equipment, and infrastructure. As such, they can be expected to vary according to the number of personnel and the size and age distribution of the stock of equipment and infrastructure assets. Operations and maintenance expenditures may also act as substitutes for other types of defense expenditure. Maintenance expenditures, for example, may to some extent reduce equipment fleet requirements by ensuring that a higher proportion of a smaller fleet is in serviceable condition and operationally ready. More generally, maintenance expenditures can offset equipment and infrastructure investment by affecting the flow of productive services from existing stocks and by extending their useful lives. Similarly, operations and maintenance expenditures may substitute for manpower as services previously produced within the military establishment, especially at the lower stages of the defense production chain, such as training, personnel support services, financial services and maintenance, are contracted out to the private sector. Tradeoffs among operations and maintenance expenditures and other categories of expenditure can again be expected to be conditioned by budget levels, defense technology, the inherited stock of capital assets, and the relative prices of defense inputs.

Expenditures for personnel and for operations and maintenance generally represent expenditures for *current* military capability. Personnel expenditures are made to maintain trained and motivated forces. Operations and maintenance expenditures are made to keep those forces at a desired level of readiness. Though this must be qualified, especially with regard to personnel expenditures, each of these two types of expenditure is used to buy an input which yields a *flow* of productive services at the time of expenditure. These inputs can therefore be distinguished as being variable over the short-run, that is over the budgetary period, which in most cases is one year.

Capital expenditures are different. They are made to ensure that the stocks of equipment and facilities are continuously modernized. They are therefore expenditures for *future* military capabilities. Thus, defense budgetary allocation decisions are always statements about inter-temporal choice. With a given defense budget, what is spent on capital today is at the expense of current military capabilities. Any budget exercise therefore always implies an explicit tradeoff between current capabilities and future capabilities. Accordingly, the budgetary implications of spending on capital differs markedly from the implications of spending on manpower and consumables. Annual expenditures on manpower and operations and maintenance are reasonably good indicators of the flow of productive services which they contribute to the production of defense capability. By contrast, annual expenditures on capital bear almost no relationship to the production of current capability.

While the stock of capital assets is being continuously augmented by annual flows of capital expenditures, it is also being continuously reduced through the growing obsolescence, both technical and military, of assets acquired in the past. In a steady state, that is for a constant capital stock, the reduction occurring in any one year will be precisely offset by new additions in that year, not necessarily in terms of one-for-one replacement but in terms of the amount of military capability represented by the capital stock. Net investment is then zero. When additions exceed removals, that is when net investment is positive, the stock of capital will be growing and, other things being equal, military capability will be potentially increased or at least be made more capital intensive. This net investment, however, is at the expense of acquiring more manpower or more consumables, and hence it represents a loss of current military capability. On the other hand, when removals exceed additions, net investment is negative, the stock of capital falls, and, again, other things being equal, potential military capability is reduced or becomes less capital intensive. In this case, which represents a process of disinvestment or living off one's assets, current military capabilities gain at the expense of future capabilities.

Much of the complexity in defense resource allocations arises out of this stock-flow nature of capital expenditure. Annual expenditures for equipment and infrastructure can represent only a small proportion of the stocks of these assets. Stocks can represent a multiple of two to four times a nation's total defense budget, and perhaps ten to fifteen times its annual expenditure for those assets. As a result, under normal circumstances, stocks are built up or reduced only very slowly. It can therefore take a very long period of time to significantly alter the composition and size of these stocks. Equipment and infrastructure, as inputs into the defense production process, are therefore variable only in the long-run. This period of time, the time required for complete recapitalization, which might amount to fifteen or twenty years, therefore represents the time period required to arrive at an appropriate mix of all defense inputs, including manpower, operations, and maintenance. Accordingly, successful defense planning, at least in theory, requires the management of budget allocations not for a particular point in time nor even for a few years into the future, but rather as a dynamic allocation over very long periods.

Because capital expenditures add nothing to current military capabilities but only to future capabilities, and because they affect those capabilities only after significant periods of time, they have the property of being eminently deferrable. Combined with defense planners' expected high time preferences for forces-in-being as opposed to potential forces, defense budgets, particularly in times of constant or falling budgets, can be expected to be biased toward expenditures on manpower and on operations and maintenance rather than capital. When budgets are tight, as they normally always are, there exists a natural tendency to preserve current force structure and near-term readiness at the expense of investment in infrastructure and equipment modernization. There will thus be a tendency to maintain manpower at levels above the level appropriate to the existing stock of infrastructure and equipment in the optimistic anticipation that future defense budgets will eventually allow capital deficiencies to be made up.[1] All the while of course, this hoarding of manpower and the increasing costs of operating and maintaining ageing equipment will make the availability of budget room for capital investment even more difficult to come by, leading ultimately to a cycle of capital disinvestment. Public choice theory would tend to support this bias toward manpower hoarding on the basis that higher levels of manpower mean more promotion opportunities and also higher budgets since expenditures for employment purposes might be more politically attractive than expenditures for weapons.

There is another peculiarity associated with capital expenditure, especially expenditure for equipment, which makes it difficult to achieve an optimal allocation of defense budgets. As Kirkpatrick (1995) has observed, when the typical time profile of life-cycle costs for a piece of equipment is examined, this profile will normally show a peaking of costs and expenditures in the procurement phase of the life-cycle. But there are likely to be many investment projects underway at the same time. With a limited capital budget, these projects will have to be time-phased or staggered such that procurement peaks lie within annual budgetary ceilings. Capital expenditures must in effect be squeezed down and pushed forward in time. Since defense ministries cannot generally borrow and lend to smooth out the differences between budgetary income and investment expenditures — though a case on the grounds of economic efficiency could be made to permit them to do so — the investment program must be extended through time such that all projects fit within the annual budget constraints over the planning period. The net effect is to postpone investment expenditures with the inevitable result of increased operations and maintenance costs and the reinforcement of the tendency toward a vicious cycle of disinvestment.

The ultimate consequence of the high time preference of defense planners, the bias toward expenditures for manpower, and the existence of artificial capital budget limits is a pattern of capital investment characterized by long periods of low rates of investment, usually negative net investment, such that stocks become diminished. Over this period of deferred replacement investment and diminishing stocks, internal pressures can build up for a major recapitalization effort and a radical change in the level and distribution of defense budgets. While an investment boom could be set off internally, especially when there arise serious questions about the continued viability of the defense effort, typically the spark is provided by some external development. Often this major change in defense spending will be accompanied by significant changes in defense policy, major reorganizations of the defense establishment, and the introduction of new budgeting and management techniques, all designed to ensure that the neglect of capital investment does not happen again. Inevitably, though, this boom is followed by another long period of capital neglect. All of this gives rise to a cyclical pattern of equipment investment which is characterized by boom and erosion and echoes of boom and erosion. It gives rise, too, to block obsolescence and the consequent requirement to replace much of the equipment inventory at the same time. As Lewis (1994) suggests, this self-replicating boom-erosion pattern of capital investment has become a *de facto* strategy of recapitalization in defense organizations.

These complexities on the input side of the defense production process make the evaluation of defense budgetary allocations very challenging. It is made even more so by the lack of an objective measure of the output of that process. Without a measure of output, there can be no measures of the relative productivities of inputs, and hence no objective basis for allocating expenditures among them. As an output measure, the concept of defense capability defies measurement, and probably definition. It is perhaps possible to talk about the level of performance of individual components of a military organization in terms of their training, equipment, readiness, leadership, and so on, but aggregating these to obtain some global measure of military capability for the defense organization as a whole could not be done in any meaningful way (Kirkpatrick, 1995). In any event, the effectiveness of military capability is a relative concept: it is always relative to the performance of potential rival military organizations. Hence it can only be determined in actual combat. But, as a matter of practical budgetary practice, defense planners must be assumed to deal with some notion of output. For most, given the abstract nature of the idea of defense capability, the focus is very likely to be on force structure.

Force structures, however, are only assemblages of defense inputs, that is of manpower, consumables, equipment, and infrastructure. Inputs are visible and measurable, and defense planners will understandably be more comfortable with these ideas in making defense budgetary allocations than with more abstract and elusive ideas of defense output. There are a number of alternative input-based approaches which could be used. The first, stylized and overly simplified as the "arm the men" approach, focuses on manpower. A manpower level is chosen and funded, and the required operations and maintenance expenditures are allocated to support both this level of manpower and the inherited stock of equipment and infrastructure. What remains is allocated to replacing or possibly augmenting the existing stocks of equipment and infrastructure. In this approach, then, capital expenditure is determined as a residual in the budgetary process. Such an approach may be expected to be typical of manpower-intensive organizations, especially of armies. However, the existence of boom-erosion-echo cycles in capital expenditures, which seem to be typical of defense organizations as a whole, would suggest that this approach prevails more generally.

A second approach to input-based planning focuses on the stock of equipment as the planning variable. In this case, again grossly simplified, a desired stock of equipment is identified, the additions required to bring the existing stock up to this level are determined, these additions are funded, operations and maintenance expenditures are allocated to support the new stock of equipment and whatever level of manpower can then be afforded. This "man the arms" approach treats manpower as a residual in the planning and budgeting exercise and might be expected to be typical of capital-intensive defense organizations, especially of navies and air forces. Where budget allocations are made in this way, it could be anticipated that manpower, rather than capital investment, would be subject to boom-erosion-echo cycles.

An alternative to focusing on either manpower or capital alone would be to approach defense budget allocations on the basis of the equipment-manpower ratio which the budget could support. Such a ratio would represent a measure of the average capability of the military force. The "arm the men" approach, where capital expenditure is determined as a budgetary residual, would tend to result in low equipment-manpower ratios. The opposite would be true of the "man the arms" approach, where manpower becomes the residual. However, where the ratio of equipment to manpower is made the objective of defense planning, rather than the absolute level of either, it should be possible to make much more explicit the potential tradeoff between manpower levels and average capability.

Whatever approach is taken to dealing with the concept of defense output, one extremely important issue that budget allocations may affect is the relationship between output and budget levels. If this relationship is nonlinear, then a budget may be too low in the sense that it is largely providing overhead and very little in the way of defense capability (Lewis, 1994). Reductions in defense budgets may therefore result in support costs taking a larger share of the budget leading to disproportionate reductions in operational capability. On the other hand, a budget may be too large if increments to capability are possible only with very large increases in the total budget. This phenomenon can be considered to be a problem of scale, where larger budgets allow fixed costs, infrastructure, and support services to be spread over greater output. It will be reflected in changing internal allocations of the defense budget as budgets rise or fall. Well designed economic models of defense budgeting should be able to provide some insight into these changing allocations.

Modeling defense expenditures and budgets

Defense budgeting and resource allocation would seem to offer a rich field for economic analysis. Interesting challenges certainly abound. Among these would be the identification and explanation of the structural relationships which describe defense budgeting as a complete system. A drawing of the broad lines of relationships among the various parts of the system in this way might permit us to see how all the major parts fit together and how changes in one part of the system affect changes in the other parts, not only in the present but over time. Such a framework would provide a basis for examining how the system reacts to relative price changes, to changes in the defense budget, to inflation, and to changes in ways of producing defense. Specifically, it should provide some idea of how readily the system reacts to these changes in terms of substitutions among the inputs. It should also provide some idea about the time required to complete these substitutions. Similarly, such a framework should permit a systematic investigation of such issues as whether defense budgeting is inherently manpower-biased or whether defense budgeting systems are inherently disposed to producing cycles of investment expenditure.

Despite this richness, the literature of defense economics and management is remarkably bereft of comprehensive and rigorous analyses of the internal structure and dynamics of defense budgets and production. There is, of course, a vast literature dealing with individual areas of defense budgeting and with individual defense inputs. Studies of military manpower, for example, abound, as do studies on logistics and weapons procurement. Little, however, has been written on how these are all related within the context of defense budgeting. There are exceptions. Cooper and Roll (1974) constructed a series on the rental cost of capital to show that, relative to the price of military manpower in the United States, the price of capital was falling. Assuming that defense planners were cost-minimizers, they concluded that capital should be substituted for manpower. On the basis of the same assumption, Smith, Humm, and Fontanel (1987) used a particular form of the defense production function to estimate the elasticity of substitution between manpower and capital based on 1976 cross-sectional data for 23 countries. In a similar analysis, Ridge and Smith (1991) employed an interactive demand and supply model to estimate the elasticity of substitution between military manpower and capital for the United Kingdom for the period 1952-1987. Owen (1994) has compared military manpower-equipment ratios for 23 countries in two different time periods and has made comparisons of these ratios with equivalent ratios in civil aviation and manufacturing. The implications of the rising ratio of unit-costs to defense budgets have been examined by both Pugh (1993) and Kirkpatrick (1995). Defense investment cycles have been discussed by, among others, Mulhern (1993) and Clark (1993). A recent contribution toward more comprehensive modeling of defense planning has been made by Correa, Scott, and Skovran (1997). Based on the concepts of inter-industry analysis, their framework emphasizes the interdependencies among defense activities and links changes in final output activities to an entire system of interconnected support activities.

Among more institutionally oriented works, Lewis (1994) has examined the internal structure of US defense budgets and observes that there has been a convergence over time in the budget shares allocated to the three services, that capital investment expenditures move disproportionately to changes in the total budget, rising more quickly when total budgets rise and falling more quickly when they fall, and that there has been a gradual shift in the share of expenditures going to support functions at the expense of operational functions. Snider (1993) and Snider, Gouré, and Cambone (1994) raise fundamental questions about the allocation of declining US defense budgets between expenditures for current readiness, in terms of current force structures, and expenditures for modernization, in terms of equipment procurement and research and development. Thompson and Jones (1994) apply the concepts of the economics of institutions and organizations to analysis and prescription for defense management in the US. Among the challenges they consider is the management of budget reductions, particularly as these reductions affect the stock of equipment and expenditures for research and development. Their recommendations for managing the complexity of defense resource allocation include the establishment of a system of buyer-seller and transfer pricing arrangements between operational units and support units.

This chapter describes an attempt to model the relationships between defense output and defense inputs in terms of a system of simultaneous equations. Like any economic model it represents a drastic simplification of reality. Defense institutions are complex institutions and the process of defense budget-making is a complex process, one which undoubtedly reflects political and bureaucratic interests more than any notion of allocative efficiency. Nevertheless, even defense departments must conform to the laws of arithmetic and certain accounting principles, and for those reasons alone there are bound to be regularities in the budgeting process that can be observed and modeled. If nothing else, such models help to organize data about the defense resource allocation process and that in itself is a useful step toward understanding the process. In any event the usefulness of economic modeling lies less in its accurate portrayal of a detailed reality than it does in providing a framework for tracing cause and effect among a small number of key variables. They are especially useful in tracing out relationships which involve feedback effects, effects which are typical of defense budgeting and defense expenditures.

Defense budget models are therefore simplified skeletal systems. They inevitably represent a tradeoff between realism and manageability. If well devised, however, they bring out features of interdependence among defense expenditure categories that are not easily recognized or comprehended without their help. Relationships among these categories are therefore made more explicit and are more easily tested for reasonableness and consistency when presented in the form of a mathematical model.

The Model

The point of departure for this model is the defense budget identity. This equation expresses the defense budget as the sum of four expenditure categories: personnel, operations and maintenance, equipment, and infrastructure. With the exception of personnel expenditures, which are singled out for more elaborate explanation, each of the variables on the right-hand side of this equation is expressed in terms of price and quantity components. Personnel expenditures are defined in a second equation as the sum of expenditures on military personnel and on civilian personnel, again expressed in terms of price and quantity components. Military manpower is then defined as the sum of operational manpower and support manpower. The demand for total support personnel is hypothesized to depend upon the total size of operational manpower, the stock of equipment, the stock of infrastructure, and the basing structure, assumed to be represented by the number of military bases and establishments. Military support manpower is determined as a proportion of total support personnel where the proportion is assumed to be a defense planing choice. The number of civilian personnel is then the difference between total support personnel requirements and military support personnel. Operations and maintenance expenditures are hypothesized to depend upon the number of military operational personnel, the total number of support personnel, the infrastructure stock, the equipment stock, and the number of bases.

Infrastructure expenditures are treated in the context of a partial stock-adjustment mechanism. Investment in any year is expressed as a proportion of the difference between a desired stock of the asset and the depreciated existing stock at the beginning of that year. In other words, it is assumed that, for financial or technical reasons, adjustments in the infrastructure stock are made with a time lag. Only a proportion of the required adjustment in any time period is made in that time period. Infrastructure stock is then calculated in each period as the accumulation of past investment expenditures net of depreciation. In this model, the desired stock of infrastructure assets is assumed to depend upon the number of operational military personnel, the total number of support personnel, the equipment inventory, and the number of military bases and establishments. Actual infrastructure investment expenditures in any year are the product of investment and the infrastructure procurement price index.[2]

Equipment expenditures are treated in one of two ways depending upon whether the output proxy is taken to be total manpower or the equipment-manpower ratio. Where manpower is assumed to be the planning variable, investment expenditures are determined as the residual expenditure after all relationships among the other expenditure categories have worked themselves out. When the equipment-manpower ratio is assumed to be the planning variable, the treatment of equipment expenditures is very similar to that described for infrastructure expenditures. Actual equipment expenditures will be expressed as a proportion of the difference between a desired stock of equipment and the depreciated existing stock, such that the adjustment in any time period is necessarily incomplete. The existing stock is then calculated as the summation of past expenditures on equipment net of depreciation. The desired stock of equipment is defined as the product of the planned equipment-manpower ratio and total operational manpower. In this version of the model, assuming a fixed budget, manpower becomes the residual variable.

The detailed specification of the model is given below. Definitions of the variables and policy parameters are given in Table 3.1.

The defense budget allocation model

The budget identity:

(3.1) $B_t = P_t + po_t O_t + pF_t I_{Ft} + pw_t I_{Wt}$

Personnel expenditures and demands for personnel:

(3.2) $P_t = pM_t M_{Mt} + pc_t M_{Ct}$

(3.3) $M_{Mt} = M_{Ot} + M_{MSt}$

(3.4) $M_{MSt} = k M_{St}$

(3.5) $M_{St} = \pi_0 + \pi_1 M_{MOt} + \pi_3 F_t + \pi_4 W_t + \pi_5 E_t$

(3.6) $M_{Ct} = M_{St} - M_{MSt}$

Operations and maintenance expenditures:

(3.7) $O_t = \phi_0 + \phi_1 M_{MOt} + \phi_2 M_{St} + \phi_3 F_t + \phi_4 W_t + \phi_5 E_t$

Infrastructure expenditures:

(3.8) $I_{Ft} = \lambda_F \left[F_t{}^* - (1 - d_F) F_{t-1} \right]$ (lagged adjustment to desired stock)

(3.9) $F_t = \alpha_0 + \alpha_1 M_{MOt} + \alpha_2 M_{St} + \alpha_4 W_t + \alpha_5 E_t$ (desired stock)

(3.10) $F_t = (1 - \delta_F) F_{t-1} + I_{Ft}$ (infrastructure accumulation)

Equipment expenditures:

(3.11) $I_{Wt} = (B_t - P_t - p_{ot} O_t - p_{Ft} I_{Ft}) / p_{wt}$ (residual expenditure)

        or

(3.12) $I_{Wt} = \lambda_W \left[W_t{}^* - (1 - \delta_W) W_{t-1} \right]$ (lagged adjustment to desired stock)

(3.13) $W_t{}^* = r M_{Ot}$ (desired stock)

(3.14) $W_t = (1 - \delta_W) W_{t-1} + I_{Wt}$ (equipment accumulation)

Model solution

In constructing these models we start with some idea of the variables whose movements we want the model to explain. In the models described in this chapter, there are 11 such endogenous variables explained by the system when military manpower is the planning variable. Thus, manpower is an exogenous variable while the equipment-manpower variable is endogenously determined. When the equipment-manpower ratio is the planning variable, there are 13 endogenous variables, including military manpower. In both versions the remaining variables, including the defense budget, the number of bases, and the inherited stocks of infrastructure and equipment (which are actually lagged endogenous variables and give the system its dynamic character) are exogenous to the system at a given point in time. Other exogenous variables include the civilian-military share parameter for support personnel, the input prices, the lag parameters, and the depreciation rates.

Table 3.1: Variables and parameters

Endogenous Variables
P = personnel expenditures
O = O&M expenditures in units of constant purchasing power
I_W = equipment expenditures in units of constant purchasing power
I_F = infrastructure expenditures in units of constant purchasing power
M_O = number of operational military personnel
M_S = number of military support personnel
M_{MS} = number of support personnel
M_C = number of civilian personnel
M_M = number of military personnel (endogenous when equipment-manpower ratio is exogenous)
F^* = desired stock of physical infrastructure
F = actual stock of physical infrastructure
W^* = desired stock of equipment
W = actual stock of equipment
r = equipment-manpower ratio (endogenous when military manpower is exogenous)

Lagged Endogenous Variables
F_{t-1} = actual stock of physical infrastructure lagged one period
W_{t-1} = actual stock of equipment lagged one period

Exogenous Policy Variables
B = total defense budget
E = number of military bases and establishments
M_M = number of military personnel (exogenous when equipment-manpower ratio is endogenous)
r = equipment-manpower ratio (exogenous when military manpower is endogenous)
k   = civilian personnel as a proportion of support personnel

Other Exogenous Variables
p_O = price index for operations and maintenance expenditures
p_F = price index for infrastructure expenditures
p_W = price index for equipment expenditures
p_M = average unit cost of military manpower
p_C = average unit cost of civilian manpower
λ_F = infrastructure investment lag $(0 < \lambda_F < 1)$
λ_W = equipment investment lag $(0 < \lambda_W < 1)$
δ_F = depreciation rate for infrastructure
δ_W = depreciation rate for equipment

Changes in any of the exogenous variables will have one-way effects on all of the endogenous variables in the system, but the ultimate effect of changes in the exogenous variables will be realized only after all of the relationships among the endogenous variables have been played out. For example, when the equipment-manpower ratio is taken to be the planning variable and remains unchanged, the proximate effect of an increase in the defense budget will be an increase in the number of operational military personnel. The increase in military operational personnel will in turn result in an increase in the desired stock of equipment, causing an increase in investment expenditures, which, because of the lag structures, will extend over time. Both the increase in operational manpower and the increase in the capital stock will in turn lead to changes in support personnel and infrastructure requirements. All of these changes will also require changes in operations and maintenance expenditures. Ultimately, when the system has absorbed all of these changes and equilibrium is restored, each of the endogenous variables will have assumed new values. These ultimate effects are obtained mathematically by solving the model for each of the endogenous variables in terms of all of the exogenous variables in the system. The solution thus obtained can then be used to determine the ultimate effects on all of the endogenous variables which result from changes in any of the exogenous variables, including input prices, lag parameters, and depreciation rates.

When the equipment-manpower ratio (r) is the planning variable and total military manpower (M_M) is endogenous, then the solution for the operational manpower variable is:

$$(3.15) \quad Mo_t^* = v_0 + v_1 B_t + v_2 E_t + v_3 F_{t-1} + v_4 W_{t-1}$$

In this reduced form equation, the coefficients are obtained as linear combinations of the structural coefficients of the original models, the prices, the lag coefficients, the depreciation rates, and the civilian-military share parameter. The coefficient for the budget variable in equation 3.15 is also a function of r_t, the equipment-manpower ratio, which is the policy target variable for this version of the model. Each of the coefficients in the equation indicates the ultimate effect on the size of operational military manpower of a change in the respective exogenous variables. For this reason, they are often referred to as multipliers. Hence, the coefficient on the budget variable, v_1, indicates the multiplier effect of a change in the defense budget on the size of operational military manpower after all feedback effects on support personnel, operations and maintenance, equipment investment, and infrastructure investment have been taken into account. This assumes that defense planners are attempting to achieve a particular equipment-manpower ratio, r, in time period t. From this value for Mo it is possible to compute W^*, the desired stock of equipment from (3.13).

Similarly, the system can be solved for the reduced form equations for other key endogenous variables, especially the desired stock of infrastructure and the demand for support personnel:

(3.16) $F_t^* = \mu_0 + \mu_1 B_t + \mu_2 E_t + \mu_3 F_{t-1} + \mu_4 W_{t-1}$

(3.17) $W_t^* = \nu_0 + \nu_1 B_t + \nu_2 E_t + \nu_3 F_{t-1} + \nu_4 W_{t-1}$

Using the results of these four equations it is possible to compute the equilibrium values of all of the remaining endogenous variables in the system. Finally, it is possible to construct the four expenditure components of the defense budget — personnel, operations and maintenance, equipment, and infrastructure — to determine how a change in the budget, basing structure, or the desired equipment-manpower ratio will affect the budget distribution. It would be possible to perform counterfactual experiments with the size of the budget to determine, among other things, how the ratio of operational manpower to support manpower varies with budget size. Some idea could thereby be obtained of how the "tooth-to-tail" ratio is affected by budget size. Similar simulations could be performed to determine how price changes or changes in investment lags affect manpower levels, manpower distribution, or any of the other endogenous variables in the system.

   The same process is used to solve the system when manpower is assumed to be the planning variable. The reduced form equation for equipment investment expenditures, now a residual variable, becomes:

(3.18) $I_{Wt} = \theta_0 + \theta_1 B_t + \theta_2 E_t + \theta_3 F_{t-1} + \theta_4 W_{t-1} + \theta_5 M_{Mt}$

In this case, the coefficient on the budget variable, θ_1, indicates the ultimate effect on investment expenditures of a budget change, again after all feedback effects on support personnel, operations and maintenance, equipment investment, and infrastructure investment have been taken into account and assuming that defense planners are attempting to achieve a particular level of total military manpower, M_M, in time period t. The equilibrium values for all of the remaining endogenous variables can be obtained in the same manner.

   Finally, these models can also be rearranged to treat the defense budget level as an endogenous variable. In this case, both the manpower level and the equipment-manpower ratio would be established as target exogenous variables. The system would then be solved to yield the budget path necessary to provide the specified target values over a given period of time, again on the assumption that the values of all the other exogenous variables, including input prices, lag structures, and depreciation rates, are given.

Some notional results from the Canadian data

While the general models we have constructed are modest in size, econometric estimation of their structures still requires a prodigious amount of data. Thus far we have used hypothetical structural parameters based on observations on Canadian defense budgeting experience to calibrate the models as a means of testing them for internal consistency and reasonableness. We have also used estimated versions of some simplified versions of these models to perform simulations of Canadian defense budget distributions. With a view to demonstrating the potential of using economic models to provide analytical support to defense budgeting and planning, results from some of these simulations are reported in this section.

With the simplified models, data requirements are very much reduced, though this is of course at the expense of explanatory value. In these simpler versions, for example, we have aggregated equipment and infrastructure expenditures into a single category of capital expenditure and thus deal with a single capital asset stock. Similarly, military personnel were not classified into operational and support personnel. Also, only two input price indexes were employed, one for capital expenditures and one for all other input expenditures. Operations and maintenance expenditures were linked to other inputs through a regression explaining operations and maintenance expenditures in terms of total military manpower and the age distribution of the capital stock.[3]

The simplified models are used here to perform three experiments. The first experiment assumes that manpower is the exogenously determined target variable. The model then generates the time paths for capital expenditures and the resulting capital-manpower ratio which are possible with a given budget. The time path of budget distributions in terms of personnel, operations and maintenance, and capital expenditures is also determined. The second experiment takes the capital-manpower ratio as the target variable and looks at the resulting time path of manpower levels and budget distributions as an attempt is made to increase the capital-manpower ratio over a given planning period. The third experiment assumes that both manpower levels and the capital-manpower ratio are planning variables, and then asks what time-path of defense expenditure would be required to achieve both targets over a given planning period.

Over the post-cold war transition period Canadian defense expenditures have fallen from a peak of C$12 billions to approximately C$9.3 billions in 1998-

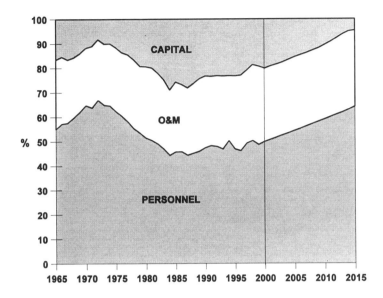

Figure 3.2: Simulated budget distributions 2000-2015: manpower target with no inflation compensation

1999. Current defense planning is based on the assumption — and it remains only an assumption and not declared policy — that the defense budget will remain at this level in real terms for the foreseeable future, that is, it will be allowed to rise in nominal terms only enough to compensate for inflation. In our first experiment, however, we are less optimistic and assume a scenario where the budget will remain at its current nominal level indefinitely. That is, there will be no compensation for inflation. Current defense planning in Canada also foresees a regular military establishment of 60,000 and a civilian establishment of 20,000. This first experiment then asks what is the effect on the capital-manpower ratio and the on distribution of the defense budget of retaining a force level of 60,000 with a budget of C$9.3 billions uncompensated for inflation over the planning period.

The results of this experiment are shown in Figure 3.2. To provide some context and perspective for the simulation results, actual and planned budget distributions for the period 1965 to 1999 are also shown. Particularly striking in this latter period is the clear cyclical pattern of the capital share and the

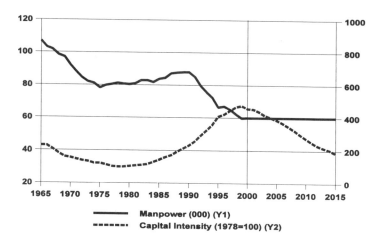

Figure 3.3: Simulated capital-manpower ratios 2000-2015: manpower target with no inflation compensation

complementary offsetting cycle in the personnel share. Not unexpectedly, given our assumptions of a constant manpower level and constant nominal defense budget, the share of capital continues to decline after 2000. In the latter part of the simulation period, capital expenditures reach the very low proportions typical of the late 1960s and early 1970s. The operations and maintenance expenditure share, it should be noted, continues the slow but incessant secular increase which has persisted since at least the mid-1970s.

The adjustments in the capital-manpower ratio required to accommodate a constant manpower level of 60,000 and constant defense budget are indicated in Figure 3.3. The capital-manpower ratio is tracked using an index with a base of 100 for 1978, the year in which the capital-manpower ratio reached its minimum level in the 1965-1999 period. Evident in the pre-2000 period is the simultaneous decline in both manpower and the capital-manpower ratio in the late 1960s and early 1970s and their simultaneous increase throughout the 1980s. With the end of the cold war, manpower began another decline but the capital-manpower ratio continued its increase both because manpower itself was declining and because capital acquisitions undertaken in the latter part of the cold war were still being completed. The simulations show the capital-manpower ratio peaking in 1998 and declining throughout the remainder of the planning period. By the end of the

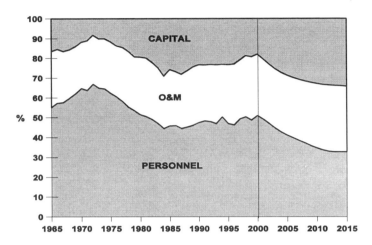

Figure 3.4: Simulated budget distributions 2000-2015: equipment-manpower ratio target with inflation compensation

period the capital-manpower ratios decline to levels previously reached in 1967, when it was on the way down, and in 1987, when it was on the way up.

The second experiment considers the effects of allowing the capital-manpower ratio to grow at a constant annual rate of growth to reach a target level at the end of the planning period.[4] In this case, the nominal defense budget is allowed to increase to compensate for inflationary changes. Manpower is allowed to vary to make budgetary room available for any required increases in capital expenditure. The results of this experiment are shown in Figure 3.4. The capital expenditure share increases dramatically at the beginning of the planning period and slows toward the end, suggesting another long cyclical boom in expenditures for capital. As a result of the increasing capital stock and changing age structure of that stock, the share of operations and maintenance expenditures also increases. Interestingly, under this scenario, by the end of the planning period, the three expenditure categories are absorbing almost equal shares of the defense budget.

Figure 3.5 shows the resulting tradeoff between capital intensity and manpower. Reaching the target capital-manpower ratio requires in this case that military manpower falls from the 60,000 planned for 1998-99 to just under 40,000 by the end of the planning period. This represents a decrease in manpower of just over one-third. In return, however, there is an increase in capital per capita

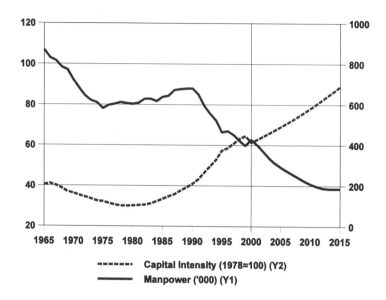

Figure 3.5: Simulated manpower levels 2000-2015: capital-manpower ratio target with inflation compensation

in the order of 75 percent compared with current levels and 350 percent above the end result obtained in the previous experiment with constant manpower levels. Tradeoffs of this sort would seem to be fundamental to defense planning. Is a one-third decrease in manpower worth, with the same budget, a 75 percent increase in how well equipped this smaller force would be? It may very well not be. The smaller force may be entirely inappropriate for stated roles and commitments. On the other hand, a larger, but less adequately equipped force may be just as inappropriate.

If appropriate combinations of force size and capital intensity cannot be attained with the current budget, then the adequacy of the budget itself must be addressed. The third experiment considers this question. In this experiment the defense budget becomes an endogenous variable while the manpower level and the capital-manpower ratio are both taken as exogenous planning variables. The model is then solved to indicate the implications for the level and distribution of the defense budget of both retaining a force size of 60,000, as in the first experiment, *and* increasing the capital-manpower ratio, as in the second experiment. The resulting expenditure levels are shown in Figure 3.6. Nominal

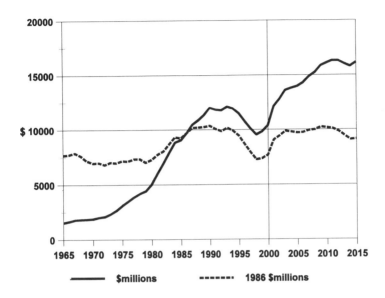

Figure 3.6: Canadian defense expenditure simulations 2000-2015: manpower and capital-manpower ratio targets

expenditures, which have been falling since 1993 and are expected to rise only slightly in 1999 and 2000, would be required to grow rather quickly between 2000 and 2010 and then stabilize at about C$16 billions thereafter. In constant dollar terms, assuming a general inflation rate of 2 percent, the budget expressed in terms of 1986C$ would stabilize quickly at approximately C$10 billions and remain at that level until about 2011 when it would decline slightly. Interestingly, a constant dollar budget of C$10 billions is almost exactly the level which prevailed in Canada over the period 1987-1994.

In terms of the distribution of the simulated budgets over this period as shown in Figure 3.7, the predominant feature is the sharp rise in the share of capital expenditures early in the period and then the leveling-off through most of the period followed by a small decline toward its end. The cyclical nature of capital investment is even more clearly suggested here than in the previous experiment. Changes in the distribution of personnel expenditure again largely mirror changes in capital expenditures. Operations and maintenance expenditures continue the slow secular increase of previous periods, but they account for a smaller share of

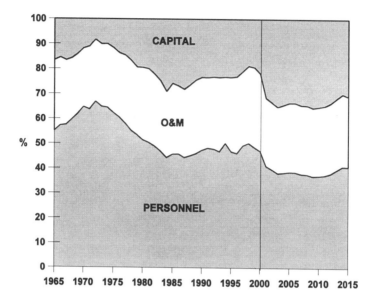

Figure 3.7: Simulated Canadian budget distributions 2000-2015: manpower and capital-manpower targets with inflation compensation

the total budget than in the previous case where the budget was fixed in real terms and capital was substituted for manpower.

Conclusion

Defense, as an economic agent, is a hugely complex institution. The process of allocating defense resources is just as complex, characterized as it is by complicated interdependencies and dynamic relationships among different types of expenditures. Disentangling such complexity is one of the significant advantages of economic analysis, especially of the model-building approach. Accordingly, the models presented here represent an attempt to bring some order and clarity to the basic relationships which govern the allocation of defense resources.

But any clarity which has been achieved has been bought at the expense of simplification and consequent loss of realism. The models presented here clearly err on the side of simplicity, but they also point to areas where further research could help to redress this imbalance. For one thing, the models are obviously very highly aggregated. This is particularly true in the sense that they implicitly deal with a single defense technology when in fact the production of defense capability requires a modern defense organization to manage many different and widely diverse technologies. Thus, a next possible step would be to disaggregate the models by identifying separate relationships for, say, individual military services, each of which uses a technology broadly different from the others, yet each of which is integrated to some extent with the others. Since individual forces produce not only final output in the form of defense capability, but also inputs used by the other forces, a useful integrating approach here would be the input-output structure described in Correa, Scott, and Skovran (1997).

Further research should also consider disaggregating the various defense inputs. This would be particularly important in the treatment of manpower. In this chapter, manpower was treated as a short-run variable input. But in concept and in reality manpower is properly considered as human capital. Manpower has to be recruited and trained before it can make a contribution to the production of defense capabilities. Expenditures for doing so represent an investment in a durable asset, one which will provide productive services over a period of time. Logically, manpower, like equipment and infrastructure, should be treated in a stock-flow context and therefore variable only in the longer run. The manpower variables used in this analysis would also be improved by explicitly including reserve forces and conscripts. It would then be possible to examine tradeoffs among these types of forces and regular forces, or even among these forces and other inputs in the production of defense capability.

A significant improvement in the models would also be achieved if operations and maintenance expenditures were separated into expenditures for overheads, equipment maintenance, equipment operation, infrastructure, and personnel. One of the key results of this modeling exercise has been to identify the pivotal role which operations and maintenance expenditures play in driving the distribution of defense budgets. As indicated in the model specifications, these expenditures are linked directly to both the level of manpower and the capital stocks. They represent, therefore, one of the key sources of interdependence among the different expenditure categories. An improved breakout of operations and maintenance expenditures would permit a clearer picture of these interdependencies and would pay dividends in terms of a better understanding of the dynamic interdependencies characteristic of defense budgeting and defense planning.

Similarly, the measures of capital stock used in this analysis would be improved through disaggregation. These stocks consist of a mixture of many different types of assets, each characterized by different life spans and different rates of depreciation. More importantly, the asset mix of the capital stock will change over time. Hence aggregate capital stocks obtained from accumulated past investment expenditures and an assumed average depreciation rate are likely to be imperfectly measured. Better measures would be obtained by separating investment expenditures by type of assets, especially within the equipment category.

Perhaps the most interesting advances which could be made in this type of work would be to apply these sorts of models to a comparison of defense budgeting and resource allocation across a number of different countries. This should not be overly difficult, especially with the simpler models. Most countries already publish defense expenditure data which is appropriately categorized, though adjustments would necessarily be required for differences in expenditure definitions. NATO already publishes standardized defense expenditure data classified into categories of personnel, operations and maintenance, equipment and infrastructure expenditures as used in these models. In any event, the construction of such models, for a single country or for inter-country comparison, even where data may be imperfect, has the very worthwhile advantage of helping to organize thinking about the economics and management of defense resource allocations, and to do so in a rigorous, integrated, and comprehensive way.

Notes

1. In an analysis of manpower-equipment ratios using a sample of 15 countries for the years 1989 and 1993, Owen (1994) found no significant general trends in reductions in these ratios. The international distribution of these ratios remains highly dispersed, especially when compared to the international distribution of similar ratios in civil aviation, suggesting a tendency of armed forces to overman equipment.

2. If output maximization was assumed to be the goal of defense planners, then the appropriate price for capital assets would be the rental price of capital, computed from the acquisition price, the depreciation rate, and an appropriate rate of interest. Given the less ambitious objectives assumed in this chapter, the simple procurement price is taken to be the relevant price variable.

3. The equation for operations and maintenance expenditure was estimated on the basis of Canadian defense expenditure data for the period 1965-1997 and was obtained from OLS as follows:

$O_t = 3729.86 + 0.0068\ M_{Mt} - 251.44A_t$ $R^2 = 0.845$
  (23.3)   (2.2)   (-12.5)   Degrees of freedom = 30

Numbers in brackets are t-values. The variable A_t represents the average age of the capital stock in years and was obtained in each year as an expenditure weighted average of the preceding fifteen years. Other variables are as defined in Table 3.1.

4. The target level was specified in terms of an actual capital-labor ratio (one million 1986 C$) rather than the index used here. The 1978 base-year level was 0.278 million 1986 C$.

References

Clark, R. (1993). "The Dynamics of Force Reduction and Reconstitution." *Defense Analysis.* Vol. 9, No.1 (April), pp. 51-68.

Cooper, R. and R. Roll (1974). *The Allocation of Military Resources: Implications for Capital-Labor Substitution.* The RAND Paper Series, No. P-5036-1. St. Monica, CA: RAND.

Correa, H., W. Scott, and J. Skovran (1997). "Military Applications of Input-Output Analysis." *Defense Analysis.* Vol.13, No.2 (August), pp. 151-167.

Kirkpartrick, D. (1995). "The Rising Unit Cost of Defence Equipment — The Reasons and the Results." *Defence and Peace Economics.* Vol. 6, No. 4, pp. 263-288.

Lewis, K. (1994). "The Discipline Gap and Other Reasons for Humility," pp.101-132 in P. Davis (ed.), *New Challenges for Defense Planning: Rethinking How Much is Enough.* St. Monica, CA: RAND.

Mulhern, J. (1993). "Defence Investment Cycles 1948-1993: The Environment of Postwar Program Management." *Defense Analysis.* Vol. 9, No.1 (April), pp.11-29.

Owen N. (1994). "How Many Men Do Armed Forces Need? An International Comparison." *Defence and Peace Economics.* Vol. 5, No.4, pp. 269-288.

Pugh, P. (1993). "The Procurement Nexus." *Defence Economics.* Vol. 4, No. 2, pp. 179-194.

Ridge, M. and R. Smith (1991). "UK Military Manpower and Substitutability." *Defence Economics.* Vol. 2, No.4, pp. 283-294.

Smith, R., A. Humm, and J. Fontanel (1987). "Capital-Labour Substitution in Defence Provision," pp. 69-80 in S. Deger and R. West (eds.), *Defence, Security and Development.* London: Pinter.

Snider, D. (1993). *Strategy, Forces and Budgets: Dominant Influences in Executive Decision Making, Post-Cold War, 1989-91*. Professional Readings in Military Strategy, No. 8. Carlisle Barracks, PA: Strategic Studies Institute, US Army War College.

Snider, D., D. Gouré, and S. Cambone. (1994). *Defense in the Late 1990s: Avoiding the Train Wreck*. Washington, DC: Center for Strategic and International Studies.

Thompson, F. and L. Jones (1994). *Reinventing the Pentagon: How the New Public Management Can Bring Institutional Renewal*. San Francisco: Jossey-Bass.

4 Challenges to NATO in the Mediterranean and beyond

Todd Sandler

Introduction

In April 1999, NATO marked its fiftieth anniversary and admitted the Czech Republic, Hungary, and Poland, thus expanding the alliance to nineteen members. NATO remains an amazingly resilient institution that has grown in size from the original twelve members while it has assumed additional chores and weathered crises (e.g., France's withdrawal from NATO's integrated command, changes in military doctrine, conflict between Greece and Turkey over Cyprus). Since the end of the cold war, NATO has been in a process of redefining itself to address security challenges both within and beyond Europe. In the latter instance, the Iraqi invasion of Kuwait in August 1990 presented threats to NATO's resource supply lines and other interests (e.g., United States' security commitment to Israel). In addition, the breakup of the Soviet Union and the fall of strong centralized governments in eastern Europe have created new risks from ethnic unrest, trade in nuclear devices, and political instabilities, which had previously been held in check by authoritarian regimes. Additional security risks have come from tribal conflicts in Africa, a spreading Islamic fundamentalist revolution, transnational terrorism, regional arms races, and the proliferation of weapons of mass destruction (WMD).

At a Rome summit on 7-8 November 1991, a new defense doctrine began to take shape as NATO assumed responsibility for ensuring European safety from threats wherever they occur (Asmus, 1997, p. 37). With the lessening of the communist challenge, NATO is becoming less concerned with guarding its perimeter than with addressing exigencies that adversely affect European economic and military security. This emerging defense doctrine of crisis management requires the development of more mobile forces that can be projected to where they are needed (Jordan, 1995). At the Oslo summit in June 1992, NATO added peacekeeping as an official NATO mission, thus increasing still further the need for rapid deployment forces and power-projection capabilities. A year and a half later, NATO Defense Ministers considered the need for Combined Joint Task Forces (CJTFs) as a means for developing mobile forces and agreed to develop these CJTFs at the subsequent summit in Brussels in January 1994. CJTFs will be drawn from NATO allies and will integrate air, land, and maritime forces that can be dispatched to crises anywhere as they develop (Thomson, 1997).

Within the Mediterranean region, threats arise from ethnic unrest in the Balkans, the spread of Islamic extremism (e.g., Algeria, Egypt, Tunisia), resource disputes over oil and water (e.g., rivers in dispute include the Euphrates, the Tigris, and the Iskendrum), the emergence of rogue states (e.g., Libya), the spread of WMD, the stalled peace process in Israel, the spillover of a possible Cyprus conflict, and persistent poverty in northern Africa. These concerns and others mean that NATO's new strategic doctrine may someday result in additional peacekeeping missions in the Mediterranean if conflicts erupt. As NATO integrates its designated entrants and considers the possible addition of other eastern European nations, there is a danger that insufficient attention will be paid to instability in the Mediterranean. To address this concern, NATO initiated a "Mediterranean Dialogue" in May 1997, whereby the alliance has begun consultations with Egypt, Israel, Jordan, Mauritania, Morocco, and Tunisia in order to promote a new partnership, not unlike the partnership between NATO and European countries (NATO, 1998). This dialogue is intended to foster mutual trust and promote regional security.

NATO also confronts a number of institutional challenges. First, NATO must determine its new membership composition. Will the alliance stop at nineteen members or will it continue to expand not only to the east but also to the south? Second, NATO must decide whether or not to alter its institutional structure in light of its new strategic doctrine and expanded membership. Expansion, thus far, calls for no change in NATO's institutional structure, but this might not be a wise decision. Third, NATO must address how to implement its new mission. This includes specifying rules for intervening in crises outside of NATO's territory. Finally, the alliance must decide how to maintain security in times of shrinking defense budgets. The primary purpose of this chapter is to evaluate NATO's challenges in the Mediterranean and elsewhere, while suggesting the best means for confronting these contingencies. A secondary purpose is to indicate how the Mediterranean countries will be influenced by the transformation of NATO.

The first section presents a brief overview of defense spending and burden sharing in NATO's Mediterranean allies. It also indicates defense spending trends in non-NATO countries in the Mediterranean. In the second section, the concerns posed by NATO's new strategic doctrine of peacekeeping and nonproliferation of WMD are addressed. The risks represented by terrorism –

terrorist groups, revolutionaries, and/or rogue states – are then assessed in the third section. NATO expansion and the issues that expansion raises are examined in section four. The final section comments on other challenges and offers concluding remarks.

NATO Mediterranean allies, burden sharing, and defense spending

There are six NATO allies near or on the Mediterranean Sea: France, Greece, Italy, Portugal, Spain, and Turkey. These countries include a nuclear ally (France), a medium-sized ally (Italy), and four small NATO allies. Although Turkey's defense spending is relatively small, it has the second largest number of troops in NATO. In Table 4.1, defense burdens for 1970-97 are displayed in terms of defense expenditures as a percentage of gross domestic product (GDP) in constant prices. For comparison purposes, NATO and US defense burdens are listed in the last two rows. Since 1975, Italy and Spain shouldered the smallest defense burdens when measured in terms of GDP for the countries listed. These two countries' defense burdens have been relatively small since 1980 when compared with NATO's defense burden, given in Table 4.1. In fact, recent defense burdens for Italy and Spain have been among the smallest, in terms of ability to pay, of the NATO allies. In contrast, Greece carried a relatively large burden, which was consistently above the average burden for NATO. This is due, in large part, to its continuing hostility with Turkey over Cyprus. Since 1970-74, only Greece and Turkey have not displayed an overall downward trend in their defense burden. This downward trend for the United States since 1985-89 is quite dramatic compared with the other allies listed, thus implying some closing of the burden-sharing gap between the United States and its NATO allies during the post-cold war era. As a group, the Mediterranean allies showed relatively little decline in their GDP-based defense burdens, which is due to three factors: distrust between Greece and Turkey; France's modernization of its nuclear weapons in this period (Fontanel and Hebert, 1997); and the already small burdens carried by Italy, Portugal, and Spain at the end of the cold war.

No single burden-sharing measure is sufficient to provide an adequate picture of an ally's contribution to the alliance (Hartley and Sandler, 1999; Sandler and Hartley, 1999); hence, Table 4.2 presents two additional measures. In the top half of Table 4.2, defense expenditure per capita levels in US dollars in 1990 prices are listed for 1975 and selected years. France carried the greatest defense burden per capita for the Mediterranean allies, followed by Greece and Italy. Given Turkey's large population, its defense spending per capita was the smallest of the allies listed. Only France exceeded or came close to the average defense burden

Table 4.1: Defense expenditures as a percentage of GDP for Mediterranean allies in NATO[a]

Country	Average 1970-74	Average 1975-79	Average 1980-84	Average 1985-89	1990	1993	1995	1997[b]
France	3.9	3.8	4.1	3.8	3.6	3.4	3.1	3.0
Greece	4.7	6.7	6.6	6.2	5.8	5.5	4.4	4.6
Italy	2.6	2.2	2.1	2.2	2.0	2.0	1.8	1.9
Portugal	6.9	3.9	3.4	3.2	3.1	2.9	2.7	2.6
Spain	n/a	2.1	2.4	2.2	1.8	1.7	1.5	1.4
Turkey	2.3	3.9	3.8	3.5	3.9	4.0	3.3	3.3
NATO	n/a	n/a	4.8	5.0	4.5	3.8	3.0	2.7
USA	7.1	5.4	5.9	6.3	5.7	4.8	3.9	3.4

[a] In constant prices; [b] estimated figures; n/a denotes not available.

Sources: NATO Office of Information and Press (1995, Table 3, p. 359). The figures for 1995 and 1997 come from NATO (1997). A different price deflator is used for 1995 and 1997 than for the other figures listed.

per capita of NATO. This same burden for the United States was quite large compared with the Mediterranean allies. In the bottom half of Table 4.2, the number of soldiers is displayed (in thousands) for 1970 and selected years. In 1997, US troop strength is only 47 percent of its troop strength in 1970 during the Vietnam war. Both NATO and the United States showed a marked decrease in troops since the end of the cold war. A more modest decline was associated with France, Italy, Portugal, and Spain in recent years. In contrast, Greece and Turkey augmented their troop strength for some of the last few years. Given French military spending and its fairly modest troop numbers, France spent a good deal on its nuclear deterrent and on sophisticated armaments (Fontanel and Hebert, 1997).

In Table 4.3, defense spending in millions of US dollars in constant prices are given annually for 1986-95 for selected Mediterranean countries. The top half of the table lists the defense expenditures for the six Mediterranean NATO allies, NATO Europe, and NATO total. Since 1990, NATO's total defense spending in

Table 4.2: Defense spending per capita and military forces for Mediterranean allies in NATO

Country	1970	1975	1980	1985	1990	1993	1997[a]
Defense expenditures per capita in US $ (1990 prices and exchange rates)							
France		591	695	739	751	710	663
Greece		356	343	438	380	366	418
Italy		332	344	392	412	409	383
Portugal		200	157	146	189	191	203
Spain		n/a	226	246	233	222	197
Turkey		65	74	71	95	103	102
NATO		n/a	652	779	761	643	543
USA		987	987	1,265	1,225	1,038	838
Soldiers (thousands)							
France	571	585	575	563	550	506	475
Greece	178	185	186	201	201	213	206
Italy	522	459	474	504	493	450	419
Portugal	229	104	88	102	87	68	72
Spain	n/a	n/a	356	314	263	204	196
Turkey	625	584	717	814	769	686	820
NATO	n/a	n/a	5,636	5,930	5,778	4,905	4,527
USA	3,294	2,146	2,050	2,244	2,181	1,815	1,554

[a] Estimated figures; n/a denotes not available.

Sources: NATO (1996, 1997). Figures from 1970 comes from NATO (1996).

Table 4.3: Defense expenditures for selected Mediterranean countries, 1986-95 in constant prices (in millions of US dollars at 1990 prices)

	1986	1987	1988	1989	1990	1991	1992	1993	1994	1995
NATO										
France	41,081	42,284	42,243	42,793	42,589	42,875	41,502	41,052	41,260	39,426
Greece	3,861	3,856	4,078	3,819	3,863	3,663	3,808	3,716	3,780	3,834
Italy	20,186	22,699	24,113	24,304	23,376	23,706	23,004	23,127	22,556	21,380
Portugal	1,504	1,563	1,738	1,824	1,875	1,925	1,977	1,908	1,861	2,088
Spain	8,827	9,995	9,345	9,668	9,053	8,775	8,113	8,823	7,940	8,037
Turkey	4,532	4,316	3,802	4,398	5,315	5,463	5,747	6,355	6,213	5,336
NATO Europe	181,025	186,653	184,668	186,223	186,375	184,601	176,253	171,513	166,043	160,114
NATO Total	527,305	529,356	520,159	518,185	504,092	464,008	470,851	451,057	430,271	407,738
Other Mediterranean Countries										
Algeria	859	875	866	847	945	926	1,289	1,666	2,027	4,962
Croatia[a]						703	845	851	1,096	1,312
Egypt	3,296	2,803	2,208	1,780	1,752	1,764	1,794	1,775	1,735	n/a
Israel	7,324	6,808	6,374	6,141	6,418	6,159	6,903	6,431	6,139	6,762
Morocco	909	916	859	933	955	992	1,070	1,020	1,019	n/a
Syria	3,675	2,283	1,731	1,770	1,642	2,687	2,525	2,449	2,302	n/a
Tunisia	249	226	261	269	248	236	235	241	249	249

[a] In 1993 prices and exchange rates. All figures for Croatia are estimated by SIPRI; n/a denotes not available. SIPRI did not list figures for Albania, Lebanon, Libya, or Serbia.

Source: Stockholm International Peace Research Institute (1996).

constant dollars has fallen by about 20 percent, while it has decreased by about 15 percent in Europe. Defense expenditure in France alone was about the same as the other five Mediterranean allies combined. Although Portugal's real defense budget increased throughout much of 1986-95, its $2 billion outlay in 1995 was relatively small by NATO standards. In fact, the minor spending status of Greece, Portugal, Spain, and Turkey is underscored when their defense spending figures are compared with the two aggregate figures for NATO. In real dollars, Greece and Turkey indicated no consistent downward trend for defense spending in the post-cold war era, unlike France and Italy. The spending patterns in Greece and Turkey were due to their mutual hostility and, in Turkey, was also the result of its internal conflict with a Kurdish minority.

In the bottom portion of Table 4.3, the real defense spending figures for selected non-NATO Mediterranean nations are given. Apparently, the end of the cold war had little impact on defense spending in any of the countries listed. Algeria increased its defense expenditures by the greatest amount in recent years because of its ongoing civil war. Defense spending showed little change in Egypt, Israel, Morocco, or Tunisia since 1989. The rise in this spending in Croatia was clearly due to conflicts in the region. Only Syria has decreased its defense spending in recent years. As the largest spender among these countries, Israel's defense budget was typically greater than the Turkish budget but less than the Spanish budget. By NATO spending standards, most of these countries possessed modest defense budgets; however, these budgetary figures do not reflect a country's stockpile of weapons or its possession of WMD. For example, Syria and Libya are known to have chemical and biological weapons, and ballistic missiles to deliver them, while Egypt probably possesses chemical weapons and Israel has nuclear, chemical, and biological weapons (International Institute for Strategic Studies, 1996; Klare, 1995). In 1995, there were sizable tank inventories in the arsenals of Libya (2,210), Syria (4,600), Egypt (3,650), and Israel (4,095) (International Institute for Strategic Studies, 1995, 1996).

During 1987-95, arms sales to most Middle East countries declined drastically except for Egypt and Israel (International Institute for Strategic Studies, 1996, Tables 6-7). Although these Mediterranean countries can pose a threat to regional stability, NATO can field sufficient forces, given the resolve, to address crises in any of these countries. Currently, the most worrisome concern is the maintenance of defense spending patterns in the Mediterranean region, the presence of chemical and biological weapons, and politically destabilizing forces.

NATO's strategic doctrine of crisis management

Following the Gulf War of 1991, NATO adopted a new strategic doctrine to ensure European security within NATO allies and beyond (Sandler, 1997; Thomson, 1997). This doctrine recognizes that NATO's security requires that resource supply lines from the Middle East, North Africa, and elsewhere must be protected so as to guard NATO's economic interests. Furthermore, the doctrine acknowledges that conflicts outside of NATO's boundaries can pose a security risk to NATO if these conflicts were to spread. At the time of writing, questions still remained among the allies as to the justification of out-of-area actions under the new doctrine.

This crisis-management doctrine is associated with a number of concerns including the composition of the CJTFs, NATO's capacity to transport these forces to trouble spots, and burden sharing for these crisis-management forces. By being multilateral, these CJTFs raise an issue as to whether allies will really permit their forces to be deployed abroad under another country's command. The United States has already indicated its reluctance to allow US troops to be deployed unless under US command and control (Thomson, 1997). If other allies follow the United States, the CJTFs will lose their ability to economize on troops and to create an integrated NATO crisis-management force. Because such forces may have to be transported to areas outside of NATO, significant power-projection capabilities are required. To date, the United States has invested heavily in power projection, while its European allies have traditionally concentrated on territorial defense (Asmus, 1997, p. 45). During the Gulf War, the United States provided about 90 percent of the military forces and much of the power-projection capabilities. Currently, the United States is considering options to augment its airlift and sealift capacity by procuring upwards of 67 C-17 transport planes and 3 roll-on/roll-off ships by 2002 (Congressional Budget Office, 1997). Germany has recently announced plans to acquire additional power-projection abilities, and France has also indicated similar plans. The United Kingdom is also expected to augment its ability to transport troops and materials. In particular, a new generation of UK aircraft carriers is under consideration to replace the current fleet of three light aircraft carriers (the *Invincible*, the *Illustrious*, and the *Ark Royal*). These new carriers, along with as-yet-unspecified new transport planes are anticipated to boost UK power projection significantly. A possibility also remains that smaller NATO allies will support power projection through the Western European Union (WEU), the military organ of the EU.

Current efforts to increase power projection are concentrated in the four largest NATO allies, thus raising the concern that this new strategic doctrine will lead to disproportionate burdens being shouldered by the larger allies, reminiscent of the first 25 years of NATO (Sandler and Hartley, 1999, Chapter 2). Power projection requires significant investments; for example, the United States is planning to spend about $20 billion during 1998-2002 (Congressional Budget Office, 1997). Unless other allies develop these transport capabilities, the alliance will have little choice but to rely on those large allies with these capabilities when crises occur. If NATO is to succeed with its new doctrine, then there must be participation by all allies. To make up for any failure to support power projection, smaller allies can offer disproportionally more of their troops for the CJTFs and allied rapid reaction corps. Because crisis management yields alliance-wide purely public benefits, free riding is clearly a concern.

Peacekeeping

NATO's adoption of peacekeeping as an official mission in line with its new strategic doctrine is motivated, in large part, by its interest in maintaining stability in the Middle East and eastern Europe. Within the Mediterranean region, ethnic conflicts plague the Balkans in Bosnia, Kosovo, and elsewhere. In Kosovo, fighting erupted in 1998 between the ruling Serbian minority and the Albanian majority, comprising 90 percent of the population. The instability of Kosovo is clearly indicated by the heightened fighting during June 1998, leading to NATO's "Determined Falcon" show of air strength over Kosovo on 15 June 1998. NATO has stated its resolve to act more quickly than in Bosnia, as

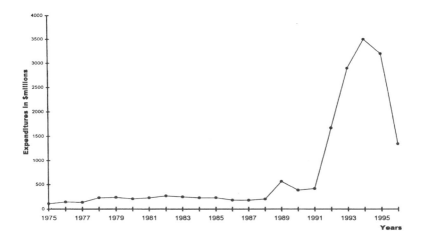

Figure 4.1: UN peacekeeping total expenditures, 1975-1996

reflected by its massive bombing campaign in 1999. A potential conflict could also begin between the Slav population and an Albanian minority in Macedonia (Larrabee, 1997). In 1997, the United States spent $11.7 million on Task Force Able Sentry to deter ethnic conflict in Macedonia (US Government Accounting Office, 1998). Another threat to peace in the Mediterranean involves hostilities among rival Islamic groups. In Algeria, for example, civil war among such groups has led to the death of tens of thousands. Islamic extremism can spread to Egypt and Tunisia, where poverty breeds discontentment. Yet another threat in the Mediterranean involves the possibility that a conflict in Cyprus would cause instability in NATO and collateral damage in the region. Given NATO's unanimity rule for intervention, the alliance may be unable to act in Cyprus because of vetoes by Greece or Turkey.

Trends in peacekeeping can be drawn from Figure 4.1, which displays UN peacekeeping spending for 1975-96 in current year dollars.[1] According to Figure 4.1, there was an increase in spending in 1978 owing to the UN Interim Force in Lebanon (UNIFIL). Essentially, UN peacekeeping spending was fairly flat until 1989,[2] at which time the United Nations assumed new missions in the Middle East, Africa, Central America, and Asia (Bobrow and Boyer, 1997; Hill and Malik, 1996; Khanna, Sandler, and Shimizu, 1998, 1999). During 1988-96, there were twice as many UN peacekeeping operations than in the first four decades of the United Nations (Khanna, Sandler, and Shimizu, 1998). UN peacekeeping spending peaked in 1994 and 1995 when $3.5 billion and $3.2 billion were spent, respectively. The current downturn in 1996 is quite misleading because most of this decline is due to NATO assuming the financial responsibility for peacekeeping in Bosnia under the NATO Implementation Force (IFOR), which began operations on 20 December 1995, based on the Dayton Agreement. Prior to IFOR, the UN Protection Force (UNPROFOR) mission in Bosnia cost $1.7 billion in 1995 and involved only 30,000 troops (International Institute for Strategic Studies, 1996, p. 293). IFOR consisted of about 60,000 troops with 20,000 from the United States, 30,000 from other NATO countries (e.g., 10,500 from France and 12,500 from the United Kingdom), and 10,000 from non-NATO countries (International Institute for Strategic Studies, 1996, pp. 33-35). Non-NATO participants included 12 European countries, Egypt, Jordan, Malaysia, and Morocco. Given its 60,000 troops, IFOR was surely more expensive than UNPROFOR, so that total peacekeeping in 1996 was as large as or greater than in 1994 or 1995. Beginning in December 1996, the Stabilization Force (SFOR) replaced IFOR in Bosnia, thus continuing NATO heightened spending on peacekeeping. Recent US Department of Defense estimates of US support burdens for Bosnia peacekeeping amounted to $2.5 billion in 1996, $2.2 billion in 1997, and $1.6 billion in 1998 (US Government Accounting Office, 1998, p.

2). In fact, this last figure for 1998 is only a partial-year estimate. These three US expenditure figures indicate that peacekeeping spending is really greater than in 1995 and is easily 20 times the annual average amounts during cold war years, once other countries' spending in Bosnia are also included.

Peacekeeping spending displayed in Figure 4.1 for the post-cold war period also does not include other non-UN-financed peacekeeping and peace-enforcement operations such as Operation Deny Flight (April 1993 to December 1995 in Bosnia), Desert Shield and Desert Storm, and Operation Provide Comfort (following the Gulf War in northern Iraq). The cost of Desert Shield and Desert Storm topped $61 billion, which overshadows UN peacekeeping spending for the entire decade since 1986 (US Department of Defense, 1992).

This increase in peacekeeping spending raises a number of issues. First, burden sharing is a concern, because crisis-management activities provide a purely public benefit in terms of political stability to the world at large and, as such, encourage free riding. Since nations nearer to the instability — e.g., European nations near Bosnia — gain more from peacekeeping, it is these nations that are anticipated to assume a greater burden of peacekeeping. Thus, NATO was destined to take over from the United Nations when Bosnian operations stretched UN financial and logistical capabilities. Within NATO, the richer allies are anticipated to shoulder a disproportionate burden in terms of the share of GDP devoted to peacekeeping. A recent study has supported this supposition for the post-cold war era, especially when non-UN-financed missions are included (Khanna, Sandler, and Shimizu, 1998). This suggests that future patterns of peacekeeping burden sharing will have both NATO and the richest allies within NATO assuming ever-greater financial burdens of peacekeeping and crisis management for the world.

Next, there is the issue as to whether the United Nations or NATO should be providing peacekeeping. If the United Nations undertakes peacekeeping, then it can rely on its *assessment accounts* to partly circumvent free riding, provided that nations pay their obligations. Given NATO's efforts to acquire power-projecting assets, the United Nations may, however, have no choice but to rely on these assets, as it has done in Kuwait and Bosnia, for large-scale operations. In recent years, the United Nations has overextended its peacekeeping capacities as it expanded its missions. NATO must be careful not to make the same mistake. A comparative advantage of peacekeeping can be distinguished for these two international organizations. Crises in Europe or involving economic or security interests of NATO allies in the Mediterranean are best addressed by NATO, whose troops are near to any contingency and whose allies are properly motivated to participate. For more distant crises, less germane to NATO's interests, the United Nations is the more appropriate body to assume responsibility. Peace-enforcement missions requiring a great deal of sophisticated weapons and well-trained troops are better provided by NATO, insofar as the procurement process in the United Nations can be lengthy. When reaction time is a crucial consideration, NATO would have a comparative advantage over the United Nations in those cases where allies' tastes are more homogeneous regarding an intervention than those of the Security Council members.

Another concern over the recent upturn in NATO peacekeeping operations involves the issue of force structure and command. NATO forces are still configured to fight the cold war; obviously, a reconfiguration is needed. Peacekeeping operations require different weapons, logistics, and training than those of the cold war era. Improvements in the allied rapid reaction corps and the formation of CJTFs are motivated to acquire the proper force structure for crisis management. An enhanced capacity to manage large-scale terrorism campaigns is also needed. The United States and terrorism-plagued EU countries have been allocating many more resources to the terrorist threats (Enders and Sandler, 1999). NATO must also address whether the military structure of the alliance needs changing to accommodate peacekeeping missions that may be near or far from the European theater (Sandler and Hartley, 1999, Chapter 8; Thomson, 1997). For example, should CJTFs have their own command on par with the Supreme Allied Command Europe (SACEUR) and the Supreme Allied Command Atlantic (SACLANT), or should CJTFs have a command subordinate to SACEUR and SACLANT?

Nonproliferation of WMD

Another aspect of NATO's new strategic doctrine involves *managing* the proliferation of weapons of mass destruction (WMD), including nuclear, biological, and chemical weapons. The Nuclear Nonproliferation Treaty of 1 July 1968, which entered into force on 5 March 1970, has 179 states as parties. Nevertheless, a number of nations — e.g., India, Pakistan, China, Israel — have developed nuclear weapons, while others — e.g., Iran, Iraq, North Korea — have been trying to develop these weapons. The Biological Weapons Convention (BWC) was signed on 10 April 1972 and entered into force on 26 March 1975, but the BWC has not stopped nations from acquiring such weapons (e.g., Iran, Iraq, Israel, China, Libya, Syria). More recently, the Chemical Weapons Convention (CWC), signed on 13 January 1993 and entered into force on 29 April 1997 (see Sandler and Hartley, 1999, Table 1.2), prohibited the development, production, stockpiling, and use of chemical weapons. The shortcoming of these treaties is the lack of an enforcement mechanism. Consider North Korea's violation of the Nuclear Nonproliferation Treaty in 1994. Only the

United States took a tough stance to get an "agreed framework" from the North Koreans to achieve compliance. In February and March 1998, the United States again took a leading role to persuade Iraq to permit UN weapons inspectors from UNSCOM less-restricted access to Iraqi sites. In the future, NATO must take a more united stance on nonproliferation of WMD if proliferation of these weapons is to be managed. Without a united stance, would-be proliferators can divide allies, as did Saddam Hussein in early 1998. There is also the danger that the American public will react negatively to free riding by its allies, which could lead to policy fatigue, whereby Congress withdraws its support for US efforts. Nuclear tests in India and Pakistan during June 1998 highlight the challenges to the world community to inhibit proliferation.

These WMD are particularly troublesome for the Mediterranean where chemical and biological weapons are already possessed by Iran, Iraq, Libya, Syria, Israel, and Egypt. Iraq and Syria have already displayed the resolve to use these weapons. In many ways, WMD pose the greatest danger to the Mediterranean region where religious extremists may stop at nothing to spread the revolution.

Terrorism

Terrorism is the premeditated use, or threat of use, of extra-normal violence or brutality to gain a political objective through intimidation or fear. To qualify as an act of terrorism, an action must be politically motivated; that is, the act (e.g., a bombing, a skyjacking, a kidnapping) must attempt to influence government policy at home or abroad. By exploiting their ability to strike at a variety of targets, terrorists try to create an atmosphere of fear where people perceive a general threat to their safety. If targets and modes of attack are varied sufficiently, the authorities have a more difficult task to thwart these activities. When terrorists are able to attack with impunity, a democratically elected government, which is expected to protect life and property, appears ineffective and loses support. This loss of support further compromises the government's ability to confront the terrorists. In extreme situations, the government may view the cost of an ongoing terrorist campaign as too high, and, thus, may seek an accommodation with the terrorists. Governments face a real dilemma when choosing an effective counter-terrorism policy. If the government reacts too strongly or seeks revenge on suspected supporters of political change (e.g., forming death squads), the government may appear tyrannical and worse than the terrorists, thus driving more followers into the terrorists' camp. If, however, the government is too permissive, it may seem inept, which will also damage its legitimacy.

Terrorism is distinguished according to domestic and transnational events. Domestic terrorism is homegrown and does not transcend a host country's borders. If the terrorists, their targets, their support, and/or their demands solely involve the host nation, then the terrorist event is domestic. When, in contrast, a terrorist incident is planned in one country and executed in another, or includes targets, victims, institutions, or demands involving another country, the terrorist event is transnational. State-sponsored terrorism, whereby one country assists the terrorists' actions in another country, is transnational. This sponsorship can include training, logistical support, intelligence, or resources. Bombings of NATO infrastructure by the Popular Forces of 25 April (FP-25) in Portugal constitute a transnational attack as does an FP-25 mortar attack on the US Embassy in Lisbon during November 1984. In Spain, attacks by the Basque Liberty and Homeland (ETA) against foreign tourists or French interests are transnational events.

In the post-cold war period, there has been a significant decline in transnational terrorism (Enders and Sandler, 1999), which can be attributed to reduced state-sponsorship as East-West confrontations have relaxed and to antiterrorist initiatives by European countries as threats have escalated. Another factor has been the demise of a number of Marxist terrorist groups (e.g., the Red Brigade, Action Direct, the Combatant Communist Cell, the Red Army Faction, and the Revolutionary Cell) (Chalk, 1996). Yet another factor may be reduced Middle East state-sponsorship by Syria and other countries that want better relations with the West. Normalization between the United States and Iran could bolster this downward trend. Whatever the cause, the downward trend is impressive (US Department of State, 1997). Unfortunately, domestic terrorism does not display a similar trend (Jongman, 1992, Table 2).

Despite the downward trend in transnational terrorism, terrorism still presents a number of concerns for NATO and the Mediterranean region. First, WMD may be acquired by terrorists. Aum Shinrikyo's sarin attack on the Tokyo subway on 20 March 1995, in which 12 people died and over 5,000 were injured, represents a disturbing omen. If their organization in Japan had not been crushed, Aum Shinrikyo had the financial and logistical means to murder hundreds of thousands (Campbell, 1997). Religious extremists and rogue states in the Mediterranean may be prepared to use such weapons. Stopping such groups or nations from acquiring WMD presents coordination problems for NATO, which has, to date, shown little explicit coordination of arms trading. Acts to inhibit the acquisition of these weapons also present free-riding problems as nations have an incentive to wait until others take the initiative.

Second, Islamic extremists have relied on terrorism in Algeria and Egypt to destabilize these regimes, and can be expected to continue to do so (Maddy-Weitzman, 1996). In Algeria, a brutal struggle between the Algerian military and rival Islamic fundamentalist groups (i.e., l'Armé Islamique du Salut (MIA) and the Group Islamique Armé (GIA)) has resulted in the death of tens of thousands, with no end in sight.[3] MIA is the military wing of the Front Islamique du Salut (FIS), which is the primary opposition group to the government. The discontentment with the ruling Front de Libération Nationale (FLN) has been rooted in rapid population growth, government corruption, and depressed oil prices. An Algerian population explosion has created abject poverty, high unemployment, and despair, from which extremist views can gain a foothold. Similar circumstances have existed in Egypt, where militant Islamic extremists have engaged in a reign of terror that has included political assassinations (e.g., Al-Jihad's assassination of President Sadat in October 1981), bombings, and armed attacks (e.g., against tourists and foreigners) (Podeh, 1996). Egypt's political stability depends on current economic measures in improving the well-being of its growing population. If the Islamic revolution succeeds in Algeria, it can spread to neighboring Tunisia, where some extremist terrorist incidents have already taken place. Even Turkey faces the possibility of an Islamic takeover. In the December 1995 Turkish national elections, the Islamic Refah party captured just over 21 percent of the total votes, making it the largest single party (Lapidot, 1996).

Third, terrorism has been prevalent as a tool in other struggles in the region. In southern Lebanon, Hezbollah continues to employ terrorism to create instabilities. Terrorism still plagues the Israeli-Palestinian peace process. Groups opposed to peace on both sides have resorted to terrorism as a means to divert the process and have been successful. Within Palestine, Fatah and Hamas have engaged in terrorism as a tactic in their civil war to control Palestine.

Fourth, by providing an inexpensive means for destabilizing a political regime, terrorism has been attractive to both state-sponsors and small groups with modest resources. Just about any kind of group can resort to terrorism and present a significant threat. Modern society's dependence on communication systems, computer networks, electrical grids, and transportation networks makes it susceptible to terrorist attacks. While terrorism is relatively cheap to engage in, it is expensive to protect against since an attack can come from almost anywhere in a variety of forms, making terrorism a cost-effective tool for the weak to use against the strong.

Fifth, terrorism poses some troublesome trade-offs for governments. If a government introduces measures to secure against one kind of attack, a terrorist group can respond by substituting into a related unguarded mode of attack. Thus, metal detectors, installed in airports in 1973, drastically reduced skyjackings, but appeared to increase kidnappings (Enders and Sandler, 1993). Governments must anticipate the interrelationships among terrorist attack modes when designing policies. Another trade-off involves wasteful policy choices made by two or more allies, targeted by the same terrorist group. Efforts to divert an attack abroad can result in the allies spending more on deterrence without necessarily improving their safety from an attack (Enders and Sandler, 1995). Unless allies are prepared to coordinate deterrence decisions, these negative trade-offs will persist.

Sixth, terrorism can have negative economic consequences in terms of reduced tourism that can rob a country of much-needed foreign exchange. This is a particular concern in Egypt where tourists have been massacred on a number of recent occasions. Additionally, terrorism can dissuade net foreign direct investment (NFDI), which is an important source of savings for many Mediterranean countries such as Egypt, Portugal, Spain, and Greece. Terrorism can reduce NFDI through an atmosphere of intimidation and heightened financial risks. In a recent study, a measurable and significant impact of terrorism on NFDI is found to exist for Spain and Greece, but not for Portugal, which experienced much-reduced levels of transnational terrorism for a 1975-1991 sample period. On average, transnational terrorism reduced annual NFDI in Spain by 13.5 percent, while it reduced annual NFDI in Greece by 11.9 percent. Such a reduction can have important growth effects. In Portugal, however, an average year's terrorism curbed NFDI by a trivial 0.05 percent (Enders and Sandler, 1996).

Challenges posed by NATO expansion

NATO expanded in early 1999 with the addition of the Czech Republic, Hungary, and Poland.[4] If this expansion goes smoothly, then a second set of entrants might include Romania and Slovenia. Seven further nations — Slovakia, Macedonia, Bulgaria, Albania, Estonia, Latvia, Lithuania — have expressed an interest in joining. The most significant forerunner to the NATO expansion decision was the Brussels summit on 10-11 January 1994, where the leaders of the NATO allies launched the Partnership for Peace (PFP) within the framework of the North Atlantic Cooperation Council. The PFP was originally intended to improve security links between NATO and the ex-communist countries in the post-cold war era. By establishing a bilateral relationship between a PFP country and NATO, which often included joint military exercises, the PFP enhanced security in the region and promoted a more efficient melding of forces during crisis. The PFP later evolved to permit prospective NATO allies to prepare their armed forces to interact alongside those of NATO by fostering interoperability of forces and standardization of weapons (Sandler and Hartley, 1999, Chapter 3). By joining the PFP, entrants were given a NATO commitment to consult any member which perceives a threat to its territory or security. As of 17 December 1996, PFP members from the Mediterranean include Albania, Bulgaria, and Macedonia.

To prepare a country for NATO membership, the PFP promotes a number of measures. First, the country's military should be in civilian control, where military processes are transparent. Second, the country's armed forces must be able to interact with those of NATO. This interaction is achieved through joint exercises, upgrades of equipment, standardization of weapons, and adoption of common logistical procedures. Third, PFP members are expected to settle border disputes and to address ethnic conflicts. These preconditions for membership bode ill for the inclusion of Albania, Bulgaria, and Macedonia. Macedonia is, for example, beset by ethnic unrest between the Slavic majority and a sizable Albanian minority (Khalizad, 1997). Furthermore, Albania and Bulgaria also face potential ethnic strife owing to sizable minorities. Additionally, Albania could get drawn into the conflict in Kosovo, where the Albanian majority's wishes for autonomy from Serbian rule resulted in ethnic cleansing and NATO's intervention.

The cost of expanding the alliance to include the three designated entrants varies greatly depending on whose estimates are consulted.[5] Only the modernization costs beyond the expenses that these allies would have to make anyway should be included. Potential expansion costs derive from direct enlargement expense (e.g., infrastructure, reinforcement reception facilities), added risks of conflict, joint exercises, the thinning of NATO forces, and decision making. To assess whether or not another ally should be admitted, expansion benefits must also be identified and weighed against expansion costs. These expansion benefits can include enhanced defense capabilities, promotion of democratic reforms, greater political stability, improved burden sharing, and cost savings for larger production runs of weapons. If the net benefits of including another ally is positive for the alliance, and if, moreover, each ally perceives a net benefit from the expansion, then the ally should be admitted. By choosing entrants whose border disputes and ethnic unrest are settled, the PFP process eliminated a number of important expansion costs, thereby making it more likely that the expansion can satisfy the sufficiency conditions.

NATO may be reluctant to expand much further until it can truly determine whether the Visegrad entrants foster the net benefits of the allies. Most Mediterranean countries — e.g., Albania, Bulgaria, Macedonia, Egypt, Algeria, Tunisia — are unlikely candidates owing to their instability and their failure to meet most of the PFP conditions. Moreover, NATO may be preoccupied for some time to come with the expansion currently underway, which will surely focus NATO's attention away from the Mediterranean despite declarations to the contrary. A downside of this attention diversion is that a crisis in the Mediterranean may become fairly intense before NATO responds.

NATO expansion is apt to lengthen decision time when responding to crises, because the 19 allies will have to agree unanimously to take an action under Articles 4-5 of the NATO treaty. Although expansion currently calls for NATO's structure to remain the same, this may not be prudent if the expanded membership size and heterogeneity greatly augment the time needed to achieve consensus on the desired response. The trade-offs between decision costs and political externality costs (of being in the minority) must be weighed when determining an alternative decision rule.

Other challenges and concluding remarks

Many other challenges remain for the post-cold war NATO. Given the downturn in defense expenditures in the 1990s (Hartley and Sandler, 1999), there is an even greater rationale for enhanced cooperation within the alliance. Security can be increased greatly if allies were able to agree to exploit their comparative advantage among missions rather than trying to be self-sufficient in all manner of operations. If freer trade in weapons among NATO allies could be achieved, there would be less need to export weapons outside the alliance in order to reduce per-unit production costs by spreading the fixed cost of weapon development over a greater production run (Sandler and Hartley, 1999, Chapter 5). By relying on arms sales to achieve these scale economies, NATO allies risk that these arms may get into the hands of hostile regimes, as was the case in Iraq. This scenario is particularly germane to the Mediterranean if Islamic extremists were to gain control.

Another challenge concerns the exploding population in northern Africa. Population growth of this magnitude can breed poverty and discontentment, which can, in turn, create political instability and migration. If this political instability is sufficiently great, then violence can erupt, thus creating a potential need for peacekeeping forces. Migrants from northern Africa are already flooding into Europe. If past is prologue, a few of these migrants can use Europe as a staging area for terrorist events, intended to publicize economic and political conditions at home. A plot to bomb the World Cup, uncovered in March 1998, is a case in point.

NATO surely faces many challenges in the post-cold war era. Even though the tension between western Europe and the East has been eliminated, the world remains a dangerous place. The types of challenges that NATO confronts today are different and, as such, require different forces and logistics. Much remains to be done if NATO is to be adequately transformed to meet these challenges.

Notes

The author gratefully acknowledges research support provided by a NATO-EAPC Fellowship for 1998-2000. All views expressed are solely those of the author.

1. The peacekeeping spending data used in Figure 4.1 come from United Nations (various years), *Financial Reports*, for 1975-85, while for 1986-96 the data come from Sam David, UN Information Centre. David estimated these eleven years of spending amounts based on UN budgets.

2. The slight downturn in 1985 is more a result from switching data sources than a true decline.

3. Facts in this paragraph about the Algeria civil way come from Maddy-Weitzman (1996).

4. Material in this paragraph is drawn in part from Sandler and Hartley (1999, Chapter 3). The interested reader should consult this chapter for an in-depth study on NATO expansion.

5. Estimates have been made by RAND, the Department of Defense, and the Congressional Budget Office. These estimates' values and assumptions are reviewed by Sandler and Hartley (1999, Chapter 3).

References

Asmus, R.D. (1997). "Double Enlargement: Redefining the Atlantic Partnership after the Cold War," pp. 19-50 in D.C. Gompert and F.S. Larrabee (eds.), *America and Europe: A Partnership for a New Era*. Cambridge: Cambridge University Press.

Bobrow, D.B. and M.A. Boyer (1997). "Maintaining System Stability: Contributions to Peacekeeping Operations." *Journal of Conflict Resolution.* Vol. 41, No. 6, pp. 723-748.

Campbell, J.K. (1997). "Excerpts from Research Study 'Weapons of Mass Destruction and Terrorism: Proliferation by Non-State Actors'." *Terrorism and Political Violence.* Vol. 9, No. 2, pp. 24-50.

Chalk, P. (1996). *Western European Terrorism and Counter-Terrorism: The Evolving Dynamic.* Houndmills, UK: Macmillan.

Congressional Budget Office (1997). *Moving US Forces: Options for Strategic Mobility.* Washington, DC: US Government Printing Office.

Enders, W. and T. Sandler (1993). "The Effectiveness of Anti-Terrorism Policies: Vector-Autoregression-Intervention Analysis." *American Political Science Review.* Vol. 87, No. 4, pp. 829-844.

Enders, Walter and Todd Sandler (1995), "Terrorism: Theory and Applications," pp. 213-249 in K. Hartley and T. Sandler (eds.), *Handbook of Defense Economics, Vol. 1.* Amsterdam: North-Holland.

Enders, W. and T. Sandler (1996). "Terrorism and Foreign Direct Investment in Spain and Greece." *KYKLOS.* Vol. 49, No. 3, pp. 331-352.

Enders, W. and T. Sandler (1999). "Transnational Terrorism in the Post-Cold War Era." *International Studies Quarterly.* Vol. 43, No. 1, pp. 145-167.

Fontanel, J. and J.P. Hebert (1997). "The End of the 'French Grandeur Policy'." *Defence and Peace Economics.* Vol. 8, No. 1, pp. 37-55.

Hartley, K. and T. Sandler (1999). "NATO Burden Sharing."*Journal of Peace Research.* Vol. 36, No. 4 (forthcoming).

Hill, S.M. and S.P. Malik (1996). *Peacekeeping and the United Nations.* Aldershot, UK: Dartmouth.

International Institute for Strategic Studies (1995). *The Military Balance 1995/96.* Oxford: Oxford University Press.

International Institute for Strategic Studies (1996). *The Military Balance 1996/97.* Oxford: Oxford University Press.

Jongman, A.J. (1992). "Trends in International and Domestic Terrorism in Western Europe, 1968-1988." *Terrorism and Political Violence.* Vol. 4, No. 4, pp. 26-76.

Jordan, R.S. (1995). "NATO's Structural Changes in the 1990s," pp. 41-69 in S.V. Papacosma and M.A. Heiss (eds.), *NATO in the Post-Cold War Era: Does It Have a Future?* New York: St. Martin's Press.

Khalilzad, Z. (1997). "Challenges in the Greater Middle East," pp. 191-217 in D.C. Gompert and F.S. Larrabee (eds.), *America and Europe: A Partnership for a New Era.* Cambridge: Cambridge University Press.

Khanna, J., T. Sandler, and H. Shimizu (1998). "Sharing the Financial Burden for UN and NATO Peacekeeping, 1976-1996." *Journal of Conflict Resolution.* Vol. 42, No. 2, pp. 176-195.

Khanna, J., T. Sandler, and H. Shimizu (1999). "The Demand for UN Peacekeeping, 1975-96." *Kyklos.* Vol. 52, No. 1 (forthcoming).

Klare, M. (1995). *Rogue States and Nuclear Outlaws: America's Search for a New Foreign Policy.* New York: Hill and Wang.

Lapidot, A. (1996). "Islamic Activism in Turkey since the 1980 Military Takeover." *Terrorism and Political Violence.* Vol. 8, No. 2, pp. 62-74.

Larrabee, F.S. (1997). "Security Challenges on Europe's Eastern Periphery," pp. 166-190 in D.C. Gompert and F.S. Larrabee (eds.), *America and Europe: A Partnership for a New Era.* Cambridge: Cambridge University Press.

Maddy-Weitzman, B. (1996). "The Islamic Challenge in North Africa." *Terrorism and Political Violence.* Vol. 8, No. 2, pp. 171-188.

NATO (1996). "Financial and Economic Data Relating to NATO Defence." NATO Press Release (96)168, 17 December, NATO Headquarters, Brussels.

NATO (1997). "Financial and Economic Data Relating to NATO Defence." NATO Press Release M-DPC-2(97)147, 2 December, NATO Headquarters, Brussels.

NATO (1998). "The Mediterranean Dialogue." NATO Basic Fact Sheet No. 16, NATO Headquarters, Brussels.

NATO Office of Information and Press (1995), *NATO Handbook* (Brussels: NATO).

Podeh, E. (1996). "Egypt's Struggle against the Militant Islamic Groups." *Terrorism and Political Violence* Vol. 8, No. 2, pp. 43-61.

Sandler, T. (1997). "The Future Challenges of NATO: An Economic Viewpoint." *Defence and Peace Economics.* Vol. 8, No. 4, pp. 319-353.

Sandler, T. and K. Hartley (1999). *The Political Economy of NATO: Past, Present, and into the 21st Century.* Cambridge: Cambridge University Press.

Stockholm International Peace Research Institute (1996). *SIPRI Yearbook 1996: World Armaments and Disarmament.* Oxford: Oxford University Press.

Thomson, J.A. (1997). "A New Partnership, New NATO Military Structures," pp. 79-103 in D.C. Gompert and F.S. Larrabee (eds.), *America and Europe: A Partnership for a New Era.* Cambridge: Cambridge University Press.

United Nations (various years). *Financial Report and Audited Financial Statements for the Biennium Ended 31 December 19_ and Report of Auditors,* General Assembly. New York: United Nations.

United States Department of Defense (1992). *Conduct of the Persian Gulf, Final Report to Congress,* PB92-163674. Washington, DC: US Department of Defense.

United States Department of State (1997). *Patterns of Global Terrorism 1996* Washington, DC: US Department of State.

United States Government Accounting Office (1998). *Bosnia: Operational Decisions Needed Before Estimating DOD's Costs*, GAO/NSIAD-98-77BR. Washington, DC: US Governmental Accounting Office.

PART II:

THE MEDITERRANEAN

5 Military tension and foreign direct investment: evidence from the Greek-Turkish rivalry

Emmanuel Athanassiou and Christos Kollias

Introduction

As recent events clearly indicate, the Balkans still remain an area of turmoil and strategic instability. In the fragile security environment of the area, Greece and Turkey, both members of NATO, are considered by many to be the principal adversaries in the region. Their ongoing rivalry is well documented in the international relations literature and both rank, in relative terms, as the highest defense spenders in the alliance (Wilson, 1979; Constas, 1991; Larrabee, 1992; Gurel, 1993; Clogg, 1991). For example, during the period 1970-1995 Greece allocated an average 5.7 percent to defense and Turkey 4.5 percent as compared to a NATO average of about 3.2 percent for the same period (Kollias, 1995b; Sezgin, 1997).

In broad terms, the literature on the Greek-Turkish dyad may be separated into two groups. The first includes studies that focus on the empirical estimation of the degree of mutual interaction. They either employ an arms race framework resulting in mixed empirical findings: unidirectional, bidirectional, and absence of causality have been found (Majeski and Jones, 1981; Majeski, 1985; Stavrinos, 1992; Georgiou, 1990; Georgiou *et al.*, 1996; Kollias and Makrydakis, 1997b). Alternatively, they employ the estimation of demand functions using various empirical methodologies (Kapopoulos and Lazaretou, 1993; Kollias, 1995b; 1996; Chletsos and Kollias, 1995; Avramides; 1997). The second group of studies examine the economic impact of Greek and Turkish defense expenditures (Athanassiou *et al.*, 1998; Chletsos and Kollias, 1995; Antonakis, 1997a; 1997b; Kollias and Refenes, 1996; Sezgin, 1997; Kollias and Makrydakis, 1997a; 1999; Kollias, 1994; 1995a). Here, too, the reported results are mixed. On the one hand, findings point to growth-retarding effects mainly through investment crowding-out. But on the other hand aggregate demand stimulation and growth-enhancing effects through modernization have also been reported. Furthermore, one also has to allow for the fact that defense spending has a high opportunity cost since the resources used in defense could potentially find more productive and socially beneficial uses in other sectors of the economy such as education, health, and so on (Athanassiou *et al.*, 1998).

Adverse effects of defense spending spread wider than the mere crowding-out of investment or the opportunity cost entailed by such expenditure or indeed the self-reinforcing nature of military spending in an arms race context. High defense spending is an indication of tension between countries, tension that could potentially lead to armed conflict. As Goertz and Diehl (1986) point out, high defense budgets and weapons build-up can be regarded as an early warning sign of impending armed conflict. This may adversely affect the flow of investment capital from abroad by influencing the decision to invest or to postpone investment in a country. In other words the perceived institutional (country) risk, relative to risk elsewhere in the world, may be adversely influenced by military tension. Since foreign direct investment (FDI) represents privately held funds, such investment is both highly mobile and intensely competitive. It should therefore be sensitive to the level of risk and its variations. Given that the flow of FDI is important not only because it may increase employment and expand productive capacity but also because of the potential transfer of technology and know-how involved and the externalities this can induce, an increase in uncertainty may well carry grave effects upon the development potential of a country.

Using a military tension index, the purpose of this chapter is to examine the impact of the tense Greek-Turkish bilateral relations on foreign direct investment flows in each country. The approach adopted is based on the premise that military tension between rival states increases the institutional uncertainty that foreign capital has to take into consideration when deciding to invest in a country. Thus, *ceteris paribus*, one would expect that fluctuations in tension would be reflected in such flows.[1] This study thus departs from more traditional approaches that have concentrated primarily on the empirical investigation of the macroeconomic impact of high defense expenditures.

Greek-Turkish friction and a military tension index

In order to quantitatively capture the effect that uncertainty emanating from the possibility of armed conflict may have on FDI, it is necessary to find some index

Table 5.1: Major incidents in the Greek-Turkish conflict

1963	Inter-communal fighting in Cyprus
1974	Turkish forces invade Cyprus
1976	Crisis over proposed Turkish oil explorations in Aegean disputed waters
1986	Frontier incident
1987	Crisis over proposed Turkish oil explorations in Aegean disputed waters
1994	New international treaty allowing extension of territorial waters to 12-miles
1996	Turkish troops land on uninhabited Greek island of Imia
1997-98	Intended procurement of Russian S-300 anti-aircraft system by Cyprus

that tracks the fluctuations in military tension between the countries involved. Fluctuations in military tension between two countries may be seen through the waning and waxing of the various issues of friction and conflict.

Resulting from their antagonistic interests, Greece and Turkey have on a number of occasions come close to war (Clogg, 1991): one such incident occurred in 1963 due to the outbreak of inter-communal fighting in the then newly independent state of Cyprus; another occurred in 1974 when Turkish troops invaded Cyprus; and yet another in 1987 as a result of a Turkish attempt at oil explorations in disputed areas of the Aegean. Tension flared in late 1994 when a new international treaty allowing countries to extend their territorial waters to 12 miles came into force, and again in 1996 when Turkey claimed that the status of certain uninhabited Greek islands was not clearly defined by the relevant treaties and landed troops on one of them. On all of these occasions the armed forces of the two countries were placed on full alert. In 1997-98 tensions were once again rising over the future deployment of an anti-aircraft system in Cyprus.

As can be seen in Table 5.1 above, there appears to exist a ten year cycle in the frequency of major military crises between the two countries. It seems that the two countries are currently at the apex of the most recent one. This increased tension between Greece and Turkey in recent years is reflected in the number of air force engagements and shows of force in disputed areas of the Aegean air space.

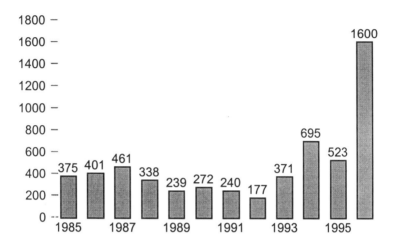

Figure 5.1: Air space violations over the Aegean Sea, 1985-1996

Source: Greek Ministry of Defense.

The data presented in Figure 5.1, published by the Greek Ministry of Defense, are the total number of violations of Greek air space by Turkish fighters in the period 1985-96. Comparing the peaks in the time series with the incidents referred to in Table 5.1, it appears that airspace violations can be used as a tension index between the two countries since periods of deteriorating bilateral relations are associated with an increase, while periods of reduced tensions result in a reduction in the number of such incidents.[2] Clearly, there are important limitations and shortcomings associated with the selection of any index chosen as a proxy quantifying such a complex interaction and therefore any conclusions resulting from its use must be used with due restraint.[3]

Military tension, institutional risk, and FDI flows

Institutional uncertainty emanates from non-market transactions and forms an integral part of business risk in the sense that uncertainty as to the outcome of these transactions may directly or indirectly affect the future outcome of a business venture. For the purposes of this discussion, institutional risk may be separated into two categories, the risk emanating from the workings of economic institutions and the uncertainty arising from institutional breakdown (Furubotn and Richter, 1997).

Market risk depends on the degree of adequate coordination of decentralized decisions through market exchange. Institutional arrangements affect the efficiency of this coordination mechanism in two ways. On the one hand they substitute for market failure, thus providing a complement to the coordination mechanism while, on the other hand, institutions provide a framework for the working of the market itself thus affecting the efficiency of decentralized decision making. In both cases the efficiency of the resource allocation mechanism would be affected.

Uncertainty emanating from the threat of institutional breakdown would appear as the threat of a major disruption to the market process rather than affecting the level of risk due to the level of market efficiency. In fact this is a form of pure uncertainty, in that the results of an event cannot be adequately quantified beforehand. This is particularly true of uncertainty associated with war.[3] The result of armed conflict could range from a temporary slow down in the workings of institutions (e.g., due to the increased demand for resources from the military sector), to disruption of supply lines and access to markets, change of institutional rule implementation in case of victory or of defeat, and finally to institutional collapse.

The difficulty in quantifying the economic impact of war for front-line states implies that the standard expected utility calculus would not adequately describe the decisions of agents in such situations. It has long been recognized that where substantial irreversibility in investment is present, there is economic value in postponing the investment decision, and this should be incorporated in the cost-benefit calculus. Irreversibility implies high sunk costs which cannot be recovered once a firm is committed to a particular business venture (Pindyck, 1991). Thus as long as resources have not been committed to a project, the option of doing so at some future date remains open and has economic value. This would certainly be true of investments directed toward regions where a substantial risk of war prevails.

To analyze problems set by irreversibility, techniques of option pricing have been adopted for the analysis of a firm's investment decision. The results show that, in general, a higher threshold level has to be satisfied for investment to be undertaken as compared to that of traditional present value calculations. This is due to the fact that under option pricing at the time of the investment decision the present value of the benefits of a project will have to cover both sunk costs and the opportunity cost of waiting, i.e., the value of keeping the investment option open (Dixit and Pindyck, 1994).

Consider an investment project in a two-period framework, where the values of the pertinent variables for the second period are subject to uncertainty (Serven, 1997). For simplicity assume that the project can take two values during the second period depending on the state that will obtain then. Thus the present value of the project at the beginning of period one for investor i is

$$(5.1) \quad V_{i0} = -P_K + R_0 + \rho E(R_{i1}) = -P_K + R_0 + \rho[\pi R_{i11} + (1 - \pi)R_{i12}]$$

where P_K is the price of the capital good, ρ is the discount rate, π the probability of state one occurring and R_{ijk} the contingent returns where $R_{i11} > P_K > R_{i12}$. Note that the return for period two is less than the purchase price of capital. We have also made the simplifying assumption that only potential returns in period one differentiate between investors. This implies that either expectations or circumstances vary across investors.

If the agent decides to postpone his decision, taking the decision to invest at the beginning of period two, the state that then prevails becomes known to the investor. In this case the expected value of this option at the start of period one will be

$$(5.2) \quad V_{i1} = \pi \left[\rho(-P_K) + \rho R_{i11}\right]$$

If the favorable state obtains, the investment will be carried out. Otherwise the investor knowing that he will incur a certain loss will not invest. This is the value of waiting, evaluated at the start of period one. If $V_{i1} - V_{i0}$ is positive, the value of waiting is superior to the classical present value, therefore it is profitable to delay the investment until more information is available. Thus if

$$(5.3) \quad W_{i0} = V_{i1} - V_{i0} = (1 - \rho\pi) P_K - R_0 - \rho (1 - \pi) R_{i12}$$

is positive, the decision will be postponed, otherwise investment will take place immediately. Note that the value of the option is dependent on the unfavorable outcome alone. This is the *bad-news principle*. Examining the properties of the option we have

(5.4)
$$\frac{dW_{i0}}{dR_{i12}} = -\rho\,(1-\pi) < 0$$

An increase in the return of the unfavorable outcome will reduce the incentive to postpone the investment.

(5.5)
$$\frac{dW_{i0}}{d\pi} = -\rho P_K + \rho R_{i12} < 0$$

An increase in the probability of the unfavorable outcome will increase the incentive to postpone.

(5.6)
$$\frac{dW_{i0}}{d\rho} = -\pi P_K + (1 - \pi)R_{i12} < 0$$

An increase in the discount rate will favor immediate action

(5.7)
$$\frac{dW_{i0}}{dR_0} = -1 < 0$$

An increase in the immediate return will also favor immediate action

(5.8)
$$\frac{dW_{i0}}{dP_K} = (1 - \rho\pi) \gtrless 0 \ as \ 1 \gtrless \rho\pi$$

Finally an increase in the (certain) purchase price of capital will tend to postpone investment if the discount rate and the probability of the favorable outcome are small enough, and the reverse if those figures are sufficiently high. In fact if the current value of capital increases, this will postpone action, while if the present value of the expected purchase price of capital increases there is an incentive to invest right away.

In what follows we will assume that institutional uncertainty enters as a shift variable in the probabilities of the two states. Thus if θ is an index of institutional risk,

(5.9) $\pi(\theta)$ *with* $\dfrac{d\pi}{d\theta} < 0$

We assume that expectations as to the evolution of the other variables entering the investment decision calculus are static through different institutional risk regimes. This heroic assumption needs elaboration. What we are in fact assuming, in the interests of simplifying the presentation, is that the shift in all other variables would be such as to reinforce the sign change that would result from the variation in the level of uncertainty. The qualitative properties of the model would not be affected. The main constraint we are imposing by adopting this assumption is that the expected change in the purchase price of capital goods does not overshadow the expected change in the contingent returns.

Aggregation and empirical findings

This model of investment behavior would result in discontinuous investment flows for a single firm. Alternatively, firms could postpone particular projects while going ahead with others. Finally it is possible that different firms have different investment thresholds. The decision to invest may well depend on the individual firm's recent track record, i.e., on whether or not there is indivisibility as well as irreversibility at play (Caballero *et al.*, 1995). At any one point in time, a firm that previously found it optimal to postpone investment may go ahead with it after all and vice versa. Thus in the aggregate there will be a continuous flow of investment variations which could be explained in part by the number of individual firms crossing the threshold at each point in time. Aggregate investment would depend on the distribution of threshold levels amongst firms. In our example, differentiation amongst threshold levels is given by the perceived potential returns for each firm alone (Caballero and Engel, 1993).

The option-pricing technique allows for the adaptation of the decision to invest one unit of capacity. It does not answer the question as to the amount to be invested, if the modified criteria are satisfied. This would depend on expectations of the growth in the market in question. Finally, taking these considerations into account, if the level of risk associated with the workings of economic institutions is stable for every level of institutional breakdown risk, aggregate investment would have the following general functional form:

$$(5.10) \qquad FDI = G[\phi(W_0), Y, \pi] = G[\phi(R_{i12}), \psi, Y, \pi]$$

where $\phi (R_{i12})$ is the distribution of potential returns, ψ is a vector of variables affecting the mean level of ψ (Caballero and Engel, 1991), Y is the expected activity level, and π is the level of institutional risk.

The empirical analysis was carried out using quarterly data extending from 1992:1 to 1997:4.[4] The form of the empirical tests, i.e., the OLS regressions that were actually estimated for each country, was dictated largely by the availability of comparable data in order to use a single index of the changing probability of war to examine the impact on FDI flows into Greece and Turkey. The variables that were found to significantly affect FDI flows were different in each case. This is partly, but not wholly, explained not only by the significantly different levels of economic, political, and institutional development of each country but also by the different level of FDI flows into each country: in Greece this is more than double than that of Turkey and given the relative size of the two countries, FDI *per head* in Greece in more than tenfold that of Turkey and has been at that level for a considerable length of time. FDI in Turkey took off in 1987-88 to reach the current comparative level. On this count alone the Greek economy may be seen to be considerably more open to international markets than the Turkish one. One also has to allow for the fact that Greece has been an EU member since 1981 which is a factor influencing FDI. Given the data availability problem, the equation estimated for Greece for the mentioned time-period, was:

$$(5.11) \qquad FDI = c + \alpha_1 \, TMAN + \alpha_2 \, VIO(1)/VIO + \alpha_3 \, STO/STO(-1) \\ + \alpha_4 \, CIP/PETP + \alpha_5 \, EGR$$

where FDI is foreign direct investment in Greece; TMAN is manufacturing output; VIO is the number of airspace violations; STO is the ratio of industrial firms reporting increased levels of stocks to industrial firms reporting decreased level of stocks; CPI is the consumer price index; PETP is the price of petroleum products; and EGR is the exchange rate.

In broad terms, the results obtained from the fitted equation are as one would expect (see Table 5.2). The explanatory power of the equation is satisfactory, the variables enter with the expected signs, even though their statistical significance varies, and the diagnostic tests of the equation are satisfactory given the data

Table 5.2: OLS results for Greece

Dependent variable: FDI

	Independent variables			*Summary statistics*	
	coefficient	*t-stat*	*p-value*		
Constant	-6.31	-0.11	0.92	R^2	0.91
TMAN	5.19	8.89	0.00	Adj. R^2	0.88
VIO(1)/VIO	-3.29	-2.53	0.02	s.e.	1.09
STO/STO(-1)	2.82	5.24	0.00	D.W.	2.01
CPI/PETP	-1.06	-1.96	0.07	Akaike criterion	5.00
EGR	-0.80	-6.26	0.00	Schwarz criterion	5.30
				F-stat	3.33
				Prob-value	0.00

limitations and the relationship that is being estimated. As expected FDI reacts positively to the level of manufacturing activity. This would imply either that expectations are static or that the current level of activity is an adequate predictor of future trends. The reaction to the expected rate of growth of airspace violations is negative. Investment seems to be sensitive to the build-up of tension, since the rate of the growth of violations one period hence is significant. The rate of growth of the net number of firms reporting increases in stocks is positively related to FDI. This variable acts as a proxy for changes in the distribution of the values of the options across firms. Thus an increase in the level of stocks at the firm level may signal an upturn of future sales, and hence leads to realization of investment at the micro level. The ratio of the consumer price index to petroleum product prices may be taken as a measure of the profitability of the economy. It is negatively correlated to FDI implying that there is a counter-cyclical relation at play. Finally the exchange rate is negatively correlated to FDI. This may be due to the fact that an appreciation of the local currency tends to affect immediate installation costs, while a devaluation would tend to affect future returns.

Turning to the case of Turkey the equation fitted was as follows:

$$(5.12) \quad FDT = \alpha_1 \, INPRT/INPRT(-1) + \alpha_{21} \, CPT/PENT + \alpha_3 \, VIO(-1) \\ + \alpha_4 \, LXT(1)/LXNT + \alpha_5 \, ORDT/STOT \\ + \alpha_6 \, ORDT(-1)/STOT(-1) + \alpha_7 \, GFGDT$$

where FDT is foreign direct investment in Turkey; INPRT is industrial production; CPT the consumer price index; PENT is the price of energy; VIO is the number of airspace violations; LXT is the ratio of the number of firms

Table 5.3: OLS results for Turkey

Dependent variable: FDT

	Independent variables				*Summary statistics*	
	coefficient	*t-stat*	*p-value*			
Constant	-4.27	-3.89	0.00		R^2	0.85
INPRT/INPRT(-1)	4.84	4.61	0.00		Adj. R^2	0.79
CPT/PENT	2.93	3.67	0.00		s.e.	3.13
VIO(-1)	-0.17	-2.67	0.02		D.W.	2.55
LXT(1)/LXNT	-2.57	-3.79	0.00		Akaike criterion	7.15
ORDT/STOT	-0.30	-2.59	0.02		Schwarz criterion	7.55
ORDT(-1)/STOT(-1)	-0.43	-4.40	0.00		F-stat	1.25
GFGDT	-5.19	-2.60	0.02		Prob-value	0.00

expecting to increase employment over those expecting to decrease employment; ORDT is the same ratio as above concerning orders received; STOT is the same ratio as above concerning stocks; and GFGDT is the ratio of gross fixed capital formation over GDP.

Overall the performance of the estimated OLS regression for Turkey is less satisfactory when compared to that of Greece. The first two coefficients are positive indicating a positive effect of the rate of industrial production on FDI, as well as that of the current profit rate. The level of tension has a negative effect on FDI, albeit with a one quarter lag. The next three variables are proxies for the distribution of the option-value across firms. The ratio of the net number of firms expecting to increase employment one period hence to the number of firms holding unchanged expectations as to employment conditions during the current period are consistent with expectations of increased future labor costs. This would induce the firms expecting to expand to postpone investment. It is also possible that choice of labor expansion is an alternative strategy to capital expansion. This would affect those firms that have no pressing need to replace equipment, i.e., those that have already invested relatively recently. The ratio of the net number of firms reporting increased orders over those reporting increased stocks is negatively related to FDI, indicating that firms will be more influenced by bad news to postpone investment than by good news to speed it up. Finally the gross fixed capital formation ratio to GDP seems to indicate a crowding-out effect.

Overall, the empirical results for each country appear to indicate that there might exist a negative relation between FDI flows and military tension. Given the fact that the form of the empirical tests, i.e., the OLS regressions estimated for each country, was dictated largely by the availability of comparable data in order to use a single index of the changing probability of war to examine the impact on FDI flows into each country, the findings may broadly be considered as satisfactory. An interesting fit to the data was found to exist for aggregate FDI flows for Greece while a less robust relationship was found for FDI for Turkey (FDT). This may be due to the fact that Turkey is exposed to more than one military source of tension. It is also possible that the relatively low level of FDI in Turkey vis-à-vis that of Greece may indicate a different degree of openness to the international economy, hence a different type of investor behavior in the two countries. This seems to be corroborated by the different set of variables found to have a significant fit for the two countries. Finally, an additional factor differentiating investor behavior may be the successful stabilization of the Greek economy in recent years.

Concluding remarks

High defense spending is an indication of tension between countries, tension that could potentially lead to armed conflict. Indeed, high defense budgets and weapons buildup between rival states can be regarded as a sign of enduring armed tension. The economic effects on growth as well as the opportunity cost of military spending have been extensively researched in relevant literature. However, military tension and weapons buildup may also adversely affect the flow of investment capital from abroad by influencing the decision to invest or to postpone investment in a country. This possible impact has largely been ignored in the relevant literature. Given that the flow of FDI is important not only because it may increase employment and expand productive capacity but also because of the potential transfer of technology and know-how involved and the externalities this can induce, an increase in uncertainty due to military tension may well have grave effects upon the development potential of a country.

This chapter, using Greece and Turkey, two countries with tense bilateral relations and disputes that have on a number of occasions brought them to the brink of war, estimates the impact of bilateral military tension on the flows of FDI in each of them. This study thus departs from traditional approaches that have concentrated mainly in the empirical investigation of the macroeconomic impact of high defense expenditures. Due to data shortcomings, among other things, the empirical investigation leaves much to be desired; still, the reported results appear to suggest that at least in the case of Greece and Turkey such a negative impact of military tension on FDI flows is probably present. If indeed this is the case then this points to the need for further research along these lines using other dyads as case studies. Finally, one may also add that understanding the enduring rivalry of countries embroiled in arms races could be enhanced by concentrating on the asymmetries regarding these countries' circumstances. These could among other things include the degree of openness of the economies, the macroeconomic policies undertaken, and their position in the international specialization of production.

Notes

The authors gratefully acknowledge useful comments and constructive suggestions by the editors of this volume on earlier drafts of this chapter. The views expressed in this chapter are those of the authors and are not necessarily shared by their institutions.

1. It is also true that one would expect that military tension would affect the level and composition of FDI flows to a region. But this question is outside the scope of this chapter.

2. Although the legal technicalities behind what constitutes sovereign air space are of no immediate concern for the purposes of this chapter, as long as one party considers the flight path of the other party's air force as a violation of national air space and attempts to intercept, then such incidents can be viewed as reflecting the level of bilateral tension between the two countries.

A further shortcoming of this index is that the data come from a Greek source; using these to estimate a risk function for Turkey may not be appropriate since the investment risk in the country that suffers the airspace violations may be systematically different from the investment risk in the country generating the violations. However, for the time being, the absence of Turkish data on such incidents forces us to use the publicly available data.

3. The existence of persistent and high levels of threat of institutional breakdown may dictate particular forms of economic institutions, e.g., certain forms of risk hedging, elimination of some types of markets, etc., that could affect market performance. Such a situation may also partly determine the type of investment flows into a country.

4. Apart from data from the Greek Ministry of Defense, data was obtained from the IMF *International Financial Statistics*, and OECD *Main Economic Indicators* and *Indicators of Industrial Activity*. In particular, data for FDI and exchange

rates were found in the IMF *International Financial Statistics*, various issues. FDI is defined as investment amounting to more than 10 percent of the value of the beneficiary firm. The proxies for the variations in the distributions of firms' particular circumstances are from the OECD *Indicators of Industrial Activity* series. They are based on a fixed sample of firms for each country. While they refer to industrial firms only, this shortcoming is counterbalanced by the fact that this is precisely the kind of firm that would be more affected by irreversibility. All other data where acquired from the OECD *Main Economic Indicators* series.

References

Antonakis, N. (1997a). "Defence Spending and Growth in Greece: A Comment and Further Empirical Evidence." *Applied Economics Letters*. Vol. 4, No. 10, pp. 651-655.

Antonakis, N. (1997b). "Military Expenditure and Economic Growth in Greece, 1960-90." *Journal of Peace Research*. Vol. 34, No. 1, pp. 89-100.

Athanassiou, E., C. Kollias, and S. Zografakis (1998). "The Opportunity Cost of Defence: The Case of Greece." Paper presented at the conference "*The Economics of Military Expenditure in Developing and Emerging Economies*," Middlesex University, London, 13-14 March.

Avramides, C. (1997). "Alternative Models of Greek Defence Expenditure." *Defence and Peace Economics*. Vol. 8, No 2, pp. 145-187.

Caballero,R.J. and M. Engel (1991). "Dynamic (S,s) Economies." *Econometrica*. Vol. 59, pp. 1659-1686.

Caballero, R.J. and M. Engel (1993). "Microeconomic Rigidities and Aggregate Price Dynamics." *European Economic Review*. Vol. 37, pp. 697-717.

Cabellero, R.J., M. Engel, and J.C. Haltiwanger (1995). "Plant Level Adjustment and Aggregate Investment Dynamics." *Brookings Papers*. Vol. 2, No. 2, pp. 1-35.

Chletsos, M. and C. Kollias (1995). "Defence Spending and Growth in Greece 1974-90: Some Preliminary Econometric Results." *Applied Economics*. Vol. 27, No. 3, pp. 883-890.

Clogg, R. (1991). "Greek-Turkish Relations in the Post-1974 Period," pp. 12-23 in D. Constas (ed.), *The Greek-Turkish Conflict in the 1990s*. London: Macmillan.

Constas, D. (ed.) (1991). *The Greek Turkish Conflict in the 1990s*. London: Macmillan.

Dixit, A., and R. Pindyck (1994). *Investment under Uncertainty*. Princeton: Princeton University Press.

Furubotn, E.G. and R. Richter (1997). *Institutions and Economic Theory*. Ann Arbor: University of Michigan Press.

Georgiou, G. (1990). "Is There an Arms Race between Greece and Turkey? Some Preliminary Econometric Results." *Cyprus Journal of Economics*. Vol. 3, No. 1, pp. 58-73.

Georgiou, G., P. Kapopoulos, and S. Lazaretou (1996). "Modelling Greek-Turkish Rivalry: An Empirical Investigation of Defence Spending Dynamics." *Journal of Peace Research*. Vol. 33, No. 2, pp. 229-239.

Goertz, G. and P. Diehl (1986). "Measuring Military Allocations." *Journal of Conflict Resolution*. Vol. 30, No. 3, pp. 553-581.

Gurel, S. (1993). "Turkey and Greece: A Difficult Aegean Relationship," in A. Balkir and C. Williams (eds.), *Turkey and Europe*. London: Pinter.

IMF (various years). *Yearbook of International Financial Statistics*. Washington, DC: IMF.

Kapopoulos, P. and S. Lazaretou (1993). "Modelling the Demand for Greek Defence Expenditure: An Error Correction Approach." *Cyprus Journal of Economics*. Vol. 6, No. 1, pp. 73-86.

Kollias, C. (1996). "The Greek-Turkish Conflict and Greek Military Expenditure 1960-92." *Journal of Peace Research*. Vol. 33, No. 2, pp. 217-228.

Kollias, C. (1995a). "Preliminary Findings on the Economic Effects of Greek Military Expenditure." *Applied Economics Letters*. Vol. 2, No. 1, pp. 16-18.

Kollias, C. (1995b). "Country Survey VII: Military Spending in Greece." *Defence and Peace Economics*. Vol. 6, No. 4, pp. 305-319.

Kollias, C. (1994). "The Economic Effects of Defence Spending in Greece 1963-90." *Spoudai*. Vol. 44, Nos. 3-4, pp. 114-130.

Kollias, C. and S. Makrydakis (1999). "A Note on the Causal Relationship Between Defence Spending and Growth in Greece: 1955-93." *Defence and Peace Economics*. (Forthcoming).

Kollias, C. and S. Makrydakis (1997a). "Defence Spending and Growth in Turkey 1954-1993: A Causal Analysis." *Defence and Peace Economics*. Vol. 8, No. 2, pp.189-204.

Kollias, C. and S. Makrydakis (1997b). "Is There a Greek-Turkish Arms Race? Evidence from Cointegration and Causality Tests." *Defence and Peace Economics*. Vol. 8, No. 4 pp. 355-379.

Kollias, C. and A. Refenes (1996). "Modelling the Effects of Defence Spending Reductions Using Neural Networks." *Peace Economics, Peace Science and Public Policy*. Vol. 3, No. 1, pp. 1-12.

Larrabee, S.F. (1992). "Instability and Change in the Balkans." *Survival*. Vol. 34, No. 2, pp. 31-49.

Majeski, S. and D. Jones (1981). "Arms Race Modeling. Causality Analysis and Model Specification." *Journal of Conflict Resolution.* Vol. 25, No. 2, pp. 259-288.

OECD (various years). *Indicators of Industrial Activity.* Paris: OECD.

Pindyck, R. (1991). "Irreversibility, Uncertainty and Investment." *Journal of Economic Literature.* Vol. 29, No. 2, pp. 1110 - 1148.

Serven, L. (1997). "Uncertainty, Instability and Irreversible Investment." Policy Research Working Paper No. 1722. Washington, DC: World Bank.

Sezgin, S. (1997). "Country Survey X: Defence Spending in Turkey." *Defence and Peace Economics.* Vol. 8, No.3, pp. 381-409.

Stavrinos, V. (1992). "Defence Expenditure in Arms Competition: Modelling and Causality Analysis." *Greek Economic Review.* Vol. 14, No. 1, pp. 115-128.

Wilson, A. (1979). "The Aegean Dispute." *Adelphi Papers.* No. 195. London: International Institute for Strategic Studies.

6 The defense-growth relation: evidence from Greece

Selami Sezgin

Introduction

In a series of papers, Sezgin (1997, 1998, 1999a) examined Turkey's defense-growth relationship. The results suggested that the Turkish defense sector stimulates economic growth in Turkey. The aim of this chapter is to analyze Greece's defense-growth relationship so as to compare the results with those obtained for Turkey. Greece and Turkey show similarities. Both countries allocate large budgets to their defense sector as compared to other NATO countries and they both started to produce their own military equipment during the 1980s. One might therefore suspect that Greece's defense-growth relationship is similar to that found for Turkey.

The relationship between Greek defense spending and economic growth is estimated, first, with a supply-side (Feder-type) model using ordinary least squares (OLS) estimation for the time-period 1958 to 1994, and, second, with a demand and supply-side (Deger-type) model using OLS, 2SLS, and 3SLS, for the same time-period.

Following this introductory section is a brief review of the Greek economy. The next section critically analyzes Greece's defense economy, followed by a review of the extant literature on Greek defense-growth studies. This is followed by the empirical analysis, in two parts. The first analyzes the relationship with a supply-side (Feder-type) model. The model and its specifications are described, data sources and calculations are given, and the estimation procedures and results are discussed. In the second part, the Deger-type demand and supply-side analysis is performed. Again, the model, specifications, data sources, and estimation results are described and discussed. The final section summarizes the main findings.

The Greek economy

Greece is a small country with a population of over 10 million and is located at the southern edge of the Balkan peninsula. It is a member of the European Union and NATO. Until 1950, its economic development was retarded by historical factors (World War II and the civil war between 1939-1949). After 1950, important transformations took place in the economy. Between 1954-1974, the Greek economy achieved high GDP growth but after the first oil shock and the subsequent recession of the mid-1970s, Greece's economy showed unsatisfactory performance. During the 1980s, the Greek economy stagnated. It isolated itself from the mainstream of industrial development, and its exports specialized in low value-added products (OECD, 1993). The low growth rate of the Greek economy continued until 1994 but gathered strength in 1996 (OECD, 1997). Traditional Greek industrial sectors are food, beverages, tobacco, textiles, clothing, leather, furniture, and cement. An expanding shipbuilding sector was mostly involved in repair services (Avramides, 1995).

Macroeconomic trends in Greece can be summarized as follows. Greece's population growth rate was very low during the period 1954-1995 when its population grew from 7.9 million people in 1954 to 10.5 million people in 1995. The inflation rate was low until the mid-1970s and increased thereafter to between 10 to 30 percent. Due to a large wave of emigration, especially during the 1950s and 1960s, the unemployment rate has been very low but shows an increasing trend after 1980. The growth of gross national product (GNP) between 1958 and 1994 averaged 4.8 percent annually. Per capita income increased until the 1980s when it began to stagnate. The investment/GNP ratio showed a downward trend during the period. A slight increase was shown in the government consumption/GNP ratio but the ratio declined after 1985. All in all, Greece had rapid economic growth from 1954 to the mid-1970s; thereafter, the Greek economy is characterized by high inflation and macroeconomic stagnation (OECD, 1996).

Greece's defense economy

The Greek defense burden is the highest among NATO and European Union members. Table 6.1 shows indicators of Greek defense expenditures between 1958 and 1996. Defense expenditures are given in 1990 constant prices. The growth rate of defense expenditure averaged 4.9 percent per annum. Due to the Cyprus-Turkish war, this rate peaked in 1975 at 7.0 percent. During the entire period, economic growth also averaged 4.9 percent per annum. On average,

Table 6.1: Selected indicators of Greek defense expenditure

Years	ME	ΔME (%)	ΔGNP (%)	ME/GNP (%)
1958	135	- 2.4	2.0	4.7
1960	148	4.8	4.7	4.8
1965	171	10.5	11.7	3.5
1970	330	6.2	6.9	4.7
1975	612	70.1	6.1	6.6
1980	630	- 8.1	2.1	5.5
1985	830	10.2	2.4	7.0
1990	612	0.8	- 0.3	4.8
1991	588	- 3.9	3.6	4.4
1992	617	5.0	0.4	4.6
1993	605	- 2.1	- 0.3	4.5
1994	615	1.7	1.4	4.5
1995	629	2.3	1.9	4.4
1996	662	5.2	1.4	4.5

Sources: SIPRI (various years); IMF (various years), NATO (1998).
Notes:
• ME: Military expenditure in 1990 constant Greek billion drachmas
• ΔME: Real growth rate of military expenditure
• ΔGNP: Real growth rate of gross national product
• ME/GNP: Share of military expenditure in GNP

Greece's defense burden is higher than both Turkey and NATO. As regards the share of military expenditure in the central government budget (CGB), Greece's ME/CGB ratio is higher, on average, than that of NATO but lower than for Turkey. Per capita military expenditure of Greece is also lower than for NATO but much higher than Turkey's.

Frequently, defense spending is divided into personnel, equipment, infrastructure, and other operational expenditures. In this respect, Greek defense expenditure devoted to personnel is higher than Turkey's, whereas equipment and infrastructure expenditures are lower than Turkey's. While between 1990 and 1994, an average of 63 percent of Greek defense expenditure goes to personnel expenditure, the figure for Turkey is only 50 percent.

When compared to the size of its population, Greece has very large armed forces at about 212,000 in 1995, which is equivalent to about 5.9 percent of the total labor force. About 73 percent of the armed forces personnel are male conscripts. National military service currently lasts for about 19 months and is compulsory for all able-bodied males. For the near future, compulsory military service seems likely to remain in Greece due to the perceived Turkish threat in Aegean Sea and on Cyprus. But Greece's low population growth rate and large armed forces are likely to create a problem in territorial defense (Kollias, 1995a).

Similar to the Turkish situation, Greece has started to supply its own military requirements but still imports most of its military equipment, and its arms exports are extremely low. Greece ranked as the 10th highest arms importer in 1995 (US ACDA, 1994). The main reason for establishing a defense industry in the 1970s was strategic rather than economic. Leading defense companies were founded and operated by the state (Avramides, 1995) with ownership residing in the state and military forces (Bartzokas, 1992). The goal was to develop self-sufficiency in defense requirements in areas such as aeronautics, military vehicles, and shipyards. Most activities involve licenced production. The defense industry also created new jobs for the Greek economy (Avramides, 1995).

In sum, the Greek economy shoulders a very high defense burden, a high proportion of its labor force is allocated to its armed forces, and it has been developing an indigenous defense industry. (Indeed, the development of Greece's defense industry is very similar to Turkey's.) The defense sector thus appears to be an important element in Greece's economy.

Previous defense-growth studies concerning Greece

In recent years, the study of the Greek defense-growth relationship has attracted a number of authors. Kollias (1995b) analyzed the relationship using techniques of cointegration and error-correction methods. The study covers the period of 1963-1990 and found that defense spending had a positive impact on Greek GDP.

Chletsos and Kollias (1995) investigated the relationship using OLS regression, covering 1974-1990. They hypothesized that military spending entails direct positive effects through aggregate demand stimulation and other spin-off effects and negative effects through crowding-out of investment. Their model is based on a typical Keynesian national income equation (GDP = C+I+G), and their findings are as predicted: defense spending positively affects consumption and, through it, gross domestic product but induces a negative impact on investment.

Antonakis (1996) analyzed the defense-growth relationship by means of a simultaneous equation model, using 3SLS estimation. His findings are contrary to Kollias (1995b) and Chletsos and Kollias (1995). Negative effects on growth

Table 6.2: Defense-growth empirical studies on Greece

Author	Model	Sample Period	Remarks	Conclusion
Kollias (1995b)	Production function *(ad hoc)*	1963-1990	Single equation, cointegration and ERM	Positive and significant effect of defense on growth
Chletsos and Kollias (1995)	Keynesian national income equation	1974-1990	Four equations, consumption, investment, military and GDP equations, OLS estimations	Positive direct effect of defense on growth, negative impact on investment
Antonakis (1996)	Demand and supply side (Deger) model	1958-1990	Three equations, defense, saving, and growth equations, 3SLS	Negative directs effect of defense on growth, positive indirect effect. Net effect is negative
Antonakis (1997)	Feder model	1958-1991	Single equation, two sectors model, military, nonmilitary, OLS	Defense had a negative impact on growth

and positive effects on saving are found, and the overall net effect is negative. Finally, Antonakis (1997) used a Feder-type model to estimate the defense-growth relationship for Greece for 1958-1991, concluding that Greek defense spending is detrimental to its economic growth.

Table 6.2 summarizes these inconclusive studies. The studies contain several shortcomings. Kollias' (1995b) model is not based on a theoretical framework, but it employed recent, advanced econometric techniques. In Chletsos and Kollias (1995), theory entails *ad hoc* justification of the chosen regression, and the sample period is relatively short. The short time period might have led to the introduction of bias in the estimates. To provide a better understanding of defense-growth relationship in Greece, this chapter estimates first a supply side (Feder-type) model and, second, a demand and supply-side (Deger-type) model. The analysis will also give us an opportunity to compare the Greek defense-growth relationship with that of Turkey.

Empirical analysis

Sezgin (1997, 1998) found that Turkish defense spending is positively related to its economic growth. Of course, these results cannot be generalized across countries. To facilitate comparison, the Greek defense-growth relationship is therefore empirically analyzed in this chapter using highly similar specifications and sample periods to those employed in Sezgin (1997, 1998).

The data for this analysis came from several sources. Defense expenditure data were taken from various SIPRI yearbooks. GNP, investment, population, savings (calculated from national accounts), balance of trade (exports of goods and services minus imports of goods and service in the national accounts), and inflation rates were taken from various IMF *International Financial Statistics* (IFS) yearbooks. All financial data were deflated to 1990 billion Greek Drachmas using IFS GNP-deflators. Data for the share of Turkish defense spending in GDP and average NATO defense burdens of NATO members were taken from various SIPRI yearbooks.

Supply-side (Feder type) analysis

Feder (1983) developed a model to investigate export-growth relationships. His model divides the economy into two sectors. One is an advanced sector export (X) and the other is a domestically oriented, non-export, sector. The export sector provides positive externalities to the rest of the economy. Ram (1986) and Biswas and Ram (1986) applied this model to the study of defense spending and economic growth in a cross-section of 58 less developed countries (LDC's) for the period 1960-1977. Since then, many researchers have employed the Feder-model to investigate the defense-growth relation.[1]

In this model it is assumed that the economy consists of two sectors, namely, a civilian sector (C) and a defense sector (M). Externalities emanate from the defense sector to the civilian sector. The main inputs to the sectors are capital (K) and labor (L). Subscripts refer to each sector:

(6.1) $M = M (K_m, L_m)$

(6.2) $C = C (K_c, L_c, M)$

The major advance of this model is that it considers externalities from sector M to sector C and offers much for the empirical study of defense-growth relationships (Deger and Sen, 1995). In particular, it may also explain defense spending's size- and externalities effects as well as sectoral factor-productivity differentials. At the same time, the model is relatively parsimonious in its data needs, generally a big problem when studying developing countries. A further advantage of this model is that it describes the supply constraints which are important for developing countries such as Greece.

For the Feder-type model used here, the econometric form of the models used are:[2]

$$(6.3) \qquad \frac{\Delta Y}{Y} = \alpha_0 + \alpha_1 \frac{I}{Y} + \beta \frac{\Delta L}{L} + \left(\frac{\delta}{1+\delta} + C_m \right) \frac{\Delta M}{Y} + \epsilon$$

and, with separate externality-effect and factor-productivity differentials of defense expenditure:

$$(6.4) \qquad \frac{\Delta Y}{Y} = \alpha_0 + \alpha_1 \frac{I}{Y} + \beta \frac{\Delta L}{L} + \left(\frac{\delta}{1+\delta} - \theta \right) \frac{\Delta M}{Y} + \theta \frac{\Delta M}{M} + \epsilon$$

In equations (6.3) and (6.4), growth of productivity is a function of:

- physical capital $\left(\alpha \frac{I}{Y} \right)$

- changes in labor $\left(\beta \frac{\Delta L}{L} \right)$

- the total effect of defense expenditure $\left(\left(\frac{\delta}{1+\delta} + C_m \right) \frac{\Delta M}{Y} \right)$

- the size effect of defense spending $\left(\left(\frac{\delta}{1+\delta} - \theta \right) \frac{\Delta M}{Y} \right)$

- and the externality effect of defense spending $\left(\theta \frac{\Delta M}{M} \right)$.

Furthermore, equation (6.4) shows the relative marginal productivity of defense spending (δ) on economic growth, as compared to the rest of the economy.

The variables used in the estimation are:

$\Delta Y/Y$ The model's dependent variable is the annual rate of growth of output, measured as the difference between current-year real GNP and previous-year real GNP, divided by previous-year real GNP.

ΔL/L   The labor-force growth rate, proxied by population-growth data since labor-force data are unavailable for Greece.

I/Y   The investment-to-GNP ratio, measured as real gross fixed capital of Greece, divided by the previous year's real GNP.

ΔM/Y   The difference of real military expenditure between current-year and previous-year, divided by previous-year real GNP.

ΔM/M   The real growth rate of defense expenditure, calculated as for the above-mentioned variables.

Empirical results

Equations (6.3) and (6.4) were estimated using ordinary least squares (OLS). The results (not shown here) indicated that the coefficient of investment is statistically significant and positive in both estimations. They are as expected because economic growth of a developing country is mainly stimulated by its increasing capital stock. In contrast, the coefficient of population growth is not statistically significant. The reason for this may be that population is not a good proxy for labor force. The total effect of defense spending as represented in equation (6.3) is estimated as statistically insignificant. Estimates for equation (6.4) also gave statistically insignificant results for the defense-size and defense-externality variables. This implies that the defense sector has no important effect on Greece's economic growth. The factor-productivity differential between the defense sector and the rest of economy is positive. This means that the defense sector is more productive than the civilian sector and is contrary to the findings in Sezgin (1997). This result may explain why the Greek defense sector has no apparent negative effect on its economic growth. The sector seems productive.

In a separate study, Sezgin (1999b) showed that Greek equipment-defense spending negatively affects its economy but non-equipment defense spending (personnel, infrastructure) is positively correlated to the Greek economy. The positive productivity impact of defense on Greece's economic growth may therefore come primarily from spending on personnel and military infrastructure. For comparison, in the case of Turkey defense size correlated positively to economic growth while externalities from the defense sector to the rest of the economy were negative (Sezgin, 1997, 1999a).

The diagnostic tests for the OLS estimations of equations (6.3) and (6.4) were weak. For example, the time-series data generally show a trend and a trend variable should therefore be added into the equation. Moreover, in July 1974,

Turkey intervened militarily in Cyprus, greatly affecting Greek defense spending as from 1975 (Kollias, 1995a). Consequently, a Cyprus dummy variable should be included in the models as well, taking a value of one between 1975 and 1981 and zero for all other years.

Rerunning the regressions for (6.3) only with the trend variable added, resulted in a statistically significant coefficient for the trend and improved estimation and diagnostic statistics, but the defense variable remained statistically insignificant. Rerunning the regressions only with the dummy variable, the dummy coefficient turned out to be statistically insignificant. Finally, including both the Cyprus dummy and the trend variables resulted in similar findings. While the investment and trend variables show significant and positive relationships with Greek economic growth, the Cyprus dummy and defense variables were not statistically significant. The same procedure applied to equation (6.4), the one including separate size- and externality-effects of defense spending, resulted in statistically insignificant coefficients for all the defense variables in all three estimations but the diagnostics were improved by the inclusion of the trend and the Cyprus dummy variables.

In a further step, I tested the stationarity of variables, the same procedure as used in Sezgin (1999a). There, due to non-stationarity of some variables (investment, labor force), first-differences of these variables are used for the final version of the estimation and resulted in highly improved empirical results for Turkey. Thus, here, the Greek data were tested for unit-roots and became stationary after taking first-differences.

In the final estimations, then, the results of which are shown in Tables 6.3 and 6.4, first-difference versions of equations (6.3) and (6.4) are used. Consider first Table 6.3. The trend variable is omitted here because after first-differencing of the variables, the trend ceased to exist, but a Cyprus dummy is retained. As may be seen from Table 6.3, the results are almost identical to those discussed before: statistically significant and positive results are obtained for investment but the defense variables and the Cyprus dummy resulted in statistically insignificant coefficients in all four estimation runs. This suggests that Greek defense spending has no important effect on its economic growth.

Although the investment and labor force variables are non-stationary and needed first-differencing, the defense variables actually were stationary. Therefore, another estimation was performed using first-differences only for the

Table 6.3: Estimates of equations (6.3) and (6.4) with first-differencing of all variables

Dependent variable: Economic growth (1959-1994); first differences

	Eq. (6.3)	Eq. (6.3)	Eq. (6.4)	Eq. (6.4)
Constant	-0.02	-0.01	-0.01	0.01
	(-0.01)	(-0.04)	(-0.01)	(-0.59)
Investment (first diff.)	0.82***	0.81***	0.81***	0.81***
	(3.60)	(3.53)	(3.53)	(3.47)
Population growth (first diff.)	1.70	1.68	1.55	1.52
	(1.19)	(1.16)	(1.01)	(0.97)
Defense size (first diff.)	0.84	0.84	-0.21	-0.28
	(1.26)	(1.23)	(-0.06)	(-0.07)
Defense externality (first diff.)			0.05	0.05
			(0.29)	(0.30)
Cyprus dummy		0.01		0.01
		(0.09)		(0.12)
Factor productivity differential			0.05	
R^2	0.32	0.32	0.32	0.32
DW	2.88	2.87	2.87	2.87
F-stat	5.086***	3.698**	3.728**	2.891**

t statistics in parentheses
** significant at the 5 percent level
*** significant at 1 percent level

investment and labor variables. While the diagnostic tests improved, the substantive results remained almost identical (see Table 6.4).

I also estimated the Greek defense-growth relation using another four different versions of the Feder-model (i.e., those by Biswas and Ram, 1986; Ward *et al.*, 1991; Ward and Davis , 1992; and Alexander, 1991). The results are not shown here. At any rate, the investment parameter was statistically significant and positive in three cases and the population growth variable resulted in an insignificant coefficient in all four estimations. Importantly, the defense parameters (size and externality) were not statistically significant in any of the four cases. Once again, no significant effect of defense spending on Greece's economic growth was found.

When these results for Greece are compared with those found for Turkey (Sezgin 1997, 1998, 1999a), one finds that the investment variable is positively

Table 6.4: Estimates of equations (6.3) and (6.4) with first-differences only for the investment and labor-force proxy variables

Dependent variable: Economic growth (1959-1994)

	Eq. 6.3		Eq. 6.4	
	Coeff.	*t-stat*	*Coeff.*	*t-stat*
Constant	0.09***	(8.23)	0.09***	(8.03)
Investment (first diff.)	0.48***	(2.57)	0.49***	(2.55)
Population (first diff.)	1.80	(1.53)	2.03	(1.51)
Defense size	0.25	(0.33)	2.01	(0.42)
Defense externality			- 0.08	(- 0.37)
Trend	- 0.1***	(- 4.91)	- 0.01***	(- 4.85)
R2	0.55		0.56	
DW	1.54		1.51	
F-stat	9.84***		7.68***	

*** significant at 1 percent level

correlated to economic growth of both Turkey and Greece. As regards population, the population-growth variable is positively correlated to Turkish economic growth but is statistically insignificant for Greece.

Turning to defense variables, the total effect of defense spending is positive for Turkey and externalities from the defense sector to the rest of economy are negative. In contrast, for Greece the effects are insignificant. This suggests that whereas Turkish military expenditure stimulates its economic growth, Greek defense spending has no important effect on Greece's economy. Put differently, the results suggest that the effect of defense spending differs across the countries, even though the selected sample countries and sample time-periods were very similar.

Furthermore, running the four additional Feder-type models generally resulted in small positive but no statistically significant effects of Greek defense spending on economic growth.

Demand and supply-side (Deger-type) analysis

The results reported thus far are all based on various versions of the Feder-type model. To study whether these results are model-invariant, this sub-section runs the data through a Deger-type model, essentially the same used for analyzing

Turkey (Sezgin 1997, 1998). For Turkey, both model-types showed that Turkish defense spending is positively correlated to its economic growth. The results for Greece are reported below.

The bulk of the empirical studies using the Deger-type simultaneous equation model are summarized by Deger and Sen (1995) as follows:

Growth equation:

$$(6.5) \quad \frac{\Delta Y}{Y} = a_0 + a_1 \frac{S}{Y} + a_2 \frac{M}{Y} + a_3 \frac{B}{Y} + a_4 E_1$$

Savings equation:

$$(6.6) \quad \frac{S}{Y} = b_0 + b_1 \frac{M}{Y} + b_2 \frac{\Delta Y}{Y} + b_3 \frac{B}{Y} + b_4 E_2$$

Trade balance equation:

$$(6.7) \quad \frac{B}{Y} = c_0 + c_1 \frac{M}{Y} + c_2 \frac{\Delta Y}{Y} + c_3 E_3$$

Defense equation:

$$(6.8) \quad \frac{M}{Y} = d_0 + d_1 E_4$$

where $\Delta Y/Y$ is the growth rate of GDP, S/Y is the savings ratio, M/Y is the share of defense expenditure in GDP, B/Y is the trade-balance share in GDP, and E_i are a set of exogenous variables chosen through data specifications. E_4 in particular depends on strategic, security, and wealth variables.

The results reported here derive from equations (6.5) to (6.8) and used data for the time period 1958-1994. Exogenous variables were chosen considering Greece's economy and defense sector. In addition, level-data rather than share-data are used (see Sandler and Hartley, 1995). The equations are constructed as follows:

Growth equation:

$$(6.9) \quad Y = a_0 + a_1 S + a_2 M + a_3 B + a_4 P$$

Savings equation:

$$(6.10) \quad S = b_0 + b_1 M + b_2 Y + b_3 B + b_4 INFRT$$

Trade balance equation:

(6.11) $B = c_0 + c_1 Y + c_2 M + c_3 EXCRT$

Defense equation:

(6.12) $M = d_0 + d_1 PCI + d_2 DUMCYP + d_3 TUR_{-1} + d_4 NATO_{-1}$

where Y is real gross national product, S is real gross savings, B is the real balance of trade, M is real defense expenditure, P is population, PCI is per capita income, INFRT is the inflation rate, EXRT is the real exchange rate, TUR_{-1} is lagged Turkish military expenditures as a share of GDP, $NATO_{-1}$ is the lagged average defense burden of NATO countries (excluding Greece and Turkey), DUMCYP is a Cyprus war dummy variable for the years 1975 to 1981. Although Greek defense expenditures continued to increase after 1981, this increase depended on other security considerations.

The growth equation (6.9) includes three endogenous explanatory variables (savings, the balance of trade, defense expenditure) and, exogenously, population as a proxy of labor force. In the second equation (6.10), saving (S) is affected by defense expenditure, the balance of trade (as a proxy of foreign savings), growth (Y), and the inflation rate (INFRT). Equation (6.11) for the balance of trade contains defense expenditure (M), growth (Y), and the exchange rate (EXRT). For the defense equation (6.12), a fairly standard demand function for military expenditures is used.

The hypothesis that savings (S) and population (P) are positively correlated to economic growth, see equation (6.9), is standard in any basic growth-theoretic model (Deger and Sen, 1983; Deger and Smith, 1983; Faini *et al.*, 1984; Deger, 1986a; Lebovic and Ishaq, 1987; Scheetz, 1991). The sign for the coefficient of the balance of trade (B) should be negative because a trade-balance deficit implies net capital inflows from abroad which stimulate economic growth. The defense spending coefficient is hypothesized as a direct positive effect on economic growth through Keynesian aggregate demand and modernization effects.

Regarding equation (6.10), Benoit (1978) argued that in developing countries only a small part of any income not spent on defense is put into highly productive investment. Most of the income goes into consumption and social investment, such as housing and does not stimulate economic growth much. It is not a productive investment but rather contributes to consumer satisfaction (Benoit, 1978). Consequently, an increase in defense spending may not imply an equivalent decrease in investment or vice versa. Following life-cycle theories of consumption, savings depend on growth. Higher income and growth tend to generate higher savings. Thus, the growth effect on savings is hypothesized to be positive. The external-sector coefficient (B) is expected to be positive as it affects savings through income multipliers and trade taxes (Scheetz, 1991). Finally, inflation is included in the savings equation. Inflation certainly affects savings. Deger (1986b) assumed inflation to cause forced savings and therefore it is expected to be positively correlated to savings.

In equation (6.11), defense expenditure is generally held to be negatively related to the balance of trade. If there are domestic supply constraints an increase in defense spending may reduce exportable goods and/or may result in increased total imports. It is true that Greece has greatly benefitted from military transfers from the US and the NATO alliance. The burden on the balance of trade equation therefore should be obviously lower. As regards the exchange-rate variable, it is included to account for the effects on exports and imports of a change in the international purchasing power of domestic currency and is expected to have a positive impact on the balance of trade equation. Finally, economic growth should affect the trade balance. Deger (1986b) argued that the effect for countries following export-promoting strategies should be positive and negative for countries following import-substitution industrialization. Greece followed both of these strategies. Therefore, the sign of the coefficient cannot be hypothesized.

The defense equation (6.12) differs from previous studies. For this equation, a standard demand function for military expenditures is used. In general form, the estimating equation for defense expenditures is:

(6.13) Defense spending = f (income, spill, threat, prices)

Sandler and Hartley (1995) explain that income is a crucial determinant of military expenditures. There is a positive relationship between defense spending and a country's GDP. As GDP rises, a nation has both more resources to protect and greater means to provide protection. In equation (6.13), "spill" captures real defense spending of allies and "threat" is the defense spending of rivals. "Prices" denotes the relative price of defense as compared to non-defense goods. Regrettably, such prices are generally not available and therefore cannot be included in the estimation of the equation. "Spill" and "threat" are frequently lagged by one year when time-series data are used because a nation must experience the threat and/or spill before responding to it (Sandler and Hartley, 1995).

In light of this discussion, the determinants of Greek defense expenditures are, in addition to a dummy variable for the Cyprus war, per capita income (PCI),

NATO military spending for the "spill" effect (in real terms, exclusive of Greece and Turkey), and Turkey's military spending for the "threat" effect. If Greece is a free rider, the coefficient of NATO will be negative; but if Greece's defense planners adopt a follower mode of response, the coefficient should be positive. TUR is Turkish military expenditure as a share of GDP, capturing the "threat" to Greece. An increase in Turkish defense expenditure will be responded to by increased Greek defense spending.

Turkish and Greek bilateral relations have rarely been smooth. Their disputes have often threatened war. Several empirical studies find evidence in support of the notion that an arms race exists between the two countries. For example, Kollias (1996) found that Greek defense spending is primarily influenced by Turkish defense spending. Both countries engaged, in recent years, in the modernization and upgrade of their military capabilities (Kollias, 1996). Kollias (1995a) also finds support for the existence of an arms race between the two countries. Therefore the TUR variable is included in the equation and it is expected that its coefficient be positive and statistically significant. In spite of Sandler and Hartley's admonition (1995), these two variables (NATO and TUR) are proxied as a *share* of defense expenditures in GDP, because using real level-values is not possible in this case due to the conversion-into-common-currency problem. The dummy variable (DUMCYP) is intended to capture the effect of the war between Turkey and Cyprus at the end of 1974.

Empirical results

Table 6.5 reports the estimates for the equation system (6.9) to (6.12) using OLS, 2SLS, and 3SLS estimation techniques. The variables were first tested for unit-roots and, due to non-stationarity, all variables were first-differenced after which they became stationary. Turning to the estimation results, in the growth equation (6.9), the savings and defense variables are statistically significant and positively correlated to economic growth. These results for Greece are consistent with the Turkish case (Sezgin, 1998). But the balance of trade variable, as a proxy for capital inflows from abroad, and the population variable, as a proxy for labor force, both showed statistically insignificant results. Perhaps they are inadequate proxies. All three estimations — OLS, 2SLS, and 3SLS — show highly similar results.

The savings equation (6.10) suggests that national income is positively related to savings. But defense expenditures exert a negative effect, suggesting that increasing defense expenditures in Greece cause lower savings levels, hence lower investment. The results are consistent across the three estimations. In contrast, Turkish defense spending (Sezgin, 1998) showed no significant effect

Table 6.5: Estimation results for (6.9) to (6.12) with lagged response, 1958-1994

	Exogenous variables	OLS	2SLS	3SLS
Growth equation (6.9)	Constant	241.33 (4.63)***	242.19 (3.47)***	218.66 (6.02)***
	ΔS	0.95 (7.78)***	1.24 (7.99)***	1.23 (10.61)***
	ΔB	-0.06 (-0.70)	-0.01 (-0.02)	-0.09 (-0.31)
	ΔM	1.20 (2.58)**	1.99 (2.84)***	2.47 (3.86)***
	ΔP	5.58 (0.07)	212.01 (0.21)	30.06 (0.09)
	Diagnostic tests	R^2: 0.66 DW: 1.33	σ: 171.92	σ: 181.57
Saving equation (6.10)	Constant	-137.5 (-4.46)***	-162.30 (-4.42)***	-178.23 (-5.55)***
	ΔM	-0.96 (-2.28)**	-2.78 (-2.68)**	-2.12 (-3.79)***
	ΔB	0.02 (0.20)	-0.04 (-0.19)	0.02 (0.11)
	ΔY	0.63 (7.60)***	0.75 (7.45)***	0.81 (10.71)***
	ΔINF	-1.77 (-0.61)	-5.88 (-1.11)	0.01 (0.01)
	Diagnostic tests	R^2: 0.68 DW: 1.99	σ: 142.92	σ: 149.54
Trade balance equation (6.11)	Constant	-5.97 (-0.16)	-1.18 (-0.02)	-0.69 (-0.01)
	ΔY	-0.06 (-0.73)	-0.09 (-0.73)	-0.09 (-0.78)
	ΔM	-0.70 (-1.72)*	-0.26 (-0.35)	-0.15 (-0.21)
	$\Delta EXRT$	-0.16 (-0.21)	-0.21 (-0.20)	-0.20 (-0.19)
	Diagnostic tests	R^2: 0.12 DW: 2.49	σ: 183.13	σ: 183.33
Defense equation (6.12)	Constant	1.13 (0.07)	1.13 (0.07)	-3.00 (-0.20)
	ΔPCI	0.18 (0.54)	0.18 (0.55)	0.24 (0.75)
	$\Delta TUR(-1)$	2.40 (0.11)	2.40 (0.11)	-0.80 (-0.04)
	$\Delta NATO(-1)$	53.20 (0.71)	53.20 (0.74)	19.07 (0.26)
	DUMCYP	52.78 (2.09)	52.78 (2.12)**	56.29 (2.34)**
	Diagnostic tests	R^2: 0.17 DW: 2.01	σ: 57.53	σ: 57.85

Explanatory notes are on p. 131.

on its savings rate. The Greek balance of trade and inflation variables did not result in statistically significant coefficients.

The third equation (6.11) did not give any significant results, except for a weakly significant coefficient for military spending in the OLS run where R^2 is very low (0.12) and no other variables are significant at commonly accepted levels. Again for comparison, Sezgin (1998) found that the Turkish balance of trade is mainly affected by its exchange rate and Turkish national income. The results for Greece are unexpected. It could of course be that the Greek balance of trade is determined by factors other than those included in the equation. Alternatively, the data used might be inappropriate. Even though two different sets of data were used to represent the balance of trade (exports of goods and services in national accounts minus imports of goods and services in national accounts, and merchandise exports minus merchandise imports), both proxies gave very similar — statistically insignificant — results.

The final equation in this estimation is the defense equation (6.12). Only the Cyprus dummy variable resulted in a positive and statistically significant coefficient in the 2SLS and 3SLS estimations: the Cyprus war increased Greek defense spending. In contrast to Turkey where lagged Greek and NATO military spending were positive and statistically significant (Sezgin, 1998), in the case of Greece examined here the lagged variables ΔTUR_{-1} and $\Delta NATO_{-1}$ resulted in insignificant coefficients, a finding corroborated by Dunne and Nikaladou (1998).

It may well be that Greek military spending does not react with a lag to Turkish military spending but instead reacts *instantaneously*, a possibility entertained by Kollias and Makrydakis (1997) who indeed found empirical evidence in support of an arms race between the two countries. Therefore, I reran the equation system (6.9) to (6.12), replacing the lagged variables ΔTUR_{-1} and $\Delta NATO_{-1}$ with ΔTUR and $\Delta NATO$. The results are shown in Table 6.6.

The first three equations result in very similar coefficient estimates but with improved diagnostics. But the estimation of the defense equation (6.12) greatly improved. Nearly half of the variation in Greek military spending is explained by the variables in this equation, and the effect of Turkish military spending on Greek military spending (ΔTUR) is particularly strong (positive and statistically significant).

But, once again, the balance of trade equation (6.11) performed very weakly. Therefore, in one final run, this equation is altogether omitted from the system and equations (6.9), (6.10), and (6.12) are run as a simultaneous three-equation system, with the addition that an inflation variable is added to the defense spending equation (since inflation can lower real defense spending). The results are reported in Table 6.7.

Table 6.6: Estimation results for (6.9) to (6.12) with instantaneous response, 1958-1994

	Exogenous variables	OLS	2SLS	3SLS
Growth equation (6.9)	Constant	241.33 (4.63)***	236.16 (3.43)***	220.87 (5.15)***
	ΔS	0.95 (7.78)***	1.26 (7.91)***	1.25 (8.50)***
	ΔB	-0.06 (-0.70)	-0.04 (-0.08)	0.01 (0.01)
	ΔM	1.20 (2.58)**	2.08 (2.49)**	2.41 (3.41)***
	ΔP	5.58 (0.07)	-249.96 (-0.26)	-46.94 (-0.10)
	Diagnostic tests	R^2: 0.66 DW: 1.33	σ: 175.24	σ: 180.78
Saving equation (6.10)	Constant	-137.5 (-4.46)***	-160.73 (-4.07)***	-174.09 (-4.66)***
	ΔM	-0.96 (-2.28)**	-2.81 (-2.60)**	-1.99 (-2.54)**
	ΔB	0.02 (0.20)	-0.24 (-0.61)	-0.18 (-0.50)
	ΔY	0.63 (7.60)***	0.76 (6.86)***	0.78 (7.67)***
	ΔINF	-1.77 (-0.61)	-9.12 (-1.46)	1.27 (0.42)
	Diagnostic tests	R^2: 0.68 DW: 1.99	σ: 156.72	σ: 150.19
Trade balance equation (6.11)	Constant	-5.97 (-0.16)	-6.82 (-0.18)	-9.64 (-0.26)
	ΔY	-0.06 (-0.73)	-0.65 (-1.13)	-0.63 (-1.12)
	ΔM	-0.70 (-1.72)*	-0.06 (-0.73)	-0.06 (-0.71)
	ΔEXRT	-0.16 (-0.21)	-0.19 (-0.24)	-0.28 (-0.39)
	Diagnostic tests	R^2: 0.12 DW: 2.49	σ: 135.53	σ: 135.59
Defense equation (6.12)	Constant	-2.98 (-0.26)	-1.01 (-0.09)	-2.58 (-0.24)
	ΔPCI	0.48 (1.79)*	0.40 (1.47)	0.53 (2.00)**
	ΔTUR	54.77 (3.29)***	54.28 (3.30)***	45.00 (2.93)***
	ΔNATO	123.92 (1.87)*	101.4 (1.64)	134.92 (2.43)**
	DUMCYP	39.76 (1.98)**	40.0 (2.00)**	42.24 (2.39)**
	Diagnostic tests	R^2: 0.47 DW: 2.26	σ: 45.95	σ: 46.39

Explanatory notes are on p. 131.

Explanatory notes to Table 6.5:

- t-statistics in parentheses
- ***, **, * statistical significance at the 1, 5, and 10 percent levels, respectively
- For 2SLS estimation; loglik= -748.13 T= 36 and LR test of over-identifying restrictions: $Chi^2(21) = 300.97 [0.0000]$
- For 3SLS estimation; loglik= -736.07 T= 36 and LR test of over-identifying restrictions: $Chi^2(21) = 276.85 [0.0000]$

The variables were measured as follows:

- ΔY= real gross national product (first difference)
- ΔS= real gross saving (first difference)
- ΔB= real balance of trade (first difference)
- ΔM= Real defense expenditure (first difference)
- ΔP= Population growth (first difference)
- ΔPC= Per capita income (first difference)
- $\Delta EXRT$= Real exchange rate (first difference)
- ΔTUR_{-1}= Lagged Turkish military expenditures as a share of GDP (first difference)
- $\Delta NATO_{-1}$= Lagged average shares of defense burden of NATO countries (excluding Greece and Turkey) (first difference)
- DUMCYP= Dummy variable took value of one for the years 1975 to 1981 and zero elsewhere.

Explanatory notes to Table 6.6:

- t-statistics in parentheses
- ***, **, * statistical significance at the 1, 5, and 10 percent levels, respectively
- For 2SLS estimation; loglik= -817.88 = 37 and LR test of over-identifying restrictions: $Chi^2(13) = 421.61 [0.0000]$
- For 3SLS estimation; loglik= -790.57 T= 37 and LR test of over-identifying restrictions: $Chi^2(13) = 366.99 [0.0000]$

The variables were measured as follows:

- ΔY= real gross national product (first difference)
- ΔS= real gross saving (first difference)
- ΔB= real balance of trade (first difference)
- ΔM= Real defense expenditure (first difference)
- ΔP= Population growth (first difference)
- ΔPCI= Per capita income (first difference)
- $\Delta EXRT$= Real exchange rate (first difference)
- $\Delta INFRT$= Inflation rate (first difference)
- ΔTUR= Turkish military expenditures as a share of GDP (first difference)
- $\Delta NATO$= Average share of defense burden of NATO countries (excluding Greece and Turkey) (first difference)
- DUMCYP= Dummy variable took value of 1 for the years 1975 to 1981 and zero elsewhere

For both tables, all computations used PC-GIVE 8.0 and PC-FIML 8.0 (see Doornik and Hendry, 1994; 1995).

Table 6.7: Estimation results for (6.9), (6.10), (6.12) with instantaneous response, 1958-1994

	Exogenous variables	OLS	2SLS	3SLS
Growth equation (6.9)	Constant	241.33 (4.63)***	244.89 (3.75)***	204.65 (5.34)***
	ΔS	0.95 (7.78)***	1.29 (7.80)***	1.26 (7.82)***
	ΔB	-0.06 (-0.70)	0.05 (0.28)	-0.04 (-0.26)
	ΔM	1.20 (2.58)**	2.35 (3.14)***	2.27 (3.11)***
	ΔP	5.58 (0.07)	-416.47 (-0.45)	211.48 (0.58)
	Diagnostic tests	R^2: 0.66 DW: 1.33	σ: 185.26	σ: 183.01
Savings equation (6.10)	Constant	-137.5 (-4.46)***	-159.49 (-4.00)***	-173.48 (-4.58)***
	ΔM	-0.96 (-2.28)**	-2.83 (-3.02)***	-2.00 (-2.85)***
	ΔB	0.02 (0.20)	-0.06 (-0.44)	0.04 (0.38)
	ΔY	0.63 (7.60)***	0.78 (6.91)***	0.80 (7.39)***
	ΔINF	-1.77 (-0.61)	-9.36 (-1.60)	-1.05 (-0.38)
	Diagnostic tests	R^2: 0.68 DW: 1.99	σ: 158.70	σ: 146.88
Defense equation (6.12)	Constant	-1.99 (-0.19)	-1.99 (-0.19)	-3.45 (-0.34)
	ΔPCI	0.46 (1.72)*	0.45 (1.75)*	0.54 (2.18)**
	ΔTUR	34.93 (1.99)**	34.93 (2.02)**	30.96 (2.33)**
	$\Delta NATO$	92.70 (1.58)	92.70 (1.61)	115.03 (2.68)**
	ΔINF	-2.88 (-2.39)**	-2.88 (-2.43)**	-2.41 (-2.23)**
	DUMCYP	38.98 (2.06)**	38.98 (2.09)**	41.54 (2.82)***
	Diagnostic tests	R^2: 0.54 DW: 2.15	σ: 41.88	σ: 43.25

Notes:

▸ t-statistics in parentheses
▸ ***, **, * statistical significance at the 1, 5, and 10 percent levels, respectively
▸ For 2SLS estimation; loglik= -620.57 T= 37 and LR test of over-identifying restrictions: $Chi^2(8) = 371.95$ [0.0000]
▸ For 3SLS estimation; loglik= -538.03 T= 37 and LR test of over-identifying restrictions: $Chi^2(8) = 206.87$ [0.0000]

Explanatory notes are continued on p. 133.

Explanatory notes to Table 6.7 (continued):

The variables were measured as follows:
- ▸ ΔY= real gross national product (first difference)
- ▸ ΔS= real gross saving (first difference)
- ▸ ΔB= real balance of trade (first difference)
- ▸ ΔM= Real defense expenditure (first difference)
- ▸ ΔP= Population growth (first difference)
- ▸ ΔPCI= Per capita income (first difference)
- ▸ ΔINFRT= Inflation rate (first difference)
- ▸ ΔTUR= Turkish military expenditures as a share of GDP (first difference)
- ▸ ΔNATO= Average share of defense burden of NATO countries (excluding Greece and Turkey) (first difference)
- ▸ DUMCYP= Dummy variable took value of 1 for the years 1975 to 1981 and zero elsewhere

For Table 6.7, all computations used PC-GIVE 8.0 and PC-FIML 8.0 (see Doornik and Hendry, 1994; 1995).

The results suggest that Greek economic growth (6.9) is positively and statistically significantly affected by its gross savings and defense expenditure. Greece's gross savings (6.10) are positively affected by changes in national income but negatively affected by its defense expenditures. Finally, Greece's defense spending (6.12) is positively correlated to changes in per capita income level, Turkish contemporaneous defense expenditures, and the Cyprus war dummy variable, and negatively affected by inflation. The NATO variable is statistically significant only in the 3SLS run.

Conclusion

This chapter briefly surveyed the Greek economy and intensively investigated its defense-growth relation. The results were compared to an earlier, similar study performed on Turkey (Sezgin, 1998). To ease comparison, in both cases Feder-type models (supply-side) and Deger-type models (demand and supply-side) were employed for the time-period 1958-1994.

The following summary conclusions may be drawn:

- ▸ Both Greece and Turkey carry a high defense burden, and both use large, conscripted armed forces. Both began to establish an indigenous arms industry at a similar time. Even so, both are major arms importers and only minor arms exporters. But with respect to the economic impact of military spending on their respective economies, the countries differ significantly.

▸ The estimation of the Feder-type supply-side models suggest that Greek defense expenditure is not correlated to its economic growth as the defense size- and externality-effects are insignificant. With regard to factor-productivity differentials I also found that the defense sector appears more productive than the Greek civilian sector.

▸ But when a Deger-type demand and supply-side model is estimated, the results are different. They suggest (see Table 6.7) that Greek defense spending has a statistically significant positive direct effect on economic growth but an indirect and statistically significant negative effect on gross savings. The net effect is positive. The estimated model also suggests that the major determinants of Greek defense spending are its per capita income, contemporaneous, rather than lagged, Turkish defense spending, the Cyprus war in 1974, as well as NATO's military expenditures.

▸ In sum, the empirical evidence would suggest that the defense-growth relation for Greece is inconclusive. While the Feder-type model suggest no significant tradeoff between defense and growth, the Deger-type model suggests a positive net effect of defense spending on economic growth.

▸ Finally, the effect of defense spending differs across countries even when the countries are similar, as in the case of Turkey and Greece (similar defense burden, economic structure, threat, defense industrial base). Very similar time periods and the same models were deliberately used to estimate Greece's and Turkey's defense-growth tradeoff in this chapter and in Sezgin (1997, 1998, 1999a). Although Turkey's defense sector appears to stimulate its economic growth, the results are inconclusive for Greece.

Defense expenditures are generally divided into personnel, equipment, maintenance, and infrastructure expenditures. Their effects on economic growth could be different for different countries. When compared, it turns out that Turkey spends less on personnel but more on equipment, infrastructure, and maintenance than Greece does. The differential effects of military spending on the economies of Greece and Turkey might be due to the different composition of their respective military spending.

Notes

1. See Sandler and Hartley (1995), Dunne (1996), Ward *et al.* (1991), Ward *et al.* (1995), and Sezgin, (1997) for a detailed literature review and the derivation of the model.

2. Derivation of the model is available from the author.

References

Antonakis, N. (1996). "Military Expenditure and Economic Growth in Less Developed Countries: A Simultaneous Equation Approach with An Application to Greece, 1958-90." *Economia Internazionale.* Vol. XLIX, No. 3, pp. 329-346.

Antonakis, N. (1997). "Defense Spending and Growth in Greece: A Comment and Further Empirical Evidence." *Applied Economic Letters.* Vol. 4, pp. 651-655.

Alexander, W. Robert J. (1991). "The Impact of Defense Spending on Economic Growth: A Multi-Sectoral Approach to Defense Spending and Economic Growth with Evidence from Developed Economies." *Defense Economics.* Vol. 2, No. 1, pp. 39-55.

Avramides, A.C. (1995). "An Analysis of Greek Defense Expenditure." Unpublished Ph.D. Thesis. University of Reading, UK.

Bartzokas, A. (1992). "The Developing Arms Industries in Greece, Portugal, Turkey," in M. Brzoska and P. Lock (eds.), *Restructuring of Arms Production in Western Europe.* Oxford: Oxford University Press.

Benoit, E. (1978). "Growth and Developing Countries." *Economic Development and Cultural Change.* Vol. 26, No. 2, pp. 271-280.

Biswas, B. and R. Ram (1986). "Military Spending and Economic Growth in Less Developed Countries: An Augmented Model and Further Evidence." *Economic Development and Cultural Change.* Vol. 34, No. 2, pp. 361-372.

Chletsos, M. and C. Kollias (1995). "Defense Spending and Growth in Greece 1974-90: Some Preliminary Econometric Results." *Applied Economics.* Vol. 27, No. 9, pp. 883-889.

Deger, S. (1986a). *Military Expenditure and Third World Countries: The Economic Effect.* London: Routledge and Kegan Paul.

Deger, S. (1986b). "Economic Development and Defence Expenditure." *Economic Development and Cultural Change.* Vol. 35, No. 1, pp. 179-196.

Deger, S. and S. Sen (1995). "Military Expenditures and Third World Countries," chapter 11 in K. Hartley and T. Sandler (eds.), *Handbook of Defense Economics.* Amsterdam: Elsevier.

Doornik, A.J. and F.D. Hendry (1995). *PC-GIVE 8-0: An Interactive Econometric Modeling System.* London: Chapman and Hall.

Dunne, J.P. (1996). "Economic Effects of Military Expenditure in Developing Countries: A Survey," chapter 23 in N. Gleditsch, O. Bjerkholt,, A. Cappelan, P.R. Smith, and D.P. Dunne (eds.), *The Peace Dividend.* Amsterdam: Elsevier.

Dunne, P. and E. Nikolaidou (1998). 'Military Spending and Economic Growth: A Case Study of Greece, 1960-1996." Paper presented at the International Conference on Defense Economics and Security in Mediterranean and Sub-Saharan Countries, Technical University of Lisbon (June).

Faini, R., P. Annez, and T. Taylor (1984). "Defense Spending, Economic Structure and Growth: Evidence among Countries and over Time." *Economic Development and Cultural Change*. Vol. 32, No. 3, pp. 487-498.

Feder, G. (1983). "On Exports and Economic Growth." *Journal of Economic Development*. Vol. 12 , pp. 59-73.

International Monetary Fund (various years). *International Finance Statistics Yearbook*. Washington, DC: IMF.

Kollias, C. (1995a). "Country Survey VII: Military Spending in Greece." *Defense and Peace Economics*. Vol. 6, No. 4, pp. 305-320.

Kollias, C. (1995b). "Preliminary Findings on The Economic Effects of Greek Military Expenditure." *Applied Economic Letters*. Vol. 2, pp. 16-18.

Kollias, C. (1996). "The Greek-Turkish Conflict and Greek Military Expenditure 1960-92." *Journal of Peace Research*. Vol. 33, No. 2, pp. 217-228.

Kollias, C. and S. Makrydakis (1997). "Is There a Greek-Turkish Arms Race? Evidence from Cointegration and Causality Tests." *Defense and Peace Economics*. Vol. 8, No. 4, pp. 355-379.

Lebovic, J.H. and A. Ishaq (1987). "Military Burden, Security Needs and Economic Growth in the Middle East." *Journal of Conflict Resolution*. Vol. 31, No. 1, pp. 106-138.

NATO (1998). *NATO Review* (Spring 1998). Brussels: NATO.

OECD (various years). *Economic Surveys Greece*. Paris: OECD.

Ram, R. (1986). "Government Size and Economic Growth: A New Framework and Some Evidence from Cross-Section and Time-Series Data." *American Economic Review*. Vol. 76, No. 1, pp. 191-203.

Sandler, T. and K. Hartley (1995). *The Economics of Defense*. Cambridge: Cambridge University Press.

Scheetz, T. (1991). "The Macroeconomic Impact of Defence Expenditures: Some Econometric Evidence for Argentina, Chile, Paraguay and Peru." *Defence Economics*. Vol. 3, No. 1, pp. 65-81.

Sezgin, S. (1997). "Country Survey X: Defense Spending in Turkey." *Defense and Peace Economics*. Vol. 8, No. 4, pp. 381-409.

Sezgin, S. (1998). "An Empirical Analysis of Turkey's Defense-Growth Relationship with A Multi-Equation Model (1956-1994)." Paper presented to the conference on The Economic of Military Expenditure in Developing and Emerging Economies. Middlesex University, London (March).

Sezgin, S. (1999a). "A Note on Defense Spending in Turkey: New Findings." *Defense and Peace Economics.* Vol. 10 (forthcoming).

Sezgin, S. (1999b). "Defense Expenditure and Economic Growth in Turkey and Greece: A Disaggregated Analysis." Unpublished manuscript. Centre for Defense Economics, and Department of Economics and Related Studies, University of York, UK.

SIPRI (various years). *SIPRI Yearbook: World Armaments and Disarmament.* Oxford: Oxford University Press.

US Arms Control and Disarmament Agency (1994). *World Military Expenditures and Arms Transfers 1991-1992.* Washington, DC: US Government Printing Office.

Ward, M.D., D. Davis, M. Panubarti, S. Rajmaria, and M. Cochran, M. (1991). "Military Spending in India: Country Survey 1." *Defense Economics.* Vol. 3, No. 1, pp. 41-63.

Ward, M.D. and D. Davis (1992). "Sizing Up the Peace Dividend: Economic Growth and Military Spending in the United States 1948-1996." *American Political Science Review.* Vol. 86, No. 3, pp. 748-755.

Ward, M.D., D. Davis, and C.R. Lofdahl (1995). "A Century of Tradeoffs: Defense and Growth in Japan and the United States." *International Studies Quarterly.* Vol. 39, pp. 27-50.

7 The defense-growth relation: evidence from Turkey

Onur Özsoy

Introduction

Since the 1960s, the relation between military expenditures and economic growth has been extensively investigated and debated, especially among development economists, peace and defense economists, and political economists (Hitch, 1960; Benoit, 1973, 1978; Adams *et al.*, 1991; Lim, 1983; Babin, 1989; Atesoglu and Mueller, 1990; Alexander, 1990; Biswas and Ram, 1986; Rothschild, 1973; Deger and Sen, 1983; Deger 1986a, 1986b; Macnair *et al.*, 1995; Sandler and Hartley, 1995).[1]

Analyzing how military spending affects economic growth both in less developed countries (LDCs) as well as developed countries (DCs) is an empirical as well as theoretical issue. It is also crucial in determining new economic policies, allocation and adjustment of government resources among alternative government programs and spending, i.e., whether to spend more on education, health, housing, or other types of welfare programs, or to increase military outlays.

In this chapter, following Feder (1983), Ram (1986), and Biswas and Ram (1986), a three-sector neoclassical economic growth model is developed to empirically analyze and test for the impact of defense spending on economic growth in Turkey. The time-period used is 1950-1992. It is assumed that there are three sectors in the economy, N, M, and C, representing the nonmilitary public sector, the military public sector, and the civilian sector, respectively. Each of these sectors is assumed to contribute to the total output at each period in time. Each sector uses three inputs, namely, capital (K), labor (L), and human capital (H). I include human capital in each of the sectoral production functions and allow for differentiated, relative contributions of less educated and more educated labor to total output. Unlike others, my model is designed to detect the externality effect of an adversary's defense spending (Greece) on the economic growth of the country investigated (Turkey). The relative contributions of each input to total output and to the total externality and productivity effects are investigated. Additionally, wherever possible, the externality and productivity differentials are estimated separately.

This chapter makes several contributions to the literature. First, this study covers a longer period than most of the earlier studies. The results are likely to be more robust and recent. Second, because of the design of the model, the study provides insight into which of the sectors are relatively more efficient and contribute to economic growth and well-being in Turkey. Third, regarding budget allocations, the study might assist in the determination of more effective future government policies, i.e., either to spend more on defense or on other types of programs, such as education and health.

The chapter proceeds with a review of the relevant literature. Next, the model is developed, followed by results and interpretation of the empirical analysis. The chapter concludes with summary observations and policy implications and suggestions.

Literature review

Since 1986, multi-sector neoclassical growth models have been used extensively to study the relation between military expenditures and economic growth (Ram, 1986; Biswas and Ram, 1986; Alexander, 1990; Adams *et al.*, 1991; Linden, 1991; and Macnair *et al.*, 1995).[2]

Ram (1986) and Biswas and Ram (1986) modified Feder's (1983) model of export-led economic growth and estimated the impact of the military sector on the civilian sector for 58 LDCs for the time-period 1960-1977.[3] Following Ram (1986) and Biswas and Ram (1986), a number of other development economists used versions of the Feder-Ram[4] type of multi-sector neoclassical growth models to test for the relation between military spending and economic performance, especially economic growth in LDCs (Ward *et al.*, 1991; Linden, 1991; Ward *et al.*,1993; Stevenson and Mintz, 1995). A consensus finding has not emerged.[5]

The model

Sectoral production functions

(7.1) $N = N(K_n, L_n, H_n)$

(7.2) $\quad M = M(K_m, L_m, H_m, N, D)$
(7.3) $\quad C = C(K_c, L_c, H_c, N, M, D)$

where the lower-case subscripts denote the sectors.

The civilian sector (C) is affected by the nonmilitary (N) and military (M) public sectors of the economy. In addition, the military public sector of the rival country (D) is modeled not only to affect the country's military sector but also to affect its civilian sector. Positive externalities can occur "when the activity of one sector augments output in another sector, and this positive interdependency is uncompensated by the market activities" (Macnair, 1995).

Three inputs are allocated among the sectors at each point in time. Each input contributes to the production of the total output, Y, which is defined as:

$$Y = N + M + C$$

The reduced-form of equations of (7.1) to (7.3) is:[6]

(7.4)[7]

$$\frac{\dot{Y}}{Y} = \alpha_0 + \alpha \left(\frac{I}{Y}\right) + \alpha_1 \left(\frac{\dot{L}}{L}\right) + \alpha_2 \left(\frac{\dot{H}}{H}\right) + \alpha_3 \left(\frac{\dot{N}}{N}\right) \left(\frac{N}{Y}\right)$$
$$+ \alpha_4 \left(\frac{\dot{M}}{M}\right) \left(\frac{M}{Y}\right) + \alpha_5 \left(\frac{\dot{D}}{D}\right) \left(\frac{D}{Y}\right) + \epsilon$$

where
α_0 = constant term;
$\alpha = C_K$ (the marginal productivity of the capital stock);
$\alpha_1 = \gamma / g$ (the marginal productivity of the labor force);
$\alpha_2 = \gamma_1 / g_1$ (the marginal productivity of human capital);
$\alpha_3 = [(\delta_n/1 + \delta_n) + C_N + (M_N/1 + \delta_m)]$;
$\alpha_4 = [(\delta_m/1 + \delta_m) + C_M]$;
$\alpha_5 = [(M_D/1 + \delta_m) + C_D]$.

Sectoral productivity differentials and externalities

The model can be used to estimate the externality and productivity differentials separately.[8] Following Feder (1983), it is assumed that the nonmilitary public sector, the military public sector, and the rival's military public sector affect the production of the civilian sector of the economy with constant elasticities, i.e.,

$$C = C(K_c, L_c, H_c, N, M, D) = N^{\theta 1} M^{\theta 2} D^{\theta 3} \phi (K_c, L_c, H_c)$$

where θ_1, θ_2, and θ_3 are parameters. It can then be shown that

$$\partial C/\partial N \equiv C_n = \theta_1(C/N); \quad \partial C/\partial M \equiv C_m = \theta_2(C/M); \quad \partial C/\partial D \equiv C_d = \theta_3(C/D).$$

Making use of the marginal and average product of labor and human capital in (7.4), the following reduced-form equation is obtained for estimation purposes:

(7.5)

$$
\begin{aligned}
\frac{\dot{Y}}{Y} &= \alpha_0 + \alpha \left(\frac{I}{Y}\right) + \alpha_1 \left(\frac{\dot{L}}{L}\right) + \alpha_2 \left(\frac{\dot{H}}{H}\right) \\
&+ \alpha_3 \left(\frac{\dot{N}}{N}\right)\left(\frac{N}{Y}\right) + \alpha_4 \left(\frac{\dot{M}}{M}\right)\left(\frac{M}{Y}\right) + \alpha_5 \left(\frac{\dot{D}}{D}\right)\left(\frac{D}{Y}\right) \\
&+ \theta_1 \left(\frac{\dot{N}}{N}\right)\left(\frac{C}{Y}\right) + \theta_2 \left(\frac{\dot{M}}{M}\right)\left(\frac{C}{Y}\right) + \theta_3 \left(\frac{\dot{D}}{D}\right)\left(\frac{C}{Y}\right) + \epsilon
\end{aligned}
$$

where
α_0 = constant term;
$\alpha = C_K$ (the marginal productivity of the capital stock);
$\alpha_1 = \gamma/g$ (the marginal productivity of the labor force);
$\alpha_2 = \gamma_1/g_1$ (the marginal productivity of human capital);
$\alpha_3 = [(\delta_n/1+\delta_n) + (M_N/1+\delta_m)-\theta_1]$;
$\alpha_4 = [(\delta_m/1+\delta_m) - \theta_2]$;
$\alpha_5 = [(M_D/1+\delta_m) - \theta_3]$;
θ_1 (the externality effect of nonmilitary public sector outlays on the civilian sector);
θ_2 (the externality effect of military public sector expenditures on the civilian sector);
θ_3 (the externality effect of rival country's military public sector expenditures on the other country's civilian sector);
ϵ (the error term).

Extended model

The model can be modified to include the civilian and military public sectors in the nonmilitary public sector's production function as well as to include the civilian sector in the production function of the military public sector, as in equations (7.6) to (7.8) below. The main purpose of this is to measure externality effects and productivity differentials of the military public sector and the civilian sector on the nonmilitary public sector. As before, there are three sectors, three inputs, and three production functions. The main difference is the addition of M and C to the nonmilitary public sector's production function.

In this specification, I also dropped the rival's defense spending from the production function of the civilian sector (equation 7.8). The reason for this is that when the rival's defense sector expenditures affect the military public sector of the home country, they indirectly affect the civilian sector as well.

The new production functions are:

(7.6) $N = (K_n, L_n, H_n, M, C)$
(7.7) $M = (K_m, L_m, H_m, N, C, D)$
(7.8) $C = (K_c, L_c, H_c, N, M)$

In equation (7.6), M and C are included in the production function of the nonmilitary public sector to capture the combined externality effect and productivity differentials of the military and civilian sectors on the nonmilitary public sector. Total externality effects and productivity differentials of N, C, and D on the military public sector are captured in equation (7.7). Finally, in equation (7.8), N and M are included to explore externality effects and productivity differentials between the civilian sector and the nonmilitary and military public sectors, respectively. Put differently, equation (7.8) permits to detect relationships between the military and nonmilitary public sectors and the rest of the economy. The reduced-form equation for this model is:[9]

(7.9)
$$\frac{\dot{Y}}{Y} = \alpha_0 + \alpha_1 \left(\frac{I}{Y}\right) + \alpha_2 \left(\frac{\dot{L}}{L}\right) + \alpha_3 \left(\frac{\dot{H}}{H}\right) + \alpha_4 \left(\frac{\dot{N}}{N}\right) \left(\frac{N}{Y}\right)$$
$$+ \alpha_5 \left(\frac{\dot{M}}{M}\right) \left(\frac{M}{Y}\right) + \alpha_6 \left(\frac{\dot{C}}{C}\right) \left(\frac{C}{Y}\right) + \alpha_7 \left(\frac{\dot{D}}{D}\right) \left(\frac{D}{Y}\right) + \epsilon$$

where
α_0 = constant term;
α_1 (the marginal product of capital stock in the civilian sector of the economy);
α_2 (the elasticity of the labor force);
α_3 (the elasticity of human capital);
α_4 (the relative productivity and externality effect of the nonmilitary public sector on the civilian sector);
α_5 (the relative productivity and externality effect of the military public sector on the civilian sector);
α_6 (the effect of the civilian sector on total output);
α_7 (the effect of rival country's defense expenditures on the civilian sector);
ϵ (the error term).

In similar fashion, equation (7.10) below was calculated to capture the externality effects of the civilian sector on the nonmilitary and the military public sectors. It also allows to find the total effects of each sector on economic growth.

$$\frac{\dot{Y}}{Y} = \alpha_0 + \alpha_1 \left(\frac{I}{Y}\right) + \alpha_2 \left(\frac{\dot{L}}{L}\right) + \alpha_3 \left(\frac{\dot{H}}{H}\right)$$

$$+ \alpha_4 \left(\frac{\dot{N}}{N}\right) \left(\frac{N}{Y}\right) + \alpha_5 \left(\frac{\dot{M}}{M}\right) \left(\frac{M}{Y}\right) + \alpha_6 \left(\frac{\dot{C}}{C}\right) \left(\frac{C}{Y}\right)$$

$$+ \alpha_7 \left(\frac{\dot{D}}{D}\right) \left(\frac{D}{Y}\right) + \theta_1 \left(\frac{\dot{N}}{N}\right) \left(\frac{C}{Y}\right) + \theta_2 \left(\frac{\dot{M}}{M}\right) \left(\frac{C}{Y}\right)$$

$$+ \theta_3 \left(\frac{\dot{D}}{D}\right) \left(\frac{C}{Y}\right) + \theta_4 \left(\frac{\dot{C}}{C}\right) \left(\frac{M}{Y}\right) + \theta_5 \left(\frac{\dot{C}}{C}\right) \left(\frac{N}{Y}\right) + \epsilon$$

(7.10)[10]

where
α_0 = constant term;
$\alpha_1 = C_K$ (the marginal productivity of the capital stock);
$\alpha_2 = \gamma /g$ (the marginal productivity of the labor force);
$\alpha_3 = \gamma_1/g_1$ (the marginal productivity of human capital);
$\alpha_4 = [(\delta_n/1+\delta_n) + (M_N/1+\delta_m)]$;
$\alpha_5 = [(\delta_m/1+\delta_m) + (N_M/1+\delta_n)]$;
$\alpha_6 = [(N_C/1+\delta_n) + (M_C/1+\delta_m)]$;
$\alpha_7 = (M_D/1+\delta_m)$;
θ_1 (the externality effect of the nonmilitary public sector outlays on the civilian sector);
θ_2 (the externality effect of military public sector expenditures on the civilian sector of the economy);
θ_3 (the externality effect of rival country's military public sector expenditures on the other country's civilian sector);
θ_4 (the externality effect of the civilian sector on the military public sector);
θ_5 (the externality effect of the civilian sector on the nonmilitary public sector);
ϵ (the error term).

Theoretical expectations for equation (7.4)

The expected signs, despite some misgivings, might be characterized as follows:

α This effect, the marginal product of capital stock in the civilian sector of the economy, should be positive. As is well known, investment spending plays a very important role in the development process. The growth rate of Turkish GDP averaged 5 percent annually during the time period 1960-1993 (Turkish State Planning Organization, 1995). The sudden output growth of the Turkish economy after the 1970s was the result of infrastructure investment made in the late 1950s and early 1960s in almost every part of the economy. Investment in productive areas of the economy has been a crucial element in explaining the successful growth of output. It is therefore plausible to expect the coefficient of the capital stock in the civilian sector of the Turkish economy to be positive.

α_1 This effect, the elasticity of the labor force, is also expected to be positive. The reason is that an increase in the quantity and quality of the labor force is the main source for economic growth and development. Total productivity and economic growth can be enhanced both by larger and by more highly qualified work forces.

α_2 is the elasticity of human capital; a positive effect is expected. Human capital plays an important role in the economic development and growth process (Romer 1986, 1990). For example, in Romer (1990) human capital is the key input to the research sector that generates the new products or ideas that underlie technological progress. Countries with greater initial stocks of human capital experience a more rapid rate of introduction of new goods and thereby tend to grow faster.

α_3 captures the relative productivity and externality effects of the nonmilitary public sector on the civilian sector of the economy. As stated, there have been a number of studies dealing with the relationship between nonmilitary government expenditures and their impact on the civilian sector of the economy. Findings are usually mixed: they can be positive, negative, or neutral.

α_4 measures the externality effect and productivity differences between the military public sector and the civilian sector; the effect is expected to be negative. It is assumed that the civilian sector benefits from the military public sector if there is a highly developed, heavy military-industrial complex in the country in question. However, Turkey has no major military-industrial complex. Therefore, the externalities of the nonmilitary public sector for Turkey should be negative.

α_5 computes the externality effect and productivity differentials of the military public sector of the rival country on the other country's civilian economy. *A priori*, the sign of this coefficient is ambiguous. The direction of the impact depends strongly on the pattern of the military expenditures.

Theoretical expectations for equation (7.5)

α is the marginal productivity of capital stock. As before, it is assumed to be positive.

α_1 and
α_2 are the marginal productivity of labor and human capital, respectively. Both are assumed to be positive. As stated in the previous subsection, in any successful economic development process, the quality and quantity of labor force play a crucial role.

α_3 is the size effect of the nonmilitary public sector. In developing countries, the nonmilitary public sector is very important in the process of infrastructure investment, such as schools, hospitals, bridges, roads, railways, etc. All are thought to make major contributions to development and economic growth. Therefore, the coefficient of nonmilitary public sector's contribution to the growth process is expected to be positive.

α_4 is the size effect of the military public sector. The impact of military expenditures on economic growth should be negative. The military sector can contribute to economic development positively if, and only if, a country has a major military industry and thus a major military research and development sector which entail civilian applications and spill-over effects. Since Turkey has no major military complex, its limited resources and foreign exchange reserves will go to the purchase and import of arms and related products from developed countries. This will reduce the availability of export commodities, ordinarily a more productive and growth-promoting sector than the military sector is. As a result of importing military equipment, the balance of payments will worsen and the purchase of intermediate goods needed for more productive sectors, such as the civilian sector, will be hindered. Therefore, military spending will worsen economic well-being as well as economic growth in Turkey. Consequently, the effect of military expenditures on economic growth of Turkey is expected to be negative.

α_5 is the size effect of the rival country's defense spending. This effect on the home country's military public sector and on its civilian economy will depend on the direction (increasing or decreasing) and magnitude of the rival's defense spending and might therefore be positive, negative, or neutral.

θ_1 is the externality effect of nonmilitary public sector spending on the civilian economy. A positive θ_1 means that production in the government sector has a positive externality effect on the civilian sector. Conversely, a negative sign indicates that the externality effect is negative.

θ_2 defines the externality or spill-over effect of the military public sector on the civilian economy. A positive sign suggests that the military sector positively affects the output of the civilian sector and overall economic growth. In contrast, a negative sign is evidence of a negative impact of military spending on the civilian economy and thus suggests slower or negative economic growth.

θ_3 shows the externality effect of the rival country's defense spending on the civilian sector of the home country's economy. Again, a positive sign means that the rivals' defense spending contributes to the other's economic growth.

Theoretical expectations for equations (7.9) and (7.10)

α_1, α_2, α_3 are the coefficients of marginal product of capital stock, marginal product of labor force, and marginal product of human capital; all are expected to be positive for the same reasons as given above.

α_4 is the combined productivity and externality effect of the nonmilitary public sector. It is expected to positively influence the economy.

α_5 is the coefficient of the combined productivity and externality effect of military public sector on the rest of the economy. As argued above, its sign is expected to be negative.

α_6 is the combined productivity and externality effect of the civilian sector on overall economic growth and is expected to be positive.

α_7 is the total effect of the rival's defense spending on the other country's economy and its sign depends on the direction and magnitude of the rival's military spending.

The theoretical expectations for equation (7.10) are similar.

Data, empirical results, and interpretation

The data set covers the time-period 1950 to 1992 for Turkey. Real gross domestic product (RGDP), real gross investment (RGI), and real government expenditures (RGE) data are measured in constant 1985 US dollars. They were obtained from the Penn World Table (Mark 5.6a), denoted as PWT5.6a,[11] and growth rates were computed. Labor force data also come from PWT5.6a. Human capital data were obtained from the World Bank, the United Nations Educational, Scientific and Cultural Organization (UNESCO), and the Turkish State Planning Organization (TSPO). Military expenditure data come from Stockholm International Peace Research Institute *Yearbooks*.

Nonmilitary public expenditures were computed by subtracting the military public sector expenditures taken from SIPRI from RGE. It is generally difficult to obtain good labor force statistics for LDCs. I follow Ram (1986) and others to also use the growth rate of population as a proxy for labor. The annual growth rate of human capital is calculated from secondary school enrollment ratios (total number of student enrolled in secondary schools over total number of students), a measure of the quality of the labor force.

The main sources for military expenditures data were SIPRI, the US Arms Control and Disarmament Agency (ACDA), National Government Accounts, and the International Institute for Strategic Studies (IISS). Problems of reliability and quality of the military expenditures data have been addressed by many scholars. Researchers tend to agree that the most reliable data source is SIPRI which constructs its measure by adding military spending, military pensions, military interest payments, and military spending on paramilitary forces, then subtracting spending on police force and net foreign military aid, i.e., military aid to other nations minus military aid obtained from other nations (Hewitt, 1992, p. 112). In this chapter, I use SIPRI data to compute the impact of the annual growth rate of military spending on economic growth.

Definition of variables

To empirically estimate the parameters of equations (7.4), (7.5), (7.9), and (7.10), the following dependent and independent variables were computed and utilized:

$\dot{Y}/Y$ the dependent variable which is the annual rate of growth of real GDP. Calculated as log (Y/Y(-1)) or log Y - log Y(-1).

| I/Y | the investment share in GDP, computed as total real investment over real GDP. Its use allows to find the impact of investment on economic growth in Turkey. |

$\dot{L}/L$ the annual rate of growth of total population used to proxy for labor force and computed as log $(L/L(-1))$ or log L - log L(-1). This permits to capture the marginal contribution of the quantity of labor force to the annual rate of economic growth.

$\dot{H}/H$ the annual rate of growth of human capital, found as log $(H/H(-1))$ or log H - log H(-1). This captures the impact of labor force quality on economic growth.

$\dot{N}/N$ the annual rate of growth of real nonmilitary public expenditures, found by subtracting military public sector expenditures from real government expenditures. Computed as log $(N/N(-1))$ or log N - log N(-1), it produces the size effect of nonmilitary public spending on economic growth.

$\dot{M}/M$ the annual rate of growth of real military spending, computed as log $(M/M(-1))$ or log M - log M(-1). This is the size effect of military public sector spending on economic growth.

$\dot{C}/C$ the annual rate of civilian sector growth, computed as log $(C/C(-1))$ or log C - log C(-1), and measuring the impact of the civilian sector on overall economic growth.

$\dot{D}/D$ the annual rate of growth of Greece's real military spending, computed as log $(D/D(-1))$ or log D - log D(-1). This explains the impact of Greece's defense spending on Turkey.

Empirical analysis

Annual data from 1950 to 1992 for Turkey were used to estimate equations (7.4), (7.5), (7.9), and (7.10). Using OLS, Table 7.1 presents the results for equations (7.4) and (7.5), and Table 7.2 presents the results for the other two equations. Equation (7.4) was also estimated using 2SLS to address the endogeneity problem. Endogeneity was corrected by using instrumental variables, such as population size, percentage of urbanization, population density, and real money supply, and exogenous variables.

Let us examine Table 7.1 first. In almost all instances, the coefficients' expected signs for equation (7.4) were obtained although only a few resulted in statistically significant values. The estimated coefficients for equation (7.5) allow the computing of the combined productivity differentials and externality effects of the nonmilitary public sector, and the combined and separate productivity differential and externality effect of the military public sector. Equation (7.5) also permits to capture the total impact of Greece's defense sector on Turkey's economic growth.

The coefficient for the investment share is positive in both equations but statistically significant only in (7.4). This is in agreement with expectations. As pointed out, infrastructure investments made in the late 1950s and throughout the 1960s played a very important role in the Turkish development process. The coefficient for the marginal productivity of the labor force is negative in both equations, but neither is are statistically significant. This is contrary to *a priori* expectations. The human capital coefficient is positive for (7.4) and negative for (7.5). Again, neither is statistically significant, also in contravention to expectations.

The estimated coefficient of nonmilitary public sector spending on economic growth is positive and statistically significant in both equations (0.066, 0.115, respectively), even though they are small in magnitude. This suggests that the nonmilitary public sector played a role in the development process of Turkey during the time-period 1950-1992. In addition, the coefficient of the externality effect of the nonmilitary public sector on the civilian economy (equation 7.5) is positive and statistically significant at the 5 percent level. It may thus be said that positive externalities flow from the nonmilitary public sector to the civilian sector. The coefficient of military public sector spending is positive and statistically significant at the 1 percent level for (7.4) but negative and insignificant for (7.5). The total effect (productivity differential and externality effect combined) of the military public sector on economic growth is significant and positive but the externality effect of the military public sector is statistically insignificant.

The positive impact of defense spending on the Turkish economy may have been generated by technology transfer, technical support, or military aid received from other nations. Therefore, these findings indicate that defense spending has likely not been a burden on Turkish economic growth over the time-period 1950-1992. The coefficient of the adversary's (Greece's) defense sector is negative but statistically insignificant in both equations. Greek military spending apparently does not affect Turkey's economic performance. The externality effect of Greek defense expenditures is also statistically insignificant. One may conclude that Greek defense spending imposes no external cost on the Turkish economy during

Table 7.1: OLS estimates of coefficients for equations (7.4) and (7.5); Turkey, 1950-1992 (dependent variable: growth rate of real GDP)

Variable	Equation (7.4)	Equation (7.5)
Constant	0.030	0.036
	(0.621)	(0.657)
Investment	0.143***	0.227
	(2.494)	(1.227)
Labor	-0.839	-2.228
	(-0.323)	(-0.691)
Human capital	0.006	-0.118
	(0.022)	(-0.364)
Nonmilitary public sector	0.066***	0.115**
	(3.208)	(2.239)
Military public sector	3.455***	-0.103
	(2.493)	(-0.011)
Rival's military sector	-1.810	-3.161
	(-1.524)	(-0.538)
Externality effect; nonmilitary public sector on civilian sector		0.051*
		(1.851)
Externality effect; military sector		0.380
		(0.545)
Externality effect rival		-0.887
		(-0.704)
Std. error of regression	0.042	0.041
R-squared	0.490	0.576
Adjusted R-squared	0.403	0.440
Durbin-Watson statistic	2.281	2.34
F-statistic (zero slopes)	5.626	4.224

Note: t-statistics are in parentheses; ***, **, * denotes statistical significance at the 1, 2.5, and 5 percent levels, respectively.

Table 7.2: OLS estimates of coefficients for equations (7.9) and (7.10); Turkey, 1950-1992 (dependent variable: growth rate of real GDP)

Variable	Equation (7.9)	Equation (7.10)
Constant	0.011	0.007
	(0.227)	(-0.246)
Investment	0.264	0.212
	(1.255)	(1.559)
Labor	-1.939	0.008
	(-0.732)	(0.119)
Human capital	0.029	0.017
	(0.351)	(0.085)
Nonmilitary public sector	0.037**	-6.463
	(2.060)	(-1.457)
Military public sector	2.668**	-3.031
	(2.186)	(-0.457)
Rival's military sector	-0.962	1.322
	(-0.838)	(0.278)
Civilian sector	0.495***	0.514
	(3.056)	(0.380)
Externality effect of nonmiliary sector		1.484**
		(2.093)
Externality effect of military sector		0.733
		(0.972)
Externality effect; rival		0.007
		(0.014)
Externality effect; civilian on nonmilitary public sector		-3.664
		(-0.621)
Externality effect; civilian on military public sector		-3.738
		(-0.524)
Std. error of regression	0.038	0.031
R-squared	0.500	0.417
Adjusted R-squared	0.391	0.178
Durbin-Watson statistic	2.325	1.879
F-statistic (zero slopes)	4.586	1.723

Note: t-statistics are in parentheses; ***, **, * denotes statistical significance at the 1, 2.5, and 5 percent levels, respectively.

the time period under study.

The factor-productivity differential of the military public sector is found to be negative, 0.383, leading to an inconclusive result.[12] In contrast, the factor-productivity differential for the nonmilitary public sector cannot be found because M_D is unknown.

Let us turn now to examine Table 7.2. Again, most of the expected signs are obtained. The estimated coefficient of the investment share is, as expected, positive in both runs but statistically insignificant. The coefficients for labor and human capital are also statistically insignificant. The coefficients for the nonmilitary and military public sectors are positive and statistically significant at the 2.5 percent level only in equation (7.9). This suggests that the impact of both the nonmilitary public sector and the military public sector on economic growth are positive: an increase in spending in those sectors positively affected economic growth of Turkey during the time-period 1950-92.

Regarding equation (7.10), the externality effect of the nonmilitary public sector is positive and statistically significant. All other coefficients for this equation are statistically insignificant. Moreover, due to the possibility of multicollinearity, it is not possible to compute the externality and total effects separately to find the sectoral productivity-differentials and to determine which sector is more efficient.

The civilian sector coefficient in equation (7.9) is positive (0.495) and statistically significantly different from zero, meaning that the Turkish civilian sector made a positive contribution to overall economic growth in Turkey. As a result, more resources should be employed in the civilian sector of the economy to obtain higher future rates of economic growth.

Finally, Table 7.3 presents the estimated coefficient for equation (7.4) using 2SLS estimation for the time-period 1950-1992. The main reason for using the 2SLS estimation technique is to correct for a possible endogeneity problem that might exist between some of the independent variables and the growth rate of RGDP.

Endogenous variables are determined by the model and correlated with the error term. In the estimated models in this study, potential endogenous variables are investment share and human capital. Investment is a function of interest rates and interest rates are affected by money supply. Therefore, money supply may be correlated with the endogenous variable, investment share. The correlation between money supply and investment was 0.417. As a result, money supply can be used as an instrumental variable for eliminating the problem of endogeneity.

Another potential endogenous variable is human capital. It is assumed that if the rate of growth of RGDP increases, there would be more resources available for education. Thus, human capital may be influenced by the level of total output.

Table 7.3: 2SLS estimates of equation (7.4); Turkey, 1950-1992

Variable	*Coefficients*
Constant	0.088
	(0.798)
Investment	-0.833
	(-0.816)
Labor	6.910
	(0.614)
Human capital	-0.096
	(-0.223)
Nonmilitary public sector	0.041
	(1.175)
Military public sector	3.297*
	(1.765)
Rival's military sector	-0.705
	(-0.358)
Std. error of regression	0.053
R-squared	0.161
Adjusted R-squared	0.014
Durbin-Watson statistic	1.780

Note 1:   Instruments: Constant , Population, Nonmilitary Government Sector,
Civilian Sector (-1), LogGDP(-1), Log Public Sector, Military Sector
(-1) and Log Military Sector.

Note 2:   t-statistics in parentheses; ***, **, * denotes statistical significance
at the 1, 2.5, and 5 percent levels, respectively.

Demographic variables, such as size of population, population density, and percentage of urbanization were used as instruments to remove endogeneity. The correlations were high between human capital and population (0.989), human capital and population density (0.97), human capital and urbanization (0.95). Consequently, they are all eligible to serve as instrumental variables.

Still, almost all of the estimated coefficients of equation (7.4) were statistically insignificant for the time-period 1950-92 (see Table 7.3), possibly because of the low quality of the instrumental variables that were used.

Conclusion

This chapter adds to the ongoing defense-growth debate using data for Turkey for 1950-1992. The empirical estimation of model parameters suggests that there has been a positive relationship between defense spending and economic growth in Turkey during this time period. The total and the externality effects of Turkey's military public sector on economic growth were found positive and statistically significant. The productivity differential of the military public sector turned out positive, suggesting that the military public sector is more efficient than the civilian Turkish economy. Moreover, the net impact of the military public sector on overall economic growth was positive because both the externality and productivity differentials are positive.

Nonmilitary public sector spending has also positively influenced economic growth in Turkey, suggesting that an increase in nonmilitary public sector spending would increase overall economic growth in Turkey. It is believed that especially in LDCs government spending is a crucial component of aggregate demand. Increased government demand for goods and services induces economic activities and boosts economic growth. Yet the factor-productivity differential of the nonmilitary public sector was found to be negative, indicating that the nonmilitary public sector is not as efficient as the civilian sector in Turkey. Nevertheless, the net effect of the nonmilitary public sector on the civilian economy is still positive, leading to the conclusion that the nonmilitary public sector has also been an important part of Turkish development. In addition to these findings, Greek defense spending on Turkish economic growth was found to be statistically insignificant.

Contrary to expectations, the marginal contributions of labor and human capital to economic growth were found to be negative in some cases and positive in others. All of them were statistically insignificant. But the estimated coefficient of investment was, as expected, positive and significant, indicating that formation and accumulation of capital stock were important factors in Turkish economic growth over the period examined. Inclusion of the civilian sector in the model showed that there has been a positive relationship between the civilian sector and economic growth. The estimated coefficient of the civilian sector was found to be large in magnitude and statistically significant.

A 2SLS procedure was used in an attempt to correct for endogeneity. Instrumental variables chosen in the model were correlated with the potential endogenous variables (investment and human capital) but were uncorrelated to the error term. The log of the rate of growth of money supply was used as an instrument for investment because investment is a function of the interest rate and the interest rate is a function of money supply. Therefore, money supply was selected as an instrumental variable for investment.

These results and findings are consistent with a number of comparable studies, including Atesoglu and Mueller (1990), Mueller and Atesoglu (1993), and Mintz and Huang (1990) for the case of the US, Ward *et al.* (1991) for the case of India, and Ward *et al.* (1993) for the case of Taiwan, and Stevenson and Mintz (1995) for a cross-sectional study of 103 countries. These and other researchers found positive relations between military spending and economic growth. The results reported in this study are also consistent with and support studies that found a positive impact of the nonmilitary public sector on economic growth, especially in LDCs. These include Landau (1986), Ram (1986), Ward *et al.* (1991), Ward *et al.* (1993), and Stevenson and Mintz (1995). Due to the positive effects of the nonmilitary and military sectors on Turkish economic growth, the results reported here suggest that the Turkish government should not make drastic resource-allocation changes between nonmilitary and military public spending.

Further research might focus on gathering disaggregated data and testing the impact of different components of military sector spending on economic growth. Additionally, as more disaggregated data are made available by the governments of different nations, future research can benefit by estimating simultaneous multisectoral economic growth models.

Notes

The author is grateful to Jurgen Brauer for his helpful comments and suggestions.

1. The list of studies mentioned here is only a small part of a relevant literature.

2. For details, see Ram (1986), pp. 192-194 and Biswas and Ram (1986), pp. 367-368.

3. Dividing the economy into export and nonexport sectors to investigate the sources of growth for a group of semi-industrialized less developed countries, Feder (1983) found that the export sector had a higher marginal productivity than the nonexport sector. Thus he concluded that economic growth can be created both by increasing the aggregate level of labor and capital and by the reallocation of resources from the less productive to the more productive sector.

4. This term is first used by Macnair *et al.* (1995).

5. Possible reasons for the disparate findings include the following. Different data sets and estimation techniques generate different results. The major data sources for military spending are SIPRI, ACDA, IISS, and government statistical offices. Due to the nature of military activities, the reliability and quality of these data sources is questionable. In addition, different variables included in the model result in different findings, and cross-sectional findings differ from those of time-series studies (Chan, 1986).

Sample size and characteristics also tend to generate different results. For example, some studies do not distinguish among sample countries and include those with similar characteristics as well as those with dissimilar characteristics in terms of per capita income levels, resource constrains, literacy levels, quality of labor force, and capital and technology availability. Obviously, adding a country's data to or subtracting it from a sample, or stratifying countries into similar groups, produces different empirical results as does the use of varying econometric models and estimation techniques employed by researchers. For further details, see Deger and Smith (1983).

6. Derivation of the reduced-form equations are available from the author.

7. The major difference between equation (7.4) and those used by Feder (1983), Ram (1986), and Biswas and Ram (1986) is my addition of human capital and the rival country's defense spending into the production function.

8. This shows that factor productivities among the different sectors differ from unity by δ. If $\delta < (>) 0$, increased military public output will imply a lower (higher) rate of growth of total output.

9. The derivations are available directly from the author.

10. Derivation available directly from the author.

11. The Penn World Table (Mark 5.6a) is an extended version of Summers and Heston (1991).

12. The coefficient for the military public sector in (7.5) is $[(\delta_m / 1 + \delta_m) - \theta_2] =$ - 0.103, which leads to the calculation of a factor-productivity differential, δ_m, of 0.383.

References

Adams, F.G., J.R. Behrman, and M. Boldin (1991). "Government Expenditures, Defense and Economic Growth in LDCs: A Revised Perspective." *Conflict Management and Peace Science*. Vol. 11, pp. 19-35.

Alexander, W. R. J. (1990). "The Impact of Defence Spending on Economic Growth: A Multi-Sectoral Approach to Defence Spending and Economic Growth With Evidence from Developed Economies." *Defence Economics*. Vol. 2, pp. 39-55.

Benoit, E. (1973). *Defense and Economic Growth in Developing Countries*. Lexington, MA: Heath.

Benoit, E. (1978). "Growth and Defense in Developing Countries." *Economic Development and Cultural Change*. Vol. 28, pp. 271-280.

Barro, R.J. (1991). "Economic Growth in a Cross-Section of Countries." *Quarterly Journal of Economics*. Vol. 106, pp. 407-444.

Biswas, B. and R. Ram (1986). "Military Expenditures and Economic Growth in Less Developed Countries: An Augmented Model and Further Evidence." *Economic Development and Cultural Change*. Vol. 34, pp. 361-372.

Chan, S. (1985). "The Impact of Defense Spending on Economic Performance: A Survey of Evidence and Problems." *Orbis*. Vol. 29, pp. 403-434.

Deger, S, and S. Sen (1983). "Military Expenditure, Spin-off and Economic Development." *Journal of Development Economics*. Vol. 13, pp. 67-83.

Deger, S., and R. Smith (1983). "Military Expenditure and Economic Growth in Less Developed Countries." *Journal of Conflict Resolution*. Vol. 27, pp. 335-353.

Feder, G. (1983). "On Export and Economic Growth." *Journal of Development Economics*, Vol. 12, pp. 59-73.

Hewitt, D. (1992). "Military Expenditures Worldwide: Determinants and Trends, 1972-1988." *Journal of Public Policy*. Vol. 12, pp. 105-152.

Lim, D. (1983). "Another Look at Growth and Defense in Less Developed Countries." *Economic Development and Cultural Change*. Vol. 31, pp. 377-384.

Linden, M. (1991). "The Dynamics and the Instability of the Middle East Military Expenditures in Years 1955-84." *Defence Economics*. Vol. 2, pp. 199-208.

Macnair, E., *et al.* (1995). "Growth and Defense: Pooled Estimates for the NATO Alliance, 1951-1988." *Southern Economic Journal*. Vol. 61, pp. 846-860.

Ram, R. (1986). "Government Size and Economic Growth: A New Framework and Some Evidence from Cross-Section and Time-Series Data." *American Economic Review*. Vol. 76, pp. 191-203.

Romer, P.M. (1986). "Increasing Returns and Long-Run Growth." *Journal of Political Economy*. Vol. 94, pp. 391-408.

Romer, P.M. (1990). "Endogenous Technological Change." *Journal of Political Economy*. Vol. 98, pp. S71-S102.

Rothschild, K.W. (1973). "Military Expenditure, Exports and Growth." *Kyklos*. Vol.26, pp. 804-814.

Sandler, T., and K. Hartley (1995). *The Economics of Defense*. Cambridge: Cambridge University Press.

SIPRI (various years). *SIPRI Yearbook: World Armaments and Disarmament*. Oxford: Oxford University Press.

Turkish State Planning Organization (1995). *Statistical Yearbook of Turkey*. Ankara: TSPO.

Summers, R., and A. Heston (1991). "The Penn World Table (Mark 5): An Expanded Set of International Comparisons, 1950-1988." *Quarterly Journal of Economics*. Vol. 2, pp. 327-368.

Ward, M.D., *et al*. (1993). "Military Spending and Economic Growth in Taiwan." *Armed Forces and Society*. Vol. 19, pp. 533-550.

Ward, M.D., *et al*. (1991). "Country Survey 1: Military Spending in India." *Defence Economics*. Vol. 3, pp. 41-63.

8 Political and economic tensions in the western Mediterranean

Carlos Pestana Barros

Introduction

France, Spain, and Portugal comprise the northern border of the western Mediterranean. They are European, Catholic countries, economically members of the EU and militarily members of the NATO alliance. The southern border of the Mediterranean consists of Algeria, Libya, Tunisia, and Morocco. They are African, Muslim countries, members of the Arab Defense Council. The recent rise of Arabic fundamentalism poses an immediate threat to the internal security of the Muslim countries and a potential threat to the security of the Catholic countries. Considering the economic disparity between the two sides of the sea, the EU launched in 1985 the *Forum Euromed*. Formed to promote cooperation and economic growth, the *Forum Euromed* is not performing adequately and, at present, is not promoting economic growth as intended.

In the absence of international cooperation, internal political tension may induce increased military spending, thereby weakening economic performance. Indeed, the study of the demand for military expenditure has attracted a considerable amount of empirical research, and the majority of studies conclude that military expenditure is detrimental to economic growth. Military expenditure, a process of collective choice, may adversely affect growth, crowding out resource availability for the private sector, especially savings and investment, and may aggravate economic inefficiency.

The dynamics come in two phases. In the first phase, we see an increase in internal security expenditure in Muslim countries due to rising fundamentalism and to cultural differences highlighted by efforts to promote international cooperation in *Forum Euromed*. In the second phase, the ineffectiveness of economic cooperation may then translate into increased military expenditure on both sides, reinforcing confrontation and stalling economic development.

In this chapter I test the hypothesis that ineffective economic cooperation and Muslim fundamentalism combine to induce increases in military expenditure and stall the economic development of the region. The model allows for cultural differences and the effect of fundamentalism. The econometrics uses pooled data.

The model

A number of models have been employed to study the demand for military expenditure (see Sandler and Hartley, 1995, Chapter 3). This chapter adopts a demand-side approach similar to Smith (1980, 1989), Beenstock (1993), Dudley and Montmarquette (1981), and Wall (1996). In Smith's model, government maximizes welfare subject to the restrictions of the strategic environment and the resource tradeoff between civilian well-being and national security. In Beenstock's model, military expenditure is modeled as a form of self-insurance against possible losses from invasions. Dudley and Montmarquette's model employs a median-voter approach. Wall's model is derived from a maximization of the government welfare function subject to government budget constraints and a production function for national security.

Although these approaches differ in their theoretical bases, the empirical results are very similar and can be considered as a family of models that analyses the demand for military expenditure. The major finding of this empirical research is that, in cross-national studies, military spending is a normal good and that population, whenever it is used as an explicit variable, can be negatively related to military expenditure if a rise in population lowers per capita income, or negatively related to military expenditure if tax shares decrease with increases in population size (Dudley and Montmarquette, 1981).

In my model I assume that government, at some point in time, associates an internal political movement with the existence of a security threat, e.g., Muslim fundamentalism. If the expected cost associated with the threat exceeds the expected cost associated with making concessions, government will either negotiate or allocate sufficient resources to nullify the threat. But if the expected cost associated with threat is less than the expected cost of concessions, government may continue to operate "normally".

To model decision choices for a representative government confronted with security issues, government utility is maximized over security determinants. The arguments of the welfare function are Y, the per capita income, and S, the security function:

(8.1) $U = U(Y, S)$

subject to a national-security production function:

(8.2)   S = F (ME, X)

where ME is military expenditure and X stands for a vector of socio-economic variables. In this standard set-up, the maximization of government utility subject to the national-security production function allows us to obtain the level of military expenditure as the first-order condition (see, e.g., Smith, 1980, and Wall, 1996):

(8.3)   ME = G (Y, X)

The estimation of the model

The model to be estimated is the following:

(8.4) $\log ME_i = \beta_{0i} + \beta_{1i} \log \text{Income} + \beta_{2i} \log \text{Population} + \beta_{3i} \log \text{Total} + \beta_{4i} \text{Fund} + \beta_{5i} \text{SPILLA} + \beta_{6i} \text{DSPILLN} + \epsilon_i$

where ME is military expenditure in millions of US$ taken from SIPRI (converted at constant prices using the GDP-deflator, *World Bank Tables*, 1987=100). This specification implies that the price of military activity changes proportionally to the price level in the private sector (SIPRI, 1984, pp.195-211). Income is per capita GDP in US$ at constant 1987 prices, taken from the *World Bank Tables*; Population is the country's population, taken from the *World Bank Tables*; Total is the total number of armed forces, taken from SIPRI; Fund is a dummy variable that takes the value of zero between 1972 and 1980 and one between 1981 — the year President Sadat of Egypt was assassinated — and 1995; SPILLA represents spill-in effects to the side under consideration and is measured by the aggregated military expenditure of the respective allies; this variable is lagged by one period to order to reflect the Nash-Cournot independence assumption whereby a nation chooses its military expenditure based upon the choices of its allies; SPILLN represents the spill-in effect of non-allies, measured by their aggregated military expenditure.

Country data are shown in Table 8.1. Lack of complete data for Libya led me to drop it from the analysis.

Table 8.1: Descriptive data (average values, 1972-1995)

Variables	Algeria	France	Morocco	Portugal	Spain	Tunisia
Population (in millions)	21	54.9	21.1	9.7	37.6	7. 0
GNP per capita (constant 1987 US$)	2,096	16,111	1,031	8,235	9,509	1,524
Military expenditure (constant 1987 US$ in millions)	7.61	293.76	9.68	25.14	62.16	3.65
Total armed forces (in thousands)	110	482	140	84	275	30
Army (in thousands)	95	288	122	58	179	24
Navy (in thousands)	5.6	67	5	14	45	3.2
Air force (in thousands)	8.8	98	10	12	35	2.6
Paramilitary (in thousands)	19	82	32	14	65	11
Food production (1989-91=100)	82	93	70	80	85	77

Per capita military expenditure is lower in the Muslim countries than in the European ones, as is per capita GNP. Per capita total armed forces are also lower in Muslim countries. These differences highlight different development levels between the two sides.

Applying OLS to equation (8.4) I adopted Hendry's general-to-specific modeling procedure (Hendry, 1986). The results of the estimation are shown in Tables 8.2 (for the Catholic countries) and 8.3 (for the Muslim countries).

The results do not confirm the hypothesis that we may see an increase in security expenditure in Muslim countries due to rising fundamentalism and cultural differences highlighted by efforts to promote international cooperation. The fundamentalism variable (FUND) was dropped from the regression analysis because it resulted in a statistically insignificant coefficient. Moreover, the estimated model shows that for the European countries per capita GDP, population, total armed forces, and the spill-in effects are the main determinants of military expenditure. For the Muslim countries, the determinants of military expenditure are past military expenditure, and present and past income, suggesting inertia effects on military spending. The determinants of military expenditure of the Catholic countries are in line with previous empirical studies,

Table 8.2: Estimates of equation (8.4) for Catholic countries

Variables (independent variable: log ME)	*OLS estimates*	*t-statistics*
CONSTANT	-10.363	(-9.902)**
log INCOME	1.171	(17.293)**
log POPULATION	-1.683	(-15.084)**
log TOTAL	0.22	(2.941)**
SPILLA $_{t-1}$	-0.351	(-7.258)**
R2-adjusted	0.933	
F test (zero slopes)	246.959	
DW	1.408	
Number of observations	71	

Note: ** significant at the 1 percent level.

Table 8.3: Estimates of equation (8.4) for Muslim countries

Variables (independent variables: log ME)	*OLS estimates*	*t-statistics*
CONSTANT	-3575	(-2.909)**
log INCOME	1.11	(2.765)**
log INCOME $_{t-1}$	-0.895	(-2.255)*
log ME $_{t-1}$	0.693	(5.700)**
R2-adjusted	0.694	
F test (zero slopes)	53.95	
Number of observations	71	

Note: ** significant at 1 percent level; * significant at 5 percent level.

e.g., Murdoch and Sandler (1986).

Concluding remarks

The aim of this chapter was to test the proposition that rising fundamentalism and the ineffectiveness of *Forum Euromed*, result in increased military expenditure and stalled economic development in the Muslim countries. The empirical test does not accept this hypothesis. The results show that military expenditure in the European, Catholic countries is primarily explained by GDP, population, the total size of the armed forces, and spill-in effects of allies military spending. For the Muslim, African countries, military spending is explained by current and lagged income and lagged military expenditure, an inertia effect.

Notes

I am grateful to Todd Sandler for comments on a previous version of this chapter, and to Jurgen Brauer for comments on the final version.

References

Beenstock, M. (1993). "International Patterns in Military Spending." *Economic Development and Cultural Change*. Vol. 41, pp.633-649.

Dudley,L. and C. Montmarquette (1981). "The Demand for Military Expenditure: An International Comparison." *Public Choice*. Vol. 37, pp. 5-31.

Hendry, D.F. (1986). "Empirical Models in Dynamic Econometrics." *Applied Economics Discussion Paper*. No. 1. Oxford: Oxford University Press.

Murdoch, J.C. and T. Sandler (1986). "The Political Economy of Scandinavian Neutrality." *The Scandinavian Journal of Economics*. Vol. 88, No. 4, pp. 583-603.

Sandler, T. and K. Hartley (1995). *The Economics of Defense*. Cambridge: Cambridge University Press.

Smith, R.P. (1989). "Models of Military Expenditures." *Journal of Applied Econometrics*. Vol. 4, pp. 345-359.

Wall, H.J. (1996). "Is the Military Really a Luxury Good? An International Panel Study on LDC's." *Applied Economics*. Vol. 28, pp. 41-44.

9 The Algerian drama: consequences of a bureaucratic-socialist experiment

Jacques Fontanel and Fanny Coulomb

Introduction

Strong interactions between strategic discourses, political decisions, Islamic influences, and national socio-economic outcomes have marked the post-colonialist history of the Algerian economy. Algeria offers an interesting example of the inextricable links between ideologically-based governmental will and the government's role as the main economic agent. Because of the anti-colonialist and pro-socialist line followed by Algeria in its early post-colonial history, it refused dependence on international markets and on Western defense systems. Instead, it developed macroeconomic planning based on heavy-industrial development and an industrialization process managed by the state. In this chapter, the study of the Algerian economy only tangentially concerns defense economics *per se*; instead, it looks at the totality of Algerian economic, political, and security considerations within which defense economics may play its role.

Since independence, Algeria has exerted an important influence on international socialism. It even played a prominent role in building the concept of a New International Economic Order: indeed, Algeria spearheaded the demands of the less developed countries. Yet Algeria's internal economic and political "self-centered" strategy, whose principles were widely declared by official authorities, was more discourse than reality. Marked by cultural contradictions and sterile internal political struggles, it experienced progressively growing political and economic difficulties.

Long attached to Soviet anti-imperialist policy, Algeria strove to develop close links with this "main combatant against capitalism". Even while adjusting them to local needs, it tried to imitate Soviet notions of public planning and economic organization. This had three main consequences:

- The strong political links with the USSR progressively gave rise to bad economic working relations with capitalist, developed countries.
- The search for a progressive and planned economy accelerated, with the demise of the USSR, the degeneration of the Algerian economy.
- The Algerian civil war called into question the great economic potential of the country, where each temporary respite from economic crisis is susceptible to destruction by political crisis.

This chapter examines each of these three consequences in turn.

Links with the USSR and withdrawal from capitalist developed countries

During decolonization, the USSR became for Algeria the primary anti-imperialist example, not only a political ally but an alternative to capitalism. At the same time, various Algerian governments were very active in the Third World movement. Algeria's links with Western countries, notably with France, deteriorated (Kadri and Fontanel, 1996).

The USSR: anti-imperialist "big brother"

To Algeria, the Soviet Union provided both intellectual attraction, based mainly on socialist ideology, and strong military relations with the leader of the Warsaw Pact. With decolonization, the USSR and the United States engaged in a struggle of influence and power in which decolonized countries were voluntarily and directly involved. The Soviet strategy had as its main aim the thwarting of Western influence in the newly independent countries, particularly in the Middle East and in Asia, and to secure strategically important supplies. Early on, this led the USSR to support independence movements and progressive regimes in the Third World notably by means of military aid. But the early 1980s marked the end of Soviet power expansion in the Third World, weakened as it was by the Afghan war. To reinforce its position, the USSR switched emphasis from providing military aid to promoting the economic efficiency of its financial aid and to establish new links with more solvent partner countries, especially oil producers such as Algeria (Isaev, 1991).

For Muslim Algeria, even if the materialist side of the socialist system should be rejected, rigid Soviet economic planning constituted an interesting way of fostering national development. The Algerian political apparatus become convinced that centralized, national economic management was necessary. Moreover, as less developed countries revolted against economic oppression, they perceived the USSR as a military resource, a great nuclear power able to protect them against American imperialism. Great artisan of the ideas of the New International Economic Order, Algeria borrowed some of her anti-colonialist slogans from Marxist analyses developed by Soviet people. But it was a marriage of convenience based only on intellectual attraction; the cultures of the two countries were very different and their efforts at cooperation did not always succeed.

Algeria asked for Soviet military aid as early as 1962. The USSR became Algeria's privileged arms supplier (but without gaining monopoly status) and an important partner regarding military assistance and military questions without however being directly associated with the organization of Algerian defense. From the late 1960s, Algeria did seek occasional help from western countries, notably France, for technical and advisory missions. Tables 9.1, 9.2, and 9.3 show Algerian military spending, arms imports, and other indicators as well as the USSR's role in comparison with other Algerian arms suppliers.

Table 9.1: Algerian arms imports (in millions of dollars) and main suppliers (in percent), 1974 to 1995

Years	Amount	USSR	US	France	UK	Other NATO	Other ex-Warsaw Pact
1993-1995	395	65.8	2.5	0	0	7.6	15.2
1987-1992	2,490	80.3	0.8	0	0	0	17.3
1982-1986	3,730	83.1	5.9	2.7	4.3	2.7	0.5
1974-1982	2,575	84.3	0	0.8	0.6	12.4	0.5

Source: US ACDA (various issues).

Table 9.2: Algerian arms transfers and trade balance

Years	Arms imports (mn 1995 US$)	Arms imports/ total imports (in percent)	Trade balance (mn 1995 US$)
1975	151	1.5	- 3,817
1980	869	4.8	+ 5,738
1985	685	5.1	+ 4,110
1986	801	6.5	- 1,870
1987	906	9.9	+ 1,535
1988	1,061	11.6	+ 993
1989	749	6.6	+ 430
1990	356	3.2	+ 3,700
1991	144	1.7	+ 5,560
1992	5	0.1	+ 2,749
1993	21	0.3	+ 2,574
1994	144	1.5	- 502
1995	230	2.2	- 10

Source: US ACDA (1997) for 1985-1995; earlier issues for earlier years.

Table 9.3: Algerian military expenditures, arms imports, and ratio of military expenditures to GDP

Year	Military Expenditures	Arms Imports	% ME/GDP
1988	555	n/a	1.9
1989	542	n/a	1.7
1990	(606)	n/a	(1.5)
1991	593	n/a	1.2
1992	868	n/a	(1.9)
1993	1,067	15	2.6
1994	1,298	161	3.2
1995	1,235	332	3.0
1996	1,401	5	3.4
1997	1,550	-	n/a

Note: In millions of constant 1995 US dollars.[1]
Source: SIPRI (1998); n/a = non available; figures in brackets are estimated.

Beginning in 1963, future Algerian marine officers were sent to the USSR to be trained in Soviet naval academies. In the same year, Soviet supplied military personnel and material participated in mine clearing operations in Algeria, mainly along its borders. Between 1968 and 1969, financed by a $100 million credit, 2,000 Soviet air force and army advisers and another 2,000 marine advisers came to Algeria (Pineye, 1982). Until 1974, Algeria was the second-largest buyer of Soviet armaments, with about 22 percent of such exports for the period 1955-1974, behind Egypt which accounted for 67.5 percent of Soviet arms sales and transfers. These figures are not based purely on political factors. The USSR charged much lower prices than Western countries wanted, it granted steep discounts (of up to 40 percent), and delivery times were relatively short.

Military relations between Algeria and USSR developed especially from December 1974, when the Madrid agreement concerning the sharing of the Western Sahara between Mauritania and Morocco was signed. The resulting tension on the Algerian-Moroccan border drove Algeria to develop air superiority against Morocco.[2] In 1975 and 1976, the USSR granted further credits of $500 million for new arms purchases, requiring repayment in convertible currency.[3] Additional terms of this credit included an agreement on economic cooperation that entailed a long-term (25 years) development plan by Soviet experts regarding Algeria's oil resources and fuel-stop rights at south-Algerian airports granted to Soviet airplanes to carry arms for the socialist movement in Angola's civil war.

While the USSR remained Algeria's main supplier, from 1978 the United States, the Netherlands, Italy, and France obtained an increasing role, notably for technical and advisory missions and for the formation and organization of the state police force. Still, owing to financial constraints that required the reduction of hard-currency outflows and impeded supply-diversification attempts, Algeria bought 75 to 80 percent of her military equipment from the USSR. Moreover, given the predominance of Soviet equipment, maintenance was naturally obtained from the USSR as well.

Socialist activity of Algerian governments

Socialist activity of Algerian governments was expressed by their strong involvement in the Non-Aligned Movement and the New International Economic Order. During the Boumedienne era, Algeria progressively became a forerunner of the non-aligned countries, together with Cuba, Yugoslavia, India, and Egypt. In United Nations agencies, developing countries often appeared as natural allies of the USSR, notably in their condemnation of Western imperialism. Leftist intellectuals embraced anti-capitalist or anti-American theses. It is a paradox of history that "progressive" people condemned capitalism as exploitative while human rights violations multiplied in the USSR.

Algeria was very involved in this behavior. It took an active part in the debates about the construction of a New International Economic Order. In Algiers, a summit of non-aligned countries in September 1973 stated that the failure of United Nations development strategies was caused by the unwillingness of developed countries to change and help, and imperialist policy was characterized as open economic aggression against the people that capitalism does not cease to exploit. Established international trade, based on an unequal North/South division of labor, and stemming from the mode of determination of international prices, was held responsible of the deterioration of the terms of trade. The best hope for economic development would therefore consist of reaching and preserving unity among Third World countries and to press for collective autonomy (Fontanel, 1995).

But the Algiers conference also revealed fragility. The ideals of the movement of non-aligned countries were formally based on notions of peaceful coexistence, support to liberation movements, refusal to join military alliances and engage in bilateral great-power military-aid agreements, and rejection of foreign military bases on indigenous territory. Yet, these criteria were obviously not respected by most of the movement's own members, in part because of the excessiveness of its ideological claims. Still, Western countries were depicted as the main cause of economic underdevelopment, and this favored, given the lack of non-capitalist alternatives, the development of commercial exchanges between the South and the East. In 1974, Algeria's president, viewing the economic order as an hindrance to development, suggested LDC's development be thought of from "a perspective of struggle on the international level" and advised LDC's to "count on themselves and on their own means from an internal point of view" (Destanne de Bernis, 1977). He proposed the nationalization of natural-resource industries (so as to keep its earnings), launching of an integrated and coherent development process involving the entire agricultural and industrial potential, mobilization of the international community for economic equity, reduction of the debt burden, and an aid program for the poorest countries. The strategy consisted of devising a "self-centered" development policy. The economic reality, however, was that hydrocarbons accounted for 90 percent of exports and of 20 to 30 percent of GDP and obliged him to temper his discourse.

Algeria's declining links with Western countries, notably France

The degradation of Algerian links to Western countries was the consequence of the after-effects of decolonization, fractious cultural and weak economic cooperation, and reduced economic aid due to Algeria's socialist stance. One of the after-effects of decolonization concerned the continuing immigration problem between France and Algeria. Another was that Algeria inherited a totally non-structured economy, as it was actually marked by two diverging ideologies of state control (Muslim-Arabism and socialism). Claiming status as an equal with France, Algeria was replete with contradictions, such as how to develop relations with France while refusing neo-colonialism, how to advocate socialism while accepting the assistance of a capitalist country, and how to search for normal relations with France in spite of reciprocal resentments stemming from the national war of liberation.

By 1962, the Algerian economy was totally torn down, unbalanced, and financially, technologically, and commercially dependent on France. Moreover, the departure of more than 900,000 Europeans left an economic and social vacuum, leading to the cessation of many industrial activities, decreased production, and above all to a relative lack of executive, technical, and skilled personnel. Excessive recourse to foreign technical assistance, notably from France, generated a new dependency, even as the Algerian state did not want France to have a monopoly on cooperation and wished to cooperate with socialist countries.

In this climate, cultural cooperation was thought of by both as a stabilizing element in the political relations between Algeria and France, and it was the only permanent link between the two countries. But in 1971, an "Arabization" program began with the objective to remove Algeria from French cultural influence and language. Difficulties of adapting the Arab language to the modern, technological world, and the lack of skilled teachers, then brought about a near dismantling of science and the university system in Algeria. The linguistic problem and attempts to "Arabize" the whole of society served as vehicles to Islamic fundamentalism. On 5 July 1998, the government decided on the total Arabization of the country.

Even before the first oil crisis, France and Algeria experienced numerous difficulties in reaching agreement on oil prices. France argued that historical links, cultural cooperation, and its active engagement in Algerian oil production gave her some rights. Algeria, even before taking its strong anti-imperialist, anti neo-colonial stance, wanted to obtain prices that would permit it to engage in its own economic development and to diversify its international economic relations. The famous privileged bilateral agreements were not satisfactory to Algeria and became a decisive factor in its progressive attraction to socialism and the USSR. Economic aid from France and Europe was reduced in like measure. Justifications were numerous. Algeria's behavior in international organizations was judged as not always friendly, "flirting" as she was with the USSR during the cold war. Algerian emigration to France was an important foreign-exchange resource for Algeria but France reduced transfer possibilities. In short, bilateral agreements became less and less privileged.

Those that benefitted from Soviet bloc assistance were newly independent, developing countries, and especially those that chose a socialist way of economic development based on heavy industry and/or on the construction of an enormous public sector (India, Egypt). But, rapidly, other economic considerations prevailed. At the end of the 1960s and the beginning of the 1970s, the USSR proposed civilian as well as military assistance, the idea being that it would often be more desirable to import products and raw materials from developing nations than to produce them at higher costs in the USSR itself (Valkenier, 1983). The Soviet Union thus reoriented its aid program toward solvent countries, particularly those with natural resources.

From planned progression to degeneration

After independence, the objective of the Algerian state was to induce a total break with the colonial system. Exercising political will through a strong state and a single-party system, development was to take place by recuperation of national wealth via a state-controlled development strategy. Indeed, the Algiers Charter of 1964 clearly spoke of the necessary and major role of centralized planning in a non-Marxist, but socialist, type of development strategy. Therefore, the post-colonial Algerian transition commenced under the guidance of the state, public-sector industrialization being perceived as the core of development, financed by oil earnings. But the chosen strategy, strongly inspired by the Soviet model and the "developmentalist" thesis (Lamchichi, 1991), showed its limits as early as the mid-1970s. It eventually led Algeria, and other ex-socialist countries, to reject a system and development model vulnerable to external shocks and unfit for international trade.

Uncertain plans: between desired ideal and concrete reality

The Soviet model of organizing power (with the single-party principle) inspired, especially since 1965, the organization of the Algerian economy, as did the economic theories of the "developmentalist" school that became the fundamental reference point of Algeria's industrialization model. This centralist method of economic organization, along with a hierarchical decision system (Goumeziane, 1994), was very similar to the Soviet one.

But there were shortcomings, especially with regard to the (misinterpreted) concept of planning, insufficient Soviet aid, and ill-focused international relations. Economic planning was reduced to the strict determination of investments allowed in the public industrial sector. Economic development was centrally controlled, through direct state intervention, so as to exclude all foreign economic influence. The model was based on the promotion of the public industrial sector, able to produce necessary goods for other economic sectors (unbalanced growth). This was thought of as the only way to build an independent and fully integrated economy. Financial resources were used in the planning system so as to bring about the industrial objectives determined by the state, the single economic agent able both to set industrial investment programs (public for the most part) and to nationalize foreign assets, particularly those involving oil activities. Thus, the Algerian development plans determined investments in primary industries only (iron and steel, manufacturing, electricity, and hydrocarbon industries), and not, as in the USSR, in all economic activities. The functional ministries (Plan Administration, Finance, and Trade) did not take part in the decision process; they came into play only once the strategy and the plan were discussed for adoption in ministerial council. Oddly, the Plan Administration was progressively marginalized. The economic outcomes were disappointing (Kadri and Fontanel, 1996).

Soviet aid was insufficient and mostly based on arms. Though based on comparable ideological principles, the bilateral political relations between Algeria and the USSR were marked by increasing difficulties that explain the limited amount of Soviet aid to Algeria, except for armaments. Soviet aid was limited to a few developing nations, mostly countries of the Middle East and potential "progressive" belligerents. Arms sales to Algeria reflected relatively clear strategic priorities, as the logic and the nature of the East-South trade were not, in principle, economic. Moreover, military transfers were often in compensation for oil sales, owing to comparative advantages. For the Eastern countries, the economic reasons behind this arms-for-oil trade were as strong as the strategic and political reasons. "Military material was the only type of equipment for which the East could pretend to be in quasi-technical parity with the West, in some cases even with superior quality or performance relative to price" (Portes, 1979). Soviet military aid was geographically highly concentrated, and it became very intense in the 1970s, especially with Middle-East countries. Thus, the relations between Algeria and the USSR were paradoxical: commercial trade was weak but military trade was high (90 percent of the Algerian army was equipped with Soviet material).

Actually, relations between Algeria and the countries of central and eastern Europe have always been minor and may lead one to think that commercial realism has always been stronger than political considerations. Algeria and the USSR, countries with different levels of development but specialized on the same groups of primary products, were rather in a situation of competing for the same world oil and natural-gas markets, hydrocarbons constituting, to diverse degrees, key elements of both economies (Locatelli, 1992). Algeria and the Soviet Union participated in the global oil market with different objectives. Both were highly dependent on oil exports, supplying them with convertible currency, but Algeria intended to use its earnings to finance its industrial development strategy whereas the USSR needed currency to modernize its production apparatus. For both, oil served to finance the necessary imports. Therefore there really existed no complementarity between the Algerian and Soviet economies, explaining the low level of bilateral commercial trade as well as the highly developed political relations.

Lost reference point

With the disappearance of the USSR, Algeria lost its major political and economic point of reference. Today Algeria is neither socialist, nor capitalist; economically, it occupies a no-man's land between liberalism and socialism. It is destitute, and its economic performance is a cause for worry.

After independence, the prevailing idea was to get rid of underdevelopment by building a socialist society. Post-colonial transition led to a system dominated by oil rents and speculation. Oil price increases in the 1970s and early 1980s financed the reform of the political economy but the vulnerability of this strategy was revealed with declines in oil prices after 1986. Mass mobilization accelerated industrialization, but economic policy did not lead to economic development. The Algerian model of "self-centered" development, one that sacrificed agriculture and celebrated industrial development, failed.

For many years, the Algerian economy encountered severe macroeconomic and macro-financial constraints which deeply limited its dynamics and openness. Its grave situation is sometimes attributed to financial crisis and sometimes to the failure of her economic system. It is a crisis of organization and regulation, generating the need for a quick transformation of the entire economy toward a market economy. The increasing importance of the trade imbalance, foreign debt, foreign exchange shortages, and the ill-functioning of the economy all gave rise, in 1987, to an economic reform process and to Algeria's rapprochement with international institutions, such as the IMF and the World Bank. The reform program entered in 1987 and 1988 marked the official break with the centrally administered economy. And as from 1989, military expenditures, which had grown until then, progressively decreased until 1993 (see Table 9.4).

Table 9.4: GNP, armed forces, military expenditures, GNP per capita, and ratio of military expenditures to GNP, 1985-1995

Year	GNP (millions, 1995 US$)	Armed forces (000')	Military expenditures (millions, 1995 US$)	GNP per capita	ME/GNP (%)
1985	38,690	170	982	1,744	2.5
1986	38,300	180	1,121	1,676	2.9
1987	38,700	170	1,086	1,648	2.8
1988	37,570	126	1,225	1,559	3.3
1989	39,600	126	1,175	1,602	3.0
1990	39,150	126	801	1,544	2.0
1991	38,270	126	643	1,473	1.7
1992	39,000	139	741	1,465	1.9
1993	38,500	139	1,091	1,413	2.8
1994	37,880	126	1,257	1,358	3.3
1995	38,940	120	1,238	1,365	3.2

Source: US ACDA (1997).

The fall of export earnings contributed to growth in the demand for short-term credit and the decline of the world oil market resulted in underutilization of productive capacities (which, however, recovered from 35 percent utilization in 1988 to 50 percent in 1992). Oil sales represented 91 percent of export earnings in 1980, 85 percent in 1985, 89 percent in 1990, and more than 85 percent in 1994. That is, despite large oil exports, falling oil prices did not allow Algeria to diversify its economy. It remained fundamentally dependent on this market without benefitting from induced multiplier effects.

The reform program suggested by international financial organizations led first to a policy of money depreciation, then to macroeconomic measures such as price liberalization. Inflation, only 6 percent in 1988, rose to 31.7 percent in 1992, then fell to 20.5 percent in 1993, and rose again to 28.6 percent in 1995.

Algeria's economic crisis was not merely a financial crisis but also a systemic crisis, necessitating a total break from the former mode of economic management. Exclusively based on oil and natural-gas exports, once virtually the only source of finance for industrialization (Hadjseyd, 1994), Algeria today remains characterized by her dependency on hydrocarbon-based natural resources. This is a consequence of the first quadrennial plan that laid out investment priorities in basic and hydrocarbon-based natural-resource industries at the expense of agriculture, consumption-goods industries, and export-oriented industries.

In 1986, the brutality of the Algerian economic collapse raised the problem of systemic vulnerability to fluctuations in external markets and therefore to economic indebtedness in the context of oil-rent depletion. External support became unavoidable owing to insufficient internal saving and to firm's incapacity at self-financing. The state's principle of resource centralization did not allow self-financing. Enterprises were subject to a centralized system of resource allocation and to central planning of investments. Small, private enterprises had no interest in investing either, as they were not officially allowed to derive benefits or to reinvest freely. However, savings from the private sector were directed toward a shadow market where yields were much better.

To prevent the industrialization process from slowing down, it became indispensable for Algeria to take up loans from the international markets. Algerian indebtedness, then, is not recent, but its size is new and now constitutes a huge burden for society (see Table 9.5). As with all semi-industrialized countries, Algerian indebtedness accelerated. Until 1985, Algeria had no strategy of external debt management (Guillaumont, 1985), and debt service absorbed three quarters of her export receipts. In fact, potential oil and gas earnings were considered sufficient guarantees to mobilize credits on international financial markets.

According to IMF criteria, Algeria is placed among moderately indebted countries, since two of three important debt-ratios do not reach critical levels: total debt to GDP, at 57.4 percent in 1993, placed Algeria in the little-indebted countries category and the ratio of total debt to exports (216.6 percent in 1993) placed her in the moderately- indebted countries category. But the ratio of debt *service* to exports was 76.9 percent (in 1993) and shows that Algeria was heavily indebted. The debt burden imposed a strong constraint on export receipts and led to excesses — exports at any price or contraction of imports. But debt service is a short-run problem, linked exclusively to oil price and dollar volatility. Algeria is not structurally indebted, but it must offer securities and face the repayment of her debt.

The IMF reform program (stand-by agreement) for Algeria of 3 June 1991 emphasized macroeconomic measures, notably price liberalization of subsidized products, the total liberalization of foreign trade, and a 60 percent devaluation of the Algerian dinar (to quickly match the exchange rate in the parallel market). The desperate situation of the Algerian economy leads us to question her future.

Table 9.5: Algerian foreign debt (in millions US$)

Years	1972	1973	1974	1975	1976	1978	1979	1980	1981	1982	1983
Total debt	2,991	3,366	4,633	6,114	10,600	15,736	18,501	19,359	18,367	17,636	16,261
Long term debt	2,991	3,366	4,633	6,114	8,914	13,751	16,568	17,034	16,060	14,885	14,304
Short term debt	-	-	-	-	1,686	1,985	1,933	2,325	2,307	2,751	1,957

Years	1984	1985	1986	1987	1988	1989	1990	1991	1992	1993	1994
Total debt	15,883	18,243	22,634	24,395	26,038	26,999	27,637	27,919	26,349	25,757	29,470
Long term debt	14,124	16,381	19,482	23,080	24,417	25,160	26,846	26,680	25,557	24,587	28,500
Short term debt	1,759	1,862	3,152	1,315	1,621	1,840	791	1,239	793	700	970

Source: World Bank (1994a and 1994b).

Economic potential in political crisis

The army remains Algeria's major internal force but terrorism rages on. Economically, Algeria is faced with globalization requiring strong restructuring. And culturally, Algeria has lost her landmarks.

The grave political question

Algeria's political crisis may last for decades. Islam is a cross-national phenomenon, but the Algerian conflict is purely internal. The Algerian regime is not a democracy, nor really a dictatorship. For three decades, the army comprised the core of the state. Composed of 1,300,000 men, 20,000 gendarmes, and 30,000 auxiliaries to cover a territory four times the size of France, it was the country's only organized strong force. Structured along Soviet lines, it was mainly defensive in posture and strongly hierarchical. Over time, army officers, despite diverging interests, came to hold (and to hold on to) government power. Violent groups do not only threaten Algeria *per se*, they also reject democracy and the application of basic human rights. But Algerian Islamic groups have few leaders and their violent actions are not concerted. Islamism is primarily the political expression of economic despair resulting from failed industrialization, ruined agriculture, unemployment of 28 percent (IMF, 1998), and widespread, endemic corruption.

In January 1995, the Algerian opposition (composed of 16 political parties, including the National Liberation Front) gathered in Rome so as to restart dialogue on possible solutions to the Algerian crisis. The tragic national situation was judged to stem from the interruption of democratic processes, resulting in armed confrontation between state forces and terror groups, threatening the very existence of the country itself. The opposition meeting in Rome called for restoration of a democratic, sovereign Algerian State, within Islamic principles, conforming to the declaration of 1 November 1954. It called on Algeria's army to give up all political activity and to limit itself to territorial defense. In contrast, the Armed Islamic Group (AIG) asks for the application of God's law and for the dissolution of communist and atheist parties. The Rome accord was rejected both by the government and by the AIG which called for the installation of an Islamic regime by means of war. The elections of 16 November 1995 marked the victory of Liamine Zéroual and of the army, but massacres continued.

Having acquired revolutionary legitimacy in the liberation war, the Algerian army suffered a political set-back with the results of the democratic process of 1990-1991 that favored an Islamic state in gestation. Its defenders then advocated "total war". In spite of the conscription of some 15,000 men, the result was not a strengthened army even if it recovered control over some towns such as Blida. Instead, one observed reinforcement of a repressive state apparatus and the "privatization" of violence as 15,000 militiamen were armed to combat Islamic guerrillas. These groups may even wish to perpetuate a situation which on occasion allows them to enrich themselves. Moreover, some paramilitary groups sent by the Algerian government to infiltrate Afghan Islamic groups during that war have never been broken up upon their return to Algeria.

Algeria, Europe, and Mediterranean countries

Meeting in Corfu in June 1994, the European Council decided to stabilize relations between Europe and the Mediterranean which was quickly becoming a zone of strategic importance for the European Union. Emphasis was put on matters relating to energy, migration, trade, and — of special importance — direct foreign investments. The Council even foresees free trade in agricultural products by 2010, provided that the Mediterranean countries install free-market economies. A follow-up conference in Barcelona in November 1995 proposed the promotion of peace, stability, and security of the European-Mediterranean region, advocating lasting and balanced social and economic development so as to build a shared zone of prosperity. The final document, the so-called Barcelona declaration, includes references to and underlines human rights, citizens' fundamental liberties within the state, people's right to self-determination, and states' obligation to fight terrorism.

To attract international institutions and private investors, the European Commission put some amount of co-financing at the disposal of Mediterranean countries. A further follow-up conference in Triest (1996) asked Mediterranean countries to agree to European standards in terms of investments, trade liberalization, harmonization of investment legislation and regulations, development of natural gas and electricity networks, and settlement of a system of guarantees for energy investments.

All this may be useful to Algeria but Algeria opposes the constraining character of the charter which it judges inappropriate to its interest.

In 1983, a transmediterranean pipeline, Transmed, was put in service. It runs between Algeria and Italy, via Tunisia. Its capacity has since then been more than doubled, financed by the European Bank. In addition, a Maghreb-Europe pipeline (MGE) links Algeria to Spain and Portugal, via Morocco. The European Union financed part of that project. Another European program, MEDA, was designed to unify various resources and to define sectoral choices. Toward this end, to create new development zones, energy trade, and new economic and social infrastructure, six billion dollars were allocated from 1996 to 1999. The receiving countries must however agree to respect human rights and make progress toward free trade and the establishing of a free-market economy.

Algeria generates fears in Europe (terrorism, migration, and political instability) and its partnership with Europe therefore faces periodic difficulties. Even though the mentioned projects are profitable, it was necessary for the European Union to reassure partners on all sides so as to allow Algeria to conclude new export contracts. The pipelines in particular are of fundamental importance for Mediterranean cooperation.

An uncertain economic recovery

In an econometric study, covering the period 1971-1995, Teboul and Moustier find the following major relations among economic variables:

▸ Algeria's GDP is positively related to exports, investment, indebtedness, and government expenditures ("Keynesian" stimulants).
▸ Algeria's GDP is negatively related to inflation and to imports (more consumptive than productive in nature).

Findings such as these are distorted not only by the fact that Algeria's disposition of oil earnings leads to aggravated internal inequalities but in that they fail to consider the state's ability to make its creditors wait and to extract financial aid and resources based on oil-guarantees. For example, under France's insistence, creditors consented to a series of debt reschedulings for Algeria. This ability to manipulate public finance does not change people's daily life but reinforces the position of Algeria's governing military class.

Still, a one-year IMF stand-by agreement signed on 10 April 1994 provided for a macroeconomic and macro-financial stabilization program, based on price and trade liberalization, restrictive monetary and fiscal policies, a rigorous incomes policy, and efficiency improvements in the public sector. It also included provisions to reschedule Algeria's external debt.[4] The financial stabilization was a real success (see Table 9.6 for some performance indicators) and Algeria entered a virtuous cycle of debt reduction combined with a strong trade and current-account balance.

In June 1997, the IMF recognized the Algerian government's commitment to economic liberalization. At the same time, it cited market uncertainty regarding privatization of the oil sector and the fact that the envisioned privatization process does not extend to small and medium-sized firms. A privatization process was finally engaged in from September 1997, but foreign direct investment did not develop as expected, owing to continued risk perceptions.

Table 9.6: Indicators of Algerian economic performance (1994-1998)

Variables	1994	1995	1996	1997	1998(p)
Population (million)	27.4	27.9	28.3	28.8	29.3
GDP (billions of 1995 dinars)	1,910	1,966	2,108	2,135	2,161
Growth rate	- 1.1	3.9	3.8	1.3	1.2
GDP (dollars) per capita	1,532	1,479	1,615	1,613	1,626
Inflation rate	28.1	28.6	22.2	6.1	5.0
Exports	8.89	10.26	13.21	13.82	13.39
Imports	9.15	10.10	9.09	8.13	9.08
% foreign debt / GDP	70.0	78.4	73.4	63.4	67.0
Gross official reserves	2.64	2.11	4.23	8.04	8.71
Debt service ratio (in percent of current external receipts)	48.6	42.5	29.2	29.8	n/a
Real effective exchange rate (percentage change)	-14.1	-16.2	2.5	9.6	n/a
Budgetary balance (% GDP)	- 4.4	-1.4	3.0	2.4	0.7
Unemployment rate	26.5	28.1	28.3	28.6	28.0
Gross investment / GDP	31.7	32.2	26.6	20.6	n/a

Source: IMF (1998); n/a = not available; p = preliminary.

Eventually, Algeria escaped the umbrella of IMF supervision, but the rescheduled debt payments are due shortly. For 1998, the government proposed to limit public expenditures, modernize the way the economy is financed, rationalize and privatize the part of the public sector that competes with the private sector, progressively contract-out monopolistic public services, rebuild housing, sustain employment, and develop agriculture.

The relatively favorable economic environment is due, in part, to the failure of the Islamic guerrilla movement to dispose of President Zéroual or to engage in decisive attacks against targets such as the country's gas and oil installations. But unemployment keeps rising (28 percent of the labor force, that is 2.1 million unemployed, with three quarters of those never having worked). Wage earners' purchasing power decreased considerably between 1989 and 1995 (on average by more than 20 percent per year). Only a minority of the population can buy imported goods. Oil income is extracted mainly by the army (Ellyas, 1999).

Algeria's current account improved significantly, from a deficit of 5.5 percent of GDP in 1994 to a surplus of 7 percent in 1997. This turnaround was due mainly to increased oil prices (30 percent, on average), to increased natural gas exports via a newly opened pipeline to Spain, and to the rise of the dollar. Good harvests in 1995 and 1996 also allowed reductions in food imports. Moreover, the debt restructuring supported by France and the IMF led to debt service reductions from $8.1 billion in 1993 to $4.2 billion in 1996. Whereas in 1992 and 1993, debt service absorbed 90 percent of export receipts, today it is only 30 percent. Despite this good news, gas and oil income goes into a banking and financial system controlled by political power and military *nomenclature* which does not reinvest in the country but imports European consumer goods. We see great concentration of economic power within the governing class as Algeria's population grows poorer. Increasingly, the armed forces are used to protect frontiers and profitable economic zones (the "useful Algeria") rather than its people.

The future of the Algerian economy is uncertain. Oil and gas exports will rise significantly, by about 50 percent, on account of a new gas-export agreement with Italy and Austria one the one hand, and a new oil-export agreement with Spain and Portugal on the other. There are also new export agreements with US companies (Arco, Anaderka, and Schlumberger) and European ones (Total, Repsol). However, the agricultural sector is in difficulties and private industry has collapsed (minus seven percent in 1996). Imports of equipment goods declined by 20 percent in 1997 but imports of non-food consumption goods increased by 18 percent. Algeria's main export customers are Italy (21.6 percent), the United States (17.3 percent), and France (13.3 percent), and its main import-suppliers are France (23.5 percent) and the United States (9.9 percent).

Small and medium-sized firms suffer harassment by armed groups and fail to develop the private sector. Unemployment keeps rising. The growth rate went from 3 percent in 1990 to 1.3 percent in 1997, but only 5.5 people million work out of a population of more than 29 million people. Since 1990, some 400,000 Algerians, especially intellectuals, have left the country. Investors perceive the Algerian country-risk as very high, discouraging foreign investment.

In addition to the IMF, Algerian programs are supported by the Arab Monetary Fund and the World Bank and by debt relief from the Paris and London creditor clubs. The objectives of all these programs include continued macroeconomic stabilization and reform processes to create a market-based, private-sector led economy integrated to the rest of the world. For the IMF Executive Board, Algeria's medium-term economic prospects are clouded by the risk of low export prices and, indeed, in 1998 real GDP growth slowed to 1.2 percent after two consecutive years of 4 percent growth. Industrial production continues to decline due to difficulties experienced in the ongoing restructuring process in the public sector and low foreign and domestic investment. Algeria introduced the full convertibility of the dinar for the current account and privatization of the economy is underway. The structural adjustment program is necessary and in its way successful, but it is no substitute for a development program.

Conclusion

Abdelaziz Bouteflika's election to president of Algeria in April 1999 does not solve its problems, such as the shortcomings in its democracy, lack of investor confidence, and extraction of oil and gas rents by the army. The electoral defeat of militant Islamism (Lmrabet, 1999) does not mean the end of social and national conflict. Neither do the recurring ideological references to former President Boumediène, based on the principles of socialism, authoritarianism, and concentration of economic power, necessarily create social peace . One can find in Algeria's modern history the fundamental reasons for her numerous crises. Having been a long-standing depository of the hopes of free and progressive developing countries, Algeria has failed in her own course of economic development and important elements of its society have developed an increasingly pronounced non-materialist taste. The relations (always love-hate relations) to economic development, to international relations, to France, to the USSR, and to oil failed and religious reactionism developed. Islamism is the new, big challenge for Algeria. Today, it is important to note that Algeria's main official objectives are liberalization, privatization, and globalization, denoting the end of Algeria's anti-imperialist, socialist experiment. At the same time, an emergent Muslim Algeria has not solved the problem of finding an equilibrium between God and materialism. And it is not clear at all that rapid liberalization, privatization, and globalization will provide Algeria with a way to balance these two opposite objectives between its various citizens and governments.

Notes

1. Algerian arms imports data are not really available before 1993, first because they are not computed by SIPRI and second because the data are heavily modified from one SIPRI publication to another, showing large standard deviations.

2. Algeria bought six MIG-21 and six MIG-21 MF in 1977, 25 MIG-21 MF and 20 MIG-23S in 1978 as well as tanks and land-to-air missiles (*source*: SIPRI Yearbooks 1977, 1978, 1980, 1981, 1982, 1985, 1990, 1991, 1992).

3. The arms contracts between the USSR and Algeria were in US dollars. However, some arms trade was conducted in exchange for oil. Incidentally, when we refer to "oil" in this chapter, we mean oil and natural gas, or hydrocarbon-based natural resources.

4. 15 billion US dollars due for 1994 to 1995 was rescheduled for 1998-2001 in exchange for agreement to reduce the state's budget deficit, further devaluation of the dinar, and total liberalization of foreign trade and prices.

References

Destanne de Bernis, G. (1977). *Relations économiques internationales*. Paris: Dalloz (4th edition).
Ellyas, A. (1999). "Les généraux gagnent à tous les coups." *Courrier International*. No. 440, 8 au 15 avril 1999.
Fontanel, J. (1995). *Organisation Économiques Internationales*. Paris: Masson, Collection Droit Sciences Économiques (2nd edition).
Goumeziane, S. (1994). *Le mal algérien : Économie politique d'une transition inachevée 1962-1994*. Paris: Éditions Fayard.
Guillaumont, P. (1985). *Économie du développement*. Vol. 3: Dynamique Internationale du développement. Paris: P.U.F.
Hadjseyd (1994). "L'industrie algérienne (1962-1993), Blocage du système productif et tentatives d'ajustement." Grenoble 2, Thèse, I.R.E.P./D, Juin.
IMF (1998). *IMF Economic Reviews*. No.2. Washington, DC: IMF (May-August).
Isaev, V.A. (1991). "Les relations économiques soviéto-arabes. Bilan, problèmes et perspectives," pp.143-154 in M. Capron (ed.), *L'Europe face au Sud*. Paris: Éditions l'Harmattan, (Coll. Forum du Tiers-Monde).
Kadri, K. and J. Fontanel (1996). "Les relations entre la Russie, la France et les pays en voie de développement: le cas de la Russie." *Cahiers de l'Espace Europe*.
Lamchichi, A. (1991). *L'Algérie en crise*. Paris: Editions l'Harmattan.
Lmrabet, A. (1999). "La défaite de l'islamisme militaire." *Courrier International*. No. 440, 8 au 15 avril 1999.

Locatelli, C. (1992). *La question énergétique en Europe de l'Est*. Paris: Éditions l'Harmattan (Collection Pays de l'Est).

Pineye, D. (1982). "Les fondements économiques de la nouvelle approche soviétique de l'Afrique septentrional." *SLOVO: Revue de l'Institut National des Langues et des Civilisations Orientales*. No. 4, pp. 65-84.

Portes, R. (1979). "Est, Ouest et Sud: le rôle des économies centralement planifiées dans l'économie internationale." *Revue d'Étude Comparative Est-Ouest*. Vol. 10, No. 3 (September), pp. 31-73.

SIPRI (1998). *SIPRI Yearbook 1998*. Oxford: Oxford University Press.

Teboul, R, and E. Moustier (1999). "L'aide et le financement de la croissnance au Sud de la Méditérranée," in Cartapanis (ed.), *L'Euro et al Méditerranée*. Marseilles: Editions de l'Aube.

US ACDA (1997). *World Military Expenditures and Arms Transfers*. Washington, DC: US ACDA.

World Bank (1994a). *World Tables 1994*. Washington, DC: World Bank.

World Bank (1994b). *World Debt Tables*. External Finance for Developing Countries, Volume 2 Country Tables, 1994-95. Washington, DC: World Bank.

Valkenier, E.K. (1983). *The Soviet Union and the Third World: An Economic Bind*. New York: Praeger.

PART III:

SOUTHERN AFRICA

10 The economics of civil war in Mozambique

Tilman Brück

Introduction

Despite prevailing in two world wars, Britain has seen its economy grow less rapidly than Germany this century. In fact, the German post-war economic miracle is often attributed to the opportunities for investment and political reform offered by the end of the last war. However, it is not clear if such prospect will also hold for a poor, developing country emerging from civil war.. This chapter demonstrates that while some economic effects of war are universal, others are conditioned by individual economic and political circumstances.

Four specific propositions regarding the economics of civil war are addressed for the case of Mozambique. First, while war can be expected to reduce wartime output in any economy, a developing country may not achieve high post-war growth. Second, while war will increase uncertainty and lower investment, these effects may not affect all economic sectors equally thus creating distortions and affecting the outcome of market liberalization policies. Third, war increases the need for tax revenues. Yet in developing countries with civil wars, a high tax burden may cause increasing tax evasion and black market activity thus creating large budget deficits. Fourth, a war-related budget deficit, a high debt burden, and a diminished ability to finance either may lead a government to end the war for lack of financial resources. Hence this chapter explains how the Mozambican civil war ended for endogenous, economic reasons. Such an outcome of civil war in a developing country is thus very different from that of World War II which ended only with the military defeat of Germany. Finally, this chapter examines the effects of these four propositions on the design of aid, debt, and development policies for poor countries experiencing current or recent civil war.

Microeconomic mechanisms in a civil war economy

Physical capital and investment

Civil wars are fundamental disagreements between two or more groups within a nation involving competing claims over the legal authority over some asset or territory and various methods and instruments for communicating and resolving this difference. The most noted economic effect of war is the destruction of physical capital. The easiest way of conceptualizing the impact of war on various types of capital is by analyzing its war vulnerability. This section addresses five aspects of vulnerability which are related to the characteristics of capital itself, namely visibility, mobility, specificity, duration, and legality.

Visibility makes an asset more vulnerable to attack. Agents may anticipate this vulnerability *ex ante* and reallocate their capital into a less visible form. In addition, less visible or invisible assets are preferred if they have been obtained illegally.

Mobility acts to increase capital's vulnerability by exposing it to theft (keeping the capital's value unchanged but affecting its ownership). In contrast, immobility would make an asset more subject to destruction thus reducing its value but maintaining its ownership. Expropriation by the state has the same effect as theft but may affect both mobile and immobile assets. Capital cannot be both invisible and immobile.

Specificity describes capital's degree of exclusiveness to an economic activity or sector. The more specific capital is to one activity or sector, the more vulnerable it is to military action. This affects the impact of anticipated warfare: non-specific capital may be reallocated to another activity thus harming production in the threatened sector even before hostilities commence but at least putting this capital to some use in the economy (albeit at lower productivity). In contrast, specific capital may continue to be operated even during war but once attacked may cease to be functional. This makes non-specific capital less risky compared to the all-or-nothing property of specific capital.

The duration of capital refers to the economic life span or life horizon of capital. A typical distinction is between non-durable and durable goods. The longer the life horizon of a capital good, the more vulnerable it becomes to possible future wars.

Depending on its vulnerability, portfolio holders will seek to reallocate their capital to optimize their portfolio in light of new war circumstances. Some traders may actually experience an increase in profitability, leading to further portfolio adjustments. War profiteers also exploit temporary illegitimate profit-opportunities (Keen, 1997), providing an incentive to save. Other people likely to benefit from war, who are thus confronted with portfolio choices, may be weapons traders or generals. To the extent that they view war as temporary, war profiteers are likely to show a high savings propensity. Thus government policy creates varieties of incentives and risks, co-determining capital reallocation and investment patterns.

Current investment by firms responds to the relative war vulnerability of assets, activities, and sectors through lower actual and optimal levels of capital and a decreased adjustment coefficient of investment. Actual capital is reduced through destruction or reallocation while future capital may be reduced through long-run uncertainty and increased tax rates. Under conditions of war uncertainty, the option value of investment (Dixit and Pindyck, 1994) may be very high, thus explaining why apparent liquidity in a war economy may correspond to very low levels of actual investment. From that point of view, war uncertainty is an extreme form of policy uncertainty and in effect acts as a tax on investment. The adjustment coefficient of investment may fall due to increased transaction costs in the economy and uncertainty.

The destruction and erosion of immobile and hence war vulnerable capital in Mozambique is shown in Table 10.1. Export agriculture would have suffered severely from the two-thirds reduction in operational dams and plant nurseries as compared to the pre-war capital stock. The average destruction of all categories was 40 percent. Assuming the war was at its worst during the ten years prior to the peace agreement, this implies an annual rate of war-related capital reduction of almost 4 percent.

An even higher rate of destruction was experienced by the railway system (Table 10.2), a visually obvious and politically suitable target for attacks. The table also suggests the constant, high level of military activity and subsequent insecurity experienced throughout the 1980s in Mozambique. Finally, Figure 10.1 illustrates that cattle production, a visible yet somewhat mobile activity, was strongly affected by war. Less than a fifth of its recorded 1980 cattle stock remained in 1992, the remainder having been lost both through direct (rebels killing cattle to spread terror, to halt development, and to feed their troops) and indirect war effects (lack of feed and veterinary care, short-term consumption needs of the population, and missing cattle markets for related trading and breeding activities).

Export-oriented agricultural in Mozambique suffered a particularly high war burden. Crops that are slow-growing, production that is located in the countryside (where most fighting took place), and bulky output that needs to be transported through rural areas by means of a modern transport system all contributed to the war vulnerability of the cash crop sector. In fact, the pre-war transport sector had been a large foreign exchange earner as it transported goods for the neighboring

Table 10.1: Destruction of immobile capital (measured at the end of 1992)

Immobile capital by sector	Operational units	Non-operational units	Destroyed units	Total units	Destruction (in %)	Non-operational and destroyed (in %)
Agriculture						
Irrigation systems	118	24	7	149	5	21
Dams	122	208	57	387	15	68
Seed production centers	13	9	0	22	0	41
Nurseries	38	19	4	61	7	38
Tick-cleansing tanks	70	299	40	509	8	67
Water supply						
Wells	3,057	1,071	138	4,266	3	28
Holes	1,225	530	32	1,787	2	31
Fountains	484	205	11	700	2	31
Small water supply systems	96	84	29	209	14	54
Domestic trade						
Shops	6,664	1,318	2,381	10,363	23	36
Warehouses	369	8	40	417	10	12
Banks	144	6	4	154	3	6
Savings posts	54	31	0	85	0	36
Communication						
Post offices	123	8	17	148	11	17
Rural post offices	49	90	13	152	9	68
Public Administration						
District administration	117	33	42	192	22	39
Municipal administration	99	83	120	302	40	67
Administrative residences	724	474	374	1,572	24	54

Average destruction at the end of 1992   39.7%

Source: Comissão Nacional do Plano (1993, p. 21).

Table 10.2: Destruction of CFM locomotives

	1982	*1983*	*1984*	*1985*	*1986*	*1987*	*1988*	*1989*
Units destroyed or damaged [a]	24	34	37	28	32	59	36	58
Units in operation [b, c]	222	222	249	214	178	172	146	158

Sources: [a] Stephens (1994, pp. 136-141); [b] Comissão Nacional do Plano (1990, p. 25); [c] World Bank (1990, p. 69).

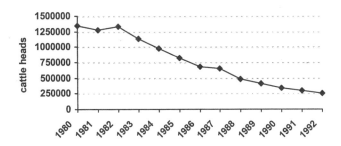

Figure 10.1: Cattle stock, 1980 to 1992

Source: Ministério da Agricultura (1994).

states of Malawi, Zimbabwe, South Africa, and Swaziland. The manufacturing sector, involving for example the processing of cash crops, produced tradable goods at source in rural areas. But the war vulnerability of these locations was high as occasional attacks even near towns were probable. The visible location of production, the storage of inventories (especially with poor transport and the seasonality of some crops), and the specificity of some inputs combined to make the export crop sector highly war vulnerable.

Despite its seeming resemblance to the cash crop sector, the agricultural subsistence sector was placed in a better position. Bare land by itself is unlikely to be attacked but fields may have been burned and livestock killed, as indicated above. Seeds benefitted from being storable, easily hidden, and edible by their

Table 10.3: Foreign direct investment in Mozambique

	mid-1985 to mid-1993		mid-1993 to mid-1994	
	Investment (mn US$)	*% of total*	*Investment (mn US$)*	*% of total*
Project status				
Active/realized	165.6	26.8	40.0	9.0
Being implemented	62.8	10.2	217.1	49.0
Implementation not started	22.5	3.6	158.2	35.7
Canceled/pending	366.5	59.4	27.6	6.2
Total approved	617.4	100.0	442.9	100.0

Source: Centro de Promoção do Investimento Estrangeiro (1995).

producers if necessary. Thus, subsistence agriculture, while the target of many attacks, was less war vulnerable compared to cash crop agriculture as it depended on very localized purchases and sales and local transport, if any. While this may be detrimental to objectives of rural development, the nature of its activities contributed to the subsistence sector being marginally more protected from the war than was the export-oriented sector. This does not imply, of course, that the countryside did not suffer a high war burden particularly in human costs (it did) but rather that some economic activities in the countryside were less affected than others. Therefore, many people were forced into extreme forms of self-reliance as the war destroyed other forms of survival. Subsistence agriculture became the default alternative for previous producers of cash crops, a deliberate choice of survival activity for some peasants, and an unattainable means of survival for a large group of landless laborers and refugees.

The data on foreign direct investment (FDI) in Mozambique illustrates how vulnerable investment is to war. Table 10.3 indicates planned annual FDI of about US$ 30 million, 1985-93, in all sectors except minerals and commerce. Actual annual FDI has been estimated conservatively at about US$ 12 million by the Mozambican government. In comparison, in the post-war period, mid-1993 to late-1994, US$ 442.8 million worth of FDI were approved under new investment legislation. This is equivalent to over two-thirds of the sum approved in the previous eight years.

Overall, the destruction of physical capital works as a step back in time for welfare: the old equilibrium level of capital may be obtained eventually but the lost welfare resulting from decreased consumption during the phase of capital re-accumulation is permanent. Hence, catching up with some hypothetical peace-time optimal output level is not possible. If post-war economies, perhaps even the defeated side, attain seemingly higher levels of output and welfare than peacetime or victorious countries, it is not due simply to the replacement of destroyed capital.

Human capital

Human capital also suffered destruction and reallocation. Table 10.4 shows the destruction and erosion of primary schools at an average annual rate of about 6 percent for the years 1983-91. A similar destruction of hospitals and health posts occurred in rural areas (Cliff and Noormahomed, 1988). The subsequent effect on the quality of human capital is not measurable, but self-evident.

Frequently, people subjected to hostilities became displaced either within their municipalities, within Mozambique, or internationally. Table 10.5 indicates that war-induced population flows increased in the late 1980s. About a quarter of all domestic residents (excluding international refugees) were displaced within Mozambique at the end of the war, a further 10 percent were international refugees, and an unknown number of Mozambicans, although remaining near their usual residence, had their livelihoods destroyed by the war. These figures suggest three things, at least. First, the extent of the displacement of human capital in Mozambique was extreme, only comparable to a very few other population movements following genocide in recent world history. Second, such

Table 10.4: War-related destruction or closure of primary schools, grades 1 to 5 (1983-91)

Year	Total number	in percent
1983-87	2,655	45.1
1988	226	3.8
1989	238	4.0
1990	77	1.3
1991	206	3.5
Total	3,402	57.8
Total number of primary schools in 1983	5,886	100.0

Source: Ministério da Educação (1994, pp. 7-8).

Table 10.5: Estimated displaced and refugee population

	Sept. 1986	mid-1989	Oct. 1992
1. Total population	14,174,300	15,166,000	14,285,000
2. Total affected [a]	n/a	2,873,957	n/a
3. Total displaced [b]	n/a	1,689,492	3,728,000
4. Total refugees [c]	250,000	1,000,000	1,390,000
5. Total affected and displaced	3,482,626	4,563,449	n/a
6. Total affected, displaced, and refugees	3,732,626 (26.3%)	5,563,449 (36.7%)	>5,118,000 (>35.8%)

Notes:
a   Affected persons are defined as those whose homes or livelihoods have been destroyed but have not fled the area.
b   Displaced persons are defined as those who have moved internally.
c   Data for refugees refer only to those persons living in neighboring countries, with 1986 and 1989 data restricted to Malawi, Zambia, and Zimbabwe.

Sources: 1986 and 1989 data: World Bank (1990, p. 67); 1986 population estimates: Comissão Nacional do Plano (various years); 1992 data: International Organization for Migration (1994, pp. 9-11) and UNOHAC (1994, pp. 8-9).

migration patterns must have been caused both by extreme insecurity and by dire economic concerns of the individuals involved. Third, such levels of migration will in turn cause unprecedented higher levels of uncertainty, transaction costs, and increased claims on fiscal and aid resources.

Table 10.6 presents figures which are unlikely to have immediate economic significance but further reinforce how profound and long-lasting the legacy of civil war in Mozambique has been and will be. The table illustrates psychological traumas experienced and crimes committed by war-affected children.

A war-induced reduction in the population through death, disability, or migration will shrink the size of the entire economy for a given capital stock and at full employment. A reduction in human capital will decrease total consumption, as fewer people now exist to consume, and it will decrease output, as less labor input is available to produce. The difference between physical and human capital lies in an asymmetry at the individual level: a reduction in physical

Table 10.6: War experiences of children from war-affected areas

War experience	*Percentage*
• witnessed physical abuse and/or torture	88
• witnessed killings	77
• served as porters for Renamo	75
• were abducted from their families	64
• witnessed rape or sexual abuse	63
• were physically abused or tortured	51
• witnessed family members being killed	37
• were trained for combat	28
• admitted to being raped	16
• admitted to killing	9
• suffered permanent physical injury	7

Note: Sample consisted of 504 children aged 6 to 15 at the time of their war experiences, originating from seven different provinces, all of whom had been resident in war-affected areas. Data collected between 1989-1990.

Source: Boothby, Uptom, *et al.* (1991, p. 21)

capital affects every individual a little whereas a reduction in human capital affects only some individuals but those very severely. In addition, the level of uncertainty concerning human capital will increase more in some sectors and areas than in others. These two effects cause distortions between actors and sectors which have a lasting impact in the post-war period.

Transaction efficiency

Civil war in a developing country does not destroy global levels of technology but it leads to significantly higher costs of market transactions, i.e., war reduces the transaction efficiency of the economy (North, 1990). This effect of war is related to the dispute over authority, i.e., to war uncertainty, and to the levels of physical, human, and social capital required to maintain transaction efficiency. Transaction inefficiency may then further decrease the speed of investment, already reduced by civil war, both through the breakdown of markets generally and the individual's reduced ability to operate effectively.

The type of civil war conducted has a huge impact on transaction efficiency. A scorched-earth policy would have a comparatively larger negative effect on technological absorption and hence transaction efficiency than would a swift, stable war. The former was in fact pursued by Renamo rebels in the rural areas of Mozambique. The rebels' aim was to destabilize through deliberately random terror and to siphon off the rural surplus as a way of financing their own war effort. However, it was not possible to achieve both aims in the long run. In fact, Renamo acted myopically: as it destroyed much social and private capital, it reduced the ability of rural areas to create output. Renamo thus damaged its own supply of war finance.

If only private assets but no social capital are affected by war, a quick restoration of private sector investment and output levels is possible soon after a war shock thus making a post-war peace dividend feasible. But if much social and private capital has been destroyed, private investment will not recover unless public investment and confidence accompany the return of peace. Transaction inefficiency in conjunction with war uncertainty may thus lead to the destruction of the development capacity of the economy. Such destruction of technological absorption and confidence will be hard to overcome even in the long run.

The war-related reduction in transaction efficiency is the most difficult to estimate. Some proxies for this effect include domestic marketing activity and transport costs. Table 10.7 lists the net changes in numbers of operational units for a variety of commercial structures (buildings and some mobile marketing units). Warehouses, shops, and trading posts may have been abandoned due to insecurity, eroded value, or complete destruction. The net decrease for all structures in the period 1982-88 was approximately 30 percent, suggesting a net annual loss rate of about 5 percent.

Another proxy for transaction inefficiency focuses on increases in distribution costs due both to insecurity (requiring protection and reducing load factors due to coordination problems) as well as to the reduced quality of transport infrastructure (reducing travel speeds and increasing breakdowns on rough or mined roads). Figure 10.2 shows distribution costs as a percentage of total costs for the two largest export and subsistence crops (by weight) in 1989, under several security and transport scenarios. Distribution costs account for a much larger share of total costs for export crops than for domestic consumption crops (as discussed above). The potential savings from security improvements are much larger than those obtained from improvements in transport infrastructure. For cashew, by total volume the largest and most valuable Mozambican export crop, distribution costs halve as one moves from war (with well protected distribution) to peace time and improved transport infrastructure. Thus war imposes a tax on output which affects cash-crops relatively more than other crops.

Table 10.7: Commercial network for agricultural marketing

Commercial structure	*Number of establishments nationally*			*Percentage change*
	1982	*1985*	*1988*	*1982-1988*
• private shops	3,582	2,452	2,187	- 39%
• agricom fixed posts	235	150	62	- 74%
• other fixed posts	393	94	99	- 75%
• all other structures	882	1,230	1,226	+39%
Total commercial structures	5,092	3,926	3,574	- 30%

Source: World Bank (1990, p. 142).

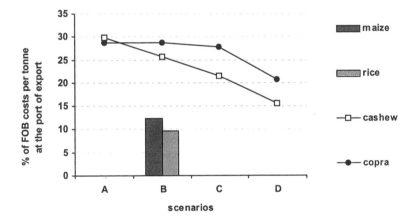

Figure 10.2: Distribution costs in the war economy

Scenario A: 1989 Mozambican situation with dedicated security force protection
Scenario B: actual 1989 Mozambican situation
Scenario C: same as B but with improved road transportation infrastructure
Scenario D: same as C but improved maritime transport and security improvements which would allow the elimination of military escort (peace scenario)

Source: World Bank (1989, pp. 75-76).

The effect of war on transaction efficiency is threefold. First, warfare reduces the aggregate size of the economy for a given size of the population and thus leads to lower welfare per capita. Second, a reduction in efficiency is likely to destroy the capacity for generating future development. Third, post-war economic policies aimed at market liberalization will find that firms previously competitive in the world market are no longer able to compete. Instead of forcing the closure of such firms, government and donors should consider investing in institutions that will lower private transaction costs.

In the case of cashew in Mozambique for example, ignoring the long-run implications of the war for transaction costs has led the World Bank to recommend the closure of cashew processing factories. An alternative policy could have been assisting these firms regaining competitiveness by investing in market institutions that lower transaction costs. Such policy, coupled with financial and training assistance following from the issues addressed above, would have also helped to maintain valuable foreign exchange earnings for Mozambique.

Risk, uncertainty, and expectations

Investment and consumption decisions are closely related to issues of risk, uncertainty, and expectations. Risk represents the subjective probabilities agents attach to the occurrence of future events including people's age at death. War is unlikely to change people's attitude to risk. Instead, their actions change as their circumstances deteriorate. That is, individuals close to the survival threshold will not become more risk averse but they will act differently in order to avoid a further deterioration of their situation. Uncertainty refers to the experience of a variety of risks in the whole economy. War uncertainty is the extreme version of state-induced uncertainty and this is distinguished by its near-perfect correlation of risks among households and hence its uninsurability.

The source of much war uncertainty is the conflict between two groups over authority and legitimacy. The erosion of either or both increases war uncertainty. Thus war uncertainty need not imply "maximum" uncertainty but rather a form of uncertainty related to fundamental state functions and actions. War uncertainty is fundamentally dependent on the type of conflict: in a stable international war, the government may have little uncertainty attached to its operations. The more likely it becomes that the opponent's aim of assuming sole leadership will be achieved, the more single-minded the government will become in placing the war effort above all other policies. That is, the more threatened a government is the more it will regulate the economy to ensure its own victory. This is plausible as regulation is the only policy tool of government and wars typically are not won by deregulating domestic activity — after all military activity is a very authoritarian and centralized affair. But a more regulated economy is also likely to be less efficient. Furthermore, such threatened leadership increases uncertainty by reducing policy credibility.

War uncertainty reduces investment due to the immobility of some forms of capital (an undesirable property of capital in times of uncertainty), due to the effect of uncertainty on savings, and due to capital flight. War uncertainty will be the more severely felt the less agents can substitute from vulnerable to less vulnerable assets or activities. The existence of vulnerability-reducing institutions such as social networks and income diversification opportunities permit a reduction of exposure to war uncertainty thereby positively affecting people's welfare.

The Mozambican government was able to build up its legitimacy in the course of the war, thus reducing war uncertainty over time. The government went through successive stages of war uncertainty from chaotic times at independence to a newly established authority soon afterwards, to then being a legitimate but threatened authority (by Renamo), and finally to becoming the fully legitimate authority. Thus at the macro level state uncertainty declined in the course of the war but it was significant throughout this period. The increased authority and legitimacy of the government created an opportunity for realizing a post-war peace-dividend, which materialized in Mozambique in the late 1990s.

At the micro level, war of this type meant that civilians as well as soldiers faced increased risks of mortality. In fact, about 95 percent of all war-related deaths in Mozambique were of civilians (Stewart, 1993). Figure 10.3 plots the national trend for average mortality rates (for all ages) and compares it to mortality rates calculated in surveys of directly war-affected populations in several provinces over various years. While the national mortality rate did not increase during the war years, directly war-affected people could face mortality rates 3.5 to 7 times the national average. The change is unlike the destruction of physical or qualitative human capital, which will not return to the pre-war levels as quickly but which was reduced by less.

Additional factors in the determination of mortality rates were the parallel occurrence of famine and the offsetting provision of humanitarian assistance to cope with famine and war. War, however, weakens the aid response to famine while famine may intensify the struggle over the control of resources thus making both factors combined more harmful than the individual components would suggest.

Finally, land mines obviously increase the risk of mutilation or death in Mozambique (Roberts and Williams, 1995). Compared to the level of atrocities committed, the impact of mines is likely to be lower in numbers of fatal injuries

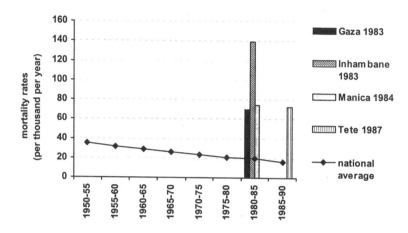

Figure 10.3: Mortality rates (war-affected areas versus national average)

Source: Cliff and Noormahomed (1988, p. 720); Comissão Nacional do Plano and Ministério da Saude (1995, pp. 21-31).

during the war, particularly among people resident in areas at the time of their mining who hence know some of the unsafe areas (unlike refugees). Yet mines will continue to threaten lives and keep land useless for years after the cease-fire thus maintaining war uncertainty beyond the end of the formal conflict.

Fiscal deficit

A government can raise resources through taxation, debt, and foreign assistance. Tax revenues (T) depend on the war experience of the population as they are also the targets of the tax authority. Negative influences on tax revenues may be counterbalanced to some extent through coercion, by increases in the tax rates, and the tax bases. Yet there will be decreasing returns to scale in such activities due to tax evasion, which itself should be easier to achieve successfully in times of internal war. Tax raising operations will be limited further by the parallel decline in transaction efficiency, human and social capital, and the increase in uncertainty. They all work to undermine the effectiveness of tax raising operations by decreasing the revenue base and reducing the morale and habits of the tax authorities and the taxable population.

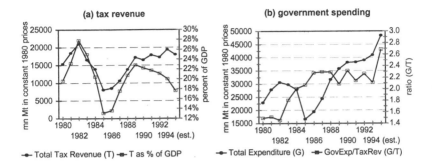

Figure 10.4: Tax revenue and government spending

Sources: Banco de Moçambique (1995); Comissão Nacional do Plano (various years); Ratilal (1990); World Bank (1990 and 1992).

Government expenditure (G) will also be affected by the type of conflict under way. Divergent styles of warfare by the two sides in a war result in different fiscal needs of both sides. The rebels' main aim in a war of destabilization may be the reduction of the government's tax base and revenue. In line with the need to raise further taxes, regulations such as production quotas, set prices, or contributions in kind will give the government further opportunities for fulfilling its need for command over resources but these also have the effect of further increasing market transaction costs.

Foreign civilian aid may be increased or decreased in times of war hence positively or negatively affecting the fiscal deficit. Typically, one would expect a reduction in investment or project-oriented aid in line with the general reduction of investment in the economy while expecting an increase in consumption and relief-oriented aid to lessen the negative human costs associated with war. The net effect of war on aid is ambiguous *a priori*: war may or may not increase the inflow of foreign aid into the economy.

The net result of war on the fiscal position is therefore likely to be a steep increase in the overall deficit of the government with consequences for policy credibility and long-run investor confidence. In fact, the data for Mozambique in Figure 10.4a indicate that the real value of total tax revenues fell by half during 1981-1985 (and by almost two-thirds on a per capita basis for 1982-1985). With the start of adjustment in 1985 revenues started rising again, possibly due to increased formal market activity (an implicit widening of the tax base).

Overall spending was volatile (Figure 10.4b). It peaked in 1982, fell until 1985, and rose until 1988 when it stabilized at an historically high level. Yet given the post-1985 recovery in spending, the trend pointed upward in most years and spending certainly rose sharply relative to revenues.

Regarding government spending, one would predict defense expenditure to increase while economically productive expenditures are likely to be squeezed. Defense spending more than doubled in real terms from 1980 to 1994, rose by almost nine percentage points as a percentage of GDP for 1980-85, and increased by 86 percent as a share of GDP between 1980 and 1987 (Figures 10.5a and b). Note that until 1980, Mozambican security was threatened by Rhodesia so that defense spending was already high at that time while the post-war levels include costs of demobilization, a peace-time cost of war. Yet defense spending was also very volatile, supporting the view that government spending contributes toward uncertainty in the economy either directly (through fighting) or indirectly (e.g., by raising demand, causing inflation, and making macroeconomic planning difficult).

Government spending on salaries, wages, goods, and services (SWGS) first declined by 60 percent but recovered after 1987 (Figure 10.5a). Yet it declined relative to other expenditures and as a share of GDP for most of the 1980s (Figure 10.5c). Hence the government was either not willing or not able to expand this type of spending in the early war years, when aid finance was not yet widely available. Economically productive spending (that is real public investment expenditure) fell to a fifth of its peak 1982 value in only three years (Figure 10.5d). Later, aid inflows permitted the resumption of public investment activity at a higher level.

The components of government spending therefore changed as expected under war conditions (increases in defense and falling other expenditures) especially in the first half of the 1980s.

The fiscal deficit consequently increased every year, except during 1985, and twice in the 1990s when the real deficit was almost unchanged (Figure 10.6a). As a proportion of GDP, the deficit more than doubled in the four years to 1984 and trebled for 1980-90 putting much strain on the domestic economy. Initially, domestic financing accounted for much of the deficit but with increased adjustment its role declined. External financing was also high initially but started to fall prior to adjustment. The renewed decline in external borrowing was presumably supply-determined through credit-rationing. These two observations suggest an important finding, namely that Mozambique was forced into structural adjustment as a result of the burden of war finance. With little Eastern bloc support forthcoming and finding it difficult to mobilize domestic resources, the

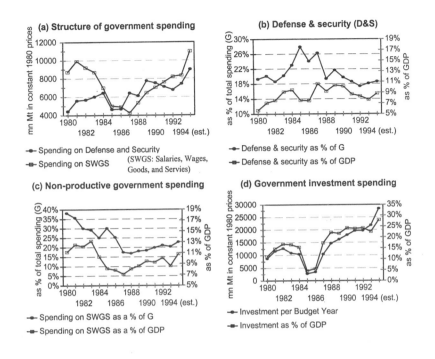

Figure 10.5: Components of government spending
Sources: Banco de Moçambique (1995); Comissão Nacional do Plano (various years); Ratilal (1990); World Bank (1990 and 1992).

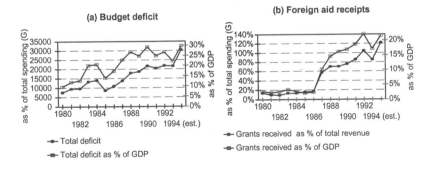

Figure 10.6: Budget deficit and foreign aid
Sources: Banco de Moçambique (1995); Comissão Nacional do Plano (various years); Ratilal (1990); World Bank (1990 and 1992).

government could not afford to self-finance both the war and Mozambique's development.

The one exception to this rule were grants. The turn from Eastern bloc support to the West facilitated a significant inflow of financial resources in support of the government. Grants increased from 2 to 3 percent to about a fifth of GDP in the early 1990s (Figure 10.6b). In fact, grants were equivalent in value to government revenue in 1992-94.

Yet the timing of the increase and the composition of the grants suggests that foreign aid is also determined by factors other than war. Aid for general use of the government is supplied even in times of war but specific aid is more readily provided by donors in an era of adjustment. Furthermore, aid in Mozambique was delivered on humanitarian grounds in times of famine or for general development purposes but not explicitly to support the war effort. Mozambique continued to attract much aid throughout the years of its internal war but not because of the war. Aid in Mozambique should thus be seen as a variable independent of the war, though the war in Mozambique was not independent from the continued inflow of aid resources.

Government debt finance has a differential welfare impact as people in the economy are differentially affected by government debt and taxation. In particular, future generations will not be affected by current spending but will have to contribute to repaying the accumulated debt. As the current leaders are likely to be rather old, they are unlikely, especially in a non-democratic society, to be taking future generations' interest sufficiently into account. Current generations hence act unsustainably by consuming too much in the present. This is made worse by the fact that a part of these resources is used in the war effort hence further reducing the productive resources left to future generations. Furthermore, government debt is a burden on the economy as it displaces capital from the portfolio of individual savers and thus diminishes the productive capacity to sustain growth now and in the future.

Government war spending therefore imposes a double burden on the economy: it reduces output and welfare in the present and, through public debt and taxation, prevents the re-accumulation of capital, output, and welfare in the future. The financing of war is thus a central concern both during the conflict and in the post-war period.

Macroeconomic implications of civil war

Output and growth

The measures used as proxies for output are gross domestic product (GDP) and global social product (GSP). While calculated according to different methodologies, both series show similar patterns, thus allowing comparisons over time. Data is expressed in constant 1980 prices (cp) using the GDP deflator and in per capita (pc) measures where appropriate, and is calculated as an index (1980 values being set to 100) so that comparisons in trends can be readily made.

The data presented in Figures 10.7a-b show that both measures of output declined until 1986-87. While GSP per capita fell more steeply and more continuously, both measures indicate a drastic decline of about 30-40 percent in output in the early and mid-1980s. The GSP data available for the mid-1970s shows output also fell by more than a third after decolonization. Such a political shock may have long-run effects akin to war (especially due to a reduction of human capital) but the output increase by about 17 percent for 1975-81 indicates that the decolonization shock was at least partially overcome when the war intensified in the early 1980s. This is related to the one-off nature of decolonization which implied expectations could adjust to the new regime (though that may have been creating uncertainties of its own). On the other hand, the large loss of physical and human capital was difficult to overcome compared to the end of the war in 1992 when much more capital (both physical and human) was available in the economy even though some war uncertainty still persisted.

However, the rise of measured output in the late 1980s indicated that war was not the only relevant factor determining output in those years. Instead, the positive effects of the reform projects and the related inflow of aid allowed an expansion of output despite the continuous destruction of capital. The war shock became relatively less important as some war variables acted in a one-off fashion. Uncertainty over life spans, for instance, would have shifted up to a higher level for each war zone but would not typically increase further thereafter. Capital destruction in some rural areas was nearly complete while the small destruction of capital in urban areas was easily being offset by aid inflows (thus preventing a further fall in consumption, see below). Yet this also indicates that the observed growth may be the result of improved measurement in certain sectors. Essentially, the war economy was characterized by significant urban-rural, formal-informal, legal-illegal, and market-subsistence dualities which strongly affect the post-war economy and reported statistics.

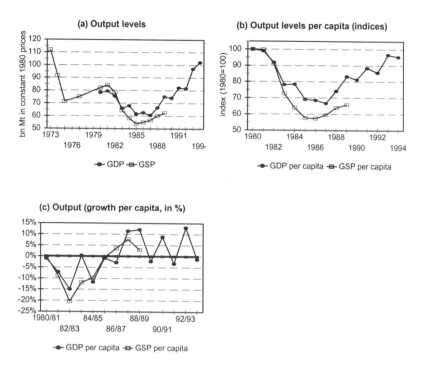

Figure 10.7: Output and growth

Sources: Banco de Moçambique (1995); Comissão Nacional do Plano (various years); Ratilal (1990); World Bank (1990 and 1992).

The actual growth rates of GDP and GSP indicate strong yearly fluctuations (Figure 10.7c). Yet the GDP series shows a small trend: while practically all pre-1988 rates are below zero, most values thereafter lie near or above zero percent growth. A possible interpretation, as argued earlier, is that the war reduced the growth rates initially and the adjustment programs helped improve this rate, but the internal war then prevented the growth rate to catch-up to hypothetical peace-time values. Therefore, the case of Mozambique gives support to the view that war damages the growth potential beyond the period of the capital destruction.

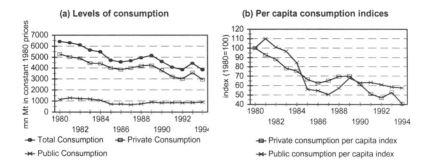

Figure 10.8: Total, private, and public consumption

Sources: Banco de Moçambique (1995); Comissão Nacional do Plano (various years); Ratilal (1990); World Bank (1990 and 1992).

Consumption

The levels of constant-price per capita private consumption declined for the first six years of the period covered in Figure 10.8a before rising slightly for three years and falling to nearly half of its 1980 value by 1994. Public consumption per capita was at a much lower level but fell similarly until 1987 before stabilizing in the period 1989-94 despite the adjustment programs in effect at that time.

Economic theory predicts that a one-off reduction in capital will lead to a curtailment of consumption so that additional investment may rebuild the capital stock. Yet this prediction will not hold for a more complex shock as war will also reduce the ability of the economy to rebuild itself, hence further decreasing output. In fact, output fell broadly equiproportionate with consumption in the period 1980-89 suggesting that agents viewed the war as permanent. In 1989 the adjustment program started to significantly cut private consumption in times of growing formal-, urban-, and service-sector output financed by aid (Figure 10.8b). Hence there were macro successes based on aid which mask declining real living standards for informal-, rural-, and agricultural-sector based poor people. Furthermore, the accumulation of a war-related budget deficit has an impact on the long-run welfare of the population yet some parts of the current population in the early 1980s may not have found their consumption to be affected thus maintaining relatively high levels of consumption initially.

Figure 10.9: Foreign debt

Sources: Banco de Moçambique (1995); Comissão Nacional do Plano (various years); Ratilal (1990); World Bank (1990 and 1992).

Debt

In times of civil war, government debt is likely to increase. Given the constraints on the Mozambican financial market (including its small size, lack of financial institutions, inflation, uncertainty, and its lack of credibility), most government borrowing had to come from foreign sources. Total foreign debt increased continuously to 500 percent of GDP after it became possible for the Mozambican government to borrow abroad in 1985 (Figure 10.9). This is a reflection of the fiscal deficits accumulated over the war years and reflects both the need for increased war spending and the reduced ability of the government to generate tax revenue domestically in times of war.

Conclusions

The above theoretical framework and the case of Mozambique suggest four conclusions concerning the economic effects of civil war.

First, as predicted, war leads to lower output and growth. The actual magnitude of these effects is strongly influenced by other economic factors, such as decolonization, government policies, and structural adjustment. War does not permit a quick restoration of output if it causes more than one-off capital destruction. The effects of government debt, uncertainty, and transaction inefficiency further undermine the economy. The long-run effects of war hence diminish the opportunities for sustainable post-war development and the realization of a peace dividend.

Second, the war in Mozambique created new economic dynamics in some sectors and disenfranchized large sections of its population from the potential benefits of specialization and trading. War directly reduces investment in war-vulnerable activities and indirectly encourages or even enforces resource reallocation into less vulnerable sectors. Output growth in a war economy predominantly occurs in non-tradable sectors which suffer less from the war-vulnerability of the tradable sector and from the Dutch Disease effects of aid. The private sector, suffering long-run uncertainty about market and taxing behavior, will not be in a position to generate growth in the worst-affected war zones. Supply-oriented policy advice often ignores this implication of civil war. Therefore, instead of introducing market *liberalization* policies in this context, government and donors should adopt market *creating* policies to reach out to the rural, agricultural, and poor households who could not participate in markets during the war. Standard structural adjustment reforms are thus unlikely to increase sustainable growth and reduce absolute poverty in highly indebted, dualistic, and poor countries suffering from war.

Third, government war taxation involves a recurrent extraction of resources from the population thus reducing their long-run welfare. The budget constraint of war-time government is particularly tight: receipts are likely to be low and spending needs high. Deliberate inflation or taxation lead to incentive problems, create distortions, and impose a heavy war burden on the economy. The obvious solution for a developing government fighting a civil war is therefore to use foreign borrowing and aid to finance its war-time spending plans. Aid in particular will permit the high investment levels needed to reduce war-related transaction inefficiency. The current highly-indebted, poor country (HIPC) debt relief initiative should thus reconsider its position on external debt relief for war-affected countries. In particular the need for a policy track record may be impossible to fulfil in war economies subject to less aid-generosity than Mozambique and where the peace process may be dependent on immediate economic benefits. Debt forgiveness and forward-looking policy conditionality should aim to create sustainable post-war development, not maximum repayment flows. In the extreme, tight adjustment programs offering few economic rewards for peaceful behavior may threaten a fragile peace process and destabilize society.

Finally, aid can extend a government's budgetary constraints significantly. This also implies that the provision of resources by donors may lead to a temporary continuation of the war. The nature of aid conditionality for war economies is thus crucial. Not all donors in Mozambique used their influence to express a preference for humanitarian over military government expenditure and work toward resolving the socio-economic issues underlying the conflict. Mozambique was driven by its dire budgetary and growth position of the mid-1980s to seek support from the IMF and the World Bank. In exchange for aid and loans the government had to accept structural adjustment and liberalization policies which placed much emphasis on complying with strict financial standards but which did not account for the realities of the war. Aid conditionality in Mozambique ignored the war and thus prevented an earlier end to the conflict and enforced policies which were unsustainable in a war economy.

By 1992, the Mozambican government had exhausted all domestic and external resources for financing core governmental functions and the war. Given the strong dependence of the war economy on external support, there existed a powerful lever for forcing the warring groups out of the conflict. This is an important lesson to diplomatic, political, and economic policymakers aiming to end civil wars in other poor, developing countries.

References

Banco de Moçambique (1995). *Boletim Estatístico*. Vol. 3, No. 7 (March).
Boothby, N., P. Uptom, and A. Sultan (1991). *Children of Mozambique: The Cost of Survival*. Durham, NC: Duke University Press.
Centro de Promoção do Investimento Estrangeiro (1995). Unpublished Data. Maputo.
Cliff, J. and A. R. Noormahomed (1988). "Health as a Target: South Africa's Destabilization of Mozambique." *Social Science and Medicine*. Vol. 27, No. 7, pp. 717-22.
Comissão Nacional do Plano (1990). *Estatísticas dos Transportes e Comunicações 1989*. Maputo.
Comissão Nacional do Plano (1993). *Plano de Reconstrução Nacional 1994-96*. Maputo.
Comissão Nacional do Plano (various years). *Informação Estatística*. Maputo.
Comissão Nacional do Plano and Ministério da Saude (1995). *Fecundidade, Mortalidade e Planeamento Familiar em Moçambique*. Maputo.
Dixit, A. K. and R. S. Pindyck (1994). *Investment under Uncertainty*. Princeton: Princeton University Press.
International Organisation for Migration (1994). *Assistance Programme for Internally Displaced Vulnerable Groups in Mozambique*. Maputo.
Keen, D. (1997). "A Rational Kind of Madness." *Oxford Development Studies*. Vol. 25, No. 1, pp. 67-76.

Ministério da Agricultura (1994). Unpublished Data. Maputo.

Ministério da Educação (1994). *Impacto da Guerra na Educação 1983-1992*. Maputo.

North, D.C. (1990). *Institutions, Institutional Change and Economic Performance*. Cambridge: Cambridge University Press.

Ratilal, P. (1990). *Using Aid to End the Emergency*. New York: UNDP.

Roberts, S. and J. Williams (1995). *After the Guns Fall Silent: The Enduring Legacy of Landmines*. Washington, DC: Vietnam Veterans of America Foundation.

Stephens, J. (1994). *The Political Economy of Transport in Mozambique: Implications for Regional Development*. Ph.D. Thesis. Brighton: University of Sussex.

Stewart, F. (1993). "War and Underdevelopment: Can Economic Analysis Help Reduce the Costs?" *Journal of Economic Development*. Vol. 5, No. 4, pp. 357-380.

UNOHAC (1994). *UNOHAC Map Series*. Maputo.

World Bank (1989). *Mozambique: Transport Sector Review*. Washington, DC: World Bank.

World Bank (1990). *Mozambique: Restoring Rural Production and Trade*. Washington, DC: World Bank.

World Bank (1992). *Mozambique: Second Public Expenditure Review*. Washington, DC: World Bank.

11 The peace dividend in post-apartheid South Africa: myth or reality?

André Roux

Introduction

It is generally proposed that high and rising defense expenditures[1] in a developing country absorb scarce resources that could otherwise have been utilized more effectively and meaningfully in non-military endeavors. By extending the argument to include the crowding-out effect, inflationary financing of defense spending, widening current account deficits, oligopsonistic market conditions, and human capital distortions the conclusion is reached that a high defense burden compromises long-run growth and socio-economic development (notwithstanding Benoit's claim to the opposite, in 1973).

In a seemingly logical extension of the argument, a sustained decline in the defense burden should therefore have the opposite — i.e., wholesome — impact on a developing country's economic and socio-economic prospects. In the case of South Africa at least, this kind of reasoning — intuitively and emotionally appealing as it may be — could be flawed on a number of counts.

First, while there can be little doubt that South Africa's economic growth and development performance between the mid-1970s and early 1990s was far from ideal, and there is no denying the fact that defense spending in that period reached unprecedented peaks, making *a priori* assumption of a causal relation between the two events could render one guilty of a number of misdemeanors. These include confusing correlation with causation; the *post hoc ergo propter hoc* fallacy; looking at reality through different eyes; and subjectivity and bias. Of course, the argument attributing poor economic performance to high levels of defense expenditure could be a valid one, even if one is guilty of faulty economic reasoning. This, however, needs to be proven.

A second potential flaw in the entire argument revolves around the interpretation one has of the concept of a peace dividend. Sandler and Hartley (1995, pp. 277-279) propose three possible interpretations and, at the same time, expose three myths surrounding the peace dividend. In essence, the uninformed (or naïve) view of the peace dividend is that it is large and instantly available for use in, for instance, redeeming the national debt, building infrastructure, or funding social services. In reality, a structural decline in defense spending requires a fundamental reallocation of resources in the economy and major adjustments in employment patterns, capital utilization, and the like.

The simple view of the peace dividend is that it will serve as a panacea to a country's economic and social problems. However, as argued earlier, this will depend on the nature of the relationship between defense spending and poor economic performance.

The final view of the peace dividend — the informed view — is that it requires a major reallocation of resources involving costs and taking time. This view dispels the myth that adjustment problems and costs of disarmament will be relatively small and localized, and therefore ignorable.

These few reflective and cautionary observations provide background to the remainder of this chapter. In an attempt to provide a scientifically justifiable answer to the question posed in the title of the chapter the analysis is essentially of a macroeconomic nature. To this end, the chapter is structured as follows: a brief review of South Africa's macroeconomic and developmental performance since 1960 is provided in the next section, followed by an analysis of defense expenditure trends in South Africa since 1960. Using econometric techniques, the chapter continues by computing the relationship between defense expenditure and various macroeconomic variables between 1960 and 1990. The ways in which the military in South Africa has affected and may continue to have a bearing on socioeconomic development are then explored, and the chapter ends with a number of concluding remarks.

South Africa's macroeconomic and development performance since 1960

Macroeconomic perspective

South Africa's economy (as measured in terms of GDP) is by far the largest in Africa. Total output of goods and services in South Africa is almost twice that of the second largest economy, Egypt. Moreover, South Africa's GDP is 2.2 times larger than the combined output of the rest of southern Africa.

However, South Africa is responsible for less than 0.5 percent of both world output and international trade. As a medium-sized, developing, and open economy, the South African economy has always been influenced, both positively and negatively, by changes and trends in the international business, financial, social, and political environments. These influences have become even more pronounced now that the country has democratized and been re-admitted into the global village.

The South African economy has been in structural decline since the 1970s. Whereas real economic growth rates of 5 to 6 percent were the rule rather than the exception until the early 1970s, between the early 1980s and early 1990s South Africans had to be satisfied with growth rates in the vicinity of 1 percent per annum (see Figure 11.1). As a result virtually no new jobs have been created in the formal sector since 1980, giving rise to serious economic and socio-political deficiencies.

Economic decline in South Africa, particularly between 1974 and 1994, was essentially brought about in at least three ways. First are inappropriate policy measures. Until the mid to late 1980s it was usually assumed, and often believed, that South Africa was a developed industrial country with mature and legitimate political institutions, and a fairly stable economic structure. This inappropriate and invalid perspective of the South African economy produced, of necessity, inappropriate strategies.

Second was an over-reliance on primary commodities. Although South Africa's mineral wealth undoubtedly played a dominant role in the economic development of the country during the first seven decades of this century, it was realized too late that a commodity switch had taken place internationally sometime during the 1970s in favor of enhanced world trade in secondary and tertiary goods, at the expense of primary goods.

Third, the international isolation of South Africa in the form of trade sanctions and, in particular, disinvestment, imposed immeasurable damage to the South Africa economy, via *inter alia*, the destabilizing and confidence-threatening impact on both investors and consumers.

The South African economy was, without any doubt, subjected to an unrelenting barrage of negative macroeconomic events, developments, and adjustments during the 1980s and early 1990s. Nonetheless, a positive — albeit very low — average economic growth rate was recorded. This provides some evidence of a remarkable degree of resilience.

Moreover, although it is early days yet, South Africa's macroeconomy is fundamentally somewhat healthier today than, say, ten years ago. For example, the new government has displayed admirable fiscal and macroeconomic discipline despite the tremendous pressure to sharply raise government expenditure on the social wage. The South African economy has recorded positive (albeit recently declining) economic growth since 1993, while the inflation rate is in single-digit territory — a combination last seen in the early 1970s.

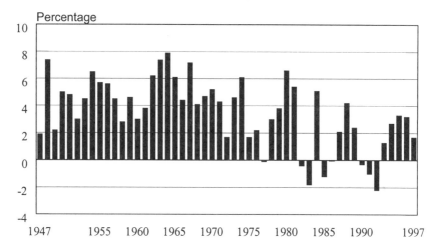

Figure 11.1: South African real economic growth, 1947-1997

Sources: South African Reserve Bank (1994); South African Reserve Bank: Quarterly Bulletin (various issues).

Development in South Africa

When viewed superficially the development effort in South Africa conveys an impression of improvement over time. Moreover, compared to other southern African states, the South African development effort has generally been above average. This cannot, however, be interpreted as justification for complacency about the supposed success that has been achieved by devoting a vast amount of resources and efforts to the provision of social and physical infrastructure, buildings, and development-linked loans.

When scrutinized more closely, South Africa's development can be diagnosed in a less favorable light. South Africa is formally classified by the World Bank as an upper-middle-income country. Socio-economic comparisons with cohorts in this category show, almost without exception, an inferior development status for South Africa (Table 11.1).

Moreover, the bipolar nature of the South African economy becomes clear when orthodox development indicators are disaggregated. Table 11.2, which entails a sample of the latest available data on South Africa's socio-economic

Table 11.1: Selected measures of socioeconomic development for countries in the World Bank's upper-middle-income category[1]

Country	1996 GNP per capita $	1996 life expectancy at birth years	1995 adult male illiteracy rate %	% of population with access to sanitation 1995	Population below $1 a day %
Poland	3 230	72	<5	100	6,8 (1993)
Slovak Republic	3 410	73	<5	51	12,8 (1992)
St Lucia	3 500	70	n/a	n/a	n/a
South Africa	**3 520**	**65**	**18**	**46**	**23,7 (1993)**
Mexico	3 670	72	8	66	14,9 (1992)
Mauritius	3 710	71	13	100	n/a
Croatia	3 800	72	<5	68	n/a
Trinidad & Tobago	3 870	73	1	56	n/a
Gabon	3 950	55	26	76	n/a
Hungary	4 340	70	<5	94	<2 (1993)
Malaysia	4 370	72	11	91	5,6 (1989)
Brazil	4 400	67	17	41	23,6 (1995)
Czech Republic	4 740	74	<5	n/a	3,1 (1993)
Chile	4 860	75	5	83	15,0 (1992)
Uruguay	5 760	74	3	82	n/a
Seychelles	6 850	71	21	n/a	n/a
Antigua & Barbuda	7 330	75	n/a	n/a	n/a
Argentina	8 380	73	4	80	n/a
Slovenia	9 240	74	<5	90	n/a

Note: (1) Those countries with per capita GNP of more than $3,115 but less than $9,636 in 1996.

Source: Compiled from World Bank (1998).

Table 11.2: Socioeconomic situation of different income classes, 1993[1]

	Income/consumption quintiles					
	Q1	*Q2*	*Q3*	*Q4*	*Q5*	*Total*
	Poorest				*Richest*	
Per capita income (R)	390	1,056	1,974	4,158	20,478	5,611
Household income (R)	2,406	6,372	11,550	22,458	82,536	30,630
Household monthly wage (R)[2]	287	546	930	1,611	4,689	1,598
Unemployed (%)	53	43	30	17	4	30
No education (%)	24	18	13	7	6	15
Less than full primary education (%)	54	42	33	21	9	35
Completed secondary education (%)	4	8	13	23	62	19
Completed tertiary education (%)	0	0	0.2	0.6	10.3	1.8
Primary enrolment (nett) (%)	85	87	88	89	90	87
Secondary enrolment (nett) (%)	46	57	67	78	83	60
Tertiary enrolment (nett) (%)	4	5	8	20	38	11
Regular wage/income (%)	23	44	67	79	65	65
Households rural (%)	76	68	46	33	15	47
Households metropolitan (%)	10	14	29	40	58	30
Households in other urban areas (%)	14	18	25	27	27	23
Households black (%)	96	93	82	68	25	73
Households white (%)	1	1	3	16	66	17
Households size (%)	6.3	6.0	59	5.4	4.2	5.5
Economically active age (16-64) (%)	49	52	n/a	n/a	n/a	57
Resident male household head (%)	50	50	n/a	n/a	n/a	61
Persons per room (%)	2.3	1.7	1.4	1.0	0.5	1.4
Households living in shacks or traditional dwellings (%)	39	32	25	15	2	23
Households with electricity (%)	15	28	49	77	98	53
Commute by car/motorcycle (%)	7	7	10	26	77	30
Treated by private doctor (%)	23	31	41	53	73	44
Stunting of children under 5 (%)	38	27	23	18	6	27
Satisfied with quality of life (%)	17	22	29	39	70	35

Notes: (1) Figures are not fully comparable across dimensions, as criteria for division into quintiles differed (e.g., income/consumption group, quintile of households/individuals, etc.).; (2) including casual labor.

Source: Van der Berg, S. (1997).

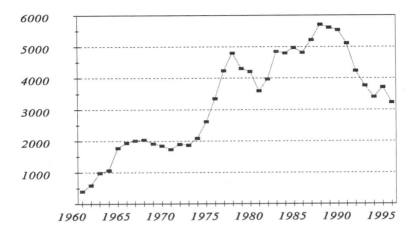

Figure 11.2: Real defense spending in South Africa, 1960-1995

Sources: RSA *Estimate of expenditures*. (various years). South African Reserve Bank. *Quarterly Bulletin* (various issues); own computations.

disparities, reveals the vast welfare chasm between, in particular, South African whites and Africans.

Defense expenditure trends in South Africa since 1960

When real defense expenditures in South Africa are examined (see Figure 11.2), three phases are discerned. Two, commencing during the early 1960s and mid-1970s respectively, involved a brief but pronounced surge in spending which took defense expenditure to new and higher structural levels which were maintained for a number of years. The third phase commencing at the end of the 1980s, heralded the first decline in defense expenditure to a sustained lower level since the 1950s.

Throughout the period under review, but particularly from the mid-1970s to late-1980s, defense spending decisions were largely influenced by national security concerns. Indeed, a direct link can be traced between defense expenditure and the perception of threat to vital national values, where both perceptions and the evaluation of values are matters of subjective judgment.

The 1960s heralded a new era in South Africa's security situation. Internally, the shooting of protesters at Sharpeville in 1960 and the new strategy, involving sabotage attempts, adopted by the then banned African National Congress (ANC) and Pan African Congress (PAC) led to a new bout of domestic conflict. Outside developments also prompted a reappraisal of the role of the defense force.

Based on these considerations it was deemed necessary to raise the efficiency of the defense force's combat readiness by expanding the supply and quality of manpower and armaments at its disposal. The number of permanent force members (volunteers from all arms of the services) rose from 9,000 in 1960 to 15,000 in 1964, while the number of national servicemen called up by means of a ballot system grew from some 2,000 in 1960 to almost 20,000 in 1964 (Jaster, 1985). Consequently, there was a threefold increase in the total number of permanent force and citizen force members available for military purposes within a relatively short period of time. In 1968 compulsory nine-month national service for all young white males was introduced. These increases necessitated the establishment and maintenance of a number of new training units.

An extensive program was also launched to modernize armaments. This entailed not only the purchase of various types of major equipment, but also the replacement of obsolete hardware, ammunition, and military vehicles. Moreover, in reaction to the 1964 arms embargo, the government embarked upon an extensive program aimed at ultimately achieving self-sufficiency with regard to arms requirements.

The increase in military personnel and establishments, coupled to the modernization program, resulted in a considerable increase in defense expenditure. By 1965 real defense spending was almost five times greater than at the beginning of the decade, while the defense burden had risen from 0.8 percent to 3 percent of GDP over the same period. Since this was a period of rigorous economic growth and rising export revenues (real exports of goods and services rose by 35 percent) the rapid increase in defense expenditure did not exert undue pressure on the capacity of the economy to finance the enhanced military capability.

However, during the second half of the 1960s the threat of direct conventional attack on South Africa dissipated, while the economic strains of sustained rises in defense expenditure became more apparent. For example, economic and export growth started to subside, and inflationary pressures emerged (the average annual inflation rate rose from 2 percent between 1960 and 1965 to 3.4 percent between 1969 and 1970 and 4.9 percent during the 1966-1973 period). Real defense expenditure consequently leveled off between 1965 and 1973. In fact, spending in 1973 was only some 8 percent higher than eight years previously. As a result the defense burden fell to an average level of 2.4 percent over this period, as compared to 3 percent of GDP in 1964 and 1965.

During 1974-1987 a number of developments led to a reappraisal of the threat against South Africa. First, the increasing range, quantity, and sophistication of armaments, as well as military personnel, provided by the Soviet bloc to Angola, Mozambique, the ANC, and the South West African People's Organization (SWAPO) were seen as conclusive evidence of the USSR's intent to provide the military capacity to conduct a conventional war against South Africa (McWilliams, 1989). Moreover, the Soviet bloc, in collaboration with the United Nations, the Organization for African Unity (OAU), and certain black African states was seen to be instrumental in effecting the implementation of punitive economic measures against South Africa (for example, trade sanctions and disinvestment). Internally, the so-called "Soweto riots" in 1976 contributed to the growing international anti-apartheid sentiment that resulted in a mandatory United Nations arms embargo against the country in 1977. The South African government also identified a deliberate psychological warfare campaign against South Africa, aimed at isolating the country from the international community (Moore, 1987).

The perception of a growing security threat heralded the emergence of the military as a major force in the country's policymaking process (Jaster, 1985). A so-called "total strategy" was devised, whereby state security was paramount and underpinned by all aspects of society, i.e., the political, economic, social, and military structures of the country. The role of the South African defense force in thwarting the perceived threat included the adoption of an offensive strategy (including pre-emptive strikes or hot pursuits in neighboring states), and the employment of the armed forces in support of the police in preventing or suppressing internal unrest (RSA, 1986). Moreover, a strong military presence was established and maintained in Namibia (then South West Africa) to prevent a take-over of that country by SWAPO.

The immediate implications for the defense sector of the new total strategy policy were, given the 1977 UN arms embargo, to aim for a high degree of self-sufficiency in arms manufacturing. To this end Armscor was established to ensure the development and production of the arms, equipment, and ammunition required to perform a conventional task externally and counter-insurgency role internally. Implementation of the total strategy also resulted in a greater military manpower requirement. Consequently, in 1978, the initial period of compulsory military service for white male draftees was raised from nine months to two years. Thereafter, servicemen were automatically placed on active reserve for twelve years, during which time they were liable for active duty of up to 90 days a year, for a maximum of 720 days of total service during that period (Jaster,

1985). At any given time, therefore, the SA Defence Force had in excess of 100,000 men permanently under arms (including some 60,000 national servicemen), as well as over 300,000 reservists capable of being mobilized within days, and a 130,000 strong commando force (Moore, 1987; Jaster, 1985).

Levels of defense spending during 1974-1987 were consistent with the heightened threat perception and concomitant demands placed on the defense sector. In 1974 real defense expenditure was 26 percent higher than in the previous year, and within four years resources allocated to defense more than doubled. As a consequence the defense burden rose from the 1965-1973 average of 2.4 percent to 3.8 percent of GDP between 1974 and 1977. The initial surge in expenditure was followed by a eight-year leveling-off period during which spending was sustained, on average, at 1977 levels (see Figure 11.2). In fact, in 1985 real defense expenditure was only 0.4 percent higher than in 1977. However, because real GDP expanded by 22 percent over this period, the defense burden fell from 4.7 percent in 1977 to 3.9 percent in 1985. A brief increase in real spending was recorded in 1986 and 1987 as a result of the intensification of South Africa's involvement in SWA/Namibia and Angola and continued domestic conflict. As a result the defense burden rose to 4.5 percent of GDP in 1987.

Developments since 1989 have altered South Africa's strategic environment in at least four respects. First, international geo-political relationships were profoundly affected by the disintegration of the former Soviet Union, the formal termination of the cold war, and the widespread propensity to replace communism with ideologies based on political and economic freedom. Second, the states of southern Africa were no longer subject to a cycle of escalating confrontation and destabilization (Du Plessis and Hough, 1992). Thirdly, the reform initiatives introduced during the early 1990s, culminating in the country's first multiparty, non-racial elections in April 1994, served to reverse the international ostracization of South Africa. Finally, full democracy in South Africa presumably obviates the need for a strong military presence to protect or promote certain sectoral interests. Moreover, there are rising pressures on the government to divert scarce resources away from the military sector to socio-economic areas such as education, housing, health, and poverty alleviation.

Although these trends have resulted in a departure from the total strategy approach adopted during the previous era, their influence on the role of the military has been ambivalent. Whilst the imperative for an offensive military stance (particularly *vis-à-vis* neighboring states) no longer exists, increasing emphasis has been placed on the role of the defense force in assisting the police in curtailing internal instability and maintaining law and order. Nonetheless, changes were effected to the national service system whereby the initial period

Table 11.3: Government expenditure on education, health, police, and defense, 1979/80 and 1997/98

	1979/80	*1997/98*
Education	16.0	21.3
Health	9.0	10.7
Housing	< 1.0	2.2
Police	5.0	6.9
Defense	16.0	5.6

Note: figures as percentage of total government expenditure.

Source: RSA. Department of Finance (various years).

of compulsory training for white males was reduced from two years to one in 1991, and then scrapped altogether with effect from January 1994. Consequently, South Africa's armed forces are now all-voluntary.

In light of the improbability of an imminent foreign act of aggression against the country, and changing socio-economic priorities, as reflected in higher levels of spending in other state departments (see Table 11.3), defense expenditure declined in real terms to more than 50 percent lower in 1997 than in 1987. Since 1991 the defense burden has fallen below 2 percent for the first time since the early 1970s, reaching an estimated 1.7 percent of GDP in 1997.

The macroeconomic impact of defense expenditure, 1960-1990

Background

The economic growth effects of defense expenditure cannot be determined without empirical research that is customized to suit the specific and unique structural characteristics of specific countries. At the same time, such empirical research should be based on sound theoretical principles so that the conclusions reached are justifiable in terms of acceptable behavioral statements.

The research problem is particularly complex in developing nations. In some cases the constraint to economic growth may be of a demand nature, in which event military spending may lead to the fuller utilization of the country's existing productive capacity, thereby enhancing aggregate demand to the benefit of economic growth (without exacerbating inflationary pressures). Thus, an increase in the supply of savings will not be a sufficient condition for enhanced economic growth. In other cases, where there is a shortage in the supply of key growth generating resources, an increase in military expenditure may impose additional burdens on the economy and ultimately subdue the rate of growth in production.

As pointed out earlier, economic growth in South Africa has been constrained by both demand and supply forces. In order, therefore, to evaluate the effects of changes in defense expenditures on economic growth in South Africa it would seem prudent to incorporate the salient features of the traditional demand-oriented as well as supply factor growth theories, whilst taking cognisance of the structural and institutional impediments to growth.

Clearly, the relations among defense, growth, and other related variables are crucial in determining whether an increase in the military burden will raise or lower the economic growth rate. There are a number of intermediate effects and feedbacks between defense and the creation of new resources and between savings and growth that should be specified in an econometric model. In addition, various authors (for example, Deger and Sen, 1983, Maizels and Nissanke, 1987, Pilandon, 1987, Grobar and Porter, 1989, and, in particular, Joerding, 1986) have suggested that military spending is at least partly dependent on the overall performance of the economy, inasmuch as the level of domestic output represents a budget constraint on all forms of government outlays, including those for defense purposes. Whilst military spending may have been more immune to decreases in the case of lower economic growth, the degree of immunity is unlikely to have been complete. It is therefore plausible that military spending is an endogenous variable.

The multiple channels through which one variable affects another and the possibility that military spending is an endogenous variable, imply that a regression analysis limited to a single equation is too simple and possibly subject to erroneous positive correlation between military expenditure and growth. Consequently, a system of simultaneous equations is called for which, if based on properly specified behavioral theories, can separate the various effects and feedbacks within the system.

In this section such a model is specified for South Africa, the results are reported, and appropriate conclusions are drawn.

Specification and estimation of the model

The discussion of the theoretical *a priori* relationship between military expenditure and growth suggests that an econometric model should accommodate at least the following points:

▸ the direct impact of military spending on growth, which may be positive or negative;
▸ the indirect effect via the savings rate to reflect the fact that military expenditure increases government expenditure and may reallocate potential savings away from investment, thereby suppressing economic growth;
▸ the effect on resource mobilization, which is manifested in a decline in the propensity to save as consumer spending rises to offset potentially lower government expenditure on services such as education and housing;
▸ the possibility that in an open economy military imports may occur at the expense of more productive civilian imports; and
▸ the possible endogeneity of military expenditure.

Deger and Sen (1983), Deger and Smith (1983), Deger (1986), and Scheetz (1991) have estimated similar multi-equation models complying with the conditions set out above. Each model hypothesizes that military expenditure may reduce growth by lowering the savings rate. By including the latter as a determinant of economic growth it is assumed, in the neo-classical tradition, that savings automatically lead to investment, which, in turn, is translated into economic growth (see, for example, Mohr and Rogers, 1987, pp. 426-430). This kind of reasoning may, however, be flawed if the decision to save and the decision to invest are regarded as two separate decisions and that production is determined by effective demand. In recognition of this possibility, each of the mentioned models also hypothesizes potential positive direct effects of military expenditures on growth through Keynesian demand stimulation.

In accordance with the above conditions and international modeling experiments, as well as the dictates of data feasibility, a four-equation system is proposed for South Africa with four endogenous variables, namely economic growth, the domestic savings ratio, the current account balance as a percentage of GDP, and the military burden.

The growth equation is based on the premise of the neo-classical proposal that capital growth is financed by domestic savings and/or foreign capital inflows. The former is reflected in the national savings rate; the latter by the current account balance as a percentage of GDP. The military burden is used in recognition of the possible modernization benefits of military expenditure. The share of non-military government expenditure in GDP is also included to allow for the possibility of a Wagnerian relationship between growth and government outlays and in recognition of the significant role played by the government sector in South Africa. A labor force variable was discarded at an early stage as it was felt that it would serve no statistical purpose by virtue of the fact that a major portion of the annual increase in the number of economically active persons has not been absorbed into the formal labor market and has therefore not made a contribution to measured economic growth. The above translates into:

(11.1) $g = a_0 + a_1 s + a_2 ca + a_3 m + a_4 nmg$

where g = annual rate of growth of GDP; s = gross domestic savings as a share of GDP; ca = current account balance as a share of GDP; m = government defense expenditure as a share of GDP; and nmg = non-military government expenditure as a share of GDP.

The signs for the coefficients of s and nmg are expected to be positive. The sign for the coefficient of ca should be negative because a current account deficit implies net capital inflows which favor economic growth.[2] The sign for the coefficient of the military burden will be positive if military spending mobilizes unutilized resources.

The domestic savings rate (s) is deemed to be affected by the military burden and, in terms of the life-cycle theories of consumption, the economic growth rate. Government expenditure (excluding military outlays) as a percentage of GDP is added due to the potential impact of government savings (or during the 1980s, dissaving) on private savings and investment decisions in South Africa. The real prime overdraft rate is taken to exert an influence on savings decisions. Finally, the lagged savings rate was included to capture the influence of previous years' savings decisions on savings decisions in the current year. Hence

(11.2) $s = b_0 + b_1 g + b_2 m + b_3 s_{(t-1)} + b_4 i + b_5 nmg$

where i is the real prime overdraft rate. The signs of all the coefficients of g, i and $s_{(t-1)}$ are expected to be positive, and those for m and nmg negative.

The equation for the current account balance contains the military burden as an explanatory variable because an increase in military spending increases aggregate demand which, in the event of domestic supply constraints, may result in either the internal use of goods that would normally have been exported, or an increase in imports. Economic growth is expected to have a negative impact on the current account balance as the result of rising imports (particularly of capital inputs) required to meet the increase in domestic demand. Real annual economic growth in the US, which is used as a proxy for world economic growth, is added to capture the effect on South Africa's current account of foreign demand for domestic goods and services. The lagged current account is included to capture inertia effects in trade and debt interest. The equation for the current account balance is therefore

(11.3) $ca = c_0 + c_1 g + c_2 m + c_3 ca_{(t-1)} + c_4 usg$

where *usg* is the real economic growth in the US. The sign for the coefficient of *usg* is expected to be positive, and the signs for *g* and *m* negative. The sign for $ca_{(t-1)}$ cannot be predetermined.

In the final equation the defense burden is assumed to be influenced by real per capita income, thereby capturing the public good nature of defense spending. Lagged military expenditure is added to capture its inertial nature, whereby military spending in any particular year partly reflects the commitments incurred in previous years. Finally, a dummy variable is included to account for effects of war (or the perceived threat of war) on military expenditure (*D* was set at 1 for the years between 1973 and 1987, in accordance with the country's preparation for and/or actual involvement in regional conflict; and at 0 for the remaining years). The above translates into

(11.4) $m = d_0 + d_1 pci + d_2 m_{(t-1)} + d_3 D$

where *pci* is real per capita income, and *D* is the dummy variable denoting war or the perceived threat thereof. The signs of all the coefficients are expected to be positive.

Two-stage least squares was used to estimate the four-equation system, using annual data for 1960 to 1990. The model results are summarized in Table 11.4.

Interpretation of the results

The R^2 of the estimated equations are generally high enough to warrant the conclusion that the variations in the dependent variables are adequately explained by the regressions. However, some of the t-statistics — notably those in respect of the military burden and growth variables in the savings equation — are disappointingly low. Nonetheless, these coefficients are retained for the purposes of evaluating the potential interactions and feedbacks between the variables.[3]

The signs of some of the coefficients deserve some comment. In the growth equation the military burden is included as a proxy for the possible modernization effect of military expenditure. However, the negative (and significant) military burden coefficient points to the absence of any direct spin-off effects from military expenditure in South Africa. The negative sign for *N.G.* invalidates the mooted possibility of a positive Wagnerian relationship between economic growth and government expenditure and, in fact, lends credence to the allegation that government expenditure has been a factor retarding economic

Table 11.4: Results, four-equation system, 1960-1990

Coefficient	Growth rate (g)	Savings rate (s)	Current account (ca)	Military burden (m)
Intercept	15.48 (3.35)	5.11 (0.58)	9.71 (1.87)	1.77 (1.83)
s	0.54 (3.18			
ca	-0.23 (-3.13)			
m	-1.51 (-2.63)	-0.07 (-0.08)	-1.69 (-1.44)	
N.G.	-0.87 (-3.74)	0.45 (1.21)		
g		0.58 (1.19)	-1.91 (-2.70)	
s(t-1)		0.35 (1.93)		
i		-0.23 (-1.54)		
ca(t-1)			1.03 (5.88)	
usg			0.64 (2.18)	
pci				0.0003 (-1.00)
m(t-1)				0.72 (8.35)
D				0.54 (2.93)
R^2	0.64	0.49	0.75	0.87
Durbin-Watson	2.19	1.68	1.91	1.74

Note: t-statistics in parentheses; parameter estimates statistically significant at the 5 percent level.

growth in South Africa. The signs for the shares of the current account and savings respectively in *GDP* are as expected.

In the second equation the military burden plays a statistically innocuous role insofar as its direct impact on savings (and, by implication, investment) is concerned. The positive sign for *N.G.* suggests that for the period as a whole government spending may have had a positive impact on gross domestic savings and investment, although the statistical evidence in this regard is unconvincing. The signs for the remaining coefficients are in accordance with expectations.

In the third equation the sign for the military burden is, as expected, negative. The negative sign is indicative of the tendency of imports (particularly of a capital input nature) to rise and fall in reaction to domestic demand stimuli. The positive sign for the lagged current account variable proves the inertial effects in both trade and debt interest.

As expected, in the fourth equation, the military burden itself is influenced positively and significantly by lagged military expenditure, which captures longer term commitments incurred in previous years, and the dummy variable for war or threat perceptions. This suggests that, during the period under review, defense expenditure decisions were largely based on a set of pre-determined suppositions related to actual and anticipated involvement in war. The per capita income variable yielded poor statistical results, which suggests that the public good effects of military expenditure in South Africa are limited. This confirms the notion that, for the period under review, non-economic factors dominated considerations about defense outlays.

The direct and indirect impact of defense spending on economic growth, the domestic savings rate and the current account can feasibly be determined by calculating total derivatives. However, it would for a number of reasons (including potential data deficiencies, and the statistical mediocrity of the coefficients for growth and the military burden in the savings equation) be imprudent and meaningless to employ this technique with the estimated coefficients. Consequently, qualitative conclusions would be far more appropriate. In this regard the economic results suggest that in the period 1960 to 1990:

▸ the basic Benoit hypothesis that defense expenditure in developing countries is positive for economic growth did not apply to South Africa;
▸ defense spending did not influence the gross domestic savings rate, positively or negatively;
▸ the current account reacted negatively to defense expenditure; and
▸ defense spending decisions did not take cognisance of economic considerations.

In separate analyses (for example, Roux, 1995) it has also been found that:

- the direct contribution made by defense to the persistently high levels of inflation that prevailed in South Africa between 1975 and 1990 was relatively insignificant;
- the total (i.e., direct as well as implicit) costs of conscription were considerably higher than the measured costs; and
- the domestic defense industry place a disproportionately heavy strain on the country's overall industrial base, particularly during the 1980s.

Generally, South Africa's rising military burden over the 1960-1990 period can be ascribed not to economic factors, but to considerations related to actual or expected defense force involvement in military adventures. In the absence of such expectations the military burden would presumably have been less onerous. By virtue of the claim made by the military on productive and investable resources, the country's economic growth rate was ultimately lower than would otherwise have been the case.

However, another major factor contributing to the secular decline in economic growth in South Africa appears to have been an absorptive capacity constraint which partly prevented the productive investment of available resources in the domestic economy. During the second half of the 1970s the gross domestic savings rate exceeded the investment proportion of GDP by 3.5 percentage points; thus domestic savings of the order of 3.5 percent of total output were not utilized for domestic investment purposes. This constraint was exacerbated during the 1980s by the commitment to export vast amounts of investable resources in lieu of the redemption of foreign debt; hence too the increase in the current account as a share of GDP from 2.6 percent during the 1970s to 5.6 percent during the 1980s.

Defense spending and development

Theoretical and empirical considerations

The first influence that the military ostensibly exerts on development is that of modernization. The modernizing effect of the military was espoused, especially in the United States, in the belief that the military had a potentially significant role to play in newly independent Third World nations. This role involved bringing about change in cultural and societal attitudes, particularly during the embryonic phase of post-colonial independence in the late 1950s and early 1960s.

The multifarious nature of this transmission mechanism can be described in terms of factors such as progressivity, deontic forces, demonstration effects, education, and technological spin-offs.

In essence, increasing militarism in Third World nations may conceivably have a modernizing effect because the military possesses the values, attitudes, and behavior patterns associated with modernism. The military's emphasis on modern values is attributed to several factors. These include the classless nature of military training and conditions, which foster a broader, more tolerant attitude toward all social groups; the emphasis on achievement and diligence; the politically stabilizing effect of a clearly delineated hierarchical structure; and the effects of military technology and the concomitant military support of industrial development.

However, in spite of the theoretical advantages listed above, there is little evidence that militarized societies have made significant progress toward modernization. This state of affairs may be ascribed to flawed theoretical conjecture, indicating "how impossible it is to generalize about the military as an independent static institution, without careful analysis of different types of armed forces and of their relationship to the particular society in which they operate" (Kaldor, 1976, p. 462). Alternatively, it may reflect the inability of military regimes to realize and effectively utilize the potential developmental advantages offered by military intervention. Either way, arguments around modernization can be questioned on both a theoretical and an empirical basis.

Case studies on the relationship between development and the modernizing influence of the military are generally inconclusive. This is partly because researchers appear to rely largely on scanty and anecdotal evidence. It would also appear that such evidence is gathered and interpreted through a preconceived ideological bias, or from the perspective of one or other vested interest. Palmer (1980, pp. 224-225) states that "over the years, military intervention [in developing nations] appears to have slowed the process of modernization and change as often as it has advanced it. Whether or not a military regime will promote rapid development and the extent to which it will do so, therefore depends upon the values of the leaders involved, not merely their categorization as military."

A second major approach to the role played by the military in the development process in Third World nations focuses on the extent to which military expenditure affects access to goods and services. Basic human needs are both tangible, such as health, food, water, education, and transport, and non-material, such as participation and cultural identity (Streeten, 1979, p. 30). The role of the military in meeting non-material needs has been dealt with above. Therefore, for analytical purposes, the rest of the analysis is confined to the relationship between the military and measurable dimensions of economic development.

It should be stressed that the relationship between military spending and the provision of basic physical needs in developing countries is clouded by several issues of concept and definition. These relate *inter alia* to indicators of socio-economic development, and the extent to which socio-economic services should be provided by the government. In principle at least, conventional tangible basic needs can be provided by the private sector (although for a number of reasons they are normally financed partly or fully by governments) as they are in some ways similar to private (particular) goods. Defense, on the other hand, is generally regarded as being a public good *par excellence*. It could, therefore, be argued that the responsibility for government budgeting is not affected by the relationship between military spending and development. This is because the prime responsibility of the government toward its constituencies may be to provide security, with the provision of other basic needs being of peripheral importance. In reality, however, few governments, particularly in developing nations, are willing to relinquish their developmental responsibility, so that there may be a trade-off between an enhanced military burden and state spending on health, education, and other social services.

From a global point of view, defense spending could be a substitute for the provision of other basic needs. The implication of this kind of exercise in social accounting is clear: defense spending compromises the supply of basic socio-economic needs in the developing world. However, this line of thought assumes a zero-sum relationship between military and socio-economic spending. That is to say, it assumes that the resources released by a reduction in defense outlays are automatically diverted to education, health, or other forms of welfare spending. This is not always the case. In a study of an unspecified number of developing nations, McKinlay (1989, pp. 29-42) concludes that countries which expand their military expenditure more rapidly are not prone to lower rates of growth in education or health spending.

Benoit (1973, p. 277) suggests that the military may complement socio-economic development by "(1) feeding, clothing, and housing a number of people who would otherwise have to be fed, housed, and clothed by the civilian economy — and sometimes doing so, especially in LDCs, in ways that involve sharply raising their nutritional and other consumption standards and expectations; (2) providing education and medical care ... that may have high civilian utility." This kind of exposition can be questioned on the grounds that it attempts to generalize from the specific, and does not acknowledge the possibility that these beneficial forces may be negated by the negative repercussions on development of military spending.

It is not possible to draw general conclusions about this complex issue from the available empirical studies. For some countries, lower defense expenditure leads to the release of more resources, which can be used by governments to improve the socio-economic conditions of the poor. In others, the national allocation of resources between defense and social programs seems to involve contemporaneous budgetary decisions (Hess and Mullan, 1988; McKinlay, 1989). In some cases it is possible to have higher defense expenditure and more socio-economic development, but at the expense of economic growth (Deger, 1986). In others a militarized society, even though not spending large amounts on the military, may prejudice the supply of basic needs whilst promoting economic growth (Todaro, 1989, pp. 578-583).

The military and development in South Africa

In this section the analytical framework developed in the previous section will be used to evaluate the role of the military in promoting or retarding economic growth and development in South Africa. Changes in South African politics since 1989 have been accompanied by changes in the role and nature of the South African defense establishment. This culminated in the amalgamation in 1994 of the South African Defence Force (SADF), Umkhonto we Sizwe (MK), the Azanian People's Liberation Army (APLA), and the armies of the former TBVC states, as well as the termination of compulsory conscription for white males. In light of these facts, it is suggested that the nature and scope of the relationship between the military and development after 1994 differs markedly from that prevailing prior to constitutional reform. Consequently, I first review the role of the military from the end of the Second World War until the early 1990s, and then focus on the impact of the military establishment on development since 1993.

Following the Second World War, it seems on the whole that a process of militarization took root in South Africa, particularly after 1960, in response to the international arms boycott, the severing of military links with Britain and increasing tension in the subcontinent, all of which resulted in greater pressure on civil society to release resources — human, financial and physical — for national security. As the security problem was clearly defined, the so-called "total onslaught" and specific military means and goals were identified, adhered to, and allowed to permeate civilian decision-making, it may be argued that the process of militarization was accompanied by a sense of militarism. If this was the case, it raises the question of the role played by the military as a modernizer in fostering development.

The military has arguably played a significant role in South Africa in terms of technological progress and the establishment of infrastructure. However, its ability to introduce, establish, and manage change in cultural and societal attitudes was largely negated by the fact that it mainly supported the goals, aspirations, and interest of whites. Consequently, the purported deontic benefits of conscription (e.g., discipline and cohesion) were withheld from a large section of the population. Rather than contributing toward intergroup tolerance, militarism in pre-democratic South Africa concentrated power in the hands of one particular group. Therefore, not only did the SADF fail to generate popular support from all members of the population, it also suffered from a crisis of legitimacy, as it was seen by many as an extension of special sectional interests. In short, the modernizing effects of the military prior to 1994 were largely confined to those least in need of them. Put differently, the usefulness of military service as a socialization process and a training ground for modernization was largely unexploited because the military was, for all intents and purposes, the domain of whites only.

There is some evidence that military spending in South Africa has crowded out other forms of government expenditure (Roux, 1995, pp. 140-143, 190-191). As social spending by the government constitutes a major portion of state outlays, it could be argued that rising claims on government resources by the defense sector occurred at the expense of the social well-being of the population at large. According to van der Berg (1991, p. 81), if the defense burden during the period 1973-90 had remained at its 1972 level, total government savings would have amounted to some R75 billion (in constant 1990 terms). These resources, which may be considered as the first-round costs of militarization, would have been sufficient to construct 1.9 million fully serviced houses — compared with an estimated housing backlog of some 1.2 million units. However, the results of this kind of analysis depend on the absence of absorptive capacity constraints. Therefore, van der Berg (1991, p. 83) claims that a shift of financial resources toward social expenditure on education, housing, and the like may result, at least in the short run, in an increased demand for physical and human resources which could be in limited supply. This raises the cost of the social service. In addition, cutbacks in defense expenditure have had a short- to medium-run impact on certain sectors of the economy, thereby affecting the well-being of various communities connected to the defense industry.

Conventional wisdom and somewhat rudimentary evidence suggest that military spending in South Africa has had a neutral or moderately negative impact on the provision of basic needs. However, more sophisticated and specific conceptual reasoning and empirical research into the developmental opportunity costs of defense spending are necessary in order to reach unambiguous conclusions about the nature and extent of the trade-off between defense and welfare.

Conjecture about the potential role of the military in economic growth and development in a fully democratic South Africa requires investigation of the role, composition, and professional ethos of the defense force after 1993.

The political instability in individual countries may have a negative influence on southern Africa, but it is unlikely to escalate into a conventional war involving outside parties like South Africa. However, South Africa still needs to maintain a credible deterrent ability in case of a conventional threat. Moreover, as the leading economic and military power in the subcontinent, South Africa will inevitably play a dominant role in maintaining regional security in the political, economic, social, and environmental spheres. This role requires, *inter alia*, a sound military force and appropriate technology.

Internally, it is possible that the involvement of the armed forces in maintaining domestic stability will continue and even expand. Stability may be compromised by social friction and political intolerance, in the wake of dissatisfaction in certain groups with the outcome of the multi-party democratic process. The possibility of violent resistance to legal government establishments by a number of essentially uncontrollable private armies cannot be ruled out. A psychosis of violence may be further fueled by crime resulting from endemic unemployment. Thus, although the idea is inconsistent with the moral and professional ethos of the military mind (Cilliers, 1992, p. 25), until the police can enforce stability, the defense force may have to assist them.

The role of the South African National Defence Force (SANDF) in combating internal upheaval is not a new one. However, as mentioned above, its contribution toward modernization through its stabilizing influence has been marginalized by the majority view that the armed forces have reflected and represented the militarization of white society. But it is now clear that both the composition of the defense force and the status of the armed forces in future civil-military relations are changing. This new defense force could act as a modernizing influence, bearing in mind the following considerations:

▸ The primary role of any armed forces in a democracy is to deter external aggression. This requires adequate and professional training and equipment. Although there is no imminent foreign threat, the defense force in a democratic South Africa must be equipped to answer any challenge to democratic values, institutions, and practices (Cilliers and Mertz, 1990, p. 6);

▸ To be perceived as a legitimate force which represents the interest of all those who support democracy, the defense force will have to shed its image as the defender of particular vested interests. This will require the harmonious amalgamation of all the major military formations, including the former SADF, the former TBVC forces, MK, and APLA;

▸ To avoid having a defense force with divided loyalties to various political groups, it is crucial that the transformation process in society at large be matched within the defense force. Thus, the newly integrated armed forces should at all times be guided by and subordinate to the principles and values embodied in the constitution (Cawthra, 1990, pp. 1-5). The result would be a military operating within and serving a democracy, not one that is fragmented by subsidiary loyalties; and

▸ In keeping with the principles of democracy and the subjugation of the military to civil control, defense-related decisions should ultimately be sanctioned by parliament. At the same time such decisions should, as far as possible, adhere to the principle of transparency and therefore be open to public scrutiny.

Adherence to the principles and guidelines outlined above would largely negate the propensity of the armed forces to militarize society, with a bias toward certain sectoral interests and, ultimately, at the expense of broad socio-economic development. Theoretically at least, the defense force could fulfil a modernizing role through the conduits of deontism, social learning, and the maintenance of internal stability. In addition, the pool of military management skills and experience could be used for social upliftment projects. However, even under these ideal conditions the modernizing influence of the military may be minimized by the expected reduction of the defense sector, which would in turn reduce the flow of technological expertise and demand into the civilian sector. Moreover, only a limited proportion of the population is likely to be exposed to the suggested benefits of military training and discipline.

Concerning the future absorption of scarce resources by the military, the following fundamental issue is germane: it is common cause that the lives of ordinary people in post-apartheid South Africa must be improved. This entails, among other things, eliminating the restrictions and inequalities of the apartheid era. However, there is no consensus on the most effective and appropriate way of achieving widespread social upliftment. Those favoring a free market argue for reduced state intervention, while social democrats see it as the paramount duty of the state to reduce economic exploitation and poverty.

Even if it assumed that all monies saved by a decline in defense burden are channeled *in toto* to government-financed socio-economic endeavors, the tangible impact, at least in the short run, could very well be underwhelming. For instance it is possible, in light of the unacceptably high levels of criminality currently prevailing, that a significant portion of any savings generated by a reduced defense burden may be siphoned off to the police services. Moreover, failure to achieve horizontal fiscal justice within a much shorter period may lead to rising social tension and dissatisfaction with political leadership and therefore require increased military intervention to counteract internal acts of aggression. The concomitant rise in the defense burden would then dissipate any prospects of additional money to spend on development. Finally, there are racial disparities in spending in a wide range social areas (e.g., education, housing, health, and pensions). Any "peace dividend" resulting from a reduced defense burden is therefore likely to be requisitioned by more than one government department. Consequently, those relying solely upon defense savings as a means of achieving spending equality across a wide range of social areas could be disappointed by the modest progress made.

Concluding remarks

Whether the decline in defense expenditure in South Africa since the mid-1990s translates into a higher growth path and meaningful upliftment of the entire population will only really emerge in about twenty years' time. Only by then will it be possible to determine the long-run nature, effect, and even ethos of the restructured South African economy; and the concomitant character of the relationship between defense spending, the macro-economy, and development.

Moreover, as pointed out by Sandler and Hartley (1995, pp. 278-279) the dividends of peace are likely to be small in the short run and only translate into long-run benefits in the form of a larger output of non-military goods and services after the reallocation of resources, and after fairly significant adjustment costs have been absorbed. Even then, of course, the benefits will only be obtained if public policies help to minimize the costs of adjustment and conversion.

A further reason for postponing judgment for a couple of decades is related to the dictates of statistical analysis and inference. In this regard at least 20 years of data are required to conduct a useful and reliable regression analysis.

It is therefore best to conclude with a few speculative and reflective comments.

Following the country's first all-party full democratic election in 1994, there has been a paradigm switch with regard to defense matters. For instance, in the absence of the need to prepare for any imminent military confrontation the defense burden has fallen to below 2 percent. This implied reallocation of resources away from the military raises questions as to the effect on economic growth and other pertinent macroeconomic variables. Democratization is likely to remove *in toto* any semblance of structural dependency between the macroeconomy and the military, and defense spending is expected to become less and less autonomous. The country's full readmittance to the international business and financial community has distinct benefits with regard to the flow of international savings into South Africa. Although at this stage it is uncertain whether such exogenous inflows of resources will be translated into productive investment, it is crucial to avoid the temptation of transposing the empirical results of this chapter onto the future. The long-run steady state multipliers computed are exactly that — a set of multipliers that applied to a state of affairs that remained fundamentally unchanged for three decades. Evidently, the entire nature of the military-growth-savings-current account complex will differ substantially from the one displayed prior to 1990. Consequently, any attempts to precisely quantify the growth and other effects of reduced military spending, based on historical evidence, would be inopportune. Indeed, it would be a sorry situation if the structural economic relationships prevailing prior to 1990 were to persist into the 21st century. At best, a number of tentative observations may be made, namely:

▸ the reallocation of societal resources away from the military to civilian purposes should have a benign effect on overall welfare in the long run;

▸ the extent of the positive effect will be determined by the purposes for which the released resources are employed. If, for example, they are used mainly to finance the elimination of socio-economic disparities then, in the short run at least, the positive growth spill-overs will be tempered to some extent;

▸ it is not possible to speculate on the future impact of military spending on gross domestic savings. However, it does seem fair to suggest intuitively that a lower military burden will reduce the crowding-out effect on investment. The alleviation of structural rigidities with regard to the latter will then reinforce the multiplier effect of the former;

▸ reduced military spending, in conjunction with the *de facto* reduction of foreign capital account constraints, should ameliorate the balance of payments pressure, which will in turn enhance the positive multiplier effect on growth;

▸ there is a suspicion that any government resources released by lower military expenditures will make only a marginal contribution to the alleviation of poverty caused by disparate social spending in the past; and

▸ it has been shown elsewhere (Roux, 1997, p. 183) that although disarmament and conversion need not pose a major long-run threat to overall employment in the South African economy, short-run transitory job losses are inevitable. This is something that needs to be managed with care, sympathy, and strategic awareness. Any job loss in an economy floundering under the influence of a 30 percent unemployment rate is, to say the least, disastrous.

Notes

1. A brief word on nomenclature: In this chapter "defense expenditure" and "military expenditure" are used synonymously (although there may be differences in nuance and interpretation according to be some observers). Moreover, unless otherwise stated, defense expenditure shall refer to official government spending on defense. More specifically, defense spending entails disbursements by the Department of Defense in respect of personnel expenditure, administrative expenditure, the acquisition of consumables, and equipment, the purchase and hire of land and buildings, payments for professional services, and transfer payments.

2. The current account deficit is recorded as a negative number; consequently a negative sign (-) multiplied by a negative *ca* variable yields a positive impact on growth.

3. It is, of course, possible that the model would yield differing results if it was run for two different periods, namely for data up to 1987 (when threat preparation was paramount) and for data after 1987. However, the latter period (1987-1990) is too brief (i.e., contains insufficient degrees of freedom) to warrant a meaningful estimate.

References

Benoit, E. (1973). *Defense and Economic Growth in Developing Countries.* Lexington: Lexington Books.

Cawthra, G. (1990). "The Security Forces in Transition," in *Security Forces: The Future of Security and Defence in South Africa.* Occasional Paper No 38. Cape Town: Institute for Democracy in South Africa.

Cilliers, J. (1992). "Manpower Considerations for a Future Defence Force." *South African Defence Review.* Vol. 6.

Cilliers, J. and P. Mertz (1990). "The Military in a Future South Africa," in *Security Forces: The Future of Security and Defence in South Africa.* Occasional Paper No 38. Cape Town: Institute for Democracy in South Africa.

Deger, S. (1986). "Economic Development and Defense Expenditure." *Economic Development and Cultural Change.* Vol. 35, No. 1.

Deger, S. and S. Sen (1983). "Military Expenditure, Spin-off and Economic Development." *Journal of Development Economics.* Vol. 13 (Aug-Oct.).

Deger, S. and R. Smith (1983). "Military Expenditure and Growth in Less Developed Countries." *Journal of Conflict Resolution.* Vol. 27, No. 2.

Du Plessis, A. and M. Hough (1992). *Selected Official South African Strategic Perceptions, 1989-1992.* Ad hoc publication. Pretoria: Institute for Strategic Studies.

Grobar, L.M. and R.C. Porter (1989). "Benoit Revisited: Defense Spending and Economic Growth in LDCs." *Journal of Conflict Resolution.* Vol. 33, No. 2.

Hess, P. and B. Mullan (1988). "The Military Burden and Public Education Expenditures in Contemporary Developing Nations: Is There a Trade-off?" *Journal of Developing Areas.* Vol. 22 (July).

Jaster, R.S. (1985). "South African Defence Strategy and the growing Influence of the Military," in W.J.F. Foltz and H.S. Bienen (eds), *Arms and the African: Military Influences on Africa's International Relations.* New York: Yale University Press.

Joerding, W. (1986). "Economic Growth and Defense Spending: Granger Causality." *Journal of Development Economics.* Vol. 21, No. 1.

Kaldor, M. (1976). "The Military in Development." *World Development.* Vol. 4 (June).

Maizels, A. and M.K. Nissanke (1987). "The Causes of Military Expenditure in Developing Countries," in S. Deger and R.L. West (eds.), *Defence, Security and Development.* London: Francis Pinter.

McKinlay, R.D. (1989). *Third World Military Expenditure: Determinants and Implications.* London: Printer Publishers.

McWilliams, J.P. (1989). *Armscor: South Africa's Arms Merchant.* London: Brassey's.

Mohr, P. and C. Rogers (1987). *Macroeconomics.* Johannesburg: Lexicon.

Moore, J.D.L. (1987). *SA and Nuclear Proliferation.* London: MacMillan.

Palmer, M. (1980). *Dilemmas of Political Development.* (2nd edition) US: Peacock Publishers Inc.

Pilandon, L. (1987). "Quantitative and Causal Analysis of Military Expenditures," in C. Schmidt (ed.), *The Economics of Military Expenditures.* New York: St Martin's Press.

Roux, A. (1995). "Defence Expenditure and the Economy: Burden or Prop? An Economic Analysis." Unpublished Ph.D. Dissertation. Stellenbosch: University of Stellenbosch.

Roux, A. (1997). "Defence Expenditure and Development in South Africa." *Development Southern Africa*. Vol. 14, No. 4.

RSA. (1986). *White paper on Defence and Armaments Production 1986*. RSA: Department of Defence.

RSA. Department of Finance (various years). *Budget Review*. Cape Town: Government Printer.

Sandler, T. and K. Hartley (1995). *The Economics of Defense*. Cambridge: Cambridge University Press.

Scheetz, T. (1991). "The Macroeconomic Impact of Defence Expenditures: Some Econometric Evidence for Argentina, Chile, Paraguay and Peru." *Defence Economics*. Vol. 3, No. 1.

South African Reserve Bank (1994). *South Africa's national Accounts, 1946-1993*. Supplement to *Quarterly Bulletin*. June. Pretoria: SA Reserve Bank.

South African Reserve Bank. *Quarterly Bulletin* (various issues). Pretoria: SA Reserve Bank.

Streeten, P. (1979). "From Growth to basic Needs." *Finance and Development*. (September).

Todaro, M. (1989). *Economic Development in the Third World*. (4th edition) London: Longman.

Van der Berg, S. (1991). "Redirecting Government Expenditure," in P. Moll, N. Nattrass, and L. Loots (eds.), *Redistribution: How Can It Work in South Africa?* Cape Town: David Philip.

Van der Berg, S. (1997). "South African Social Security Under Apartheid and Beyond." *Development Southern Africa*. Vol. 14, No. 4.

World Bank (1998). *World Development Indicators 1998*. Washington, DC: Oxford University Press.

12 International migration and security in southern Africa

Michael Hough

Introduction

The end of the cold war has been characterized by an increase in intra-state conflict, with a resultant focus on domestic political and security issues, especially in developing countries. Likewise non-military threats which manifest domestically, but often also have external links, have become important, again especially for developing countries, although they also affect developed countries.

One of the threats in this regard is the increase in illegal migration. In this chapter a case will be made that illegal migration, but also certain other facets of migration, form part of official threat perception, especially in the case of South Africa. The concept of national security in developing countries will therefore first be analyzed.

The concept of national security

Several attempts to change the meaning of "national security" have been made since the end of the cold war. Primarily, this is reflected in an extension of the previously military-dominated interpretation as defense or deterrence against external aggression, to include issues such as environmental security, individual security and an increased emphasis on international security. In this regard, it is, however, still being argued that war should remain the central focus (Schultz, *et al.*, 1997).

The United States' "National Security Strategy of Engagement and Enlargement" subscribes to the above view, but still emphasizes external threats (also called transnational phenomena) such as terrorism, narcotics trafficking, environmental degradation, natural resource depletion, rapid population growth, and refugee flows as having security implications for US policy (US, 1995, p. 1).

Although the traditional (and specifically the Western) concept of national security has therefore been broadened to include non-military concepts such as economic and environmental security, it still tends to focus on the external dimension. It is true that some analysts distinguish between national security (pertaining to external security), and domestic security, but concede that this distinction more properly applies to developed or so-called "strong states". The risk, in their view, of applying the concept of national security to include domestic security (which is very often a priority for "weak states"), is that it could serve to legitimize domestic violence and lead to a confusion between regime security and state security. Yet, it is conceded that if domestic threats are not viewed as part of the national security problem, other serious difficulties arise (Buzan, 1991, pp. 105-106).

More recent studies on Third World security have in fact started to emphasize the importance of the internal dimension of security and the spectrum of threats to domestic security. Imobighe, for instance, writes:

"By far the most potent security challenges facing the countries of Sub-Saharan Africa relate to those threats that have tended to undermine the national cohesion of these states as well as their internal socio-economic and political stability and progress" (Imobighe, 1993, p. 88).

It was added with specific reference to sub-Saharan Africa that corruption and resource mismanagement are two particular vices, in addition to the problem of poor leadership (Imobighe, 1993, p. 89).

The specific insecurity dilemma of Third World states as compared to the security issues pre-occupying developed countries are also emphasized, namely the lack of a single nation, the lack of regime legitimacy, the lack of effective institutional capacities, and the fact that threats are predominantly internal rather than external (Job, 1992, pp. 17-18). Third World states are therefore preoccupied with internal rather than external security (Job, 1992, p. 18).

National security, as used in this chapter, therefore includes external and internal (domestic) security. It is also used in the context of describing threats that are of such a magnitude that core values are implicated, and requiring a national response. Furthermore, it is used in a broader sense than the traditional concept of state security or regime security to also include individual security.

Normal challenges and competition should obviously not automatically be labeled national security threats, and weak states, especially, tend to have a very broad view of what constitutes a threat to national security. The intensity of a threat, the probability of its occurrence, and the weight of its consequences are obviously also some important factors in determining the implications for national security (Buzan, 1991, p. 115).

International migration and security

Migration and refugee issues have increasingly been linked to security and stability, not only in the sending country, but also in the receiving country. Migration and refugee flows are partially a reflection of economic and security conditions in the sending country, but the flight of people from a country can in turn cause further instability. Similarly, as far as the receiving countries are concerned, migration and other flows have generated conflicts within and between states. Examples include the rise of right-wing parties in western Europe who have anti-immigrant and in some cases xenophobic policies; and the refugee issue in the Great Lakes region in Africa. It has been reported that racial violence increased by 25 percent in Germany during 1997, and crime attributed to the far right-wing by 34 percent (*Beeld*, Johannesburg, 28 April 1998).

A security/stability framework for international migration, although at times complementary to a political economy framework, often yields different results. A political/economic perspective may argue that movement of people from a poor to a rich country is mutually advantageous, while a security/stability perspective may point out the risks associated with changes in the ethnic composition of the receiving country (Weiner, 1993, pp. 3-4).

Economic determinants can be one factor in international population movements, but they are not the only factor. Governments vary in their ability to control entry, although they all want to control the entry of people to a greater or lesser extent. Overemphasis of economic factors or internal upheavals also tends to obscure the fact that some governments are eager to reduce or eliminate selected social classes and ethnic groups from their territory (Weiner, 1993, pp. 4-5).

In addition to the security concerns referred to above, which are factors that shape the policies of governments toward international migration, governments are often also concerned that admittance policies that are too liberal might "open the floodgate". In this regard, it has been stated that:

"States that are capable of defending themselves against missile, tank and infantry attacks are often unable to defend themselves against the intrusion of illegal migrants infiltrating across a border ... Governments want to control the entry of people and regard their inability to do so as a threat to sovereignty" (Weiner, 1995, p. 134).

Whether migration (legal, illegal, or in the form of refugee flows, but especially in the latter two instances) is viewed as a threat will of course largely depend on perceptions. An influx of migrants may be perceived as a threat by one ethnic group but not by another. The business community, trade unions, and the general public may differ over the employment of migrant workers, and the governing party (or factions in the governing party) may have yet different perceptions regarding migration. Countries that are more homogeneous may also have a more restrictive policy than a heterogenous society (Weiner, 1995, p. 135).

As far as the specific types of threats posed by migration are concerned, a distinction should be drawn between legal migration, refugees, and illegal migration, although there is some overlap. What are termed "real and reasonably perceived threats" should also be distinguished from extreme xenophobia. In some instances, regional policies have to be taken into account as neighboring countries are often largely both the source of migration to the receiving country as well as a potential part of the attempt to find a solution. Similarly, international conventions and human rights charters in national constitutions may limit the freedom of action of governments as far as aspects of migration and especially refugee flows are concerned, although these conventions have often been ignored (UNHCR, 1993, p. 163; Naldi, 1992, p. 102; see also Adelman and Sorenson, 1994).

Five broad categories of situations in which migrants or refugees may be perceived as a threat have been identified. These threats could exist as far as the sending or receiving country is concerned, or in as far as it affects relations between sending and receiving countries.

The first potential threat arises when refugees and immigrants pose a threat to their home regime. This may occur with or without support from the receiving country. The United States, for instance, armed Cuban refugees in an attempt to overthrow Castro. Numerous other examples exist. Migrants (legal or illegal) may similarly be hostile to the regime of the country from which they have fled. Overseas Chinese, for instance, supported dissidents in China after the repression of the demonstrations in Tiananmen Square in 1989 (Weiner, 1995, pp. 136-138).

Opposition to their home regime by refugees and immigrants may strain relations between countries as the host country may be held responsible for the activities of the refugees and migrants, even if the activities are lawful. For instance, Iran has been accused of using agents to assassinate Iranian dissidents living abroad. Of course, if a host country has gone as far as arming refugees against their home country, the situation is aggravated. The Pakistani government's arming of Afghan refugees is a case in point here (Weiner, 1995, p. 137; US, 1997, p. 23).

A second type of threat arises when migrants and refugees form a direct risk to the host country. This could include involvement in crime, the launching of terrorist attacks, forming an alliance with domestic opposition, participating in arms and drug trafficking, and becoming involved in conflict with nationals of the host country as a result of being viewed as undesirable, for reasons of, for instance, being viewed as unfair competition in the labor market (Weiner, 1995, p. 139).

Third, migrants and refugees can also be perceived as a threat to cultural identity and lead to the rise of anti-migrant political parties that could threaten the government in power or result in attacks on foreigners. In Germany, for instance, right-wing attacks on foreigners increased to 790 in 1997, the highest in three years (*Beeld*, Johannesburg, 8 May 1998).

Fourth, migrants and refugees may also cause a reaction in a particular society because of the economic costs they impose or because of negative social behavior associated with their presence, such as criminality or welfare dependency. In less developed countries, refugees have come to be seen as a security and ecological threat (this was the case in the former Zaire and Tanzania, with the latter eventually closing its borders to refugees, and Kenya is currently ordering refugees to hand over illegal weapons). The definition of a refugee according to the Organization of African Unity (OAU) is broader than that of the United Nations: it provides for individuals fleeing violence or war and not only from persecution. Given the continuing civil war in many African countries, this has swelled the refugee population (Naldi, 1992, p. 102; *The Star*, Johannesburg, 27 December 1996; *Business Day*, Johannesburg, 24 June 1998).

In this regard, Weiner writes:

"Migrants and refugees often have a disproportionate impact on particular regions of the receiving country. Wherever migrants, refugees, and illegals are concentrated, the infrastructure costs for the community, with respect to schools, public transportation and health services are often high" (Weiner, 1995, p. 142).

There are of course those that argue that even illegal aliens often contribute to the economy of the receiving state as they are prepared to do jobs that the local population will not undertake. On the other hand, they do not normally pay income tax.

Fifth, immigrants may also be used as hostages by the receiving country. The Iraqi government, for instance, indicated its willingness to treat migrants of countries that did not send troops to Saudi Arabia during the Gulf War (such as India), more favorably than countries that did. There have also been reports of Libyan threats to expel migrants of governments voting for the UN Security Council resolution involving sanctions against Libya over the Pan Am incident (Weiner, 1995, p. 145). Germany recently announced that it would consider terminating all aid to countries who are not prepared to accept back those of their citizens who are being expelled by Germany. At present, this involves some 270,000 foreigners from countries such as Ghana, Nigeria, Togo, Gambia, Sudan, Pakistan, and Vietnam (*Beeld*, Johannesburg, 13 May 1998).

Whether migrants and refugees are seen as a security threat is partially shaped by the perceptions of the receiving country. For example, is there a deliberate attempt at "population dumping" by the sending country? Genuine conflicts of interest among countries regarding migrants and refugees do exist and governments have often had to adopt coercive measures, and even force, to stop population flows from another country. These measures may include cooperation with the sending country, for example, assisting in developing the economy of the neighboring country to reduce the flow of illegal (economic) migrants.

The issue of illegal aliens has been addressed by the UN General Assembly. It adopted, on 20 December 1993, a resolution on the *Prevention of the Smuggling of Aliens*, requesting, *inter alia*, states that have not done so to take the necessary measures to prevent their airports, means of ground transportation, and air carriers from being used by smugglers of aliens, and to increase efforts to prevent the smuggling of aliens on ships (UN, 1993).

The South African situation

The extent of the illegal alien population and the refugee population in South Africa, and a selection of official statements regarding migration and security, especially as far as illegal migrants in South Africa are concerned, will be presented, followed by other perceptions regarding the issue.

Extent of the illegal alien and refugee population in South Africa

The debate regarding illegal aliens in South Africa has, in the first instance, revolved around numbers. Official figures regarding the removal of illegal aliens from South Africa have generally speaking shown a steady increase, although this could partially be due to increased law enforcement. The statistics do not specifically indicate multiple removals (i.e., removal of the same individual on

Table 12.1: Number of immigrant removals from South Africa, 1988-1997

Year	Number of removals
1988	44,225
1989	51,550
1990	53,418
1991	61,345
1992	82,575
1993	96,600
1994	90,692
1995	157,000
1996	180,713
1997	176,351

Source: RSA. Department of Home Affairs (1998).

more than one occasion in any given year). In addition, the number of over-stayers (foreign nationals who have breached the conditions of their temporary permits by exceeding their period of legal residence in South Africa) also has to be taken into account when calculations of the number of illegal aliens in South Africa are made. This number is, however, a cumulative total for a given number of years, and the exact number of over-stayers present in South Africa is therefore impossible to determine.

It has been calculated that removals by the authorities at most involve 10 percent of the total number of illegal aliens in any given year, and in some calculations it is as low as five percent. Table 12.1 depicts removals for the period 1988 to 1997. For 1997, the highest number involved nationals from Lesotho (4,077), Mozambique (146,285), Swaziland (1,055), and Zimbabwe (21,673). This is broadly a repeat of the pattern experienced during 1996. A further 178 deportation orders (ministerial orders for removal) were executed during 1997 on foreign nationals convicted of offences specified in the *Aliens Control Act*.

Estimates of the numbers of illegal aliens present in South Africa vary widely. These estimates have varied from a few hundred thousand to eight million. A Human Sciences Research Council Survey during 1995 found that there were between 2.4 and 5.1 million non-South Africans resident in South Africa, of whom approximately 50 percent are thought to be illegals. These surveys have been criticized, for instance by the Canadian academic Jonathan

Crush, but convincing alternatives are not offered (Minnaar and Hough, 1996, pp. 126-130; *Business Day*, Johannesburg, 30 June 1997).

In his speech during the 1997 debate on the Home Affairs Appropriation Bill in Parliament, the South African Minister of Home Affairs, Mangosuthu Buthelezi, stated that the illegal alien population was estimated at between 2.5 million and 5 million (RSA, 1997a, column 1243).

The South African *Draft Green Paper on International Migration* of 1997, made no specific assessment of the total number of illegal migrants in South Africa, but merely cast doubt on some of the assessments. In the case of over-stayers, the Green Paper estimated that there were 425,000 pre-1996 long-term over-stayers still in the country with a further 233,000 short-term over-stayers. During 1997 alone, according to Minister Buthelezi, 6,420 individuals from the United Kingdom, 6,011 from Germany, 2,494 from France, 2,256 from the US, 2,068 from the Netherlands, and 1,247 from India had transgressed their temporary residence permits, to name but a few examples (RSA, 1997b, p. 29; RSA, 1998, p. 7).

The preliminary results of the 1996 population census in South Africa calculated a figure of between 500,000 and 1.5 million illegal aliens in South Africa. The Central Statistical Service was convinced that most illegal aliens had been counted in the census, which is of course a highly debatable issue (*Business Day*, Johannesburg, 4 September 1997).

Ultimately, all the parties to the debate do seem to agree on one issue and that is that the exact number of illegal aliens in South Africa (or any country for that matter) can never be accurately determined. These estimates can obviously also be deliberately deflated (as they sometimes are) or inflated to serve certain purposes. Some estimates seem to rely to a greater extent on empirical data and research while others seem to be mere guesses.

As far as refugees are concerned, by the end of 1997 there were 20,365 asylum seekers in South Africa, growing at 7,200 a year. The status of 4,000 refugees has already been approved. In addition, up to 300,000 Mozambicans who initially fled the civil war in Mozambique, were given a refugee-type status in some of South Africa's former homelands. They have not yet returned to Mozambique and may qualify to become permanent residents under a further amnesty which is being contemplated (*The Star*, Johannesburg, 9 September 1997, 22 April 1998).

There is one other dimension, in the area of legal migration, which has some implications for southern African countries, and especially for South Africa, namely the so-called "brain drain". It was estimated that up to 10 percent of top management would emigrate from South Africa during 1998. The crime rate in South Africa seems to be one of the main factors motivating people to leave the country. Immigration to South Africa is also down from 5,407 in 1996 to 4,532 in 1997 (*Sakebeeld*, Johannesburg, 15 May 1998). This has obvious implications for economic development and security.

Selected official South African perceptions

A similar debate has been waged (and continues to be waged) regarding the effect of illegal aliens on South Africa. During 1997, Buthelezi stated that with an estimated 2.5 million to 5 million illegal aliens in South Africa, severe strain is being placed on socio-economic resources. At a cost of even just R1,000 per illegal alien to South Africa's infrastructure, illegal aliens cost billions of rands per year (RSA, 1997a, column 1243).

The cost of apprehension and removal of illegal aliens has also become part of the debate and, in some views, the tracing and removal of short-term over-stayers is considered wasteful. The South African National Defence Force (SANDF) calculates that each illegal alien caught at the border costs them R4,000. The direct cost of removals and deportations (transport) from South Africa amounted to ±R6 million for the period 1 April 1997 to 6 March 1998, while the indirect cost (including manpower in all the departments involved in tracing, removal, and detention) has been calculated to be in the vicinity of R210 million per year (RSA Department of Home Affairs, private communication; Minnaar and Hough, 1996, p. 209; RSA, 1997b, p. 29).

As far as the socio-economic impact of illegal aliens is concerned, Buthelezi has also stated that the negative impact of illegal aliens on housing, education, welfare, health facilities, and the job market, need to be taken into account. The obtaining of false identity documents could even lead to illegal aliens obtaining the vote. Correlations between illegal migration and crimes such as prostitution, drug abuse, money laundering, sale of counterfeit goods, illegal movement of arms, and vehicle hijacking (destined for cross-border markets) were also increasingly evident. This pointed to the obvious link between migration and security matters (RSA, 1998, pp. 6-7).

The *Draft Green Paper on International Migration* basically supports the above view by stating that "[U]nregulated access to South Africa's labour market could lead to unacceptable competition for jobs" (RSA, 1997b, p. 16). But the document added that citizens of the Southern African Development Community (SADC) should be afforded more opportunities in the South African economy (RSA, 1997b, p. 29).

The spread of diseases such as AIDS, malaria, cholera, and tuberculosis have all been linked to the cross-border movement of illegal aliens (Minnaar and Hough, 1996, pp. 217-218). Further references to the security implications of the presence of illegal migrants in South Africa are found in a number of official documents. The *National Crime Prevention Strategy* (NCPS) document, for instance, states that the security consequences of uncontrolled migration include increased pressure on already over-stretched socio-economic infrastructure, a reduction in employment opportunities, rising xenophobia and resistance to immigrants within local communities, increased potential for inter-group conflict, and the involvement of illegal migrants in cross-border crime (RSA, 1996a, p. 33). The NCPS document continues to state that the relatively unregulated flow of people over borders and through ports of entry poses huge challenges to law enforcement (RSA, 1996a, p. 79).

The South African *White Paper on Intelligence*, states in this regard that the main threat to the well-being of individuals and the interests of nations across the world arise from challenges such as ethnic rivalry, crime, disease, and mass migration (RSA, 1993, pp. 4-5). The South African *White Paper on Defence*, contains similar references. Regarding migration, it says that there are large numbers of refugees and displaced persons in sub-Saharan Africa and that these impact negatively on neighboring states (RSA, 1996b, p. 30).

As far as the involvement of illegal aliens in crime is concerned, no extensive official database exists, although the involvement of foreigners (including illegals) in crime is regularly reported in the South African media. The *South African Police Service (SAPS) Quarterly Report* for the period January to June 1996 states that the entry of illegal migrants into South Africa has contributed to organized crime and included the smuggling of people to South Africa. Illegal migrants also tended to bring in firearms or drugs to obtain "seed money" to enable them to settle in the country. Illegal migrants also involve others in crime, for instance, employers knowingly or unknowingly hiring them. Local officials are also involved in acts of corruption as a result of the fraudulent issuing of identity documents (SAPS, 1996, pp. 67-68).

The link between cross-border crime and the illegal movement of people is also evident in an official South African National Defence Force (SANDF) report on the illegal movement of people from Lesotho to South Africa. In the report it is indicated that large quantities of narcotics, especially marijuana, are transported from Lesotho to South Africa via clandestine routes. The Lesotho citizens are in most cases armed to protect the contraband from being hijacked or seized by South African security forces (*Salut*, Vol. 5, No. 5, May 1998, p. 41). Allegations of hired Mozambican assassins involved in the taxi violence in South Africa, have also been made (*Weekly Mail and Guardian*, Johannesburg, 29 May 1998). Although these examples do not necessarily illustrate long-term illegal residence in South Africa, it is part of the problem of illegal movement.

In the 1994 annual police report it was reported that 12,670 illegal aliens had been arrested in connection with their involvement in cases of serious crime. Illegal migrants have also been one of the factors linked to the current wave of violent attacks on farmers in South Africa. In certain cases, illegal migrants have threatened armed resistance should there be attempts to arrest them (Visser, 1998, p. 4; SAPF, 1994, p. 24; Reitzes, *et al.*, p. 2). Between January 1997 and March 1998, for example, a total of 117 Nigerian nationals were arrested in Hillbrow, Johannesburg, for drug dealing. Amongst these were refugees and illegal aliens (*The Star*, Johannesburg, 23 April 1998). The above reference to 12,670 illegal aliens being arrested seems to be incorrect, and probably refers to the total number of foreigners (including illegal aliens) arrested for crimes.

Some official views reflect different opinions. During the 1997 Home Affairs Budget vote in parliament, an African National Congress (ANC) member stated said:

"... so I would like to plead with our people. Let us stop calling people from other states in the land of our forefathers amakwere-kwere and amakwiri-kwiri. They have not come to grab our wealth. Most of them work for themselves. Even now one can see them selling in Adderley Street. They sell radios; they do not bother anybody. So why should we label them a nuisance? What problems are they giving us?" (RSA, 1997a, column 1282).

Some public perceptions

Among the responses to the *Green Paper*, the view was postulated that illegal aliens were not depriving South Africans of jobs as they were doing jobs that South Africans did not aspire to do. Given this, it was argued, the presence of (illegal) aliens is of benefit to certain sectors of the economy (RSA, 1997c; addendum 37); CDE, 1997, pp. 3-4). However, a number of violent attacks have occurred on illegal aliens and refugees (a distinction is often not made in these cases) by local hawkers in South Africa who view the foreigners as unfair competition (Minnaar and Hough, 1996, p. 186-188; *The Star*, Johannesburg, 24 April 1998).

In a public opinion survey conducted during 1996, the following emerged regarding attitudes toward illegal migrants in South Africa (see Figure 12.1). In the case of each racial group in South Africa, the majority viewed illegal migrants as a negative phenomenon. A distinction is sometimes made between nationals of member states of the Southern African Development Community (SADC) and nationals of other countries, with the former being viewed more

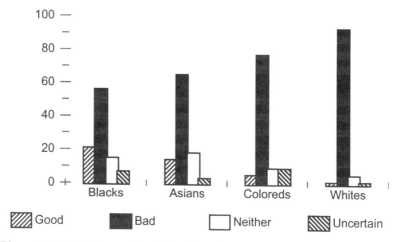

Figure 12.1: Opinion poll on illegal immigrants

sympathetically (Schutte, 1997, p. 6). This aspect will be discussed in the next section.

Refugees and illegals as a threat to their country of origin

Reference can be made here to certain members of the security forces of the late Mobuto, of the former Zaire, who had fled to South Africa after Mobuto's overthrow. While their legal status in South Africa was uncertain (they aimed to lodge a claim for refugee status), South Africa refused to extradite them despite allegations that they were conspiring to overthrow the Kabila government (*Mail and Guardian*, Durban, 20 March 1998).

South African measures to counter illegal migration

The South African *Draft Green Paper on Migration* of 1997, previously referred to, will culminate in a *White Paper on Migration* which will form the basis for any new immigration policy or legislation or amendments to the current *Aliens Control Act*. Specific legislation regarding refugees is also envisaged, and South Africa has signed both the UN and the OAU *Conventions on Refugees*. Although the *Green Paper* calls for "rights-based enforcement" regarding South African migration policy — making a clear distinction regarding the difference between illegals and refugees; and that SADC citizens, specifically, should have freer access to South Africa than others — it is in agreement with continued government action, especially with respect to long-term over-stayers. In terms of strengthening government capacity to deal with illegal migration, the *Green Paper* recommended the following (RSA, 1997b, pp. 29-30):

▸ despite the fact that employer sanctions are a viable policy option for government to reduce employment incentives for illegal migration, the Department of Home Affairs does not have the staffing capacity to enforce employer sanctions properly;
▸ although new passports and visas are more difficult to forge than old passports, some of the latter are still in circulation. Attention should therefore be paid to forgery practices, and the capacity of border officials to recognize forged documents should be strengthened;
▸ priority should be given to the strengthening of border control posts and the creation of new ones to counteract smuggling. The Department of Home Affairs and Customs and Excise should be adequately staffed and trained to execute border-post control functions properly; and
▸ South Africa's long land borders facilitate illegal entry, as it is not possible to provide effective surveillance of all the borders. However, typical crossing routes could be monitored. The SANDF estimates that one person crosses the border illegally every ten minutes, amounting to an annual influx of 50,000. However, illegal migrants from neighboring countries are engaged in a continuous pattern of oscillating movement between South Africa and their countries of origin.

In this regard, Minister Buthelezi stated in Parliament:

"When I appeal to the various service departments such as Welfare, Education, Housing and other departments, as well as the provincial governments, to request presentation of identity documents for certain services that are applied for, it is to ensure that services are focused on our own people or on those who have been granted permanent residence, and thereby to implement the will of Cabinet, indeed of Government, not that of Buthelezi" (RSA, 1997a, column 1244).

Recently, Buthelezi also stated that the South African government would deal ruthlessly with people who harbored and employed illegal aliens. He stated that a total of 195 employers had been found guilty during 1997 in this regard (*The Star*, Johannesburg, 15 May 1998). Two amnesties for certain categories of migrant workers and illegal aliens from SADC countries have also already been granted by the South African government. Obviously, it is also hoped that in the longer-run, economic development of neighboring countries would to some extent diminish the flow of illegal migrants to South Africa.

In the interim, the problem continues. A report by the US Department of State released at the beginning of 1998, indicated that an under-staffed and badly trained police force and a leaky border contributed to South Africa becoming a paradise for those involved in the drug trade (*Beeld*, Johannesburg, 2 March 1998). The same factors play a role in facilitating the illegal movement of people into South Africa. The SANDF is increasingly involved in border protection which is currently still primarily a police responsibility with assistance from the military to the police, but budget cuts severely constrain the capabilities of the military.

The southern African situation

All of the countries in southern Africa experience illegal migration to a greater or lesser extent. South Africa, Botswana, and Namibia tend to be the main receiving countries although there are illegal aliens and refugees in all southern African countries. Angola recently expelled 1,000 foreign citizens, most of them from the Democratic Republic of Congo, for illegal diamond dealing (*Africa Research Bulletin*, Vol. 35, No. 2, 20 March 1998), p. 12996). Namibia expelled a total of 1,970 illegal aliens in the 1997/98 financial year. In Zambia, the cross-border trade in stolen cars is largely blamed on foreign nationals living in Zambia, and the Tanzanian government recently expelled illegal aliens from several African and Asian countries to check increasing Islamic fundamentalism (*Beeld*, Johannesburg, 17 April 1998; *Business Daily*, Johannesburg, 23 February and 24 March 1998). The Director of Immigration in Namibia, Patrick Nanda go, stated that pressure was being placed on health, police, and other services in Namibia by illegal aliens. Statistics also showed that one out of two people involved in crime there were foreigners (*Die Republikein*, Windhoek, 13 January 1997).

Some debate has developed regarding the issue of freedom of movement of persons within the SADC. Drafts and counter-drafts of a proposed protocol have been circulated, with the current versions seemingly more restrictive than the initial SADC version which envisaged a Schengen-type of agreement (SADC, 1995).[1] In the South African parliament the proposed *Protocol on the Free Movement of Persons in the SADC* was addressed at some length by Rev K.R. Meshoe of the African Christian Democratic party (ACDP). In his view, abolishing controls on movement of people within the SADC region would be especially detrimental to health and economic conditions in South Africa. The ACDP rejected attempts to "obliterate national and geographic distinctions" on the African continent (RSA, 1996c, columns 2139-2140).

The Head of the Botswana Defence Force, Lt. Gen. Ian Khama, also stated that he did not support SADC initiatives regarding free movement of people, as South Africa and Botswana with their notable economic advantages above other countries, could be flooded (*Die Burger*, Cape Town, 10 April 1996). During the 1997 parliamentary debate on the Home Affairs Appropriation Bill, Minister Buthelezi responded to the issue by stating that although there were South African initiatives regarding the facilitation of the legal movement of persons between countries, free movement in the SADC countries, similar to that provided for in Europe in terms of the *Schengen* agreement, was not acceptable (RSA, 1997a, columns 1319-1320).

The *Draft Green Paper on International Migration* endorsed this view (RSA, 1997b, p. 15). The debate regarding freedom of movement for SADC nationals is to some extent accompanied by pressures from certain neighboring countries on South Africa specifically. The Zimbabwean Deputy Minister of Industry has appealed to South Africa to halt mass expulsions of Zimbabweans living in South Africa illegally (*Pretoria News*, Pretoria, 11 October 1994; *Sunday Tribune*, Durban, 16 October 1994). During an official visit to South Africa, President Chissano of Mozambique stated that xenophobic attitudes toward illegals should be discouraged. "Our citizens know no boundaries. They regard themselves as an integral part of each of our countries. Therefore they do not feel like aliens" (*Business Day*, Johannesburg, 2 March 1995). In addition, there are allegations of police corruption in Mozambique, involving the taking of bribes to assist Mozambicans illegally entering South Africa (AIM, *Mozambique File*, March 1995, p. 17).

The current version of the proposed *SADC Protocol* is aimed at facilitation rather than freedom of movement but certain pressures for a more extensive version will continue, also in view of the freedom of movement of people and goods envisaged with the phasing in of the continental concept of an African Economic Community by the year 2025.

While freedom of movement in southern Africa will require increased security cooperation among the countries concerned, one of the major problems will be the security of external borders. Even as far as internal borders are concerned, for instance in the countries involved in the *Schengen* agreement, reservations have been expressed about the flow of drugs from the Netherlands into, for example, France.

Multilateral security cooperation in southern Africa does currently provide, for instance, for improved border control in SADC countries but this is aimed at the smuggling of illegal and stolen goods. However, during recent discussions between South Africa, Swaziland, and Mozambique regarding the upgrading of border facilities and the opening of new border posts, delegates stated that they recognized the importance of security, particularly in the area of immigration (*Business Day*, Johannesburg, 2 April 1998).

Conclusion

In view of the broadening of the concept of national security, especially in developing countries, and given that adequate international examples exist where migration has been linked to security implications, it is clear that a security paradigm can be utilized to assess the impact of migration (and especially of illegal migrants and refugees) on both sending and receiving countries, but primarily on the latter. This is of specific importance in the case of developing countries where external (transnational) threats exacerbate existing internal threats to security.

In the case of South and southern Africa, there seem to be clear security implications linked specifically to illegal migration. Of course not all of them are on the level of national security threats. Crime, competition for scarce jobs, and some political violence seem to be the most pertinent issues in this regard. Free movement of SADC nationals, although it remains an objective of the SADC in terms of the *SADC Treaty*, is opposed, especially in its more extensive version, by those who argue that this will create even greater security threats. There is even concern, especially in South Africa, about the increasing flow of refugees who pass through "safe countries" of first asylum, *en route* to South Africa. Among the refugees are illegal aliens fraudulently claiming refugee status so that the two issues are not totally separable.

Note

1. The *Schengen* agreement entered into force on 26 March 1995 and provides for the gradual abolition of controls at the common borders of Belgium, Luxembourg, the Netherlands, Germany, France, Italy, Spain, Portugal, and Greece.

References

Adelman, H.L. and J. Sorenson (eds.) (1994). *African Refugees: Development Aid and Repatriation*. Boulder, CO: Westview Press.

Buzan, B. (1991). *People, States and Fear*. 2nd edition. New York: Harvester Wheatsheaf.

CDE, The Centre for Development and Enterprise (1997). *Response to the Green Paper on International Migration* (June).

Imobighe, T. (1993). "Security in Sub-Saharan Africa," in J. Singh and T. Bernauer (eds.), *Security of Third World countries*. Geneva: UNIDIR.

Job, J.L. (1992). "Introduction", pp. 17-18 in J.L. Job (ed.), *The Insecurity Dilemma: National Security and Third World States*. Boulder, CO: Lynne Rienner.

Minnaar, A. and M. Hough (eds.) (1996). *Who Goes There? Perspectives on Clandestine Migration and Illegal Aliens in Southern Africa*. Pretoria: HSRC Publishers.

Naldi, G.J. (ed.) (1992). *Documents of the Organization of African Unity*. London: Mansell Publishing.

Reitzes, M., et. al. (1996). *The Political, Economic and Social Impact of Immigrants in South Africa*. Centre for Policy Studies (October).

RSA (1993). *White Paper on Intelligence*.

RSA (1996a). *National Crime Prevention Strategy* (May).

RSA (1996b). *White Paper on Defence* (May).

RSA (1996c). *Debates of the National Assembly*. (3-7 June).

RSA (1997a). *Debates of the National Assembly*. (15-18 April).

RSA (1997b). *Draft Green Paper on International Migration*. Government Gazette, Vol. 383, No. 18033 (30 May).

RSA (1997c). *Executive summary of comments submitted to the Draft Green Paper on International Migration*. Pretoria: Department of Home Affairs (September).

RSA (1998). *Media Briefing by Minister M G Buthelezi*. Minister of Home Affairs. (12 February).

SADC (1995). *Draft Protocol on the Free Movement of Persons in the Southern African Development Community (SADC)*. Gaberone: SADC (June).

SAPS (1994). *A Broad Perspective on the Incidence of Crime*.

SAPS (1996). *The Incidence of Serious Crime January to July 1996*, Quarterly Report 2/96. Crime Information Management Centre, SA Police Service.

Schultz, R.H., et. al. (eds.), (1997). *Security Studies for the 21ˢᵗ Century*. London: Brassey's.

Schutte, C., *et. al.* (1997). "Public Attitudes Regarding Undocumented Migration and Policing/Crime." *African Security Review.* Vol. 6, No. 4.

United Nations (1993). General Assembly, *A/Res 48/102* (December).

United Nations High Commissioner for Refugees (UNHCR) (1993). *The State of the World's Refugees 1993.* New York: Penguin Books.

US (1995). *A National Security Strategy of Engagement and Enlargement.* Washington, DC: The White House (February).

US (1997). *Patterns of Global Terrorism, 1996.* Washington, DC: US Department of State (April).

Weiner, M. (1993). "Security, Stability and International Migration", pp. 3-4 in M. Weiner (ed.), *International Migration and Security.* Boulder, CO: Westview Press.

Weiner, M. (1995). *The Global Migration Crisis: Challenges to States and to Human Rights.* New York: Harper Collins.

Visser, J.M.J. (1998). "Violent Attacks on Farmers in South Africa". *ISSUP Bulletin* (3/98).

13 South Africa and southern Africa: toward the institutionalization of regional security

Denis Venter

Introduction

Major structural change in global society, brought about by the end of the cold war, provides a compelling reason to rethink the concept of security — now proven to have been ambiguous at best. In the past, security has often been defined in terms of a reaction to threats to the state, or to national (meaning state) interests (Du Pisani, 1992, p. 5). The conventional military definition of security ossifies it in geopolitical terms as "the spatial exclusion of threats" (Dalby, 1992, p. 98). In such circumstances, state or national security become mere code words for safeguarding a political regime and its social elite.

Traditionally security has, almost exclusively, involved military issues and threats to the state. But today, in the developing world, the notion of collective security in the form of traditional inter-state alliances at the regional, continental and international level, is more complex than it may seem (Gonçalves, 1995, p. 6; Ching'ambo, 1992, pp. 33-36; Breytenbach, 1994, pp. 26-37): it rarely offers peace and security, because it is very often non-military internal and regional factors that are of decisive importance, whether of a political, economic, social or environmental nature (Honwana, 1997, p. 58). It follows, therefore, that:

> "... national security and stability (a key element in regional security) ... largely rests on the ability of individual states to meet ... [the] economic and social needs [of their peoples], observe human rights, and afford all their citizens the opportunity to participate in ... political decision-making process[es]" (Gonçalves, 1995, pp. 7-8).

It is true to say that, for many people, security is threatened more often by the very government under whose sovereignty they live, either through oppressive policies or its incapacity to sustain a good life for all — or, put differently, to provide for the basic needs of the populace (Booth, 1993, pp. 4, 6). Governments, then, are not the sole agents of security; and this is all the more true if a broad or holistic view of security is adopted. The horizontal expansion of security (or broadening the security agenda) to include political, economic, societal, and environmental aspects *with* the military is to accept that human security is ultimately more important than the security of the state (Buzan, 1991, pp. 26-28). Individual security, however, raises a wider set of issues, including threats to human security such as poverty, malnutrition, illiteracy, unemployment, environmental degradation, and the abuse of human rights (Honwana, 1997, p. 58). Therefore, quoting Gowher Rizwi, it is clear that:

"... security no longer ... [can] be considered exclusively within the military sphere; it is concerned not only with safeguarding territorial integrity, but also with political, economic and social welfare, and above all, inter-communal harmony" (Vale, 1993, p. 33).

And a former US Secretary of Defense, Robert McNamara (1968), reminded us that:

"Security means development. Security is not military hardware, though it may include it; security is not military force, though it may involve it; security is not traditional military activity, though it may encompass it. Security is development and without development there can be no security."

This "new thinking" on security sets an agenda for radical change, and goes beyond achieving merely an absence of war to encompass the pursuit of democracy, sustainable economic development, social justice, and protection of the environment. Although military force remains a legitimate means of defense against external aggression, it is not an acceptable instrument for conducting foreign policy and for the settling of disputes. States should, therefore, mitigate the security dilemma and promote regional stability by adopting a defensive military doctrine and posture (Nathan, 1996, p. 4).

This chapter looks primarily at attempts to institutionalize regional security (including South Africa's role in the sub-continent) now that the debilitating factors of domestic insecurity (apartheid) and regional destabilization have disappeared from the scene. Security is approached from an holistic, human angle and from, essentially, a South African perspective of the southern African region.

South Africa's view of regional security encourages the development of a common security approach in southern Africa through the Southern African Development Community (SADC), acknowledges that many of the states in the region share the same domestic threats with spill-over potential into neighboring countries, and recognizes the possibility that inter-state disputes might arise over a broad spectrum of issues.

The southern African region: setting the scene

Current transitions to democracy in southern Africa are fraught with uncertainty. In fact:

> "Prevailing transitions ... make predictions difficult; the past is dying without giving rise to a manageable present or a predictable future" (Khadiagala, 1994, p. 167).

In Angola, the cease-fire agreement was thrown into turmoil when the *Uniao Nacional para a Independência Total de Angola* (Unita) rejected the results of the 1992 elections; despite numerous peace efforts, the country is sliding back into civil war. Similarly, the Democratic Republic of Congo (DRC) is slowly sinking into the quagmire of domestic turmoil and ungovernability. The government of Lesotho was subjected to the so-called "King's coup" in 1994, the legacy of which has been manifested in mutinous behavior by the police and military forces and generally poor civil-military relations, culminating in renewed instability in 1998. The negotiated settlements in Mozambique and South Africa are threatened by on-going political and criminal violence. Moreover, the fledgling multi-party system in Malawi, and the sustainability of democracy in that country, has come under serious pressure from a rather sluggish economy; and in Zambia and Zimbabwe, political manipulation by the Movement for Multiparty Democracy (MMD) and the Zimbabwe African National Union-Patriotic Front (ZANU-PF) governments have put serious question marks against long-run prospects for democracy in those countries. Swaziland is still frozen in time on the political dead-end road of a no-party, feudal monarchy. The common thread running through these hiccups is a latent conflict potential which might suddenly erupt and spill over into neighboring countries, with disastrous consequences for the region's security and stability. Obviously, this is an unsatisfactory state of affairs; southern Africa cannot hope to escape from its current economic malaise where there is no democracy. After all, a functional relationship exists between good governance, foreign investment, and economic growth.

The 1990s has witnessed southern Africa's most severe drought in 80 years, threatening several million people with starvation, continuing instability in Angola, the DRC, and Lesotho, and human massacres of unimaginable proportions in Rwanda and Burundi. Here the bases for democratic government, and in some instances even for any kind of government at all, seem to have been so thoroughly undermined that these countries are facing an uncertain and dismal future. These problems are exacerbated by the growing marginalization of southern Africa (and, indeed, Africa as a whole) in international politics and the world economy. The sub-continent, let alone the rest of sub-Saharan Africa, has never presented an attractive opportunity for foreign investment, and the ending of the cold war has greatly diminished what little strategic value it once had. This situation has been compounded, too, by the emergence of giant trading blocs in North America, Europe, and the Pacific Rim with which it cannot compete.

This state of affairs leads to some pertinent questions: can southern Africa be considered a security community, a group of states where some form of peace is predictable? Is there any possibility that the region will develop in such a way that war and the threat of war will be rejected as legitimate or possible instruments of political power? However distant it may seem, is there at least the prospect of common security developing in southern Africa: the sort of common consciousness which involves the belief that security has to be achieved with others, not against them? Common security[1] does not ignore the fact that international relations are characterized by competing national interests and the risk of hostilities. It seeks to minimize those risks by creating an environment in which disputes can be prevented through early-warning mechanisms or be resolved without resort to force; and it recognizes the interdependence of states by engaging in joint problem-solving, by developing collaborative programs on security issues, and by utilizing the potential for political and military cooperation: building military confidence and stability through arms reduction and transparency on defense matters, and negotiating multilateral security agreements (Nathan, 1996, p. 5).

The acid test of a security community is whether or not the units target each other in a military sense. To what extent does southern Africa meet these criteria? In the past, because of the offensive strategy employed by South African forces through destabilization of the region, the criteria were clearly not met. What will South Africa's strategy be in the years to come? As it drops offensive for defensive doctrines, could the region become an anomaly to Deutsch's (1957) theory — that is, as we move further into the post-apartheid era, will the sub-continent's separate units (while refraining from targeting each other) still not score highly in terms of value compatibility, economic ties, level of transnational links, institution-building, responsiveness, and mutual predictability in behavior? Although the countries of the region may not, in future, pose any military threat to their neighbors, they do face an enormous range of regional problems. Is southern Africa, therefore, not a security community but rather a community of insecurity?

But, is what is known as the security dilemma relevant to the southern African context? Apparently not (Jackson, 1992). The level of external security is relatively high because of geographical remoteness from the center of world affairs, the indifference of outside powers, and the general powerlessness of states within the region; provided, that is, that there is a clear reduction in the South African threat to the sub-region as a result of Pretoria's post-apartheid foreign policy. In terms of international politics, the states of the southern African region are relatively secure legal entities, with no significant security pressures. Internally, however, the situation has been much less satisfactory. As Khadiagala (1996, p. 6) states:

"... the African state ... [is] becoming increasingly divisible internally, overwhelmed by the centrifugal forces of ethnicity, regionalism, and competing claims for authority. Civil wars, decaying economies, and political instability ... [are] just some of the monuments to the unpreparedness of most African states to issue legitimate power and authority across geographic reaches."

Sovereignty is, therefore, threatened more from within than from without: there have been instances of significant domestic instability brought about by catastrophic ethnic massacres in Rwanda and Burundi; a state of growing anarchy in the DRC; suppression of human rights and the basic principles of democracy by the governments of Zambia and Zimbabwe; continuing scars of decades of protracted civil war in Angola and Mozambique; a clearly undemocratic no-party system in Swaziland (where trades union-inspired civil disobedience is putting the feudal Swazi monarchy under pressure); seemingly endemic local political violence in the KwaZulu Natal Province of South Africa; and factional clashes in the Lesotho armed forces, compounded by election-rigging by the governing Lesotho Congress for Democracy (LCD) party, threatening an as yet fragile democratic rebirth.

If the southern African region is relatively free of external security pressures, the implications for security policy are enormous, meaning that priority has to be given to the domestic sources of instability. Security policy must be both more multi-leveled and more multi-faceted: in other words, it must deal not primarily with states or with issues of military strategy but with a whole range of threats to a nation's well-being. It follows, then, that traditional security regimes, designed to mitigate security dilemmas, will not be as relevant to the future of southern Africa as some might think (Venter, 1996, pp. 170-171). One is inclined to agree with Khadiagala (1994, p. 177) that the region needs limited, manageable, and focused instruments for conflict resolution, rather than the comprehensive ones found in Europe. In the post-apartheid era, existing practice and *ad hoc*, flexible arrangements for problem solving already facilitate cooperation in arms control, on mass migration and refugee problems, on HIV-AIDS, and on joint action to deal with natural disasters. The experience of the frontline states and the Southern African Development Coordination Conference (SADCC) is how minimum coordination in issue areas can be fruitfully pursued within the realistic context of competing national agendas. As they also pre-empt the cost and conflict associated with comprehensive security schemes, such limited arrangements can provide the means for regular consultations over specific issues.

To institutionalize a security regime in the southern African region, several conditions (Du Pisani, 1992, p. 11) will have to be met, including (a) a strengthening and sustaining of both national and intra-regional civil society; (b) a conceiving of peace and security as social and relational phenomena, transcending the jurisdiction of individual states: this, in turn, calls for a rethinking of the concept of sovereignty;[2] (c) the developing of institutional and analytical capacities within state and other bureaucracies; (d) an expanding and improving transport infrastructure and other physical communications networks; and (e) the molding of a regional identity at both the institutional and symbolic levels. But all these measures will have little meaning (and, indeed, social peace will be impossible) without appropriate programs for poverty alleviation, migration control, basic food security, primary health care, gender equity, human resource development, and participatory democracy based on public accountability; and the stimulation of economic activity and trade-financing facilities (Green, 1996, p. 7; Du Pisani, 1993, pp. 67-68).

The southern African region will be secure only if three broad conditions are met: intra-state stability and social harmony; inter-state cooperation and solidarity; and the absence of any extra-regional threat (Honwana, 1997, p. 58). If the best route to security is ultimately through community-building, then it might be considered that cheaper transportation, efficient telecommunications systems, increased cultural exchanges, and so on, should enjoy priority on the broadened security agenda of governments in the region. This argument will sound strange to those for whom security equals defense equals military might. But it is another way of thinking about minimizing the dangers of insecurity

(Booth, 1993, pp. 16-17). Regional security must therefore be conceptualized in terms of coordination at the diplomatic level, joint mechanisms for the prevention and combat of crime, and exchange of security intelligence and information (not only on criminal matters such as drug trafficking, but also on such potentially explosive issues as uncontrolled or illegal immigration), in an attempt to eliminate the root causes of conflict at the earliest possible moment.

In summary, it should be emphasized that regional security largely rests on the ability of individual countries to improve social and economic conditions for their peoples, their observance and promotion of human rights, and their affording equal opportunity to all ethnic and other interest groups to participate in the processes of political and economic decision-making.

Security regionalism: institutionalizing peace and security

Traditionally, regionalism implies cooperation among states in geographically proximate and delimited areas for the pursuit of mutual gain in one or more issue areas (Alagappa, 1995, p. 362). In most of the successful examples of regionalism, states that are already partners to solid political processes (based on shared and complementary values) devolve collective decisions to structures that supplement rather than supplant national institutions (Khadiagala, 1996, p. 7). It is, therefore, no coincidence:

"... that the most elaborate examples of regionalism ... have occurred in regions where state structures remain relatively strong and where the legitimacy of both frontiers and regimes is not widely called into question .... Whilst regionalism may over time lead to the creation of new political organizations, regionalism and state strength do not stand in opposition to each other, and states remain the essential building-blocks with which regionalist arrangements are constructed" (Hurrell, 1995, p. 254).

If the goal of security in southern Africa is to mitigate threats in the domestic sphere, the least that could be expected of institution-building in an era of state collapse all over Africa would be a security regionalism aimed at problems left unsolved by existing continental institutions. Security regionalism acknowledges that the political infrastructures for cooperation are still in their elementary stages. And as states deal with the outcomes of failed nationhood and are increasingly consumed by primary conflicts of an internal nature, arrangements for security regionalism need to be modest measures for the prevention and containment of certain conflicts rather than the construction of elaborate institutional mechanisms. The focus needs to be on looser structures of cooperation, ones which can stabilize relations, prevent the spill-over of conflicts, secure emerging common values and, perhaps, lay the foundation for nascent security regimes.

While states in southern Africa should remain the central agents of security in their domestic settings, they should be in a position to "sub-contract" certain functions to regional institutions when they run into difficulties. Security regionalism, therefore, flows from a desire to arrest some of the outcomes of state collapse. This sub-contracting of security functions is already happening by default as weak states and their domestic opponents appeal to diverse sources for external help (Khadiagala, 1996, pp. 7-8). The participation of Executive Outcomes in the civil war in Angola, and the coup-making of the renegade mercenary forces of Bob Denard in the Comores, serve as reminders. Instead of leaving an opening for bodies like Executive Outcomes, contiguous states should take on the responsibility for separating, isolating, and conciliating domestic combatants.

South Africa and southern Africa

The leadership role in security regionalism points to hegemons assuming the roles of sub-contractors on behalf of their weaker neighbors. All regionalisms thrive on strong leadership supported by political and economic resources; and this feature is even more pertinent in the security realm. At times, leadership might also serve to mobilize external actors willing to lend much-needed support. Since southern Africa is still prone to conflict, leadership as hegemony could best find application in the containment of a conflict within this regional sub-system (Khadiagala, 1996, p. 9). South Africa's debut on the stage of regional preventive diplomacy, its efforts to broker a peaceful resolution to the 1994 "King's coup" in Lesotho (albeit in concert with Botswana and Zimbabwe), manifests this kind of leadership, compelling a return to normality in that country by judiciously using a mix of incentives and disincentives. This case also shows that hegemony works best when it can exploit geographical vulnerability and structural weakness (Venter, 1996, p. 167). In fact, the Lesotho crisis of 1994 came at an historical moment, presenting a unique opportunity. Given the timing and the circumstances, the region's leaders responded with an *ad hoc* mechanism, low-key and informal, that has proven remarkably effective. This teaches a lesson that ought not to be lost: a lesson about flexibility, pragmatism, and the advantages of minimal institutional constraints (Garba and Herskovits, 1997, p. 27).

Aware of the concerns of its neighbors:

"... South Africa has been discreet and responsible when it came to play the role of a regional policeman. During the Lesotho crisis [of 1994], it ... opted for a total blockade to asphyxiate the insular nation, instead of the military intervention contemplated by its partners" (Gonçalves, 1995, p. 7).

Equally important, leadership conducted within regional multilateral structures (under SADC auspices, and utilizing some elements of the frontline states concept) avoids the perceptions of *diktat*, particularly by multilateral partners (like Zambia, Zimbabwe, and Swaziland) who might be future candidates for similar (or other) modes of intervention (Venter, 1996, p. 167). The biggest advantage of a sub-regional approach to conflict resolution is that neighboring states are often more familiar with each other's problems than outsiders. Countries who are neighbors usually have a fairly common culture, social identity, and history, and have had similar experiences. The disadvantage, however, is that close proximity sometimes generates tension and reduces the spirit of impartiality between neighbors — even to the extent that they may sometimes become part of the problem, rather than part of the solution (Nhara, 1998, pp. 39-40). But neighboring states cannot ignore the potential repercussions of a conflict in their territorial proximity: they are familiar with the socio-cultural dimensions of a particular country, as well as the political background and ramifications of a potential conflict, and therefore have a rationale to intervene (Nkiwane-Muzenda, 1996, p. 5). And, clearly, it may be easier to intervene in an internal conflict in a smaller and weaker country, but much more difficult to do the same when a similar conflict erupts in a larger and stronger country (Omari, 1995, p. 10; Gonçalves, 1995, p. 6).

The lesson for South Africa in the Lesotho crisis of 1994 points to another avenue in rethinking leadership and security. First, there is not another regional hegemon in southern Africa besides South Africa: at the minimum, leadership entails the possession of sufficient military power to deploy in external fire-brigade situations, a reasonably viable economy to sustain such deployment, and a political elite imbued with a sense of regional mission. Second, through sustained leadership, South Africa could nurture the already existing infrastructure in southern Africa (the SADC) for building a form of regionalism lying beyond the realm of security; for the most part, therefore, a pattern of prior interaction is conducive to regionalization. South Africa has the domestic institutional capacity needed for the kind of sustained leadership necessary to effect an enhanced form of regionalism. But without the moral stature that comes from a strong sense of nationhood and domestic legitimacy, regionalism as hegemony has the potential to degenerate into the cruder forms of power over-extension long associated with sub-regional troublemakers (Khadiagala, 1996, pp. 9-10).

South Africa's role in the abortive sanctions campaign against the Abacha regime in Nigeria, however, has implications for the future discourse on the domestic underpinnings of regional leadership. The emerging debate marks:

> "... an important, though subtle, transition from the continental norm-building of state sovereignty, to a new ... [norm] of sovereignty as domestic responsibility" (Khadiagala, 1996, p. 10).

While it is understandable that South Africa's multilateral sanctions campaign was targeted at powerful international economic actors, its failure to build a strong constituency for sanctions outside southern Africa left it exposed to "populist charges of collusion with 'imperialists'". The result was that General Sani Abacha emerged, almost by default, as the "champion of the black man"; and South Africa was accused of being used in "the division and undermining of African solidarity" (Murdock, 1995). How many atrocities, perpetrated by African regimes against their own citizens, have been wiped under the carpet or papered over by invoking this rather handy notion of "African solidarity"? (Venter, 1997, pp. 91-95). Indeed, the Mandela-Abacha stand-off showed up the limitations and whittled down the remnants of the dubious consensus on "African solutions for African problems."

The burdens of hegemony might be eroded as a regional power becomes more accountable domestically, leading perhaps to a reluctant hegemon. Thus we should not expect South Africa to play a leadership role when its taxpayers demand a reduction in what appears to them to be wasteful foreign intervention (Khadiagala, 1996, p. 11). In fact, when an elite engages its people in foreign policy debates, taxpayers (while generally against grandiose foreign interventions, such as massive airlifts of food and the deployment of soldiers in unfamiliar political terrain) are likely to support a restricted use of resources for judicious contractual security roles. In the short run, through such limited contractual security engagements, a regional leader forces its neighbors to take more responsibility for managing their own affairs; and, in the long run, they create the shared reciprocity for constructing institutionalized regionalism (Hurrell, 1995, pp. 341-344).

It has been postulated elsewhere (Martin, 1991, pp. 120-121) that the most likely scenario for future relations in the southern African region may be neo-regionalism (meaning that center-hinterland relationships will continue, though with South Africa still the overall center of gravity), as opposed to the alternatives of regional restabilization, and regional break-up and peripheralization. This scenario presupposes a negotiated regional regime which would necessitate replacing some South African goods and services by other sources from within the region (for example, Zimbabwe could become an important supplier of manufactured products) and reducing transport dependence on South Africa through the upgrading of infrastructure in Mozambique and Angola. To be meaningful, therefore, neo-regionalism would require that states transcend their national goals and interests by acting and thinking regionally (Venter, 1996, p. 169). There must be a recognition that the identification of common interests throughout southern Africa, the building of common identities, and the spreading of moral and political obligations are the only dependable paths to long-run regional security (Booth and Vale, 1995, p. 297).

Clearly, a South Africa that exhibits even minimal calm and continuity is likely to remain the dominant force and the major economic, technical, financial, and military power in the region, contributing decisively to the sub-continent's security but perpetuating the existing fears of neighboring states concerning its regional pre-eminence (Patel, 1992, p. 18; Mills and Clapham, 1991, p. 6). Although the states of the region seem to have pledged themselves to cooperation and building harmonious relations, the statistics show exactly how lop-sided the regional equation really is. Militarily, and even more, economically, South Africa is the giant not just of southern Africa but of Africa, accounting for 29 percent of Africa's gross national product (GNP) and 45 percent of sub-Saharan Africa's GNP. South Africa's GNP is nearly three times greater than that of its nearest rivals, Egypt and Algeria, and more than four-and-a-half times that of Nigeria. Furthermore, South Africa's economic dominance of southern Africa is widely known: it contributes 84 percent of the total GNP of the region; and its GNP per capita is more than double that of the average for the other 13 SADC countries combined — only Mauritius and Seychelles have a higher GNP per capita, although this is put into proper perspective when one takes into account their rather minuscule populations (Esterhuysen, 1998, pp. 39, 42-43).

But South Africa's economic dominance raises the question of the country's ambitions and, more specifically, the likelihood that it might relish its role as the regional giant and use its position to enhance its own political, diplomatic, and economic power (Patel, 1992, p. 18). By the late 1980s, "giantism" had developed into one of some ten crises in South Africa's external relations (Geldenhuys, 1989, pp. 91-92); and now, a decade later, southern Africa has indeed reached a "unipolar moment" (Krauthammer, 1992, p. 297). In many ways, this is what the region has always feared. The strong resistance to the infamous Constellation of Southern African States (Consas) idea was mainly about supping with the apartheid devil, but it was also concerned with fear of South African domination. Clearly, pre-1992 SADCC planning, which always endeavored to draw South Africa into its cooperative net rather than the other way around, was aimed precisely at attenuating this very domination (Vale, 1992, p. 11).

No good intentions, no determination to create a mutually beneficial and non-dependent regional economic cooperation system, will prevent South Africa's continuing domination of southern Africa. The frustration experienced by the small states of the sub-continent brings to mind the lament of Mexican President Porfirio Diaz: "Poor Mexico, so far from God, so near to the United States." South Africa's domination of its neighbors became even greater during its long and very damaging destabilization of the region (Venter, 1992, pp. 14-34). Should the unequal distribution of power endure, southern Africa's unipolar moment might well become a permanent feature of the sub-regional scene. Now, for a number of reasons, South Africa views the region with as much uncertainty and incredulity as its neighbors. But as all sides recall their experiences, their hopes, and their fears, any equation must surely set the sub-continent's colossus beside southern Africa's many midgets. Reluctant to share the country's comparative advantage, successive South African regimes may in future dominate the region with a carrot and stick approach (Vale, 1992, pp. 12, 16).

In both the economic and security fields, the sub-region will have to find ways to accommodate, manage, even curb South Africa's superior strength. Ultimately, the principal challenge lies in the fact that this strength needs to be creatively channeled in the interests of the region as a whole (Gutteridge, 1992, p. 128); remembering, in particular, that several states in the sub-region have suffered directly from South Africa's military might in the recent past. So, whatever the character of the South African government, its neighbors will always feel some unease about its aims unless steps are taken to mitigate, or ultimately transcend, the pressures of the security dilemma. A security regime would achieve the former, a security community the latter (Booth, 1993, pp. 25-26). With South Africa now a member of the regional fraternity, its role in the sub-continent will have to be defined by its own national interests as a "regional superpower" (Gonçalves, 1995, p. 7). But tied to continental inter-state norms, a powerful South Africa is likely to have little incentive to play an overly sub-imperial role (Khadiagala, 1994, p. 178).

Moreover, widely held expectations that South Africa will become the economic engine of southern Africa may be disappointed, partly because the post-apartheid state has to generate wealth by external economic activities in areas as far removed as western and eastern Europe, Latin America, the Pacific Rim, the Middle East, and South and Southeast Asia. Nevertheless, existing regional economic organizations and relationships seem to provide relatively favorable conditions for the empirical development of mutually advantageous cooperation. And the current progressive status of South Africa's economic relationships with the rest of Africa bodes well for cooperation in other fields. The economic dynamic puts a premium on common security arrangements, especially in the areas of tourism, trade promotion and investment, transport and communications, power generation and water supply, and knowledge-creation and exchange (Gutteridge, 1992, pp. 128-129; Green, 1996, p. 6).

But strangely, meaningful debate on novel security mechanisms has lagged behind the diversity of debate on economic and political issues (Khadiagala, 1996, p. 1). Quite often politicians and diplomats, academics and intellectuals ponder at conferences and in seminars over the issue of diplomacy coordination in conflict resolution, common defense, and security — particularly for countries sharing the same geographical space. However, just how such mechanisms are to be implemented continues to be a subject of heated debate. A formal framework for regional security may not seem as premature as it did in the early 1990s. Certain scholars (Weimer, 1990; Du Pisani,1991; Gutteridge, 1992; Nathan, 1994) have argued the need for confidence-building measures in the region; the legacy left by destabilization seems to necessitate such a strategy. The end of the cold war and the resultant disengagement from regional conflicts by the superpowers have left the way clear for local initiatives to fill the power vacuum with negotiated arrangements. Nevertheless, it should be constantly borne in mind that the future of South Africa is still very precariously balanced as it faces socio-economic problems of gigantic proportions, and that the entire sub-region is in a state of flux. It would therefore be unwise for any state to leave regional security to chance. There is the danger that, if there is too much procrastination, the opportunity to properly consider regional security and cooperation may well have passed the sub-continent by.

OAU and SADC institutions and strategies for regional security

Despite the internal and global forces that propelled democracy, accountability, and participation to the forefront of African security concerns, attempts to use continental institutions to these ends have always run into the familiar problem of the limits of continentalism over domestic policy (concretized in old-style thinking about state sovereignty). But in the 1990s, agreement developed about the lofty ideals of pluralist political systems, constitutional limitations to the tenure of elected officials, independent judiciaries and civil services, and the enshrining of individual rights to life and property (Khadiagala, 1996, p. 6). Calls to review the role of the Organization of African Unity (OAU) were made against the backdrop of increasing insecurity, instability, and economic decline in many

African countries. The realization was indeed spreading throughout the continent that Africa, with the end of the cold war, needed to respond appropriately to the new challenges facing it, especially in matters such as conflict resolution, economic development, and democratization; and, to this end, the Addis Ababa OAU Summit of July 1990 passed the "Declaration on Fundamental Changes in the World and their Implications for Africa" (Nhara, 1996, p. 1).

This "paradigm shift", in the words of Thomas Kuhn (1970), was marked by new inter- and intra-state relations in Africa and led to the creation of the Division for Conflict Prevention, Management and Resolution in the General Secretariat of the OAU in March 1992. Subsequently, a Mechanism for Conflict Prevention, Management and Resolution was established at the Cairo OAU Summit in June 1993, its main focus being, most appropriately, preventive action through early warning. This development is a bold conceptual step toward peaceful intervention in domestic conflicts (Adeniji, 1996, p. 17). However, endeavors by OAU Secretary-General Salim Ahmed Salim and the United Nations (UN) to expand the OAU's capabilities in peacekeeping operations have received only lukewarm support from the majority of African countries. A crucial issue, which mitigates against the establishment of a viable regional peacekeeping capacity, is that some of the larger countries in southern Africa are wrestling with the problem of controlling their militaries under conditions of fundamental and rapid domestic political change — conditions which are often associated with revolutionary changes in the post-cold war strategic environment (Cilliers and Malan, 1996, p. 345). At the June 1995 Addis Ababa OAU Summit on peacekeeping issues, leaders grudgingly agreed to set up peacekeeping units within existing armies for peace observation roles only, instead of the widely anticipated African intervention force for peacekeeping (Thomas, 1995, pp. 1, 4-5).

Clearly, the OAU Mechanism will have to coordinate its activities with all peacekeeping initiatives in the different sub-regions. South African Foreign Minister Alfred Nzo (1995, p. 11), outlining South Africa's foreign policy priorities to the Parliamentary Portfolio Committee on Foreign Affairs, stated that:

"... any South African involvement in the prevention or solving of conflict situations elsewhere in Africa, should take place within the framework of the OAU's Mechanism for Conflict Prevention, Management and Resolution. Only if the OAU is seen to be accepting responsibility for, and dealing effectively with, its own problems, will the Organization and [the African] continent earn the respect of outsiders."

Almost simultaneously, the SADC (which has a formal mandate from member states to promote regional cooperation in the areas of politics, defense, and security) has begun to assume regional security responsibilities with its proposal to establish forums for conflict resolution, and security and defense (SADC Windhoek Communiqué, 1994; Nathan and Honwana, 1994). However, there is as yet no evidence that the prevailing apprehension among African states toward enhanced multilateralism in security matters will change in the immediate future. Since 1993 the OAU has grappled with measures to strengthen the capacity of the Mechanism to respond more rapidly and effectively to the scourge of war and conflict. These attempts have been made in recognition of the fact that Africa has to bear the primary responsibility for taking charge of its own problems. Concurrently, a firm belief has taken root that early action would contain conflicts and prevent their deterioration to a point where the OAU would be compelled to resort to complex and resource-demanding peacekeeping operations which it would find difficult to finance. It also became apparent that the Mechanism suffered from operational limitations of an infrastructural, logistical, human resource, and financial nature and, more importantly, from lack of an early warning capability: an efficient system by which the Mechanism could be alerted in a timely way to potential disputes, could inform itself quickly on incipient conflicts, and respond speedily, pro-actively and decisively to crisis situations (OAU, 1996, pp. 1-3).

What has been foremost in the minds of African leaders was the growing conviction that they must strengthen the preventive capacity of the Mechanism by establishing an OAU Conflict Management Centre to act as the focal point of an Early Warning System Network on conflict situations in Africa. Emphasis was to be put on the anticipation (prediction, even) and prevention of conflict, and concerted action in peacemaking. Such a coordinating facility would have to be capable of gathering and analyzing information to facilitate decision-making and timely, pre-emptive political action by the relevant organs of the Mechanism. Early warning is essentially a tool for preparedness, and for the prevention and mitigation of conflict, its efficiency being predicated upon a clear methodology for data collection, analysis, and information exchange; and there should be a healthy realization that the poor state of Africa's telecommunications and other high-technology support systems poses formidable obstacles in the way of any efficient early warning capability (OAU, 1996, pp. 3-4).

In southern Africa, the SADCC was replaced in 1992 by the SADC. This new institution differs from its predecessor in three important respects: it includes the regional superpower, South Africa; its primary goal goes beyond economic coordination to higher levels of regional integration; and its mandate extends to the political, military, and security realms. The SADC Windhoek Declaration

(1992:26 & 30) expressed confidence that the independence of Namibia and the transition to democracy in South Africa was taking the southern African region out of:

"... an era of conflict and confrontation to one of co-operation, in a climate of peace, security and stability. These are prerequisites for development .... Good and strengthened political relations among the countries of the region, and peace and mutual security, are critical components of the total environment for regional co-operation and integration. The region needs, therefore, to establish a framework and mechanisms to strengthen regional solidarity, and provide for mutual peace and security."

This recognition of the interrelationship among economic growth, stability, and democracy heralds an important paradigm shift within the southern African region. Similar to developments at the level of the OAU, sovereignty is no longer a holy cow and, albeit grudgingly, governments in southern Africa now have to accept that the manner in which they conduct their internal affairs is open to legitimate scrutiny (Cilliers, 1996, p. 1). On the grounds that political and military stability are essential prerequisites for development, the SADC's objectives include the evolution of "common political values, systems and institutions". Moreover, "politics, diplomacy, international relations, peace and security" are identified as one of the seven areas of regional cooperation: the others being food security, land and agriculture; infrastructure and services; human resources development, science and technology; industry, trade, investment and finance; natural resources and the environment; and social welfare, information and culture (SADC Windhoek Treaty, 1992, art. 5.1b and c, art. 21.3g). In addition, a number of strategies for advancing regional security were proposed: (a) the adoption of a "new approach to security" emphasizing the non-military dimensions of security, including the security of people; (b) the creation of a forum for mediation and arbitration; (c) a reduction in military force levels and expenditures; (d) the introduction of confidence and security-building measures; and (e) the ratification of key principles of international law governing inter-state relations (SADC Harare Framework, 1993, pp. 24-26).

But there are many constraints on the effectiveness of regional mechanisms in southern Africa: financial resources are extremely limited and it is undesirable to be overly reliant on foreign funding; national institutions are weak and this weakness is automatically transferred to regional structures; small states fear that they may be overwhelmed or undermined by strong states in multilateral forums; a tension exists between the pursuit of national and regional interests; and states are reluctant to surrender sovereignty in the sensitive areas of security, defense, and foreign policy (Honwana, 1997, p. 65; Vale, 1996, p. 382). In the light of these constraints, the following considerations should guide the formation and operation of a regional mechanism: its programs should be cost-effective and, to the greatest extent possible, financed by member states; it should have realistic objectives and a modest agenda, which could be strengthened over time; it should endeavor also to advance the national interests of states, rather than concentrate exclusively on regional goals; and its decision-making should preferably be based on consensus (Nathan, 1996, p. 9).

As southern Africa further pursues its socio-economic and developmental agenda, misunderstandings and tensions are bound to develop over issues such as harmful trade policies; differences in environmental policies and the utilization of scarce resources, such as water; cross-border health problems affecting both humans and livestock; and divergent views on migration and immigration policies. These may easily give rise to new types of conflict in the region (Mpungwe, 1998, p. 80). In southern Africa, therefore, the security focus must be on conflict prevention through preventive diplomacy, a concept popularized by former UN Secretary-General Boutros Boutros-Ghali (1992, p. 11) who defined it as:

"... action to prevent disputes from arising between parties, to prevent existing disputes from escalating into conflicts, and to limit the spread of ... [conflicts] when they occur."

Clearly, preventive diplomacy is more cost-effective than other forms of intervention: it involves information gathering and disbursement for the purpose of early warning, the use of the "good offices" of a particular government leader or international statesman, and confidence-building measures between groups of states (Nkiwane-Muzenda, 1996, p. 4). It is at the sub-regional level that preventive diplomacy, conflict resolution, mediation, and peacekeeping "by Africans, for Africans" will come to the fore. Therefore, building on the frontline states concept and the SADC's equally long-standing sectoral approach, the SADC resolved in January 1996 to establish an Organ on Politics, Defence and Security[3] (an obvious copy of the rather strange terminology adopted by the OAU):

"... which would allow more flexibility and timely response, at the highest level, to sensitive and potentially explosive situations" (Masire-Mandela Correspondence, 1996).

This decision was ratified by the August 1996 Maseru SADC Summit, allocating the chairmanship to Zimbabwe for an initial three-year term — overlapping with South Africa's three-year term as SADC Chairman. However, Zimbabwe's seeming reluctance to fully operationalize the Organ has led to a great deal of tension — especially in the light of its earlier strong support for a strictly "sectoral" approach to security, with Harare heading the proposed security sector. The SADC's sectoral approach is, by definition, a vertical one; but the horizontal expansion of security cuts across sectors, thus making a sectoral approach to security nonsensical. Naturally, Zimbabwe is anxious to maintain the leadership role it played within the frontline states context. But allocating responsibility for overall security in the southern African region to a single country would have been problematic in the extreme because of the highly sensitive, political nature of contemporary intra-state and inter-state issues.

Unfortunately, therefore, the operationalization of the Organ turned out to be a far more heavily politicized matter than had been anticipated: influential forces are pushing and pulling in different directions. Presidents Nelson Mandela of South Africa and Robert Mugabe of Zimbabwe hold diametrically opposed views on the conceptual and institutional framework for the Organ, and these dissenting positions clashed at the Blantyre SADC Summit in August 1997. South Africa insisted that the Organ must operate fully within the overall institutional framework of the SADC, with a council of ministers of foreign affairs reporting directly to the organization's chairman. Zimbabwe sees things differently, insisting that while the Organ must operate within the overall framework of the SADC, it has to maintain a certain level of autonomy under a distinct chairman and with specific summits to operationalize its activities. This sounded a clear warning that the Organ has the potential to become a source of conflict, rather than an instrument for its prevention, management, and resolution. Since then the Mauritius SADC Summit has come and gone — and a compromise solution has yet to be found.

Clearly, the Organ should work in a flexible and informal manner and respond rapidly to incidents of regional insecurity, its inspiration being the conflict prevention achieved in August-September 1994 in Lesotho and in October 1994 in Mozambique. In the Lesotho crisis, the troika of heads of state (South Africa, Botswana, and Zimbabwe) successfully applied pressure to end the King's coup and restore Prime Minister Ntsu Mokhehle to power; in the Mozambican case, they were able to muster their number at considerable speed and firmly push mid-election Mozambique back on the road to participatory democracy (Venter, 1996, p. 173; Gonçalves, 1995, p. 7). In the business of politics, preventive diplomacy, and conflict resolution, such speed is essential (and it is to the credit of southern African leaders that this line of thinking initially prevailed and was incorporated into the procedures for an embryonic regional security regime).

An informal structure might well be in line with traditional views on state sovereignty and autonomy. Some southern African countries insist that informal arrangements are preferable to formal procedures in the conduct of inter-state relations, because "structured informality" allows for a greater degree of diplomatic flexibility. This argument is based largely on the positive experience of the frontline states, through which presidents and cabinet ministers were able to communicate quickly and easily with each other without being encumbered by excessive bureaucracy (Honwana, 1997, p. 67). Yet, while informal political arrangements may have distinct benefits, they also have a number of serious shortcomings: they may be seen as disadvantaging small states; they do not regulate inter-state behavior and the settlement of disputes in an agreed and predictable manner; they are not binding on states; and, as a result, they tend to break down in times of crisis when they are needed most (Nathan, 1996, p. 12).

Although not directly involved in conflict resolution exercises, the South African government has played the important role of endorsing agreements reached by conflicting parties, preferring preventive diplomacy and peacemaking — as in Lesotho and Mozambique in 1994 (Evans, 1995). The country shows no inclination to bully its neighbors or to interfere unduly and unilaterally in their affairs (the Lesotho intervention of 1998 being the exception), a stance which may in itself boost peace prospects in the region. This does not, however, rule out quiet diplomacy in a bid to moderate the treatment of their citizens by African governments: consider the missions to General Abacha in Nigeria by Archbishop Desmond Tutu, Deputy President Thabo Mbeki, and Foreign Minister Nzo. And, since the beginning of 1996, President Mandela engaged in an intensive series of regional consultations in an effort to mitigate emerging sources of conflict in Lesotho, Swaziland, and Zambia, to assist in finding a solution to the ongoing humanitarian tragedy in the Great Lakes region, and to mediate in, what was then, an escalating conflict in eastern Zaire (now the DRC). These initiatives were a welcome departure from the apologetic diplomacy in which the region's dominant power had previously been engaged.

Generally, however, South Africa has not played a vigorous peacekeeping role in Africa: given the limitations of armed interventions to secure peace, its stance could be seen as a sign of prudence rather than indifference. And, given the "catch 22" situation facing possible South African intervention anywhere — the danger that it will be denounced as a hegemon if it does step in, and dismissed as callous if it does not — an emphasis on preventive diplomacy may well be its only option. Indeed, South Africa's neutrality is evident in the government's call for human rights to be respected world-wide, including of course in Africa, and its willingness to provide humanitarian assistance and logistical support to peacekeeping efforts in the continent (more specifically, as a member of OAU task teams in peacemaking efforts in Rwanda and Burundi, and now also in the Comores). But the country seems to be hampered by two telling factors: first, like Japan in the post-World War II period, South Africa's destabilization of the southern African region in the 1970s and 1980s make some SADC countries less inclined to trust its intentions; and second, it had (until the September 1998 intervention in Lesotho) no experience in African peacekeeping exercises.

Other SADC member states had also been reluctant to exercise regional leadership in issues related to preventive diplomacy and conflict management. One reason for this reluctance has been that certain heads of state have themselves been facing severe criticism for authoritarianism and intolerance in their own countries and, as a consequence, have been coming under intense pressure to allow a greater degree of accountability, freedom, and democracy (compare Presidents Frederick Chiluba of Zambia and Robert Mugabe of Zimbabwe). Another reason is that the Organ is still in its infancy, although it does draw from the extensive memory of the frontline states and is able to build on the existing structure of the Inter-State Defence and Security Committee (ISDSC). But of greater importance is the fact that many SADC countries do not share, to a sufficient degree, a common consensus around the political values which are reflected in the SADC Treaty. The greatest deficiency within the grouping is the absence of integrated systems, processes, and methods to deal with human rights abuses, and the advancement of democracy and good governance. Naturally, these are contentious issues about which many SADC countries are very sensitive: Swaziland is regarded as non-democratic; Lesotho, Zambia, and Zimbabwe are accused of being undemocratic in election-related practices; Angola has slid back to renewed civil war; the DRC is in a state of anarchy, its government facing an internal rebellion; and South Africa is seen to be drifting toward one-party dominance in the absence of an effective political opposition to the African National Congress (ANC).

Apart from the SADC Summit and the ISDSC, no clear mechanism is available for the pursuit of regional objectives in the areas of foreign policy and human rights. This is particularly cogent, since the SADC has become widely accepted as a regional arrangement, as envisaged in Chapter VIII of the UN Charter. It is, therefore, essential that the SADC links its efforts to deal with conflict prevention, management, and resolution with both the OAU and the UN. But the fact that the Organ is envisaged to function only at heads of state and government level, where the roles of SADC Chairman (President Mandela) and Organ Chairman (President Mugabe) are unclear, presents the SADC with a dilemma. Confusion as to leadership roles prevent the Organ from operating in an effective and pro-active manner, relegating it to a reactive or "fire-brigade" role, and this proves to be an insurmountable barrier to addressing intra-regional (and extra-regional) conflicts which may impact on peace and security in southern Africa.

In fact, renewed civil war in Angola (Venter, 1998, pp. 109-117) will affect the entire southern African region and South Africa is extremely concerned about the worsening situation in that country. Continued violence in Angola, even if it stops short of full-scale war, will displace hundreds of thousands of Angolans and exacerbate the refugee problem in the sub-region, finally destroying the country's remaining infrastructure and causing further economic devastation. South Africa has also come under increased pressure from a number of countries to launch a new Angolan peace initiative. Although circumstances might eventually force Pretoria (in concert with other SADC member states) to participate in peacekeeping operations in Angola, sending troops to that country (especially in a mission that requires troops to enforce peace when neither party is committed to peace) should be done only in response to requests by the UN and the OAU. Destabilization of Angola in the 1970s and 1980s renders any South African military presence in that country extremely sensitive. Moreover, in considering any form of intervention it may be a sobering thought that even a much reduced UN presence in Angola ran up expenses in the region of US$11 mn per month: a sum to be borne in mind by any other international body seeking to assume a similar role. For these and other reasons, neither the SADC nor any other grouping of African countries have the capacity to enforce peace in Angola.

There have also been warnings that should the conflict situation in the DRC escalate further, and if the Angolan crisis worsens, this could lead to a regional war involving several southern, central, and eastern African countries. Indeed, the need to stabilize Angola has been given fresh urgency by the anti-Kabila rebellion in the DRC. Moreover, the threat of war is being taken seriously because of Angola's aggressive military posture over the past two years. Angolan troops assisted in toppling the Lissouba government in Congo-Brazzaville and played a key role in defeating the Mobutu Sese Seko regime in the former Zaire; and Angola threatens to do the same to Zambia if that country does not prevent Unita from re-supplying from its territory. Since the *Movimento Popular de Libertaçao de Angola* (MPLA) government in Luanda apparently fears it cannot win the war on its own, is it not perhaps hoping that the SADC's sudden policy shift toward aggressive military intervention in support of so-called "established" governments (dramatically demonstrated twice during the course of 1998, in the DRC and in Lesotho) might one day benefit it? Ominously, a recent meeting of the ISDSC declared that any threat to a member of the 14-nation community could justify intervention by its allies: an allusion to backing for the DRC by Angolan, Zimbabwean, and Namibian troops to help the Kabila regime against a Tutsi-led rebellion, and the deployment in Lesotho of soldiers from South Africa and Botswana to quell an anticipated army mutiny related to disputed general election results. This points to a move to transform the SADC, almost by stealth, into a "collective security" arrangement.

It has been stated elsewhere (Le Pere and van Nieuwkerk, 1999) that the post-1994 era in South Africa has seen the predominant influence of the military and intelligence in regional affairs replaced by civilian input. However, the resurgence of "securocrats" in sub-regional affairs (almost rising like the proverbial phoenix from the ashes of yesteryear's destabilization strategy), manifesting itself in the pivotal role played by Safety and Security Minister Sidney Mufamadi and, to a lesser extent, Defense Minister Joe Modise in the ill-advised military intervention in Lesotho in September 1998, seems to contradict this viewpoint. In the southern African sub-region, the ANC government has sharply veered from its previous policy of preventive diplomacy to an approach of aggressive interventionism, despite rather feeble attempts at *ex post facto* rationalization. Operation Boleas (executed in the name, and hidden by the fig-leaf, of a flimsy "SADC mandate") must rank as post-apartheid South Africa's most serious regional blunder: something decision-makers will regret for years to come. In stark contrast, South Africa's first success in the region under a new ANC government, its diplomatic intervention in the Lesotho crisis of September 1994, was brokered by a senior foreign affairs official, former Director-General Rusty Evans. This, at least, has shown a capacity to deal with a potentially explosive situation by using a judicious mix of traditional diplomatic instruments — albeit, executed under a clear multilateral mandate.

Conclusion

Africa has acquired a reputation for the intractability of its many and diverse problems, and outside countries are showing a particular reluctance to be drawn into its peacekeeping operations. Fortunately for South Africa, it has assumed its regional and continental responsibilities at a time when a new sense of realism about peacekeeping has been emerging in Africa. Something must be done to limit conflict in Africa, which is more ravaged by civil war and other forms of armed conflict than any other part of the world. Current thinking has therefore shifted toward political rather than military intervention, to conflict prevention (through preventive diplomacy) rather than conflict management or conflict resolution.

South Africa seems poised to play its expected role in regional security, but some observers suggest that it must be cautious about being made the policeman of the southern African region or the gendarme of sub-Saharan Africa, and about putting its military capacity at the disposal of warring factions elsewhere on the continent. They argue that South Africa could not, by military involvement, have rescued the massacre victims in Rwanda, or have put an end to the on-going civil war in Angola. Where South Africa's interests do lie is in stabilizing the southern African region, if only to stop the vast and destabilizing flood of refugees and economic migrants across its borders. But that does not require military adventures or costly, and usually futile, peacekeeping operations.

If it is in South Africa's interest to make no enemies in the wider world, to trade wherever it is to its advantage to do so, and to give its modest support to international endeavors, its main interest still remains to stabilize the southern African region. This calls for patient diplomacy, to play the role of facilitator and mediator. It does not require armed excursions, nor does it require South Africa to emulate others in the futile exercise of throwing money at unstable societies. Caution has served South Africa well until recently, and it should remain its guiding principle. To quote Deputy Foreign Minister Aziz Pahad (1995, p. 8):

"... serious questions need to be asked about the effectiveness of outside military intervention to prevent or stop internal conflict .... The most important contribution that South Africa can make in preventive diplomacy, at present, is the moral authority it has derived from its own process of national reconciliation and democratization."

Southern Africa is arguably the only part of the African continent that can look forward to a truly regional dynamic. But this dynamic will be forthcoming only if there is genuine and constructive cooperation among the countries of the region. The Southern African Customs Union (SACU) is regarded as the most viable and most effective instrument of trade facilitation and customs management in the southern African region, if not in Africa as a whole. South Africa should use its energies to draw its neighbors into a functioning system of security and prosperity, which must extend real benefits. As states address the long-standing issues of domestic insecurity and work to establish viable democracies, the embrace of functional cooperation will gain legitimacy. Therefore, regional development integration and cooperation, rather than economic integration, should initially guide the future of southern Africa; policy should concentrate on developing and extending regional technical-functional networks in the areas of transport, telecommunications, water management, and power generation.

Clearly, the capability to cope with the aftermath of civil war and violent devastation, economic decline, colonialism, and apartheid in the southern African region has to be developed. Steps to consolidate security in an holistic sense (much broader than a narrow military interpretation), to restore law and order, and to prevent a recurrence of conflict are, however, likely to demand greater application and persistence than achieving the economic recovery that they will help make possible. The processes of political change in southern Africa have made possible the establishment (in name, only) of a mechanism to manage a regional security regime: the SADC Organ on Politics, Defence and Security. Although this development makes the SADC unique among regional groupings in Africa, tragically, today (more than three years later) the sub-continent still needs to operationalize a durable and credible mechanism to deal with disputes and mediate in conflicts within and between the countries of the region. The clear lesson is that, even if an appropriate focus is defined at the higher political level, this becomes blurred or narrowed if the vision is not backed up by relevant structural arrangements to implement the, albeit infrequent, political decisions of ministers and heads of state and government. A process is necessary in which a modest but meaningful agenda is articulated, and systematically expanded once member countries have exhibited a proven commitment to cooperation in clearly defined issue areas (Malan, 1998, pp. 32, 34).

One of the reasons why the SADC seems no closer to resolving the pressing issue of operationalizing the Organ is the inverted role of politicians and officials. In most inter-governmental organizations, heads of state and government, ministers and ambassadors emerge disheveled from summit meetings after fighting their points of view and achieving substantial consensus on meaningful policy directions. It is then up to senior officials to cooperate in giving effect to these broad policy guidelines. In the case of the SADC, however, politicians appear quite eager to agree to what are basically hollow policy pronouncements (that is, paying lip-service to lofty ideals, with very little in the way of substantial policy guidelines) and then leave the real policy debate to officials who, however technically competent, have to refer all the details back to their principals, since they are often left in the dark while grappling with very serious problems (Malan, 1998, p. 14). Three institutional problems also seem to hamper the operationalization of the Organ: the lack of an established political institution or framework; little, if any, provision for an early warning capacity; and the absence of a formal, horizontal link between the SADC's development and security "legs". Furthermore, at least three issue areas related to the institutionalization of regional security are part of, and underlie, these problems: (a) the challenge of dealing with sovereignty, that perennial excuse for lack of political will; (b) the issue of who are the agents of, or who are responsible for, security? — who has the power, whether willingly or unwillingly, wittingly or unwittingly, to make decisions on, provide for, or maintain security?; and (c) the apparent "downsizing" of military security and the implications thereof for creating and maintaining broader security (van Aardt, 1997; van Aardt,1998).

Finally, the collective goods that nations in the southern African region are attempting to provide are security and economic development; at least, a consensus on the need for security and economic cooperation has now developed. Bueno de Mesquita and Lalman's (1992) expected-utility model posits that the larger a regional grouping is, the more difficult collective action (the contribution of all parties to the provision of a collective good) becomes. In this context, the admission of the DRC to the SADC might well prove to have been a monumental blunder, committed collectively by all SADC member states. Geographically, the DRC does not form part of the southern African region. Having become, in essence, a grouping of sub-equatorial states (whose northern boundary now extends north of the Equator), what logical argument can be advanced to deny admission to countries such as Congo-Brazzaville, Gabon, Uganda, Kenya, Rwanda, and Burundi? Politically, and socio-economically, the DRC is a "collapsed state": an ungovernable pseudo-entity, which has become a nightmarish liability for the rest of southern Africa. Regional integration theory suggests that a regional grouping should be kept as small as possible. It would have been much more prudent for the SADC to have consolidated its position (*inter alia*, by conclusively solving the Angolan imbroglio) and to have become functionally more efficient before even the slightest consideration was given to an extension of membership. Clearly, countries such as Madagascar and the Comores would have had a more logical claim to membership of an enlarged SADC grouping.

Ohlson's (1994, p. 29) collective action theory states that the greater the share of gain one nation receives for providing a collective good, the greater the disproportionate share of the burden allotted to it.[4] South Africa especially stands to gain from regional economic cooperation; being the regional powerhouse, it will benefit from trade liberalization much more than its neighbors (hence Zambia and Zimbabwe's concern). South Africa has played a multilateral yet preponderant role in regional affairs; it is *primus inter pares* and will probably continue to be so. In terms of collective action, if South Africa upholds its role as the main donor for regional security and economic development (which it must, in view of its military and economic dominance), then these collective goods may be realized. If, however, it shirks in this regard, then a major problem will arise: no other nation will be able to fill the gap and the crucial collective goods (security and economic development) will not be optimally supplied. Indeed, unless South Africa takes the lead, either in formulating policy initiatives or footing the bill for such initiatives, very little will be achieved (Hull, 1996, pp. 47-48).

Politicians and practitioners alike should be humbled by the realization that the building or strengthening of regional security is a long, difficult, and painstaking process. Ultimately, the key question is whether the southern African region's security arrangements will be of a flexible, rapid-response variety, or whether it will become enmeshed in the bureaucratization that seems to dominate regional groupings. A clear warning is sounded by the words of Leroy Bennett (1995, p. 6):

"A rising tide of revolutionary international problems is met with the slow, evolutionary development of international institutions .... Tradition and an excessively conservative set of attitudes towards international change could easily be humankind's own worst enemy."

Let the SADC and its individual member states and governments not turn out to be their own and their peoples' worst enemies.

Notes

1. Common security expresses the acknowledgment that states are increasingly interdependent in the contemporary age of technological revolution; and in an environment of globalization, states can no longer ensure the security of their citizens through unilateral military measures. Common security, therefore, seeks to promote a culture of peaceful conflict management and resolution at the bilateral and multilateral levels (Honwana, 1997, p. 60). An opposing view is that common security is merely a statement of the mutual vulnerability of states (Nkiwane, 1993, p. 5).

2. The notion of domestic sovereignty needs fundamental rethinking. In the context of "complex interdependence", to invoke a term from Keohane's (1986) work, states actually gain in sovereignty by relinquishing some of it. The notion of "overlapping sovereignty" is particularly relevant here.

At the heart of the sovereignty problem is the issue of national pride, as well as the desire by nation-states to take care of their own security concerns rather than placing them in the hands of a supranational structure over which they fear they have very little control. Among some SADC countries, this is a legitimate concern: a fear that their membership of multilateral political and security forums will entail major infringements of sovereignty. But SADC political and security forums, as currently envisaged, are unlikely to lead to significant encroachments on sovereignty, since their emphasis will be on coordination and cooperation. It is only at higher levels of integration, such as through the formation of a defense alliance or regional parliament, that sovereignty may begin to be seriously affected (Gonçalves, 1995, p. 6; Honwana, 1997, pp. 65-66).

Significantly, the SADC Windhoek Declaration (1992, p. 30) states that regional integration does imply that some decisions which were previously taken by individual states are taken regionally, and those decisions taken nationally give due regard to regional positions and circumstances. Regional decision-making, however, implies elements of change in the locus and context of exercising sovereignty, rather than a loss of sovereignty.

3. The SADC Organ on Politics, Defence and Security is potentially an institution with a comprehensive approach to security and peace, grounded in military confidence-building, social justice, democracy, the rule of law, respect for human rights — and economic development, the SADC sectoral "leg". But, clearly, the southern African region still has a long way to go: the active, on-going, and meaningful pursuit of its inspiring array of objectives cannot occur only at an annual summit of heads of state and government, and in a system of *ad hoc* and informal arrangements. It requires the regular engagement of member states at ministerial and technical levels; in organizational terms, this is the major challenge for the structural development of the Organ.

For detailed information and comprehensive analyses of issues related to the SADC Organ, see SADC Gaborone Communiqué, 1996, p. 2 (cl. 4.1a, d, and f) and pp. 3-5 (cl. 4.2.1b-d, g, i-k, n, o-p, cl. 4.3.1 and 4.3.3); SADC Gaborone Consultative Meeting, 1996, pp. 1-2 (cl. 1.2a, j, and p); Malan and Cilliers, 1997, pp. 1-4, 6-8; Malan, 1998, p. 14.

4. For example, South Africa pays 65.07 percent of the total African contribution to the UN budget for peace-keeping operations (South Africa, Department of Foreign Affairs, 1996, p. 33).

References

Adeniji, O (1996). "Disarmament in African Security and Development." Paper presented at the Second Acdess Workshop on "South Africa within Africa: Emerging Policy Frameworks", Johannesburg, South Africa, 24-27 January.

Alagappa, M. (1995). "Regionalism and Conflict Management: A Framework for Analysis." *Review of International Studies*. Vol. 21, pp. 359-388.

Bennett, A.L. (1995). *International Organizations.* Englewood Cliffs, CA: Prentice Hall.

Booth, K. (1993). "A Security Regime in Southern Africa: Theoretical Considerations." Paper presented at a CSAS-UWC Conference on "Security, Development and Co-operation in Southern Africa", Midgard, Namibia, 23-27 May.

Booth, K. and P. Vale (1995). "Security in Southern Africa: After Apartheid, Beyond Realism." *International Affairs.* Vol. 71, No. 2 (April), pp. 285-304.

Boutros Boutros-Ghali (1992). *An Agenda for Peace.* New York: UN, Department for Public Information.

Breytenbach, W. (1994). "Conflict in Southern Africa: Whither Collective Security?" *Africa Insight.* Vol. 24, No. 1, pp. 26-37.

Bueno de Mesquita, B. and D. Lalman (1992). *War and Reason: Domestic and International Imperatives.* New Haven, CT: Yale University Press.

Buzan, B. (1991). *People, States and Fear: An Agenda for International Security Studies in the Post-Cold War Era.* Boulder, CO: Lynne Rienner.

Ching'ambo, L.J.(1992). "Towards a Defence Alliance in Southern Africa?" *Southern Africa Political and Economic Monthly.* Vol. 5, No. 8 (May), pp. 33-36.

Cilliers, J. (1996). "The SADC Organ on Defence, Politics and Security." IDP Papers No 10 (October). Institute for Defence Policy: Midrand, South Africa.

Cilliers, J. and M. Malan (1996). "From Destabilization to Peace-keeping in Southern Africa: The Potential Role of South Africa." *Africa Insight*, Vol. 26, No. 4, pp. 339-346.

Dalby, S. (1992). "Security, Modernity, Ecology: The Dilemmas of Post-Cold War Security Discourse." *Alternatives.* Vol. 17.

Deutsch, K.W. *et al.* (1957). *Political Community and the North Atlantic Area.* Princeton, NJ: Princeton University Press.

Du Pisani, A. (1991). "Ventures into the Interior: Continuity and Change in South Africa's Regional Policy, 1948 to 1991." Paper presented at a SAIIA Conference on "South Africa into the 1990s and Beyond", Broederstroom, South Africa, 15-19 April.

Du Pisani, A. (1992). "Security and Peace in Post-Apartheid South Africa." *International Affairs Bulletin.* Vol. 16, No. 3, pp. 4-16.

Du Pisani, A. (1993). "Post-Settlement South Africa and the Future of Southern Africa." *Issue: A Journal of Opinion.* Vol. XXI, Nos. ½, pp. 60-69.

Esterhuysen, P.W.(comp. (1998). *Africa at a Glance 1997/98: Facts and Figures.* Tenth Edition. Pretoria: Africa Institute of South Africa.

Evans, R. (1995). "Preventive Diplomacy in Lesotho and Mozambique." Paper presented at the SAIIA/IDP Conference on "South Africa and Peace-Keeping in Africa", Johannesburg, South Africa, 13-14 July.

Garba, J.N. and J. Herskovits (1997). *Militaries, Democracies and Security in Southern Africa. Report of the Southern Africa Security Project, 1992 to 1996.* New York: International Peace Academy.

Geldenhuys, D.J.(1989). "Ten Crises in South Africa's External Relations." *International Affairs Bulletin.* Vol. 13, No. 3, pp. 89-95.

Gonçalves, F. (1995). "Southern Africa: In Search of a Common Security?" *Southern Africa Political and Economic Monthly.* Vol. 8, No. 7 (April), pp. 5-8.

Green, R.H.(1996). "South Africa, Southern Africa and Beyond: Explorations toward Regional Integration." Paper presented at the Second Access Workshop on "South Africa within Africa: Emerging Policy Frameworks", Johannesburg, South Africa, 24-27 January.

Gutteridge, W.(1992). "Prospects for Regional Security in Southern Africa." *South Africa International.* Vol. 22, No. 3 (January), pp. 128-132.

Honwana, JB(1997). "Military and Security Co-operation in Southern Africa," pp. 57-83 in J. Hacker (ed.), *Collaborative Security in Southern Africa.* Aurora Papers No 28. Ottawa: Canadian Council for International Peace.

Hull, A.P.(1996). "Rational Choice, Security and Economic Co-operation in Southern Africa." *Africa Today,* Vol. 43, No. 1 (January-March), pp. 33-52.

Hurrell, A. (1995). "Explaining the Resurgence of Regionalism in World Politics." *Review of International Studies.* Vol. 21, pp. 331-358.

Jackson, R.H. (1992). "The Security Dilemma in Africa", pp. 81-94 in B.L. Job (ed.), *The Insecurity Dilemma: National Security of Third World States.* Boulder, CO: Lynne Rienner.

Keohane, R. (1986). *Neo-Realism and its Critics.* New York: Columbia University Press.

Khadiagala, G.M.(1994). "Southern Africa's Transitions: Prospects for Regional Security", pp. 167-179 in S.J. Seedman (ed.), *South Africa: The Political Economy of Transformation.* Boulder, CO: Lynne Rienner.

Khadiagala, G.M. (1996). "Regionalism and Leadership in African Security." Paper presented at the Second Access Workshop on "South Africa within Africa: Emerging Policy Frameworks", Johannesburg, South Africa, 24-27 January.

Krauthammer, C. (1992). "The Unipolar Moment", pp. 295-306 in G. Allison and G.F. Treverton (eds.), *Rethinking America's Security: Beyond the Cold War to a New World Order.* New York: W.W. Norton.

Kuhn, T.S. (1970). *The Structure of Scientific Revolutions*. Chicago: University of Chicago Press.

Le Pere, G. and A. van Nieuwkerk (1999). "Making Foreign Policy in South Africa". Chapter for publication in P. McGowan and P. Nel (eds.), *Power, Wealth and Global Order — International Relations for Southern African Students*. Cape Town: University of Cape Town Press.

Malan, M. (1998). *The SADC and Sub-Regional Security: Unde Venis et Quo Vadis?* ISS Monograph Series No 19, February. Midrand, South Africa: Institute for Security Studies.

Malan, M. and J. Cilliers (1997). "The SADC Organ on Politics, Defence and Security: Future Development." ISS Papers No 19, March. Midrand, South Africa: Institute for Security Studies.

Martin, W.G. (1991). "The Future of Southern Africa: What Prospects After Majority Rule?" *Review of African Political Economy*. No. 50 (March), pp. 115-134.

Masire-Mandela Correspondence (1996). Covering letter, dated 25 January, from President Quett Masire of Botswana to President Nelson Mandela of South Africa, appended to the SADC Gaborone Communiqué issued after the 18 January SADC Meeting on Politics, Defence and Security (of SADC Ministers responsible for foreign affairs, Defence, and security) in Gaborone, Botswana.

McNamara, R. (1968). *The Essence of Security*. London: Hoder & Stoughton.

Mills, G. and C. Clapham (1991). "Southern Africa after Apartheid: A Framework for Analysis." Working Paper Series, April. Belville, South Africa: University of the Western Cape, Centre for Southern African Studies.

Mpungwe, A. (1998). "Policy Considerations for the Evolution of Sustainable Peace and Stability in Southern Africa", pp. 74-82 in M. Malan (ed.), *Resolute Partners: Building Peace-keeping Capacity in Southern Africa*. IS Monograph Series No 21, February. Midland: South Africa: Institute for Security Studies.

Murdock, P. (1995). "Liberia: Nigeria Sanctions." Correspondent's Report, 7 December. Voice of America: Abidjan, Côte d'Ivoire.

Nathan, L. (1994). " 'With Open Arms': Confidence and Security-Building Measures in Southern Africa". *South African Journal of International Affairs*, Vol. 1, No. 2 (Autumn), pp. 110-126.

Nathan, L. (1996). "Formalizing Conflict Resolution and Security Arrangements in Southern Africa." Paper presented at the Second Access Workshop on "South Africa within Africa: Emerging Policy Frameworks", Johannesburg, South Africa, 24-27 January.

Nathan, L. and JB Honwana (1994). "The Establishment of SADC Forums for Conflict Resolution, and Defence and Security." Paper presented at the Eighth Conference on "Peace and Security in Eastern and Southern Africa", Araceae, Tanzania, 22-24 August.

Nhara, W. (1996). "Early Warning and Conflict in Africa." IDP Papers No 1, February. Midland, South Africa: Institute for Defence Policy.

Nhara, W. (1998). "Conflict Management and Peace Operations: The Role of the Organization of African Unity and Sub-Regional Organizations", pp 32-42 in M. Malan (ed.), *Resolute Partners: Building Peace-keeping Capacity in Southern Africa.* IS Monograph Series No 21, February. Midland, South Africa: Institute for Security Studies.

Nkiwane, S.M.(1993). "Regional Security and Confidence-Building Processes: The Case of Southern Africa in the 1990s." Research Paper No 16. Geneva: United Nations Institute for Disarmament Research.

Nkiwane-Muzenda, TC (1996). "Regionalism and Preventive Diplomacy in the Current Peace and Conflict Resolution Process in Southern Africa." Paper presented at the Second Access Workshop on "South Africa within Africa: Emerging Policy Frameworks", Johannesburg, 24-27 January.

Nzo, A. (1995). "Statement by the Minister of Foreign Affairs, Mr Alfred Nzo, before the Portfolio Committee on Foreign Affairs, 14 March", pp. 1-13 in South Africa, Department of Foreign Affairs (comp.), Policy Guidelines by the Minister and Deputy Minister of Foreign Affairs. Pretoria: Government Printer.

Ohlson, T. (1994). *The New is not yet Born: Conflict Resolution in Southern Africa.* Washington, DC: The Brookings Institution.

OAU (1996). "OAU Seminar on the Establishment of an Early Warning System for Conflict Situations in Africa". *Resolving Conflicts: OAU Conflict Management Bulletin.* Vol. 1, No. 1 (December-January), pp. 1-4, 6.

Omari, A.H. (1995). "Regional Security: One View from the Frontline States." CFR/CSAS-UWC Araceae Papers No 5, July: A Working Paper Series on Southern African Security. Belville, South Africa: University of the Western Cape, Centre for Southern African Studies.

Pahad, A. (1995). "South Africa and Preventive Diplomacy." Paper presented at an IDP/SAIIA conference on "South Africa and Peace-keeping in Africa", Johannesburg, 13-14 July.

Patel, H.H. (1992). "Peace and Security in a Changing Southern Africa: A Frontline View." Working Paper Series, April. Belville, South Africa: University of the Western Cape, Centre for Southern African Studies.

SADC Windhoek Declaration (1992). "Towards the Southern African Development Community: A Declaration by the Heads of State and

Government of Southern African States." *Southern Africa Political and Economic Monthly.* Vol. 5, No. 11 (August), pp. 26, 29-30.

SADC Windhoek Treaty (1992). "Treaty of the Southern African Development Community (SADC)." *Southern Africa Political and Economic Monthly.* Vol. 5, No. 11 (August), pp. 31, 33-36.

SADC Harare Framework (1993). *Southern Africa: A Framework and Strategy for Building the Community.* Gabarone: Botswana: SADC Secretariat.

SADC Gaborone Communiqué (1996). Communiqué of the Summit of Heads of State and Government of the Southern African Development Community, 28 June.

SADC Windhoek Communiqué (1994). Issued after the conclusion of a SADC Workshop on "Democracy, Peace and Security", Windhoek, Namibia, 11-16 July.

SADC Gaborone Consultative Meeting (1996). The SADC Organ on Politics, Defence and Security: Terms of Reference. Meeting of SADC ministers responsible for foreign affairs, Defence, and security, Gaborone, Botswana, 18 January.

South Africa, Department of Foreign Affairs (1996). Multilateral Branch. Annual Report 1995. Pretoria: Department of Foreign Affairs.

Thomas, M. (1995). "OAU Approves Peace-keeping Units." *Africa Recovery.* Vol. 9, No. 2 (August), pp. 1, 4-5.

Vale, P. (1992). "Hoping Against Hope: The Prospects for South Africa's Post-Apartheid Regional Policy." Working Paper Series, July. Belville, South Africa: University of the Western Cape, Centre for Southern African Studies.

Vale, P. (1993). "Southern Africa's Security: Something Old, Something New." *South African Defence Review.* No. 9, pp. 28-37.

Vale, P. (1996). "Regional Security in Southern Africa." *Alternatives.* Vol. 21, pp. 363-391.

Van Aardt, M. (1997). "The SADC Organ on Politics, Defence and Security: Challenges for Regional Community-Building." *South African Journal of International Affairs.* Vol. 4, No. 2 (Winter), pp. 144-164.

Van Aardt, M. (1998). "The Application of the New Security Agenda for Southern Africa," pp. 103-115 in H. Solomon and M. van Aardt (eds.), *"Caring" Security in Africa: Theoretical and Practical Considerations of New Security Thinking.* IS Monograph Series No 20, February. Midland, South Africa: Institute for Security Studies.

Venter, D. (1992). "South Africa and the African Comity of Nations: From Isolation to Integration." Research Paper No 56, March. Pretoria: Africa Institute of South Africa.

Venter, D. (1996). "Regional Security in Sub-Saharan Africa." *Africa Insight.* Vol. 26, No. 2, pp. 162-176.

Venter, D. (1997). "South Africa and Africa: Relations in a Time of Change," pp. 73-101 in W. Carlsnaes and M. Muller (eds.), *Change and South African External Relations.* Johannesburg: Thomson International Publishers.

Venter, D. (1998). "Angola: Back to the Brink?" *Africa Insight.* Vol. 28, Nos. 3/4, pp. 109-117.

Weimer, B. (1990). "South Africa and the Frontline States: From Confrontation to Confidence-Building." *Southern Africa Political and Economic Monthly.* Vol. 3, No. 11 (August), pp. 22-28.

14   Regional peace as an international public good: collective action in southern Africa

Jurgen Brauer

Introduction

Since Buchanan's (1965) and Olson's (1965) seminal works, a vast literature has developed that examines collective-action goods (see, e.g., Sandler, 1992; Cornes and Sandler, 1996). International peace among nation-states is a collective-action good. Once provided, the benefits of peace accrue to all in non-rival fashion and no one can be excluded from enjoying the fruits that peace entails. Why, therefore, contribute to peacekeeping or peacemaking? How can one avoid or mitigate the free-rider problem? This chapter

- ▸ reviews how collective goods are produced, paying particular attention to the design of institutions that are to produce peace and international security, and briefly examines the literature on economic sanctions and incentives as means to bring about or to keep peace,
- ▸ briefly characterizes the major security problems and challenges in the southern African region and provides information on the present peace-related institutional set-up in southern Africa, and
- ▸ provides suggestions for peacemaking and peacekeeping processes in southern Africa with particular attention to institutional design.

Production technologies and design of institutions

Production technology of public goods

Jack Hirshleifer (1983) examined the link between the voluntary provision of public (collective) goods and the technology used to produce them.[1] He examines three cases in particular. First, if the technology of production consists of each contributor providing one part, so that the benefits the good yields as a whole is the sum of its contributed parts (the *summation technology*), then it is likely that the good is subject to the classic free-rider problem. For instance, protecting the stratospheric ozone layer through reductions in CFC emissions abides by the summation technology: each unit of CFC reductions that any one country agrees to provides non-exclusive, non-rival benefits to all other countries. The larger the number of countries that contribute to CFC reductions, the higher the overall level of CFC reductions achieved, and the higher the sum of benefits reaped.

But if it is the only contributor to CFC reductions then costs outweigh a country's benefits. Thus, each country has an incentive to make its own contribution only if all other countries do. But if all other countries do, then it can free-ride on their efforts, benefitting from world-wide CFC reductions without contributing to any such reductions after all. This line of reasoning is correct for any, hence for all, countries. A summation technology of public goods production is therefore associated with a prisoners' dilemma game whose undesirable outcome is that no one reduces CFC emissions because it is not rational for any one to start doing so. This is a "lose-lose" game.[2]

Second, Hirshleifer refers to another production technology of public goods as *weakest-link technology*. It suggests that the benefits the public good yields are only as high as the smallest contribution to its production. Only if each party contributes will there be a public good, but if any one party withdraws its contribution there will be no public good whatsoever. An example would be nuclear non-proliferation. Any country abiding by non-proliferation standards provides non-rival, non-excludable benefits to all others. But if a single country fails to abide by non-proliferation standards, the public good of non-proliferation will not be provided at all.

Weakest-link technology is often associated with *assurance games* ("win-win" games) whose redeeming quality is the increased (but not guaranteed) likelihood of the absence of free-riding. If only country A signs a non-proliferation treaty, but country B does not, then non-proliferation does not exist at all: country B cannot obtain something (non-proliferation) for nothing. Similarly, once provided, neither party can sensibly withdraw from the non-proliferation project: if either party fails to live up to the treaty, the treaty as a whole ceases to provide benefits to either. Such situations therefore present good opportunities for incremental contributions: country A offers to make a small contribution or concession on the condition that B reciprocates; once B does, A may make another offer of a small contribution, if B does. This continues until a non-proliferation treaty is fully worked out.

Third, at the other extreme of the technology spectrum lies what Hirshleifer calls *best-shot technology* for public good production. This is associated with *coordination games*. If B contributes a cost of "two", and A contributes a cost of "three", then the level of the public good is determined by A's, the larger, contribution. But if A contributes only "one", then the level of the public good is determined by B's contribution, which is now larger than A's. The largest contribution provides the public good; everyone else gets a free ride. For example, the availability of space satellites and the potential dissemination of information gathered through them is determined by the nation(s) with the largest capacity to put such satellites into orbit. Once in orbit, information such as remote-sensing of world-wide agricultural conditions can be gathered and distributed at near-zero marginal cost (near-zero per unit of information, anyway). When any two parties are nearly equally endowed to undertake such efforts, the game theoretic question is who shall incur the cost and let the other free ride. But when two parties are unequally endowed, it is more nearly clear that the better endowed party will incur the cost purely for its own benefit (providing a free-ride to others).

I skewed this last example a bit to make two important points: (a) many international public goods are not *pure* international public goods but are mingled with private national benefits; and (b) some goods yield benefits that are in principle non-rival but excludable. For example, once the United States decides to release remote-sensing information, for instance via the Internet, it is freely available to everyone. Remote-sensing information, once provided, is non-rival indeed. But the US can decide not to release satellite information (say from spy satellites) in the first instance, thus making the good's benefit excludable to non-US parties, or make it available only at the discretion of the US government (presumably in exchange for other benefits to US wishes to acquire).

Some collective goods therefore are *joint products*. Realizing this becomes important for the design of institutions, to which I now turn.

Design of institutions producing international public goods

In areas other than questions of peace and international security, it is increasingly recognized that the institutional framework within which the production of collective goods is negotiated and carried out influences whether or not, or to what degree, the good will be successfully supplied. For example, unlike the Rio de Janeiro (1992) and Kyoto (1997) negotiations concerning global warming, the successful negotiation and implementation of the Montreal Protocol on CFC reductions stems, in part, from the recognition and acceptance of the fairly undisputed scientific consensus on the nature of the problem. The benefit of the collective good to be provided was so much more clearly spelled out, and there existed an initial cluster of highly interested and economically capable countries willing and able to pursue the issue, to drive the negotiations, and to assure their success.

In a recent book, *Global Challenges*, Todd Sandler extracts the following lessons for the design of institutions for the successful production of international public goods (Sandler, 1997, ch. 5). Here they are loosely summarized and slightly expanded upon:

▸ First, instead of reaching for the stars by insisting on all-encompassing membership, form a club with a small number of members that share similar "tastes" with respect to the problem at hand. Thereafter, build up membership gradually. If possible, invent an exclusion mechanism.

▸ Second, to increase the likelihood of contributions, and to induce more nation-states to pursue collective action, reduce and resolve uncertainty about the nature of the problem at hand (do CFCs destroy the stratospheric ozone layer? is there global warming? is Iraq building nuclear weapons? etc.). Reduce uncertainty not only about the economic cost of inaction (opportunities foregone by continued inaction), but also about the potential benefits of action (opportunities gained).

▸ Third, leadership toward achieving collective action is best provided by the nation with the potentially greatest net benefit from such action. Those who have the most to gain will most likely provide the best arguments and be most willing to put down an initial contribution toward defraying the cost of action, a down-payment on a pot of winnings which others may share if they also contribute to the pot.

▸ Fourth, in an effort to build successful coalitions, identify local or regional, not just global, benefits. For example, nations have much to gain from regional peace treaties, without any need to wait for global peace.

▸ Fifth, world media nowadays transcend nation-state boundaries and can help build awareness of collective action problems and therefore can help forge appropriate coalitions. Use them.

▸ Sixth, start with loose links among members and tighten links over time. Instead of aiming for a comprehensive solution, consider incremental improvements.[3]

▸ Seventh, do not graft a solution to one problem onto another: as the discussion of public good production technology shows, the underlying nature of the public good problem to be addressed may differ vastly from case to case.

NATO as an illustrative example

Cursorily examine a case of an international public good — international peace and security provided by NATO — and match it against Sandler's design of institutions principles. Clearly, NATO is a community of shared interests, of similar tastes or preferences. Instead of aiming at global peace, it aims at regional stability, primarily in western Europe. The benefits from the military alliance are local and regional, with international and global spill-over effects (both positive and negative).[4] Initial leadership was clearly provided by the US, France, and the UK, the nations that stood to gain extensive net benefits from the formation of the alliance. The alliance produces a joint product. Some benefits of the alliance are more nearly public ("international"), others more nearly private ("national"), and the balance between public-good and private-good production has varied from time to time. For example, when emphasis was placed on conventional forces, danger of force *thinning* (rivalry by dilution, rather than crowding) would leave any one alliance member vulnerable to attack. The good became partially rival. Thus, each alliance member contributed a larger share to conventional forces to reap private-good benefits. But when emphasis shifted toward nuclear, strategic weaponry, the good became less rival, more public in character, and contributions of individual alliance members shrunk.[5] NATO as a defense alliance is a complex good: it can be classified as an international public good, providing non-rival, non-exclusive benefits (probably protecting non-members such as France or Switzerland); it can also be classified as a partially private good providing rival, excludable benefits for specific members only; in addition, some aspects of the good NATO provides can be viewed as a common-resource pool good (rival but non-excludable), yet also as a club good (non-rival for members but excludable to non-members). Along with varying benefits are also varying costs not only for each member but for the collective of members. For instance, the larger the size of the club, the more costly it is to reach decisions, raising questions of limits to membership and optimal club size (regarding, NATO in particular, see Sandler and Hartley, 1999).

Collective action: sanctions, incentives, institutions

Making and keeping peace within and among nation-states is a collective action problem. Within states the problem is usually addressed by state-enforced coerced contributions (taxes) toward the provision of the public good ("law and order") that keeps the domestic peace. This takes place in the context of an institutional arrangement that transfers a degree of sovereignty from private individuals to some governing authority. Between and among states that governing authority — as an instance of an institutional arrangement — does not ordinarily exist and must be specifically created and some degree of sovereignty must be ceded to that governing authority (as in the case of NATO).

International peace yields benefits to those who enjoy it; but to provide peace entails costs. Yet, once provided, no nation-state can be excluded from enjoying the fruits of peaceful relations among nations in its relevant geographic region nor is there any competition or rivalry over peace. Once there is peace, there is peace for all at the same time. Thus, we expect that contributions to international peacekeeping forces and operating expenses fall short of what is needed to adequately provide the good as each nation hopes to free ride on the contributions of others, i.e., as each hopes to benefit (from peace) at the expense of others.

As in the case of NATO, peace, peacemaking, and peacekeeping is not a pure public good. It may also yield private benefits to the provider. For example, nation-states such as Canada and Norway take pride in being known for their peace loving stance. They derive private national benefits by being acknowledged worldwide as peace-loving countries: they garner stature, recognition, and international admiration. This encourages them to contribute disproportionally large shares toward international peacekeeping actions (Khanna and Sandler, 1997).

Consider recent conflicts in places such as Armenia and Azerbaijan or Haiti, Somalia, Iraq, Rwanda, the Balkan wars of the 1990s or, indeed, southern Africa. In spite of professing peace, human societies prosecute wars. If making peace is a desirable good, who shall provide it? And how? If one nation-state, external to the region, intervenes to make peace, a large number of other nation-states benefit (let alone the peoples of the directly affected nation-states). They free ride on (and benefit from) the effort of the intervener at little or no cost to themselves. Yet, if all nation-states think likewise, peacemaking will not be undertaken; it will not be provided at all or will be supplied inadequately. Thus, peacemaking and peacekeeping are desirable goods but their provision suffers from collective action problems.

Discussion of economic sanctions, for example against Yugoslavia or Iraq, or discussion of economic (dis)incentives, for example in the case of South Africa during the apartheid era, have only recently begun to be examined from the point of view of collective action (e.g., Cortright and Lopez, 1995; and Cortright, 1997). It is now recognized that economic sanctions imposed by members of international organizations, or arranged through other forms of international cooperation, do not always bring about the desired behavioral changes in the target nation or nations. Correspondingly, researchers work to identify sets of conditions under which sanctions work or fail to work. In large part, the results suggest that success or failure drives on the institutional arrangements within which collective actions, such as sanctions, are agreed upon. For example, it is now widely recognized that in order to agree to a set of sanctions in the context of an international organization, such as the United Nations, each nation in turn may need to win approval from domestically important interested parties. (Kaempfer and Lowenberg, 1988; Mansfield, 1995). By the same token, to what degree sanctions change behavior in the target nation depends, in part, on exactly who is affected in that nation. If economic sanctions hurt the ordinary population but leave the target nation's leadership untouched, and if the institutional arrangement within that country is a non-democratic, dictatorial regime, then sanctions are unlikely to result in the desired behavioral changes. In contrast, economic sanctions applied to the ordinary people in a country that is able to force leadership changes would, *a priori*, stand a greater chance of success.

An important conclusion, therefore, is simply that institutions matter. They are not an afterthought. Actions or inactions do not take place in an institutional vacuum. What actions are taken is partially determined by the institutions that make them or within which they must take effect. An equally important consideration concerns the nature of the collective action good in question. As noted, not all collective action goods are alike (Hirshleifer, 1983). One cannot merely catalog examples of sanctions (disincentives) and incentives to arrive at insights about which approach or mixture of the two "works better." Which works better depends on the institutional context. A set of sanctions imposed in one set of circumstances may work, in another it may not. Similarly, a set of incentives offered may work under some set of circumstances or institutional framework, but not in another. The design of institutions, including the transaction and coordination costs institutions entail, therefore becomes as much of a critical component as the design of particular dis/incentives themselves (Sandler, 1997). They are part of one decision-making process.[6]

In addition, as noted before, not only is the design of institutions important in its own right, but there are important sub-games that determine access to an institution and its resources. Moreover, institutions offer potential benefits at a cost to its members — and therefore induce free rider behavior. For instance, David Cortright (1997, p. 269) writes that "access to the emerging system of political cooperation and economic development among the major states ... [is] the most powerful inducement for peaceful relations in the world today." But reflect on the case of Turkey: Turkey long has sought membership in the EU, yet the EU — as a group — refuses to admit Turkey. If access to the EU is a powerful incentive for Turkey to be peaceful, so granting access is a sub-game within the EU that needs to be resolved first. Inasmuch as all EU members need to grant access, accession of Turkey to the EU will, ultimately, depend on yet further sub-games in Greece.

The emphasis to be placed on the design, cost, and operation of institutions becomes even stronger in the within-nation context of civil war, internal terrorism, arms running, drug smuggling, political assassinations, revolutionary ferment, and the like, that spill over (externality effects) into cross-nation contexts. Offering dis/incentives is not enough. Rather, the decisive questions revolve around incentives being offered to whom, that will play themselves out how, in exactly which institutional context.

Challenges to peace in southern Africa[7]

The overwhelming fact of the southern African region is the unevenness in size and strength of its countries. If one defines the southern African region as comprising the fourteen members of the Southern African Development Community (SADC), then the region contains two population giants, the Democratic Republic of Congo (the former Zaire) and South Africa, accounting for about half of the region's nearly 180 million people, six mid-size nations (Angola, Malawi, Mozambique, Tanzania, Zambia, Zimbabwe) with populations between ten and thirty million each, and six small nations (Botswana, Lesotho, Mauritius, Namibia, the Seychelles, and Swaziland) with populations below two million each (see Table 14.1).

In terms of economic achievement, South Africa alone, with one quarter of the region's population, generates a GDP three times as large as all the other SADC-members taken together (see Table 14.1). This "giantism," in itself cause for concern for South Africa's neighbors, complicates regional cooperation and integration and is an institutional feature that cannot be neglected in any attempt of thinking about peacekeeping and peacemaking in the southern African region. Not unlike the case of Nigeria in ECOWAS, a west African grouping, there cannot be any notion nor pretense of equals sitting at some negotiating table when that which is to be negotiated involves matters of economic costs and benefits.

Intra-regional asymmetries of this kind invariably create suspicion about possible domination by, and ulterior motives of, South Africa. This alone places a heavy burden on the quality of South African diplomacy in the region. In addition, threats to peace, security, and development are mounting as non-military challenges emerge, e.g., in the form of indebtedness to foreign creditors, fiscal imbalances, serious political instability in many countries, and recurrent

Table 14.1: Selected indicators, southern Africa, 1995

Country	Total population		GDP at market prices	
	'000	% of region	US$ million	% of region
Total	*178,874*	*100.0*	*166,003*	*100.0*
Angola	10,800	6.0	3,722	2.1
Botswana	1,500	0.8	4,318	2.5
Dem. Rep. of Congo	43,900*	24.5	5,268*	3.0
Lesotho	2,000	1.1	1,029	0.6
Malawi	9,800	5.5	1,465	0.8
Mauritius	1,100	0.6	3,919	2.2
Mozambique	16,200	9.1	1,469	0.8
Namibia	1,500	0.8	3,033	1.7
Seychelles	74	0.0	490	0.3
South Africa	41,500	23.2	136,035	77.3
Swaziland	900	0.5	1,048	0.6
Tanzania	29,600	16.6	3,602	2.1
Zambia	9,000	5.0	4,073	2.3
Zimbabwe	11,000	6.2	6,522	3.7

Source: World Bank, 1997; UNDP, 1997.

Note: * Data for the Democratic Republic of Congo are, for 1995, those for Zaire. The World Bank (1997) carries per capita 1995-GDP data for Zaire in Table 1a (p. 248) but does not provide an estimate of Zaire's population. The UNDP (1997) provides a population estimate as of 1994 (Table 22, p. 195). Multiplying the UNDP's population estimate with the World Bank's per capita GDP estimate provides an estimate of GDP.

droughts and the attendant crises of malnourishment, hunger, and migrant flows to hoped-for greener pastures.

Throughout the region the pace of change has shifted, and warped, accepted patterns of state behavior. The intensity of this process is expected to increase as the process of regional integration deepens. In addition, old security issues linger with great potential for damage. For example, the proliferation of weapons throughout the region — a legacy of the region's ideological past — is extremely destabilizing.

Two major forces then are clearly emerging from the major divide between South Africa and other countries on the sub-continent. First, the inability to scratch out even a meager living in a vast economic wasteland is compelling millions of hungry, poverty-stricken inhabitants to seek greener pastures elsewhere (push-forces). To most, South Africa represents those greener pastures (pull-forces). Hence the annual influx into South Africa of hundreds of thousands of illegal immigrants. Economic refugees from elsewhere in southern Africa are exerting considerable pressure on an already explosive demographic situation in South Africa. With more and more people seeking jobs and sustenance, and laying claim to the country's strained resources, the potential for violent conflict is obvious. Paradoxically, South Africa's superior economic performance and prospects relative to the rest of southern Africa contribute to its high incidence of unemployment and societal disintegration (see, e.g., IMF, 1997). As long as there are pronounced regional disparities in the sub-continent there will be an inevitable influx of illegal immigrants for many years to come. Thus, it is in South Africa's interest to make a meaningful contribution to economic development and enhanced prosperity in all southern African countries. It is far better to import goods and services from its neighbors than to import instability.

Second, recent developments have further deepened the potential for conflict. Intense problems have arisen over arranging and enforcing cease-fires and peace accords as well as in demobilizing armies and integrating former enemies into unified armed structures. Security is also threatened by the large number of unexploded land mines in countries such as Mozambique and Angola. Conflicts are also likely to emerge from declining economic activity and from the usually wrenching short-run impact of IMF Structural Adjustment Programs which could negatively affect within-state reconciliation efforts. Increasingly, too, it is apparent that change has awakened long-dormant ethnic, religious, and sub-national loyalties. State fragmentation may also take place within the region, e.g., Zanzibar, the Shaba province in the Democratic Republic of Congo, southern Angola, and northern Mozambique. Because of porous borders, change cannot be contained within any one country. As a result, conflict and other problems spill across borders, and this is now a central concern in southern Africa. And in some isolated cases, certain countries of the region are involved in border disputes or are quarreling over tracts of land.

Existing collective action institutions in southern Africa

Historically, four organizations in southern Africa have vied for ascendancy, namely the *Southern African Customs Union* (SACU), the *Southern African Development Community* (SADC), the *Common Market of East and Southern Africa* (Comesa), which grew out of the Preferential Trade Agreement (PTA), and the *Frontline States* (FLS). Each was established at a different moment in the region's turbulent past and each aimed to cope with a slightly different set of circumstances. South Africa's full readmittance into political and economic structures in the region (in 1994) has dramatically shifted the relative power of these groupings. With the exception of SACU, South Africa was previously excluded from these groups. The central challenge facing the region now is to select a single organization through which it can channel its energies in the decades ahead, and it seems that SADC is the most likely candidate. FLS disbanded as a consequence of South Africa's democratization; SACUs purpose, since 1910, is strictly limited to customs union matters and seems more likely to be incorporated into SADC than to be expanded on its own terms; Comesa might be on its way of disbandment also as SADC members signed, in 1996, a Trade Protocol with the aim of establishing a southern African free-trade area by the year 2004.

Additionally, SADC itself is expanding in membership and functions. There are now 14 member states, the Seychelles and the Democratic Republic of Congo having joined in 1997. SADC now comprises 19 functional areas (such as Trade and Investment, Agriculture, and the like), called "sectors", two "commissions", five "protocols", the latest being the 1996 Trade Protocol, and one "Organ," the "Organ on Politics, Defence and Security" (PDS) which was added in 1995. Principles and objectives of PDS are displayed in the appendix. The language of these principles and objectives suggest that the PDS Organ is, as yet, toothless.[8] It is a declaration of intentions leaving the important question of how to achieve these intentions to the future.

Taking these factors into account — South Africa's "giantism", political instability and consequent uncertainties, recurrent political and economic refugee streams, and SADC as the region's primary forum of cooperation — what steps should be taken to influence developments, especially security-related developments, in the region? The next section proposes a specific set of suggestions, drawn up in light of the discussion about the interplay of public-good production technologies, dis/incentives, and institutions.

Peacekeeping in southern Africa: some institutional suggestions

Recognizing the prevalence of conflict in the region, a fair amount of peacekeeping experience in other contexts, the general dearth of resources, as well as South Africa's relative plentitude of resources, Brooks (1997/98) suggests a five-pronged "model", or long-run strategy, to enhance regional peacemaking and peacekeeping. Brooks' model of a peacekeeping force is intended for all of sub-Saharan Africa, to be managed through the Organization of African Unity

(OAU). Since it is one of the few such models available, it merits attention and examination. But in light of the public-good production pitfalls identified by Hirshleifer (1983) and Sandler (1997), Brooks' specific suggestions strike me as unattainable, and I am therefore expanding upon and altering various components of his model to fit the context of southern Africa, SADC, and its PDS Organ. My extension of Brooks' model includes the following components of a SADC peacekeeping force (SADC PKF).

Size of SADC PKF

Sandler's (1997) suggestion that clubs be built up loosely, involve a small membership, and be build up only gradually in substance and numbers is relevant to SADC. It is significant that SADCs "Politics, Defence and Security" (PDS) Organ, while formally part of the SADC umbrella, is in fact a separate institution that will permit PDS to develop separately. SADC members need to recognize the best-shot or giantism effect that South Africa exerts. A mutual, common-defense club along the lines of NATO, say, will inevitably be dominated by South Africa's considerable military resources, armaments, experience, and sheer size and weight unless specific measures are undertaken to mitigate or altogether side-step this effect (see *Command and Control* below).

It is important to recognize that there is no automatic requirement that the regional "Mutual Defence Pact" and peacekeeping force envisioned by the PDS principles and objectives automatically include all 14 current SADC members. It is entirely possible for a sub-group to form its own peacekeeping force within SADC. For instance, there is no reason for exceedingly small countries such as Lesotho and Swaziland to pay up for their own defense forces. In case of conflict, as pre- and post-apartheid era South Africa has shown with its occasional raids into these mini-states, they simply cannot defend themselves effectively against external aggression. They might as well explicitly recognize this state of affairs, offer to integrate (but not subsume) their legitimate armed forces with South Africa's, and convert the part of their armed forces hitherto employed for purely domestic law and order functions into explicit police forces. This is especially relevant since South Africa has just undergone a period of integration of apartheid, anti-apartheid, and former "homeland" military forces and can therefore claim some expertise in this regard.

One convenient aspect of this scheme is that it takes only two SADC members to get started. Moreover, the more countries add themselves to the scheme, the higher the incentive for the remaining SADC countries' military forces: if the intent of any national military force truly is to defend its nation-state from outside aggression (and for some SADC member nations, this can be questioned), this can best be ensured by means of a fully integrated, regional PKF whose supreme commander, not inconceivably, might be a non-South African.

Early warning

The PDS objectives explicitly mention an "early warning system" to be used for "preventive diplomacy to pre-empt conflict in the region, both within and between States." Early warning is about reducing uncertainty, another one of Sandler's (1997) principles. Thus, early warning requires the setting up of channels of communication and associated consultation and decision-making among SADC members. Much of this communication, consultation, and decision-making should be explicitly designed at routine, technical, professional levels and should side-step involvement of the political level to minimize coordination costs. SADC members should agree on pre-specified trigger points at which various peacekeeping and peacemaking actions are automatically implemented. For example, in line with the PDS principle of "territorial integrity of each State and ... its inalienable right to independent existence", SADC should agree that any cross-border conflict of any sort whatsoever will automatically trigger peacekeeping forces to be self-deployed to the area of conflict. By self-deployed, I mean that the deployment decision would be made at a non-political level, for example by the commander of the PKF headquarters. Automaticity not only reduces uncertainty but also enhances credibility because certain actions are automatic (on credibility, see Martin, 1993; Mansfield, 1995; also see *Command and Control* below).

Since the PDS principles and objectives already explicitly refer to states' internal conflict, another aspect of early warning could and should involve regular reporting on equipment purchases, arms transfers, force structures, military budgets, and the like, via SADC PDS to all other SADC members. This should include reporting on sub-national activities, including arms smuggling. PDS can fulfill a highly valuable information gathering and disseminating role, and can thereby contribute to confidence-building and stability in the region. Alternatively, this information gathering and dissemination role can be subcontracted out to research institutes of the region.

The region of course lacks a well-functioning communication infrastructure (partly addressed by SADC's current telecommunications drive). But the early warning system I suggest requires more conceptual than physical inputs, for if SADC members can make a convincing case for peacekeeping outside donors are likely to assist with equipment needs, especially since prevailing research suggests some degree of positive correlation between security and peace as a basic building block of economic development.

Preparedness

Preparedness refers to the availability, on short notice, of personnel and equipment and therefore requires a willingness and ability to maintain a regional, integrated force ready for rapid deployment. As suggested earlier, South Africa's "giantism" virtually dictates that a large proportion of the capital, equipment, and human resources will have to come from South Africa and whatever donors it can attract toward this venture. This may in fact be a legitimate opportunity for South Africa to manufacture and supply appropriate defense material to a SADC peacekeeping force and to establish operations, maintenance, and training centers. Unity of equipment would assist with interoperability and serviceability of equipment across national army units that are rotated in and out of the region's peacekeeping force. If so, this would go a long way toward generating private, national interests for South Africa in the service of collective action.

The PDS objectives already call for the creation of a "collective security capacity" and a "regional peace-keeping capacity within national armies." A standing SADC peacekeeping force (PKF), consisting of national forces regularly and routinely rotated in and out of the PKF, would therefore not violate existing principles and would lie entirely within the spirit of PDS.

Force structure

Brooks (1997/98) suggests that a light infantry brigade might suffice to manage conflict at its initial stages. Brigade equipment would be distributed among and positioned at brigade headquarters and three battalion level headquarters across four countries in the region. The four headquarters would be located in the northern, southern, eastern, and western portions of the SADC territory, not only to effectively cover the region but, again, to generate private, national benefits as well. Force spreading would permit speedy responses, with additional personnel and material airlifted from brigade headquarters as needed. Of course this arrangement also avoids peacekeeping forces being held hostage inside any one SADC member country.

In keeping with Sandler's first and sixth principle of institutional design, Brooks' point of starting out with a relatively small PKF is very important. As SADC members gain mutual experience and confidence about PKF, it can be expanded gradually even to the point at which all national forces are abolished and only SADC PKF forces remain. This extreme is perhaps unlikely ever to be reached; the point however is that starting small and expanding is preferable to thinking too big and never getting underway in the first place.

Training

Peacemaking and peacekeeping missions are different from the ordinary activities of national armed forces; but like national armed forces there must be unity of mission, doctrine, and operational detail. In particular, forces must be trained to understand that peacekeeping merely involves keeping contestants apart; it does not involve the resolution of an underlying conflict *per se* by means of military intervention. Resolution of the conflict itself must remain at the political level, in line with the democratic principles of SADC and PDS. Training will also assist in leveling cultural differences among the numerous peoples of and ethnic groups within the 14 SADC members. It will foster like preferences or tastes as Sandler (1997) referred to it.

In principle, there should be no difficulty establishing peacekeeping training centers, perhaps in another four of the fourteen SADC countries, quite possibly financed by donor countries and under consultation with the emerging breed of peacekeeping and conflict resolution centers from around the world (including those that already exist in southern Africa).[9]

It is even conceivable that recruits for regular military force training be required to serve a stint at a peacekeeping training center to understand how the respective national armed forces are to serve a larger, regional peacekeeping purpose.

Command and Control

Perhaps the most important aspect of SADC PKF concerns the institutional structure of its command and control apparatus. I suggest to structure SADC PKF as a semi-autonomous institution to encourage capture by professional, multilateral peacekeepers and to avoid capture by nationalist interests (on capture, see Mansfield, 1995, especially pp. 598-604). SADC as a political organism must define pre-specified triggers that automatically calls SADC PKF into action. For example, as suggested earlier, any cross-border conflict should be immediately responded to by interspersing the PKF into the disputed area. If, in contrast, decision-making about intervention were made with veto-power at the SADC political level, then any member nation could veto any action at any time. In that case one would expect that little would ever be accomplished and the resources spent to establish PKF would go to waste.

An institutional arrangement relying on veto-power is an example of Hirshleifer's notion of weakest-link technology: if any SADC member vetoes a peacekeeping action, the public good of peacekeeping is not supplied. In contrast, a semi-autonomous PKF operating under pre-specified trigger points corresponds to a best-shot technology: it automatically and rapidly self-deploys appropriate forces to intersperse themselves and keep the peace until a political solution can be found. Once the region's PKF is established, equipped, and financed, it becomes a best-shot solution unto itself, subject only to civilian supervision by the majority of SADC members. Also note that a semi-autonomous PKF avoids the summation technology of public goods production and thereby side-steps the free-rider problem. Automaticity and non-veto power enhance credibility and thus serve as a more effective deterrent than other institutional arrangements.

Much revolves around legitimacy. It is not an encouraging sign that SADC's first chair of its Organ on Politics, Defence, and Security is Robert Mugabe, Prime Minister of Zimbabwe. His democratic credentials are unsatisfactory. But this merely reinforces the point about some fairly strong degree of institutional separation between the policy level that *determines* the trigger points and the action level that *acts upon* pre-specified trigger points.

Resources

All SADC members already expend resources on their respective armed forces. Those who wish to join a SADC PKF could agree to reduce their current military expenditures by a certain percentage and designate that percentage for SADC PKF.

In addition, South Africa in particular might deliberately tie extra-statutory resource contributions to SADC to the degree to which SADC members successfully monitor and regulate migrant flows. For instance, if the current cost of illegal migrants to South Africa is a sum X, South Africa might offer to devote that sum to specific measures enhancing SADC members' economic development efforts (e.g., education, productivity, food-security, and economic growth), i.e., it could offer would essentially amounts to "tied-aid". To South Africa the net cost of this offer is zero in the short run, but potentially positive in the long run since further economic specialization and development in neighboring SADC members will increase opportunities for intra-SADC trade and therefore is likely to reduce migrant flows.

Further, it would appear likely that certain interested non-African countries, such as the US, Canada, Norway, the UK, and Portugal (and thereby, perhaps, the EU), would be interested in contributing to a SADC PKF. Since economic decline, rather than growth, characterizes much of southern Africa, resources explicitly earmarked for a regional peacekeeping force would be helpful.

It is even conceivable that SADC and interested donors negotiate a deal along the following lines: "in exchange for a certain, guaranteed level of resources (such as equipment and training) over x number of years, we want to be part of the SADC PKF force." For instance, Canada and Norway whose peacekeeping credentials are fairly clean, might ask that a small number of their peacekeeping forces be routinely rotated in and out of SADC PKF (just as some African countries regularly contribute forces to UN peacekeeping missions or in the way that the US regularly trains future officers of foreign nations). 5 or 10 percent of the SADC PKF might be staffed in this manner and begin to generate vested interests in SADC and SADC PKF and their success.

Alternatively, major donor nations might jointly propose to SADC to fund, say, up to 50 percent of the initial costs of SADC PKF over ten years in exchange for commitments by SADC members to reduce their current military outlays to help fund the other initial 50 percent.

Leadership and missions

As Sandler (1997) points out, clubs succeed if leadership is forthcoming from those who have the most to gain. South Africa, in particular, has much to gain and should be a major driving force behind SADC PKF. Essentially, all SADC members have much to gain (as does the world community from an economically vital southern Africa), but the game-theoretic relevant question is who of the pertinent decision-makers stands to gain so much as to join a PKF. Alternatively, what incentives can be offered to national leaders (taking account of national institutional set-ups) to make it worth their while to join PKF?

South Africa's gains are evident (reduced conflict reduces migration flows into South Africa, for example), and it should be fairly straightforward to convince its leaders to participate in a SADC PKF. What about Angola and Mozambique? A potential reward that might entice leaders to contribute to and join PKF would be to direct early PKF missions at Angola and Mozambique. For example, both countries need to deal with and expend resources on land-mine clearing in any case. What if SADC and the larger international community promised substantial financial assistance for mine clearing if this activity were performed under auspices of an incipient SADC PKF? Mine clearing involves training, equipment decisions, and cooperation, it allows for reintegration of internal forces, and integration of external forces. What if the IMF and World Bank were to tie structural and development aid (for example demobilization and reintegration funds) to peacekeeping activities on account of the argument that peace fosters the preconditions necessary for economic development and growth in living standards? This proposal goes one step beyond that made by others, such as former US Defense Secretary and World Bank president Robert McNamara (1992), in that aid is not tied merely to the reduction in recipient nations' military expenditures but to the creation of and increases in mutual peacekeeping budgets.

The United States, the biggest voice in international organizations such as the IMF and World Bank, already consults regularly with SADC. It would involve a relatively small step to bring that voice to bear.

Conclusion

Peacekeeping and peacemaking are international public goods. Their provision ordinarily requires collective action. But collective action is subject to weaknesses such as free riding behavior on contributions others make. Therefore, peacekeeping and peacemaking, although eminently desirable goods, often are not supplied at all or only inadequately or belatedly.

Drawing especially on the work of Hirshleifer (1983) and Sandler (1997), this chapter examined the institutional underpinnings of peace as an international public good and advanced a variety of specific proposals for the institutional design of peacekeeping in southern Africa.

Notes

Various versions of this chapter have been read in Atlanta (Southern Economic Association annual meetings, November 1997), Chicago (Allied Social Science Associations annual meetings, January 1998), and London (Middlesex University conference on "Military Expenditures in Developing and Emerging Economies", March 1998). The Chicago and London versions were co-authored with André Roux of South Africa's Stellenbosch University (see Brauer and Roux, forthcoming). I also thank Professors Dietrich Fischer and Keith Hartley for useful comments.

1. The discussion follows Sandler (1997, pp. 46-50), although the examples are drawn from various sources.

2. That and how the Montreal Protocol to reduce CFC emissions came about anyway has to do with the design of institutions needed to avert or side-step the prisoners' dilemma game; this is addressed later on in the chapter.

3. In a happy turn-of-phrase, Jeff Dumas (of the University of Texas at Dallas) suggests to refer to this as the "dating model". When young people start dating,

they are much better off being interested solely in each other, rather discussing right away which college their eventual children might attend or where to travel once they reach retirement age.

4. Positive for non-NATO European countries that would probably have been defended in case of WTO attack (for example, France, after its withdrawal from NATO), and negative, not least with regards to the generalized worldwide anxieties that the nuclear-arms race and proliferation caused.

5. See Sandler (1992, pp. 99-106) for details and empirical results that bear out the theoretical predictions.

6. On institutions, see the recent spate of literature on New Institutional Economics (NIE), e.g., Hodgson (1998), Stiglitz (1998), and the roundtable discussion at the 1998 annual meetings of the American Economic Association (AEA, 1998).

7. This and the next section draws on Brauer and Roux (forthcoming).

8. For example, a news item in *SADC Today* of 9 September 1997 reads as follows:

09-16-97 — SADC Leaders to Meet on Angola, Regional Security

SADC leaders will meet at the end of September in Luanda, Angola to bring Angola's peace process back on track, said SADC Executive Secretary Kaire Mbuende.

The discussion will center on the conflict between the Angolan Government and UNITA. Mbuende said the lack of commitment by UNITA to fully take part in the Government of National Unity and failure to demobilize its troops remain a cause of concern. SADC leaders will also decide on who will head the SADC "Organ on Politics, Defense and Security," the organization's conflict resolution body.

But, as yet, there is no regional enforcement mechanism in place. Indeed, later on it was the UN Security Council, not SADCs PDS, that "imposed sanctions against the Angolan rebel movement, Unita, to pressure it to comply with the Lusaka peace accord signed in November 1994" (*SADC Today*, Oct. 1997, Vol. 1, No. 5).

9. See, e.g., the UN Department of Peacekeeping web site for training needs, lessons learned, and links to peacekeeping training institutes at http://www.un.org/Depts/dpko/.

References

AEA (1998). American Economic Association. Roundtable discussion on the New Institutional Economics. *American Economic Review.* Vol. 88, No. 2 (May), pp. 72-89. The participants were Ronald Coase, Oliver Williamson, Avner Greif, and Victor Nee.

Buchanan, J. (1965). "An Economic Theory of Clubs." *Economica.* Vol. 32 (February), pp. 1-14.

Brauer, J. and A. Roux (forthcoming). "Peace as an International Public Good: An Application to Southern Africa." *Defence and Peace Economics.*

Brooks, J.P.J. (Winter 1997/98). "A Military Model for Conflict Resolution in Sub-Saharan Africa." *Parameters.* Vol. 27 (Winter), pp. 108-120.

Cornes, R. and T. Sandler (1996). *The Theory of Externalities, Public Goods, and Club Goods.* 2nd edition. Cambridge, UK: Cambridge University Press.

Cortright, D. (ed.) (1997). *The Price of Peace: Incentives and International Conflict Prevention.* Lanham, MD: Rowman & Littlefield.

Cortright, D. and G. Lopez (eds.) (1995). *Economic Sanctions: Panacea or Peacebuilding in a Post-Cold War World?* Boulder, CO: Westview Press.

Hirshleifer, J. (1983). "From Weakest-Link to Best-Shot: The Voluntary Provision of Public Goods." *Public Choice.* Vol. 41, No. 3, pp. 371-386.

Hodgson, G.M. (1998). "The Approach of Institutional Economics." *Journal of Economic Literature.* Vol. 36, No..1 (March), pp. 166-192.

IMF (1997). International Monetary Fund. "IMF Concludes Article IV Consultation with South Africa." *IMF Press Information Notice.* 25 August. (Available via http://www.imf.org.)

Kaempfer, W.H. and A.D. Lowenberg (1988). "The Theory of International Economic Sanctions: A Public Choice Approach." *American Economic Review.* Vol. 78, No. 4 (September), pp. 786-793.

Khanna, J. and T. Sandler (1997). "Conscription, Peace-Keeping, and Foreign Assistance: NATO Burden Sharing in the Post-Cold War Era." *Defence and Peace Economics.* Vol. 8, No. 1, pp. 101-121.

Mansfield, E.D. (1993). "International Institutions and Economic Sanctions." *World Politics.* Vol. 47 (July), pp. 575-605.

Martin, L.L. (1993). "Credibility, Costs, and Institutions." *World Politics.* Vol. 45 (April), pp. 406-432.

McNamara, R. (1992). "The Post-Cold War World: Implications for Military Expenditure in the Developing Countries," pp. 95-125 in *Proceedings of the World Bank Annual Conference on Development Economics.* Washington, DC: World Bank.

Olson, M. (1965). *The Logic of Collective Action*. Cambridge, MA: Harvard University Press.

Sandler, T. (1992). *Collective Action: Theory and Applications*. Ann Arbor, MI: The University of Michigan Press.

Sandler, T. (1997). *Global Challenges: An Approach to Environmental, Political, and Economic Problems*. New York: Cambridge University Press.

Sandler, T. and K. Hartley (1999). *The Political Economy of NATO: Past, Present and Into the 21st Century*. Cambridge: Cambridge University Press.

Stiglitz, J. (1998). "The Private Uses of Public Interests: Incentives and Institutions." *Journal of Economic Perspectives*. Vol. 12, No. 2 (Spring), pp. 3-22.

United Nations Development Programme (UNDP) (1997). *Human Development Report*. New York: Oxford University Press.

World Bank (1997). *World Development Report 1997*. New York: Oxford University Press.

Internet sources:

SADC	http://www.sadc-usa.net/reference/protocol/organ.html
IMF	http://www.imf.org
UN Peacekeeping	http://www.un.org/Depts/dpko/lessons.
Author's web-site	http://www.aug.edu/~sbajmb/files

Appendix: Principles and Objectives of SADC's Organ on Politics, Defence and Security (PDS)

Principles (Excerpts)

▶ Sovereign equality of all member States;
▶ Respect for the sovereignty and territorial integrity of each State and for its inalienable right to independent existence;
▶ Achievement of solidarity, peace and security in the region;
▶ Observance of human rights, democracy and the rule of law;
▶ Peaceful settlement of disputes by negotiation, mediation and arbitration;

▶ Promotion of economic development in the SADC region in order to achieve for all member States, equity, balance and mutual benefit; and
▶ Military intervention of whatever nature shall be decided upon only after all possible political remedies have been exhausted in accordance with the Charter of the Organisation of Africa Unity (OAU) and the United Nations.

Objectives (Excerpts)

▶ Protect the people and safeguard the development of the region, against instability arising from the breakdown of law and order, inter-state conflict and external aggression;
▶ Promote political cooperation among member States and the evaluation of common political value systems and institutions;
▶ Develop a common foreign policy in areas of mutual concern and interest, and to lobby as a region, on issues of common interest at international fora;
▶ Cooperate fully in regional security and Defence through conflict prevention management and resolution;
▶ Mediate in inter-state and intra-state disputes and conflicts;
▶ Use preventive diplomacy to pre-empt conflict in the region, both within and between States, through an early warning system;
▶ Where conflict does occur, to seek to end this as quickly as possible through diplomatic means. Only where such means would fail would the Organ recommend that the Summit should consider punitive measures. These responses would be agreed upon in a Protocol on Peace, Security and Conflict Resolution;
▶ Promote and enhance the development of democratic institutions and practices within member States, and to encourage the observance of universal human rights as

provided for in the Charters and Conventions of the OAU and the United Nations;
▶ Promote peace-making and peace-keeping in order to achieve sustainable peace and security;
▶ Give political support to the organs and institutions of SADC;
▶ Develop a collective security capacity and conclude a Mutual Defence Pact for a responding to external threats, and a regional peace-keeping capacity within national armies that could be called upon within the region, or elsewhere on the continent;
▶ Promote the political, economic, social and environmental dimensions of security;
▶ Develop close cooperation between the police and security services of the region, with a view to addressing crossborder crime, as well as promoting a community-based approach on matters of security;
▶ Encourage and monitor the ratification of the OAU, United Nations, and other international conventions and treaties on arms control and disarmament, human rights and peaceful relations between States;
▶ Coordinate the participation of member States in international and regional peace-keeping operations; and
▶ Address extra-regional conflict which impact on peace and security in southern Africa.

Source: http://www.sadc-usa.net/reference/ protocol/organ.html

Contributors

Emmanuel Athanassiou is a Research Fellow at the Centre of Planning and Economic Research in Athens, Greece. He also lectures on institutional economics and the economics of uncertainty at the Department of Economics, University of Athens. He is currently involved in the evaluation of competition policy in Greece. Dr. Athanassiou can be reached at manath@hol.gr

Carlos Pestana Barros is auxiliar Professor of Economics at the *Instituto Superior de Economia e Gestão* of the Technical University of Lisbon. His interests include the economics of military affairs, economics, and social economics. He has published several books on these issues in Portuguese and published in *Defence and Peace Economics*. Carlos Pestana Barros can be reached at cbarros@iseg.utl.pt

Jurgen Brauer is Associate Professor of Economics at Augusta State University's College of Business Administration. His interests include economic education, the economics of military affairs, and bioeconomics. He has published several books, including *Economics of Conflict and Peace* (Avebury Press, 1997) and published in journals such as *Economic Development and Cultural Change*, *Defence and Peace Economics*, and the *Journal of Economic Perspectives*. He is vice-chair of Economists Allied for Arms Reduction (ECAAR) and can be reached at jbrauer@aug.edu

Tilman Brück obtained a M.A. degree in political economy at the University of Glasgow and a M.Phil. degree in economics at the University of Oxford. He conducted fieldwork in Mozambique in 1995 for an ODA-funded study and has since taught at the University of Oxford. In 1996, he visited the Former Yugoslav Republic of Macedonia to analyze the economics of the Balkan conflict. He returned to Mozambique in 1999 on a DFID-funded research project. He is currently completing a doctoral thesis on the economics of civil war in Mozambique at Queen Elizabeth House, University of Oxford. He can be reached tilman.bruck@economics.oxford.ac.uk

Fanny Coulomb is deputy lecturer at Espace Europe at the University Pierre Mendes France, Grenoble. Her primary research interests are the history of economic thought regarding the economics of war and peace. She can be reached at fanny.coulomb@upmf-grenoble.fr

Jacques Fontanel is professor and director of Espace Europe at the University of Pierre Mendes France, Grenoble. His interests include the economics of armament and disarmament, globalization, and geoeconomy. He has published several books, including *Les défenses militaires et le désarmement. La conversion du secteur militaire or Organisations éeconomiques internationales*, and published in journals such as *Defence and Peace Economics*, *Pax Economica*, and *Ares*. He chairs the French chapter of ECAAR (Economistes contre le course aux armements) and can be reached at jacques.fontanel@umpf-grenoble.fr

Keith Hartley is Director of the Centre for Defence Economics at the University of York in the UK and is founding editor of *Defence and Peace Economics*. Widely published with over 250 publications, he can be reached at mmc1@york.ac.uk

Michael Hough is Director of the Institute for Strategic Studies, University of Pretoria, South Africa. He also teaches in Strategic Studies and African Politics in the Department of Political Sciences at the University of Pretoria. His interests include national security, migration, and African politics. He has published numerous articles and chapters in books on these topics. Professor Hough can be reached at pulles@libarts.up.ac.za

Christos Kollias is Assistant Professor of Economics at the Department of Business Administration of the Technological Education Institute of Larissa, Greece. He has held posts as a Research Fellow at the Center of Planning and Economic Research in Athens and as an Adjunct Assistant Professor at the University of Crete. His work has been published in journals such as *Defence and Peace Economics*, *Journal of Peace Research*, *Labour*, and *Applied Economics*. Dr. Kollias can be reached at kollias@pinios.teilar.gr

Onur Özsoy is Assistant Professor of Economics at the Department of Economics, Faculty of Political Science, Ankara University since 1997. His areas of interest include defense economics, industrial organization and public regulation, health economics, and quantitative economics. He can be reached at ozsoy@politics.ankara.edu.tr

André Roux is Director of the Institute for Futures Research at Stellenbosch University, South Africa, and also Associate Professor of Economics at that University's Graduate School of Business. His interests include futures research, macroeconomics, development and labor economics, economics of defense, and knowledge economics. He recently published the sixth edition of his book *Everyone's Guide to the South African Economy* (Zebra Press, 1997), and he has had a number of articles published, both in academic journals and popular periodicals. Dr Roux can be reached at aroux@maties.sun.ac.za

Todd Sandler is a Distinguished of Professor Economics and Political Science, Iowa State University. His articles on a wide range of topics have appeared in such journals as the *American Economic Review, American Political Science Review, Quarterly Journal of Economics, Journal of Law and Economics*, and *Journal of Economic Theory*. In 1996, he co-authored *The Theory of Externalities, Public Goods and Club Goods*, 2nd edition. His recent book, *Global Challenges*, applies simple economic methods to study a range of problems including terrorism, acid rain, global warming, revolutions, treaty formation, and other topics. He and Keith Hartley have just published a book, *The Political Economy of NATO: Past, Present, and into the 21st Century* (Cambridge University Press, 1999). Professor Sandler also is former co-editor of *Defence and Peace Economics* and can be reached at tsandler@iastate.edu

Selami Sezgin is Research Assistant of Public Finance at Afyon Kocatepe University, Turkey, and DPhil student of the Centre for Defence Economics at the University of York. His interests include defense economics, especially with regard to Greece and Turkey, and the economics of law and regulation. He has published in *Defence and Peace Economics* and can be reached at ss117@york.ac.uk

John Treddenick is Professor of Economics at the Royal Military College of Canada, Kingston, Ontario. His teaching and research interests are in the areas of microeconomics and defense economics. His current work concentrates on the economics of defense budgeting and planning. He can be reached at treddenick-j@rmc.ca

Pierre Willa is a doctoral student in Politics and International Relations at the University of Geneva and Fellow at the Swiss Defense Department and the National Scientific Research Fund. His research interests are in the areas of security stability and the role of the European Union as a new kind of security organization. His doctoral thesis focuses on the Mediterranean as a case study. He can be reached at pwilla@compuserve.com

Denis Venter is the outgoing Executive Director of the Africa Institute of South Africa, Pretoria, and in-coming Managing Director of Africa Consultancy & Research cc, Pretoria. His interests are centered on African affairs, more specifically around issues of foreign policymaking, regional security, and political dynamics. He has published widely in periodicals such as *Journal of Contemporary African Studies, Africa Insight, Indian Journal of African Studies*, and *Journal of the Third World Spectrum*. He is vice-chairman of the International African Institute (IAI). Dr Venter can be reached at africore@iafrica.com

Index

NAME

ACDA, 148, 177
Adams, F.G., 139
Adelman, H.L., 250
Adeniji, O., 278
Adler, E., 40
Alagappa, M., 271
Alexander, W.R.J., 122, 139
Aliboni, R., 33
Antonakis, N., 97, 116
Asmus, R.D., 78
Avramides, C., 114
Awad, I., 31

Barnett, M., 40
Bartzokas, A., 116
Beenstock, M., 162
Benoit, E., 125, 139, 217, 236
Bensidoun, I., 35
Biswas, B., 118, 122, 139–140
Booth, K., 266, 271, 275–276
Boutros-Ghali, B., 281
Brooks, J.P., 309
Buchanan, J., 299
Bueno de Mesquita, B., 289
Buzan, B., 29, 248–249, 266

Cabellero, R.J., 104, 105
Calleya, S., 37
Cambone, S., 53
Campbell, J.K., 84
Cawthra, G., 240
CBO, 9, 78
CDE, 257

Chalk, P., 84
Chevallier, A., 35
Ching'ambo, L.J., 265
Chletsos, M., 97, 116, 117
Cilliers, J., 239, 278, 280
Clapham, C., 275
Clark, R., 53
Cliff, J., 197
Clogg, R., 97, 99
Constas, D., 97
Cooper, R., 52
Cornes, R., 299
Correa, H., 53, 67
Cortright, D., 304–305
Cox, N., 20

Dalby, S., 265
Davis, D., 122
Deger, S., 118, 124–126, 139, 228–229, 237
Destanne de Bernis, G., 172
Deutsch, K.W., 40, 268
Diehl, P., 98
Dixit, A., 101,193
Du Pisani, A., 265, 270, 277
Du Plessis, A., 226
Dudley, L., 162
Dunne, P., 15, 129

EC, 18
Ellyas, A., 183
Enders, W., 84, 85
Engel, M., 104, 105